Lecture Notes in Computer Science 7344

Commenced Publication in 1973
Founding and Former Series Editors:
Gerhard Goos, Juris Hartmanis, and Jan van Leeuwen

W0192945

Stefan Katzenbeisser   Edgar Weippl
L. Jean Camp   Melanie Volkamer
Mike Reiter   Xinwen Zhang (Eds.)

Trust
and Trustworthy
Computing

5th International Conference, TRUST 2012
Vienna, Austria, June 13-15, 2012
Proceedings

 Springer

Volume Editors

Stefan Katzenbeisser
Melanie Volkamer
Technical University Darmstadt, Germany
E-mail: katzenbeisser@seceng.informatik.tu-darmstadt.de
and melanie.volkamer@cased.de

Edgar Weippl
Vienna University of Technology and SBA Research, Austria
E-mail: edgar.weippl@tuwien.ac.at

L. Jean Camp
Indiana University, Bloomington, IN, USA
E-mail: ljcamp@indiana.edu

Mike Reiter
University of North Carolina at Chapel Hill, USA
E-mail: reiter@cs.unc.edu

Xinwen Zhang
Huawei America R&D, Santa Clara, CA, USA
E-mail: xinwen.zhang@huawei.com

ISSN 0302-9743   e-ISSN 1611-3349
ISBN 978-3-642-30920-5   e-ISBN 978-3-642-30921-2
DOI 10.1007/978-3-642-30921-2
Springer Heidelberg Dordrecht London New York

Library of Congress Control Number: 2012938995

CR Subject Classification (1998): C.2, K.6.5, E.3, D.4.6, J.1, H.4

LNCS Sublibrary: SL 4 – Security and Cryptology

Typesetting: Camera-ready by author, data conversion by Scientific Publishing Services, Chennai, India

Printed on acid-free paper

Springer is part of Springer Science+Business Media (www.springer.com)

Preface

This volume contains the proceedings of the 5th International Conference on Trust and Trustworthy Computing (TRUST) held in Vienna, Austria, during June 13–15, 2012. Continuing the tradition of the previous conferences, which were held in Villach (2008), Oxford (2009), Berlin (2010) and Pittsburgh (2011), TRUST 2012 featured both a technical and a socio-economic track. TRUST thus continues to provide a unique interdisciplinary forum for researchers, practitioners and decision makers to explore new ideas in designing, building and using trustworthy computing systems. This year's technical track provided a good mix of topics ranging from trusted computing and mobile devices to applied cryptography and physically unclonable functions, while the socio-economic track focused on the emerging field of usable security.

Out of 36 submissions to the technical track and 12 submissions to the socio-economic track, we assembled a program consisting of 20 papers. In addition, TRUST 2012 featured a poster session for rapid dissemination of the latest research results, invited talks, as well as a panel discussion on future challenges of trust in mobile and embedded devices.

We would like to thank everyone for their efforts in making TRUST 2012 a success: the members of the Organizing Committee, in particular Yvonne Poul, for their tremendous help with all aspects of the organization; the members of the Program Committees of both tracks for their efforts in selecting high-quality research papers to be presented at the conference; all external reviewers who helped to maintain the quality of theconference; the keynote speakers and panel members; and most importantly all authors who submitted their work to TRUST 2012. Finally, we express our gratitude to our sponsors Intel and Hewlett-Packard, whose support was crucial for the success of TRUST 2012.

April 2012

L. Jean Camp
Stefan Katzenbeisser
Mike Reiter
Melanie Volkamer
Edgar Weippl
Xinwen Zhang

Organization

Steering Committee

Alessandro Acquisti   Carnegie Mellon University, USA
Boris Balacheff   Hewlett Packard, UK
Paul England   Microsoft, USA
Andrew Martin   University of Oxford, UK
Chris Mitchell   Royal Holloway, University of London, UK
Sean Smith   Dartmouth College, USA
Ahmad-Reza Sadeghi   TU Darmstadt / Fraunhofer SIT, Germany
Claire Vishik   Intel, UK

General Chairs

Edgar Weippl   Vienna University of Technology and
     SBA Research, Austria
Stefan Katzenbeisser   TU Darmstadt, Germany

Program Chairs (Technical Strand)

Mike Reiter   University of North Carolina at Chapel Hill,
     USA
Xinwen Zhang   Huawei, USA

Program Committee (Technical Strand)

Srdjan Capkun   ETHZ Zurich, Switzerland
Haibo Chen   Fudan University, China
Xuhua Ding   Singapore Management University, Singapore
Jan-Erik Ekberg   Nokia Research Center
Cedric Fournet   Microsoft Research, UK
Michael Franz   UC Irvine, USA
Tal Garfinkel   VMWare
Trent Jaeger   Penn State University, USA
Xuxian Jiang   NCSU, USA
Apu Kapadia   Indiana University, USA
Jiangtao Li   Intel Labs
Peter Loscocco   NSA, USA
Heiko Mantel   TU Darmstadt, Germany
Jonathan McCune   Carnegie Mellon University, USA

Sonia Chiasson	Carleton University, Canada
Stefano Zanero	Politecnico di Milano, Italy
Sven Dietrich	Stevens Institute of Technology, USA
Tara Whalen	Carleton University, Canada
Yolanta Beres	HP Labs, USA
Yang Wang	Carnegie Mellon University, USA
Debin Liu	PayPal

Publicity Chair

Marcel Winandy	Ruhr University Bochum, Germany

Table of Contents

Socio-economic Strand

Authenticated Encryption Primitives for Size-Constrained Trusted Computing

Jan-Erik Ekberg[1], Alexandra Afanasyeva[2], and N. Asokan[1]

[1] Nokia Research Center, Helsinki
[2] State University of Aerospace Instrumentation, Saint-Petersburg

Abstract. Trusted execution environments (TEEs) are widely deployed both on mobile devices as well as in personal computers. TEEs typically have a small amount of physically secure memory but they are not enough to realize certain algorithms, such as authenticated encryption modes, in the standard manner. TEEs can however access the much larger but untrusted system memory using which "pipelined" variants of these algorithms can be realized by gradually reading input from, and/or writing output to the untrusted memory. In this paper, we motivate the need for pipelined variants of authenticated encryption modes in TEEs, describe a pipelined version of the EAX mode, and prove that it is as secure as standard, "baseline", EAX. We point out potential pitfalls in mapping the abstract description of a pipelined variant to concrete implementation and discuss how these can be avoided. We also discuss other algorithms which can be adapted to the pipelined setting and proved correct in a similar fashion.

Keywords: Trusted Computing, Platform Security, Cryptography.

1 Introduction

Trusted execution environments (TEEs) based on general-purpose secure hardware incorporated into end user devices are widely deployed. There are two dominant types of TEE designs. The first is as a self-contained stand-alone secure hardware element like Trusted Platform Module (TPM) [15]. The second is a design like M-Shield [14,11] and ARM TrustZone [1] which augment the processor with a *secure processing mode* (Figure 1).

In these latter designs, during normal operation the processor runs the basic operating software (like the device OS) but can enter the secure mode on-demand to securely execute small pieces of sensitive code. Certain memory areas are only accessible in secure mode. These can be used for persistent storage of long-term secrets. Secure mode is typically combined with isolated RAM and ROM, residing within the System-On-A-Chip (SoC), to protect code executing in the TEE against memory-bus eavesdropping. The RAM available within this minimal TEE is usually quite small, as low as tens of kilobytes in contemporary devices [9]. Often this constraint implies that only the basic cryptographic primitives or only the specific parts of some security critical architecture (such as a hypervisor) can be implemented within the TEE.

S. Katzenbeisser et al. (Eds.): TRUST 2012, LNCS 7344, pp. 1–18, 2012.

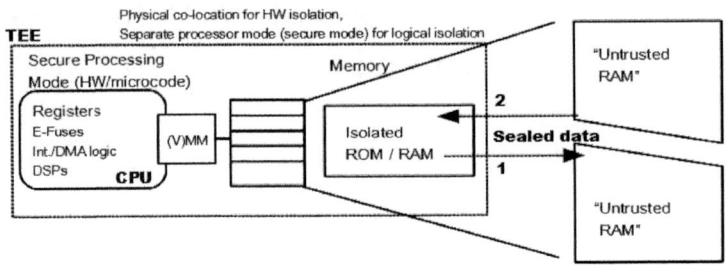

Fig. 1. TEE architecture variant: secure processor mode

In most, if not all, of these hardware architectures ([1], [11], [8]) the primary RAM on the device outside the TEE is addressable by secure mode code executing within the TEE (see Figure 1). This unprotected, and hence potentially "untrusted" RAM is significantly larger than the isolated (trusted) RAM. It is used

- to transfer input parameters for secure execution within the TEE as well as for receiving any computation results from the TEE.
- to implement secure virtual memory for secure mode programs running with the TEE.
- to store and fetch state information when multiple different secure mode programs execute in an interleaved fashion (when one program needs to stop its execution in the TEE before it is fully completed, the full state information needed to continue its execution later is too big to be retained within the TEE).

In the latter two cases, the TEE must *seal* any such data before storing it in the untrusted memory. Sealing means encrypting and integrity-protecting the data using a key available only within the TEE so that (a) the sealed data is cryptographically bound to additional information specifying who can use the unsealed data and how, and (b) any modifications to the sealed data can be detected when it is used within the TEE.

The basic requirements of a sealing primitive are confidentiality and integrity of the sealed data. These can be met by using one of several well-known *authenticted encryption* modes. Many authenticated encryption modes have been proved secure using standard reduction techniques. However, the general assumption and proof model for the execution of such a scheme is that its entire execution sequence is carried out securely and in isolation: i.e., inputs are received into isolated memory, the entire computation is securely run to completion as an atomic operation producing an output in isolated memory, and only then are outputs returned to insecure channels or untrusted RAM. This setting is unreasonable in memory-constrained TEEs. They need a *"pipelined"* variant of authenticated encryption modes where encryption and decryption can be done in a piecemeal fashion where input is read from and/or output written to untrusted

RAM gradually as the computation proceeds. In fact, interfaces specifying this sort of pipelined authenticated encryption operations are starting to appear in TEE standard specifications [7]. A natural question is whether these pipelined variants of authenticated encryption modes are as secure as the original, *"baseline"*, variants.

In this paper, we make three contributions. First, we highlight the problem of finding secure pipelined implementations of authenticated encryption primitives in the context of memory-constrained TEEs. Second, we describe how a concrete provably secure authenticated encryption mode (EAX) can be adapted for use in a pipelined fashion in memory-constrained TEEs. We prove the security of the pipelined variant by showing that it is as secure as the baseline EAX variant. We discuss other cryptographic primitives where the same approach for pipelining and security proof may apply. Third, we point out that naive realizations of pipelined EAX can be vulnerable to information leakage and describe a secure implementation.

We begin by introducing our platform model in section 2, and list the assumptions we make regarding the computing environment and algorithm implementation in section 3. In section 4 we provide proofs for pipelined EAX variants. In section 5 we discuss implementation pitfalls, and describe the full reference implementation in section 6. Related work, further work and conclusions are discussed in sections 7, 8 and 9.

2 Motivation and System Models

The hardware architecture we consider is shown in Figure 1. Authenticated secure mode programs allowed to run inside the TEE often need to store data or pass it via untrusted RAM to itself or other programs that will run in the same TEE later. In the figure this is shown by arrows labelled "sealed data": data is encrypted in trusted, isolated memory to be stored in untrusted memory and is later correspondingly retrieved and decrypted from untrusted memory to be further processed inside the TEE.

Our work is motivated by this need to produce efficient cryptographic seals for computer programs executing within a TEE on a mobile phone. The memory constraints in the TEE (isolated memory) are often severe. For example, according to [9], TEE programs in their scenario must fit into roughly 10kB of machine code and is limited to around 1-2kB of heap memory and 4kB of stack space[1]. The choice to analyze EAX rather than e.g. the more widely used CCM also stems from such constraints - EAX allows for more compact implementation.

The problem of allocating isolated memory for the ciphertext and plaintext separately, mandated by (the proof of) baseline operation of encryption primitives, can in some scenarios be replaced by in-place sealing/unsealing. In-place operation is however impractical in cases where the sealed data needs to be used also after sealing and it is never viable in cases where the seal size is larger

---

[1] The comparably lavish stack space has to be shared by e.g. cryptographic primitives when invoked, so the effective stack size is counted in hundreds of bytes.

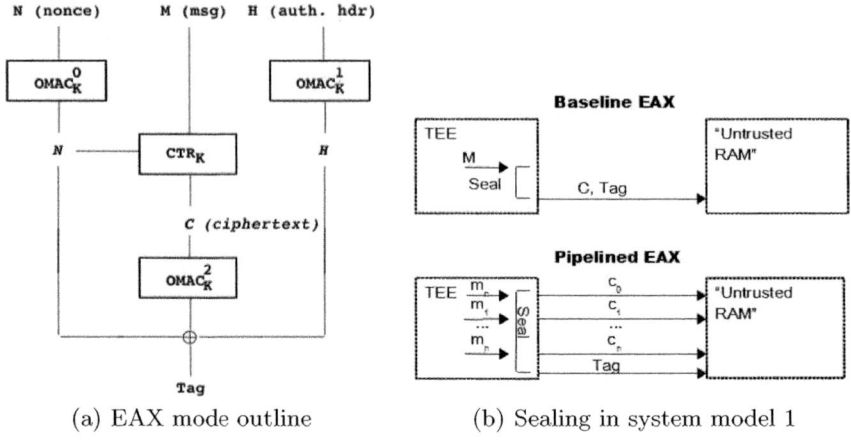

(a) EAX mode outline   (b) Sealing in system model 1

Fig. 2. EAX mode[4] and system model 1 sealing

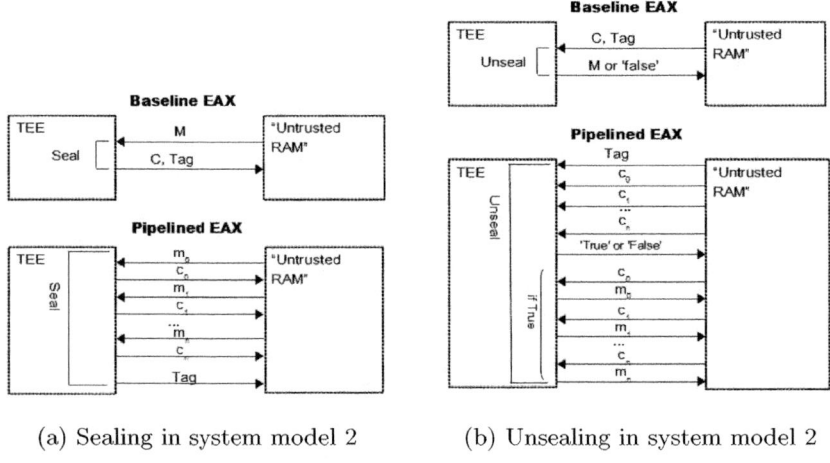

(a) Sealing in system model 2   (b) Unsealing in system model 2

Fig. 3. Sealing and unsealing in system model 2

than available isolated RAM. Such situations include the case where the TEE program needs to access only a part of the seal or when it needs to produce a large protected message say for transfer to another device or server.

We consider two models of pipelined sealing and unsealing. In *system model 1* (Figure 2(b)), the plaintext data is made available in TEE isolated memory, i.e. the decryption primitive decrypts into isolated memory from untrusted memory, and vice versa for encryption. This model is applicable e.g. for secret keys generated in a TPM, but subsequently stored in sealed format within the OS.

In *system model 2* (Figures 3(a) and 3(b)), the plaintext comes from or is returned to untrusted memory. Use cases for this approach includes streaming encrypted content, or encrypting data for network communication.

3   Assumptions and Requirements

With the motivations above, we define our problem scope:

1. The device includes a TEE that provides cryptographic services, specifically a symmetric sealing primitive, to the caller without revealing the keys used.
2. The TEE is extremely memory-constrained: It only includes a small amount (a few kilobytes) of trusted memory, but has the possibility to use external, untrusted RAM to aid the computation.
3. Encryption/decryption inside isolated memory is not an option; the amount of memory needed for the seal/unseal operations should be constant ($\Theta(1)$, rather than $\Theta(n)$ or higher) in terms of the size of the input data.

The specific problem we address is whether we can realize a pipelined variant of authenticated encryption with associated data (AEAD) with the same level of security as for the baseline (non-pipelined) in the two system models discussed above. We define "pipelined" in the computational sense: inputs to the encryption primitive are channeled from the source memory to the primitive as a stream of blocks, and equivalently that the results of the AEAD algorithm (i.e. output blocks) are channeled to target memory as they are being produced rather than when the operation completes.

The baseline setting for AEAD is one where inputs are first retrieved into the TEE, then the operation is carried out, possibly making use of secrets and a random source, and finally the results are released. This is the setting in which cryptographic primitives are usually proved correct, since it is the "natural model" for, e.g., communication security. The use of untrusted memory during algorithm execution (otherwise the pipelined setting is no different from the baseline setting) implies that more information will certainly be available to an adversary in the pipelined alternative.

We are interested in security *from the perspective of the TEE*: for a given input at the TEE boundary the pipelined variant of the AEAD implementation is as secure as the baseline variant if both produce the same output at the TEE boundary.

The code running in the TEE can be considered immutable. However such code may use two types of memory locations: isolated memory within the TEE and untrusted memory outside. We assume that an adversary can freely read and modify any untrusted memory. The classification of memory can be done for any memory location used by the AEAD implementation, including local state variables, processed input data as well as any intermediate or final result. We limit ourselves to this binary categorization, although a more complete model would also include statistical considerations caused by indirect information leakage e.g. in the form of side-channel attacks.

By necessity, we must assume that any long-term secrets (e.g., sealing keys) that are applied to the processing are stored and handled in trusted memory only. We also assume that stack and counters are fully contained in trusted memory. As with trusted execution in general, the existence of a good (pseudo)random data source inside the TEE domain is needed and assumed to be present.

For some cryptographic primitives, the system models we examine do not imply any degradation in security. For example, pipelined variants of message authentication codes like AES-CBC-MAC will not reveal any information outside the TEE until all the input data has been processed and the result is computed. This happens irrespectively of whether data input is carried out in a pipelined way or by transmitting the complete data to the TEE prior to MAC calculation. Thus pipelined operation for MACs is from a security perspective trivially equivalent to baseline operation. A similar argument holds for most common encryption/decryption modes, such as cipher block chaining or counter modes. As a rule only a few inputs and outputs for neighboring cryptoblocks affect the input or output of a given block. Therefore, if the final result is secure when the complete data is transferred to the TEE prior to the operation, so is trivially an implementation that during encryption and decryption only temporarily buffers the small set of blocks with interdependencies. In an AEAD the MAC is affected by the complete data input, but in a pipelined setting the TEE will reveal parts of the outputs prior to receiving all input for the computation of the AEAD integrity tag. This combination of confidentiality and integrity is the cause for the problem scope to be relevant, especially when applied in system model 2.

4   Proof of Security

In this section we will briefly introduce the standard reduction technique for reasoning about the security in cryptographic algorithms and protocols. Using this method we present a adversary model definition and a proof outline that covers our assumptions and requirements listed in section 3, for the system models introduced in section 2.

4.1   Technique

In this paper, we will use the same general proof method as was used for the baseline EAX variant[4]. The proof in the standard complexity-theoretic assumption, often called the "standard reduction technique", is described in detail in references [3] and [2]. On a high level the method is as follows: A security proof can include two parts. The first one is a proof in the context of chosen-plaintext attacks (CPA), where the adversary is given the ability to encrypt any plaintext using the algorithmic primitive. The opposite, the chosen-ciphertext attack (CCA) allows the adversary to set the ciphertext and observe the resulting plaintext. Each proof is constructed as a game between an adversary (A) and a challenger (C) making use of Oracles (O) that abstract the evaluated algorithmic primitive in some way, depending on the properties that are proved. In our models the oracles will represent the encryption and decryption initialized with a key, the second model adds an oracle also for OMAC[2].

The CPA (privacy) security proof is modelled by the adversary using an encrypting Oracle (O_e). The game is defined as follows:

1. A examines O_e by making q adaptive queries to it, i.e. sending any chosen plaintext to O_e and as response receiving the corresponding ciphertext.
2. In a second phase, A selects a plaintext not generated in the first step and sends it to C. C then 'tosses a coin' b and depending on the outcome either returns to A the result of submitting the received input to O_e, or in the second case a random bit string of an equivalent length.
3. Finally, A tries to determine whether the result returned from C was the random string or the actual result from O_e. The so called *advantage* of the adversary A is computed as $Adv(A) = Pr\{A^{O_e} = 1\} - Pr\{A^{\$} = 1\}$, i.e. the difference in success probability for A correctly determining b and making a random choice.

The CCA (authenticity) security proof uses two oracles: an encrypting oracle (O_e) and a decrypting one (O_d). The slightly more complex game starts out like the CPA game, but after receiving the result from C, A is allowed to continue, and submit up to σ adaptive queries to the decryption oracle O_d (of course the return string from the challenger shall not be used). Only after these extended queries A will guess the value of b. Again, the advantage of adversary A will be calculated as the difference between its probability of success with oracles usage and without it.

$$Adv(A) = Pr\{A^{O_e,O_d} = 1\} - Pr\{A^{\$} = 1\}$$

The baseline EAX mode of operation has been proved secure against CCA and CPA attacks. Since the pipelined variant is a derivation of the standard EAX we can use reduction to show that the pipelined variant is as secure as the baseline one. In this proof by reduction, we use an adversary model where an adversary B attacks baseline EAX E by using an adversary A attacking the new pipelined EAX variant E', both set up with the same parameters (keys). For the game it will also be necessary to show that the adversary B can simulate all oracles that would be used by A. The game is set up as follows: suppose there exists an adversary A which can attack algorithm E' with advantage $Adv(A) = \epsilon$. Adversary B wants to break algorithm E (for which a security proof already exists) by making use of A, such that

1. B has access to the oracles used in the proof of E
2. B forges all oracles used by A, by simulating the work those oracles would do for A, only based on its own knowledge about the baseline system E and its own oracles. This can be done with a non-negligible probability ($Pr\{OracleSim\}$).

---

[2] OMAC is a provably secure cryptographic hash construct based on the CBC-MAC primitive. Definition in [4].

3. If there exists a probabilistic polynomial time algorithm for B to attack E using A's advantage, then $Adv(B) = \epsilon * Pr\{OracleSim\}$. If $Pr\{OracleSim\} = 1$ then the respective attack advantages and thereby the security of systems E and E' are equal.

In other words the game shows that if we can attack the modified algorithm E' then we can attack the original system E in the way we built adversary B. But as a security proof already exists for E, our premise of the existence of A is disproved, thereby proving the security of E'.

4.2   Analysis

Correctness of the pipelined EAX in our first system model (Figure 2(b)) is straight-forward. Intuitively, this is because the attacker has no advantage in the pipelined setting compared to the baseline setting because inputs and outputs are not interleaved. For the sake of completeness, we present the proof in Appendix A.

In our second system model intermediate computation results are returned to untrusted memory during algorithm execution. Thus the possibility of an adaptive attack cannot be ruled out immediately. We use the terminology and definitions from [4]. In all algorithms, the **return** statement denotes the returning of data to untrusted memory, not the termination of algorithm execution. The *Read* primitive is used to explicitly indicate data input from untrusted memory. The interactions between A, B and g are shown in Figure 4.

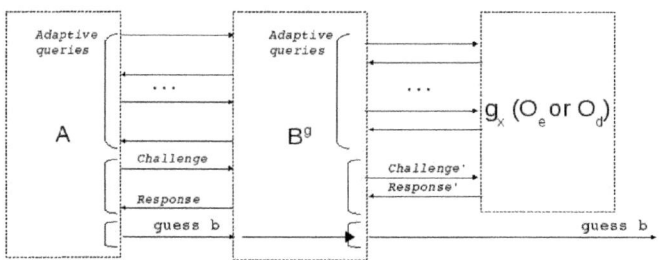

Fig. 4. Proof outline

Theorem 41. *The pipelined EAX variant presented in Algorithms 1 and 2 is as secure as original baseline EAX.*

Proof. We begin with the CPA (privacy) claim. Let $\mathcal{A}$ be an adversary using resources (q, σ) that is trying to distinguish algorithm 1 from a source of random bits. We will construct an adversary B with resources (σ_1, σ_2) that distinguishes

Algorithm 1. Encryption, model 2	**Algorithm 2.** Decryption, model 2
Input: $N, H, K, M = \{m_0, m_1, \ldots, m_{n-1}\}$	**Input:** N, H, K, C
Output: $C = \{c_0, c_1, \ldots, c_{n-1}\}, Tag$	$\{c_0, c_1, \ldots, c_{n-1}\}, Tag$
1: Read(N, H, n)	**Output:** M
2: $\mathcal{N} \Leftarrow OMAC_K^0(N)$	$\{m_0, m_1, \ldots, m_{n-1}\}$ or $Invalid$
3: $\mathcal{H} \Leftarrow OMAC_K^1(H)$	1: Read(N, H, n, Tag)
4: $\mathcal{C} \Leftarrow 0$	2: $\mathcal{N} \Leftarrow OMAC_K^0(N)$
5: **for all** $i \in 0 \ldots n-1$ **do**	3: $\mathcal{H} \Leftarrow OMAC_K^1(H)$
6: Read(m_i)	4: $\mathcal{C} \Leftarrow 0$
7: $c_i \Leftarrow m_i \oplus E(\mathcal{N} + i)_K$	5: **for all** $i \in 0 \ldots n-1$ **do**
8: **return** c_i	6: Read(c_i)
9: $\mathcal{C} \Leftarrow OMAC_K^2(c_i, \mathcal{C})$	7: $\mathcal{C} \Leftarrow OMAC_K^2(c_i, \mathcal{C})$
10: **end for**	8: **end for**
11: $Tag \Leftarrow \mathcal{N} \oplus \mathcal{C} \oplus \mathcal{H}$	9: $T \Leftarrow \mathcal{N} \oplus \mathcal{C} \oplus \mathcal{H}$
12: **return** Tag	10: **if** $T \neq Tag$ **then**
	11: **return** $Invalid$
	12: **else**
	13: **for all** $i \in 1 \ldots n-1$ **do**
	14: Read(c_i)
	15: $m_i \Leftarrow c_i \oplus E(\mathcal{N} + i)_K$
	16: **return** m_i
	17: **end for**
	18: **end if**

the OMAC algorithm[3] from a source of random bits. Adversary B has an oracle g_2 that responds to queries $(t, M, s) \in \{0, 1, 2\} \times \{0, 1\}^* \times \mathbf{N}$ with a string $\{\mathcal{M}_1, S_0, S_1, \ldots, S_{s-1}\}$, where each named component is an l-bit string. Oracle g_2 is the OMAC algorithm. Algorithm 3 describes adversary B:

We may assume that $\mathcal{A}$ makes $q > 1$ queries, so adversary B uses $3q$ queries. Then under the conventions for the data complexity, adversary B uses at most $(\sigma, \frac{\sigma}{2})$ resources. Observe that $Pr[\mathcal{A}^{Enc2} = 1] = Pr[\mathcal{B}^{OMAC} = 1]$ and $Pr[\mathcal{A}^{\$} = 1] = Pr[\mathcal{B}^{\$} = 1]$. Using Lemma 4 from [4] we conclude that

$$Adv_{Alg4}^{CPA}(A) = Pr[\mathcal{A}^{Alg4} = 1] - Pr[\mathcal{A}^{\$} = 1] =$$

$$= Pr[\mathcal{B}^{OMAC} = 1] - Pr[\mathcal{B}^{\$} = 1] \leq Adv_{OMAC}^{dist}(\sigma, \frac{\sigma}{2})$$

$$\leq \frac{1,5\sigma + 3}{2^l} \leq Adv_{EAX}^{CPA}$$

This means that the pipelined EAX, described in Alg. 1 is as private as original EAX. This completes the privacy claim.

---

[3] The construction of adversary B is adapted to a specific proof setup presented in [4], and uses a "tweakable OMAC extension" encapsulated in Lemma 4[4] and its proof. Lemma 4 asserts the pseudorandomness of the OMAC algorithm and provides an upper bound for the advantage of the adversary.

Algorithm 3. Algorithm B^g simulating O_e

1: Run $\mathcal{A}$
2: **for all** Oracle O_e calls $N_j, H_j, n_j,\ j \in 0\ldots q-1$ from $\mathcal{A}$ **do**
3:    $\mathcal{N} S_0 S_1 \ldots, S_{n_j-1} \Leftarrow g_2(0, N_j, n_j)$
4:    **for all** $i \in 0\ldots n-1$ **do**
5:        $c_{i,j} \Leftarrow m_{i,j} \oplus S_j$
6:            **return** $c_{i,j}$, in response to each Oracle O_e query $m_{i,j}$ from $\mathcal{A}$
7:        **end for**
8:        $\mathcal{H}_j \Leftarrow g_2(1, H_j, 0)$
9:        $\mathcal{C}_j \Leftarrow g_2(2, C_j, 0)$
10:       $Tag_j \Leftarrow \mathcal{H} \oplus \mathcal{N} \oplus \mathcal{C}$
11:           **return** Tag_j
12: **end for**
13: When $\mathcal{A}$ halts, get bit b
14: **return** b

For CCA (authenticity) and reusing the naming, let $\mathcal{A}$ be an adversary attacking the authenticity of algorithms 1 and 2. To estimate the advantage of $\mathcal{A}$, we construct from $\mathcal{A}$ (the authenticity-attacking adversary) an adversary B (with oracles for g_2 and g_3, intended for forging the original AES-EAX primitive). Algorithm 3 simulated oracle O_e, and algorithm 4 will simulate the decryption oracle O_d:

It is easy to see that adversary B can simulate both the oracles O_e and O_d for $\mathcal{A}$ indistinguishably from the real challenger of the AES-EAX primitive. Thus, the advantage of adversary B in forging the authenticity algorithms 1 and 2 can be calculated as follows:

$$Adv^{CCA}(B) = Pr\{B^{EAX}, forge\} - Pr\{B^{\$}, forge\} =$$
$$= Adv^{CCA}(\mathcal{A})$$

This completes the claim and the proof

5   Implementation Pitfalls

Although we proved the pipelined EAX variant correct, adequate care is needed when it is incorporated into practice. In this section, we outline two potential pitfalls.

5.1   Security for the External User

At the outset, we mentioned that our goal is to guarantee security from the perspective of the TEE. In practice, one also needs to worry about ensuring security from the perspective of the external "TEE user", for example, an application running on the operating system. As the external memory is untrusted from the perspective of the user, some form of security association between the TEE and

---

Algorithm 4. Algorithm: B^g simulating O_d

1: Run $\mathcal{A}$
2: **for all** O_e requests from $\mathcal{A}$ **do**
3:     Run simulator from 3
4: **end for**
5: **for all** O_d requests $N_j, H_j, C_j \| Tag, j \in 0 \ldots q - 1$ from $\mathcal{A}$ **do**
6:     $M_j \leftarrow g_3(N_j, H_j, C_j, Tag)$
7:     **if** $M_j = Invalid$ **then**
8:         **return** $Invalid$
9:     **else**
10:         $KeyStr \leftarrow M_j \oplus C_j$
11:         **for all** $i \in 0 \ldots n - 1$ **do**
12:             Return $c'_{i,j} \oplus KeyStr_i$, in response to each Oracle O_d query $c'_{i,j}$ from $\mathcal{A}$
13:         **end for**
14:     **end if**
15: **end for**
16: When $\mathcal{A}$ halts, get bit b
17: **return** bs

---

the user is necessary in order to ensure security from the user's perspective. This applies both in the pipelined as well as in the baseline setting.

Although it has no bearing on the security from the perspective of the TEE, the pipelined variant of the unsealing algorithm shown in Figure 3(b) is equivalent to the baseline variant only if the series of ciphertexts $\{c_0, c_1, \ldots, c_{n-1}\}$ in the first phase of the pipelined variant is exactly the same as the series of ciphertexts in second phase (after Tag is validated as $True$). In practice this can be ensured by using re-encryption: for example, in the first phase, the TEE will output encrypted blocks c'_i when processing input c_i and expects the set of c'_i to be provided to the second phase.

5.2   Mapping of Memory Locations

The risk of implementation pitfalls when mapping idealized protocols used in proofs to a real protocol is well known. Our target architecture hides an issue of such nature. Even as we now can use the reduction proofs to argue that pipelined operation of AES-EAX is secure in system models 1 and 2, a naive pipelined variant implementation unfortunately leads to a severe security flaw. Consider lines 7-10 of Algorithm 5 which illustrates how a naive implementor would map the inner loop of EAX encryption (lines 4-6 of Algorithm 7, and lines 6-9 of Algorithm 1)

At first glance, Algorithm 5 looks like a reasonable EAX implementation as shown in Figure 2(a)). It writes out each block of the ciphertext to untrusted RAM as soon as it is calculated. Step 8 corresponds to the encryption of a single block (Algorithm 7/Step 5 or Algorithm 1/Step 8). Step 10 corresponds to the incremental construction of the MAC (Algorithm 7/Step 6 or Algorithm 1/Step 9). As Algorithm 5 is realized on the architecture shown in Figure 1, the variable

---

Algorithm 5. Pipelined EAX Encryption: naive realization

Input: $k, h, n, M = \{m_0, m_1, \ldots, m_{n-1}\}$
Output: $C = \{c_0, c_1, \ldots, c_{n-1}\}, Tag$
 1: $L \leftarrow E_k(0); B \leftarrow 2L; P \leftarrow 4L$
 2: $\mathcal{N} \leftarrow E_k(E_k(0) \oplus n \oplus B)$ $\qquad\qquad$ **OMAC$_k^0$(n)**
 3: $\mathcal{H} \leftarrow E_k(E_k(1) \oplus h \oplus B)$ $\qquad\qquad$ **OMAC$_k^1$(h)**
 4: $t1 \leftarrow \mathcal{N}$
 5: $t2 \leftarrow E_k(2)$
 6: **for** $i \leftarrow 0$ to $n - 1$ **do**
 7: $\quad t4 \leftarrow E_k(t1)$
 8: $\quad \mathbf{c_i} \leftarrow m_i \oplus t4$
 9: $\quad t1 \leftarrow t1 + 1$
10: $\quad t2 \leftarrow E_k(t2 \oplus \mathbf{c_i})$ $\qquad\qquad$ **OMAC$_k^2$(c$_i$, $\mathcal{C}$)**
11: **end for**
12: $\ldots$

---

c_i will be *mapped to a memory location in untrusted memory*. So an attacker who controls the untrusted RAM will now be in a position to manipulate c_i after it is generated in step 8 but before it is used as input to $OMAC^2{}_K$ in step 10.

Clearly, the sealing primitive should release the encrypted block to untrusted memory only after both the encryption as well as the data inclusion into the integrity check value has been performed. Even though this is the intent in the abstract descriptions of Algorithms 7 and 1, the violation of this rule while mapping the algorithms to concrete realizations for our target architecture is not immediately or automatically evident to the programmer. In the baseline setting, where inputs and outputs as well as state variables are all in isolated memory this consideration causes no security issues, even for pipelined operation. In fact pipelining (or rather the fact that the input length need not be known in advance) is listed as a particular advantage of AES-EAX [4]. However, realization of pipelined EAX in our target architecture raises this subtle security issue.

The correct way of pipelining EAX sealing is outlined in Algorithm 6 in Section 6. The solution is to add an intermediary buffer in isolated memory to hold the encrypted block. For unsealing, such a buffer is also needed, but its placement is different, since the confidentiality and integrity primitives are then invoked in opposite order.

6 Reference Implementation

Based on the proofs of Algorithm 7 and Algorithm 1, and the insight on pitfalls, we have implemented and deployed EAX using AES-128 as shown in Algorithm 6. We apply a small simplification constraint to the EAX inputs. The length of the EAX associated data as well as the nonce are required to be exactly the block length of the underlying block cipher primitive. These conditions simplify the internal structures of EAX significantly since two data padding code branches can be omitted completely. Although this approach sacrifices generality, neither compatibility nor the original security proofs are affected.

Algorithm 6. Pipelined EAX Encryption

Input: $k, h, n, M = \{m_0, m_1, \ldots, m_{n-1}\}$
Output: $C = \{c_0, c_1, \ldots, c_{n-1}\}, Tag$
 1: $L \leftarrow E_k(0); B \leftarrow 2L; P \leftarrow 4L$
 2: $\mathcal{N} \leftarrow E_k(E_k(0) \oplus n \oplus B)$ $\qquad\qquad$ **OMAC$_\mathbf{k}^0$(n)**
 3: $\mathcal{H} \leftarrow E_k(E_k(1) \oplus h \oplus B)$ $\qquad\qquad$ **OMAC$_\mathbf{k}^1$(h)**
 4: $t1 \leftarrow \mathcal{N}$
 5: $t2 \leftarrow E_k(2)$
 6: $t3 \leftarrow 0$
 7: **for** $i \leftarrow 0$ **to** $FULLBL(M) - 1$ **do**
 8: $\quad$ $t4 \leftarrow E_k(t1)$
 9: $\quad$ $\mathbf{t3} \leftarrow m_i \oplus t4$
10: $\quad$ $\mathbf{c_i} \leftarrow t3$
11: $\quad$ $t1 \leftarrow t1 + 1$
12: $\quad$ **if** $i < NPADBL(M) - 1$ **then**
13: $\quad\quad$ $t2 \leftarrow E_k(t2 \oplus t3)$ $\qquad\qquad$ **OMAC$_\mathbf{k}^2$(c$_\mathbf{i}$, $\mathcal{C}$)**
14: $\quad$ **end if**
15: **end for**
16: **if** $REMBYT(M) > 0$ **then**
17: $\quad$ $t3 \leftarrow 0$
18: $\quad$ $str \leftarrow E_k(t1)$
19: $\quad$ $PART(t3 \leftarrow m_{FULLBL} \oplus t4)$
20: $\quad$ $PART(c_{FULLBL} \leftarrow t3)$
21: **end if**
22: **if** $REMBYT(M) = 0 \wedge FULLBL(M) > 0$ **then**
23: $\quad$ $\mathcal{C} \leftarrow E_k(t2 \oplus t3 \oplus B)$ $\qquad\qquad$ **OMAC$_\mathbf{k}^2$(c$_\mathbf{i}$, $\mathcal{C}$)**
24: **else**
25: $\quad$ $t3 \leftarrow ADDPADBYTE(t3)$
26: $\quad$ $\mathcal{C} \leftarrow E_k(t2 \oplus t3 \oplus P)$ $\qquad\qquad$ **OMAC$_\mathbf{k}^2$(c$_\mathbf{i}$, $\mathcal{C}$)**
27: **end if**
28: **Tag** $\leftarrow \mathcal{C} \oplus \mathcal{N} \oplus \mathcal{H}$

In Algorithm 6, input parameters consist of a key k, a block-sized header h, and a block-sized nonce n. The input data vector $\mathbf{M} = \{m_0, m_1, \ldots m_{n-1}^*\}$ is a list of block-sized units where each element is a full block except possibly the last element which may be shorter. The resulting ciphertext vector $\mathbf{C}$ has a similar construct. The resulting message integrity code m is a block-sized result. The OMAC sub-primitive calculations are marked in bold, right justified. The multiplications of value L are defined by polynomial multiplication in $GF(2)$ as defined by [4].

For increased readability we introduce a few convenience macros that hide block length calculations as well as detailed loops for simple operations over bytes in partially filled blocks. Pipelined versions are trivially constructed corresponding to the "values-known-in advance" versions listed in Algorithm 6 for readability. $FULLBL$ denotes the number of full blocks in the input data vector, and the function NPADBL(x) will for the vector x give the number of blocks that are not padded with a termination marker. $REMBYT(x)$ gives the number of bytes (if any) in the last vector element provided that it is not block-sized. AD-DPADBYTE(x) adds a termination marker to the vector block in accordance with [4], and *PART* indicates that the operation is applied to a byte vector which is not block-sized. All temporary variables $t1, t2, t3$ and $t4$ are block-sized units.

The innermost operation of EAX is clearly visible on lines 8-11. The counter (in $t1$) drives the block cipher and produces a key stream into $t4$, and the CBC-MAC is accumulated into $t2$ on each round. $t3$ is the temporary buffer that guarantees the integrity of the c_i as explained in Section 5.

The EAX implementation with the constraints outlined above is size-efficient. The algorithm supporting both encryption and decryption and implemented in C compiles to 742 bytes for an OMAP2/OMAP3 processor with ARM and an embedded AES block implementation. Algorithm memory (stack) consumption is a fixed 168 bytes, satisfying the $\Theta(1)$ requirement in Section 3.

7   Related Work

Since the concept of a hardware-assisted TCB was re-invigorated around a decade ago, a number of techniques to secure the "virtual" memory of the trusted execution environment have been proposed. One of the first results was the emergence of execute only-virtual memory (XOM) [10], an important stepping stone for trustworthy computing, but it does not consider data protection.

The work on the AEGIS secure processor [12] [13] introduced a secure computing model that highlights the operation of a security kernel running in an isolated environment, shielded from both physical and software attacks. Among other features, AEGIS implemented a memory management unit (MMU) that protects against physical attacks by deploying stateful, authenticated encryption for virtual memory blocks stored in untrusted memory regions. A comparison of cryptographic primitives suitable for implementing such a secure virtual memory manager in hardware can be found in [16].

This work examines the implementation pitfalls and security proof in the context of implementing EAX, one well-known AEAD. We prove security for that AEAD in two given models, relevant to TEE implementation. Prior work [6] [5] addressing the problem and provability of "online" encryption (system model 2) in a wider context, take another route and also provide alternative constructions for rendering a cryptographic primitive secure in this model.

8   Interpretation and Proposal

The proof approach (and the implementation pitfall) described in this paper are more generally applicable to other authenticated encryption modes as well. For example, AES-CCM, the most widely used AEAD today, uses the same confidentiality and integrity primitives as AES-EAX (AES-CTR and AES-CBC-MAC, respectively), with the main difference that in AES-CCM the integrity is calculated over the plaintext rather than over the ciphertext. Thus, the extra buffer in isolated memory needed in the implementation will still be required, although its placement in AES-CCM will, with respect to sealing/unsealing, be the mirror image of its application in AES-EAX. The Model 1 proofs are trivially adaptable to AES-CCM, but most likely also model 2 proof constructs would be similar when applied to AES-CCM.

Standardized AEAD APIs, like the Global Platform (GP) TEE API [7], includes APIs for pipelined AES-CGM and AES-CCM primitives modelled after interfaces for hash functions, i.e. with separate functions for Init, Update and Finalization. The Update function encrypt or decrypts data in pieces. These functions trivially map to a TEE implementation for pipelined encryption (Figure 3(a)). A TEE AEAD decryption primitive (Figure 3(b)) can in our model be implemented with the GP API by invoking the set of Init, Update and Finalization twice, and binding the Init parameters between the two invocation sets. It is however evidently clear that the API, as it is defined now, easily stimulates an unwary implementor to release decrypted plaintext to untrusted memory before the tag is checked, and in doing that he/she breaks the property of plaintext awareness for the AEAD primitive.

In the light of the findings in this paper, we propose that APIs for AEAD decryption inside TEE:s are changed. One option is to re-encrypt the decrypted content with a temporary key that is given out as a side-effect of a properly validated tag (integrity check) in the Finalization API method. Alternatively, the decryption Update API should not return any decrypted data at all, instead a new Keystream method would be added to return the message XOR keystream to the caller after the tag has been properly validated. Either of these solutions would force the API user to model his decryption operation in a manner that is secure from the TEE perspective.

9   Conclusion

We have described one example of an AEAD that can be proved correct in a computation context where not all data memory during the algorithm computation is assumed to be trustworthy. The hardware architecture introduced in Figure 1 is new to algorithm analysis, although devices with such properties are widely deployed. We have proved AES-EAX secure in this setup, and provide an insight into what modifications need to be done to a conventional EAX algorithm to securely realize it in the pipelined setting.

The pipelined AES-EAX presented and analyzed in this paper is commercially deployed as part of a trusted device architecture.

References

1. ARM. Trustzone-enabled processor,
   http://www.arm.com/pdfs/DDI0301D_arm1176jzfs_r0p2_trm.pdf
2. Bellare, M., Rogaway, P.: The game playing technique (2004),
   http://eprint.iacr.org/2004/331

3. Bellare, M., Rogaway, P.: Random oracles are practical: a paradigm for designing efficient protocols. In: CCS 1993: Proceedings of the 1st ACM Conference on Computer and Communications Security, pp. 62–73. ACM, New York (1993)
4. Bellare, M., Rogaway, P., Wagner, D.: The EAX Mode of Operation. In: Roy, B., Meier, W. (eds.) FSE 2004. LNCS, vol. 3017, pp. 389–407. Springer, Heidelberg (2004), doi:10.1007/978-3-540-25937-4-25
5. Boldyreva, A., Taesombut, N.: Online Encryption Schemes: New Security Notions and Constructions. In: Okamoto, T. (ed.) CT-RSA 2004. LNCS, vol. 2964, pp. 1–14. Springer, Heidelberg (2004), doi:10.1007/978-3-540-24660-2-1
6. Fouque, P.-A., Joux, A., Martinet, G., Valette, F.: Authenticated On-Line Encryption. In: Matsui, M., Zuccherato, R.J. (eds.) SAC 2003. LNCS, vol. 3006, pp. 145–159. Springer, Heidelberg (2004), doi:10.1007/978-3-540-24654-1-11
7. GlobalPlatform Device Technology. TEE Internal API Specification. Global Platform, vrtsion 0.27 edition (September 2011),
http://www.globalplatform.org/specificationform.asp?fid=7762
8. Intel Corporation. Trusted eXecution Technology (TXT) – Measured LaunchedEnvironment Developer's Guide (December 2009)
9. Kostiainen, K., Ekberg, J.-E., Asokan, N., Rantala, A.: On-board credentials with open provisioning. In: ASIACCS 2009: Proceedings of the 4th International Symposium on Information, Computer, and Communications Security, pp. 104–115. ACM, New York (2009)
10. Lie, D., Thekkath, C., Mitchell, M., Lincoln, P., Boneh, D., Mitchell, J., Horowitz, M.: Architectural support for copy and tamper resistant software. SIGPLAN Not. 35(11), 168–177 (2000)
11. Srage, J., Azema, J.: M-Shield mobile security technology, TI White paper (2005),
http://focus.ti.com/pdfs/wtbu/ti_mshield_whitepaper.pdf
12. Edward Suh, G., Clarke, D., Gassend, B., van Dijk, M., Devadas, S.: Efficient memory integrity verification and encryption for secure processors. In: MICRO 36: Proceedings of the 36th Annual IEEE/ACM International Symposium on Microarchitecture, p. 339. IEEE Computer Society, Washington, DC (2003)
13. Edward Suh, G., O'Donnell, C.W., Sachdev, I., Devadas, S.: Design and implementation of the aegis single-chip secure processor using physical random functions. In: ISCA 2005: Proceedings of the 32nd Annual International Symposium on Computer Architecture, pp. 25–36. IEEE Computer Society, Washington, DC (2005)
14. Sundaresan, H.: OMAP platform security features, TI White paper (July 2003),
http://focus.ti.com/pdfs/vf/wireless/platformsecuritywp.pdf
15. Trusted Platform Module (TPM) Specifications,
https://www.trustedcomputinggroup.org/specs/TPM/
16. Chenyu, Y., Rogers, B., Englender, D., Solihin, D., Prvulovic, M.: Improving cost, performance, and security of memory encryption and authentication. In: 33rd International Symposium on Computer Architecture, ISCA 2006, Boston, MA, pp. 179–190 (2006)

A   First System Model Analysis

The first model that we consider is the one where plaintext inside the TEE is encrypted for storage in untrusted memory, and vice versa for decryption. For the encryption primitive we will use the standard reduction technique to reason about whether the encrypted content can be released to an adversary before the whole primitive has completed.

In this model the decryption primitive is unmodified and need not be analyzed, as the decrypted plaintext is stored in the TEE and thus is not becoming available to the adversary during the execution of the primitive. An implementation must still adhere to a similar rule as with encryption, i.e. any encrypted block has to be moved to trusted memory prior to the integrity check and a subsequent decryption - otherwise an adversary has the possibility to decouple the data for the integrity check from the data being decrypted.

Algorithm 7 is an abstraction of the implementation of pipelined EAX, and returns encrypted blocks as they have been generated.

Theorem A1. *The pipelined EAX encryption variant presented in Algorithm 7 is as secure as the original baseline EAX encryption.*

Proof. We begin with the CPA claim. Let $\mathcal{A}$ be an adversary using resources (q, σ) and is trying to distinguish algorithm 7 from a source of random bits. We construct an adversary B that distinguishes the original EAX algorithm from a source of random bits. Adversary B has an oracle g_1 that responds to query $(N, H, M) \in \{0,1\}^l \times \{0,1\}^l \times \{0,1\}^*$ with a string $C = \{c_0, c_1, \ldots, c_{n-1}\}, Tag$. Each named component is an l-bit string. Algorithm 8 describes the operation of adversary B using g_1:

Algorithm 7. Encryption, model 1

Input: $N, H, K, M = \{m_0, m_1, \ldots, m_{n-1}\}$
Output: $C = \{c_0, c_1, \ldots, c_{n-1}\}, Tag$
1: $\mathcal{N} \Leftarrow OMAC_K^0(N)$
2: $\mathcal{H} \Leftarrow OMAC_K^1(H)$
3: **for all** $i \in 0 \ldots n - 1$ **do**
4:    $c_i \Leftarrow CTR_K^{\mathcal{N}}(m_i)$
5:    **return** c_i
6:    $\mathcal{C} \Leftarrow OMAC_K^2(c_i, \mathcal{C})$
7: **end for**
8: $Tag \Leftarrow \mathcal{N} \oplus \mathcal{C} \oplus \mathcal{H}$
9: **return** Tag

Algorithm 8. Algorithm B^g simulating O_e

1: Run $\mathcal{A}$
2: **for all** Oracle calls (N_j, H_j, M_j), $j \in 0 \ldots n - 1$ from $\mathcal{A}$ **do**
3:    $C_j \| Tag_j \Leftarrow g_1(N_j, H_j, M_j)$
4:    **for all** $i \in 0 \ldots n - 1$ **do**
5:       **return** $c_{i,j}$ in response to $\mathcal{A}$'s query
6:    **end for**
7:    **return** Tag_j in response to $\mathcal{A}$'s query
8: **end for**
9: When $\mathcal{A}$ halts, read its output bit b
10: **return** b

We may assume that $\mathcal{A}$ makes $q > 1$ queries to its oracle, and adversary B uses the same number of queries. Also, $\Pr[\mathcal{A}^{Alg2} = 1] = \Pr[B^{EAX} = 1]$. We assume that $\mathcal{A}$ is nonce-respecting[4], B is length-committing[5] and $\Pr[\mathcal{A}^{\$} = 1] = \Pr[B^{\$} = 1]$. Thus, we conclude that

$$Adv_{Alg2}^{CPA}(\mathcal{A}) = Pr[\mathcal{A}^{Alg1} = 1] - Pr[\mathcal{A}^{\$} = 1] =$$

$$= Pr[B^{EAX} = 1] - Pr[B^{\$} = 1] = Adv_{EAX(B)}^{CPA}$$

This completes the claim.

It is easy to see that the CCA proof follows from the CPA proof, since the decryption procedure remains unmodified. Thus, using the same logic it is possible to show that

$$Adv_{Alg2}^{CCA}(\mathcal{A}) = Adv_{EAX}^{CCA}(B)$$

and this completes the proof.

---

[4] An adversary is nonce-respecting if its queries never repeat a nonce value.
[5] Adversary B is length-committing if it consults its own oracles with the appropriate data block lengths implied by the needs of adversary A.

Auditable Envelopes: Tracking Anonymity Revocation Using Trusted Computing

Matt Smart and Eike Ritter

School of Computer Science, University of Birmingham, UK
research@mattsmart.co,
e.ritter@cs.bham.ac.uk

Abstract. In this paper, we discuss a protocol allowing the remote user of a system providing revocable anonymity to be assured of whether or not her anonymity is revoked. We achieve this via a novel use of Trusted Computing and Virtual Monotonic Counters. The protocol has wide-ranging scope in a variety of computer security fields, such as electronic cash, fair exchange and electronic voting.

1   Introduction

A number of fields in computer security consider the anonymity of protocol users to be of critical importance: in digital cash and electronic commerce, it is important that rogue users should not be able to trace the spender of a coin, or to link coins that user has spent with each other. In anonymous fair exchange protocols, multiple parties exchange items with one another, whilst wishing to remain anonymous (sometimes for obvious reasons). In electronic voting, the voter must remain unlinkable to their vote.

However, designers of each of these classes of protocol must consider that there are sometimes occasions when a user's anonymity must be *revoked* — a coin might be maliciously double-spent, or used for an illegal purchase; a party could renege on their promise as part of an exchange protocol; a voter may attempt to vote twice, or may not be a legitimate voter at all[1]. The point of this paper is not to consider for what reason anonymity revocation is required, though: instead, we note that users whose anonymities are revoked should be *made aware* of this fact. In this work, we present a solution to this problem, which is essentially a digitized version of the "sealed envelope problem" discussed in [1].

Let us consider the physical, paper abstraction of the problem. Alice lives in a country where it must be possible to link her identity to her vote (though only authorised entities should be able to make this distinction). When she collects her ballot paper, her identity is sealed inside a tamper-evident envelope, and the serial number of her ballot paper is written on the outside. The envelope is stored securely. Alice votes. Some time later, for whatever reason, someone may

---

[1] The ability to link a voter to their ballot is actually a legal requirement in the UK [2, 20, 15, 16].

S. Katzenbeisser et al. (Eds.): TRUST 2012, LNCS 7344, pp. 19–33, 2012.

wish to trace Alice's ballot back to her. After the election, Alice may wish to see whether her anonymity has been revoked or not. To do this, she merely requests to see the appropriate envelope from the authorities (i.e., that with her ballot serial number on it), and verifies that the envelope is still sealed.

We can apply this abstraction to a number of other fields, and it particularly makes sense when considering payment for goods (we discuss this more in Section 5). However, digitising the (auditable) sealed envelope is not at all trivial: it is intuitively not possible to simply give the authorities an encrypted copy of Alice's identity: if the key is provided with the ciphertext, then Alice has no way to know whether it has been used. If the key is *not* provided, then the authorities cannot do anything with the ciphertext anyway, without contacting Alice (who, as a rogue user, may deliberately fail to provide information) [1]. As a result, we must consider that some sort of trusted platform is required, in order for Alice to be convinced that her anonymity has not been revoked. In this work, we detail a protocol which uses *trusted computing*—specifically, the TPM—to assure Alice in this way.

1.1   Related Work

This paper is potentially relevant to a wide range of fields where revocable anonymity is important: digital cash, fair exchange, and electronic voting. We do not specifically address *any* of these areas, as the way in which they use the identity of the user is unimportant to us: it is the similarity in the need for the user's anonymity that matters. Very little existing work considers auditable revocable anonymity: Kugler and Vögt [11] discuss an electronic payment protocol in which the spender of a coin can determine (within a fixed period) whether their anonymity is revoked or not. Although the protocol is attractive, it requires knowledge *a priori* of who is to be traced—something which is not possible in fields such as electronic voting. More generally, Moran and Naor [12] discuss many high-level theoretical implementations of cryptographic "tamper-evident seals", but do not go into detail as to how these would be realised (and seemingly place a lot of trust in the entity responsible for generating seals).

Ables and Ryan [1] discuss several implementations of a "digital envelope" for the storage of escrowed data using the TPM. Their second solution is appealing, and uses a third party with monotonic counters. However, their solution allows only a single envelope at a time to be stored (as the TPM only permits the usage of one monotonic counter at a time), and also would require Alice herself to generate her identity (something which would not be appropriate for us).

The work of Sarmenta *et al.* [14] on virtual monotonic counters using a TPM is crucial to our work, as we use a new monotonic counter for each anonymous user, allowing each to track their own anonymity. We discuss this more in Section 2.1.

1.2   Motivation and Contribution

In this work, we introduce a new protocol, not tied to any specific class of user-anonymous security protocols (electronic commerce, voting, et cetera), which uses the TPM to assure a user of whether or not their identity has been revealed: we call this property *non-repudiation of anonymity revocation*. Our motivation is clear: if we are to have protocols providing anonymity revocation, then it must be possible for a user to determine when their anonymity is revoked. The reasoning for this is twofold: not only does a user have the right to know when they have been identified (generally, as a suspect in a crime), but the fact that anonymity revocation is traceable is also beneficial:

> ...the detectability of inappropriate actions and accountability for origination suffices to prevent misbehaviour from happening [22, p. 5]

Though protocols exist in electronic commerce which permit this ([11], for example), the techniques used are not widely applicable, for reasons discussed above. We consider preliminary discussions of "escrowed data" stored in a digital envelope which use *monotonic counters* [1], and discuss the use of *virtual monotonic counters* [14] to allow multiple tokens to be securely stored by a single entity.

1.3   Structure

In Section 2, we provide some background in Trusted Computing and the TPM. In Section 3, we discuss our trust requirements for the protocol, which itself is presented in Section 4. We discuss applicability of the protocol in Section 5, give a short discussion on the security of the protocol in Section 6, and finally conclude.

2   Background: Trusted Computing

Trusted Computing is the notion that it is possible to enforce the behaviour of a computer, through the provision of specific "trustworthy" hardware. This allows users of a machine to be convinced that it is in the correct state, and is not compromised. Trusted Computing requirements are generally realised via the use of a Trusted Platform Module (TPM) [18, 19], a tamper-resistant secure coprocessor responsible for a number of functions, including random number generation, RSA key generation, and encryption/decryption. The TPM is capable of *remote attestation* as to the state of its registers, and of *sealing* data: encrypting it such that it can only be opened by a TPM in the correct state.

The TPM has many other functionalities, including Direct Anonymous Attestation, used to anonymously attest to the state of a machine [3]. These functionalities are accessed by the host through a predefined set of commands (or API). For brevity we do not expand further on these functionalities, but instead direct the interested reader to [5], which provides a solid introduction to Trusted Computing and the TPM. It suffices to state that we do not modify the API in any way with our work.

2.1   Physical and Virtual Monotonic Counters

For us, one of the most important capabilities of the TPM is the availability of secure *monotonic counters*. Monotonic counters are tamper-resistant counters embedded in the TPM, which, once incremented, cannot be reverted to a previous value: this reduces the likelihood of replay attacks, for many applications [14].

Unfortunately, the 1.2 version of the TPM, being a low-cost piece of hardware, has only four monotonic counters, of which only one can be used in any boot cycle. As noted by Sarmenta *et al.*, the intention here was to implement a higher number of *virtual* monotonic counters on a trusted operating system. We would rather not require trusted operating systems, however. The work of Sarmenta *et al.* [14] demonstrates the creation of an unbounded number of virtual monotonic counters with a non-trusted OS.

A virtual monotonic counter is a mechanism (in untrusted hardware or software) which stores a counter value, and provides two commands to access it: ReadCounter, which returns the current value, and IncrementCounter, which increases the counter's value. The counter's value must be *non-volatile*, increments and reads must be *atomic*, and changes must be irreversible. Note that *virtual* monotonic counters are not stored on the TPM, but instead on untrusted storage, allowing a far higher number of simultaneous counters to be used.

The manner in which Sarmenta *et al.* implement their solution means that the counter is not tamper-*resistant*, but merely tamper-evident. This is sufficient for our purposes. The counter produces *verifiable* output in the form of unforgeable *execution certificates*, via a dedicated attestation identity key (AIK) for each counter. The counter uses this key, together with nonces, to produce signed execution certificates to send to users.

In the implementation of virtual monotonic counters suggested by Sarmenta *et al.* [14, p. 31], the counter mechanism is stored in full on the host (rather than on the host's TPM), and supports the following functions:

- CreateNewCounter(nonce): returns a CreateCertificate containing the ID number of the counter, and the nonce given as a parameter
- ReadCounter(CounterID,Nonce): returns a ReadCertificate containing the value of the counter, the counter's ID and the given nonce
- IncrementCounter(CounterID,Nonce): increments the counter, and returns an IncrementCertificate containing the new value of the counter, counter ID and nonce
- DestroyCounter(CounterID,Nonce): destroys the counter.

In this work, we assume availability of the virtual monotonic counters defined by Sarmenta *et al.*. To avoid use of commands that are not included in the TPM API, we adopt the first, log-based scheme which they define [14, p. 32]. As noted earlier, the TPM has a limited number of physical monotonic counters, of which only one at a time can be used. The log-based implementation of virtual monotonic counters uses a physical monotonic counter as a "global clock", where the time t is simply the value of the TPM's physical counter at a given time.

The value of a virtual monotonic counter is then the value of the global clock at *the last time the virtual counter's* IncrementCounter *command was executed*. This consequently means that the value of a counter each time it is incremented cannot be predicted deterministically—we can merely say with certainty that the value of the counter will only monotonically increase. As we discuss further in the conclusion, this does not present a problem for us.

The IncrementCounter operation is then implemented using the TPM's API command TPM_IncrementCounter, inside an exclusive, logged transport session, using the ID of the counter in question, and a nonce n_S generated by the client to prevent replay. The result of the final TPM_ReleaseTransportSigned operation is a data structure including the nonce, and a hash of the transport session log, which is used to generate an IncrementCertificate.

The ReadCounter operation is more complex, and involves the host (the "identity provider", idp, for us) keeping an array of the latest increment certificates [14, p. 33] for each virtual counter, returning the right one when the client requests it. In order to prevent reversal of the counter's value, however, the host must send the current time certificate, the current increment certificate, and all of the previous increment certificates. Verification of the counter's value then involves checking that each previous increment certificate is *not* for the counter whose ID has been requested.

We do not go into further implementation specifics, but instead refer interested readers to [14, p. 32] for further information.

3   Trust Model

In our work, we make the following assumptions:

1. Alice and the identity provider idp (discussed in the next section) trust the TPM in Alice's machine, by virtue of it attesting to its state (and therefore, the state of Alice's machine)
2. All users trust idp, by virtue of it attesting to its state (and therefore, the state of idp's machine)
3. The judge is trusted to only authorise anonymity revocation where necessary

In a strict sense, it is not necessary for users to deliberately place trust in any TPM (whether it is in the identity provider's machine, or the user's): both the user's and the identity provider's TPMs have the ability to verify the correctness of the other's TPM and host machine, where the TPM itself is assumed to be a tamper-resistant hardware module. Instead, therefore, any trust we place must be in *the manufacturer of* the TPM, to construct such a device according to its correct specification. Note as a consequence that idp is *not* a trusted third party: the fact that it is *worthy* of trust can be determined by any user.

4   Protocol

We begin by explaining our protocol from a high level, and then go into more implementation specific detail. Note that we assume the availability of standard

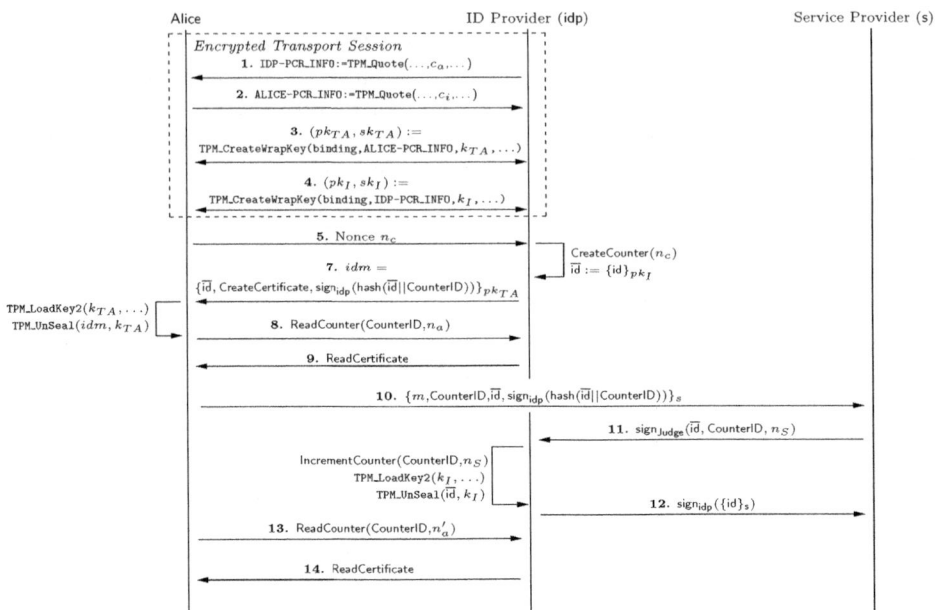

Fig. 1. Our Revocation Audit Protocol

public key cryptographic techniques, hashing and signature protocols. Our scenario is as follows. Alice wishes to engage in a user-anonymous protocol with a *service provider*, s: Alice normally remains anonymous, but s has some interest in revoking her anonymity under certain circumstances (s can obtain a signed request for the user's identity from a judge). Alice would like to know whether or not her anonymity has been revoked at some point after her interaction with s is complete.

In order to present a solution, we introduce a third party, the *identity provider*, idp. The identity provider runs trusted hardware, and attests to the state of his machine in an authenticated encrypted transport session with Alice's TPM (again, it should be noted that this means idp is *not* a trusted third party, but a party which proves that it is trustworthy). Once Alice is assured that she can trust idp's machine, and idp is likewise assured of the trustworthiness of Alice's machine, idp generates a virtual monotonic counter specifically for Alice's identity, using a nonce sent by Alice. He then encrypts Alice's identity using a key generated by Alice's TPM. This is concatenated with a certificate produced by the creation of the counter, hashed, and signed. The signature, certificate and encrypted ID—which we will refer to as a *pseudonym*—are sent to Alice, encrypted with a binding wrap public key to which only her TPM has the private counterpart.

Alice now reads the counter generated for her. She can then send whatever message is necessary to s, along with the particulars of the counter relating to her ID, and idp's signature thereof. The service provider is able to verify the validity of the signed hash on Alice's identity, and can store it for further use.

Should s request to view Alice's identity, he contacts idp with a signature generated by a judge, on the pseudonym and particulars of the certificate (the details originally sent to him). The protocol dictates that idp first increments the virtual monotonic counter associated with the certificate received, and can then load the appropriate key, and decrypt Alice's identity. Alice is later able to request the value of her monotonic counter once again, allowing her to determine whether or not her anonymity was revoked.

4.1   Implementation Steps

We now present a more detailed implementation. A diagram for the protocol is give in Figure 1. The protocol can be split into two stages: in the first, Alice registers her identity with idp, and receives a pointer to a virtual monotonic counter back. In the second, she interacts with s, who may wish to obtain her identity. She is then able to audit this process.

Stage 1. Alice begins with her TPM and the TPM of the identity provider, idp, engaging in an *encrypted transport session*[2]. She invents a nonce, c_a, and challenges idp's TPM to reveal the state of a number of its *platform configuration registers* (PCRs—a set of protected memory registers inside the TPM, which contain cryptographic hashes of measurements based on the current state of the host system), using the TPM_Quote command (with c_a being used for freshness). Alice can use this information to determine if the TPM is in a suitable state (i.e., if its host machine is running the correct software). The identity provider's TPM does the same with Alice's TPM, using a different nonce c_i. In this manner, both platforms are assured of the trustworthiness of the other.

Alice proceeds to have idp's TPM generate a fresh RSA keypair $k_I = (pk_I, sk_I)$ using the TPM_CreateWrapKey command, binding the key to the PCR information she acquired. This ensures that only a TPM in the same state as when the TPM_Quote command was executed is able to open anything sealed with pk_I. Similarly, idp's TPM has Alice's TPM generate a binding wrap keypair $k_{TA} = (pk_{TA}, sk_{TA})$, where the private key is accessible only to Alice's TPM.

Next, idp receives a nonce n_c from Alice. He then creates a *virtual monotonic counter* [14], which he 'ties' to Alice's identity, using the CreateNewCounter command with n_c. This returns a CreateCertificate, detailing the ID number of the counter, CounterID, and the nonce used to create it. idp proceeds to produce a *pseudonym* $\overline{\mathsf{id}} = \{\mathsf{id}\}_{pk_I}$ for Alice, an encryption of her identity (which we assume it knows) using the TPM_Seal command and the binding wrap key pk_I. $\overline{\mathsf{id}}$ and the ID of the counter, CounterID, are concatenated and hashed. The signed hash,

---

[2] We note that idp could also undergo *direct anonymous attestation* [3] with Alice to attest to the state of his machine. However, this is unnecessary for us, as neither Alice nor idp need to (or could) be anonymous at this stage.

pseudonym $\overline{\mathsf{id}}$ and the aforementioned CreateCertificate are sent to Alice, encrypted with the binding wrap key pk_{TA} generated for her TPM. The ID provider stores CounterID and $\overline{\mathsf{id}}$ locally. Alice has her TPM decrypt the message she receives, and then verifies the hash. Note that only Alice's TPM, in the correct state, can decrypt the message sent to her.

Finally, Alice generates a fresh nonce n_a, and contacts idp to request the value of the counter, via the ReadCounter(CounterID, Nonce) command. She receives back a ReadCertificate containing the counter's value, the CounterID and the nonce she sent.

Stage 2. The second stage, which can happen at any time in future, is where Alice communicates with whichever service provider she chooses (note that she may choose to use the same id token with multiple service providers, or may generate a new token for each—it would obviously be sensible to do the latter, to prevent linkability between service providers). Where Alice's message (which might be a tuple containing her vote, or a coin, or some exchangeable object) is represented by m, she sends the tuple

$$\{m, \mathsf{CounterID}, \overline{\mathsf{id}}, \mathsf{sign}_{\mathsf{idp}}(\mathsf{hash}(\overline{\mathsf{id}}\|\mathsf{CounterID}))\}_s$$

to s. Note that the whole message is encrypted with the public key of the service provider, preventing eavesdropping. The message m is further processed (how is outside of the scope of this paper). The signed hash is examined to confirm that it is indeed a valid signature, by idp, on the pseudonym and Counter ID provided. The service provider can then store $\langle \mathsf{CounterID}, \overline{\mathsf{id}} \rangle$ for later use.

Now, Alice can, at any point, check the value of her virtual monotonic counter. The service provider may wish to discover her identity, and so will seek a signed request from a judge, generating a nonce n_S. He sends this request, $\mathsf{sign}_{\mathsf{Judge}}(\overline{\mathsf{id}}, n_S, \mathsf{CounterID})$, to idp. Note that in order to decrypt Alice's pseudonym, idp must use the key k_I—bound to the correct state of his TPM's PCRs—which Alice selected. This means that he needs to be in the correct state. He begins by incrementing Alice's virtual monotonic counter using the command IncrementCounter(CounterID, n_S), and then loads the appropriate key k_I using the TPM_LoadKey2 command. He can then decrypt Alice's identity using TPM_UnBind. Finally, idp returns id, encrypted for s. Again, what s does with Alice's identity is outside of the scope of this paper.

At any later time, Alice can check the virtual monotonic counter value, by contacting idp and executing ReadCounter command with a fresh nonce n'_a. If idp was correctly following the protocol (which, using a verified TPM, he must have been), Alice will know—by determining whether the value of the counter has increased—if her identity has been revealed.

A key point of the protocol is that the identity provider is automatically trusted to follow it, as a consequence of the encrypted transport session in Stage 1. When Alice quotes the PCRs of the identity provider's TPM, she makes it generate a key bound to the correct machine state that it is currently in (presumably,

Alice would terminate any session where an erroneous result of TPM_Quote was reported). Even if idp were to become corrupted after the encrypted transport session, this corruption would alter its TPM's PCRs, protecting Alice's identity from rogue decryption.

5 Applicability

In this section, we discuss some use cases for the protocol: as mentioned earlier, we believe it to have a number of areas of applicability. Here we focus on digital cash and electronic voting, two classes of protocol where anonymity is critical.

5.1 When Does Alice Request a Pseudonym?

We mentioned in Section 4.1 that Alice is free to have idp generate an unlimited number of pseudonyms for her, or just one, depending on her preference. Common sense dictates that, should Alice wish the services she interacts with to be unable to link her transactions together, she should generate a fresh pseudonym for each service she uses. For services which a user uses only once (say, participating in an election), this solution is sufficient. For those which she uses multiple times—such as spending multiple coins in a digital cash system—we consider whether a solution requiring Alice to contact idp multiple times for different pseudonyms is suitable. Digital cash protocols such as [10] typically secure a spender's identity by encrypting it with a key to which only one, trusted, entity has access. When coins are withdrawn, the identities of those coins are stored with the encrypted ID of their owners in a database. Consequently, as in [10], though the digital coin itself does not contain Alice's identity, it contains pointers which which her identity can be looked up in the database.

We note that, in [10], whenever Alice withdraws a coin, she encrypts her identity using fresh symmetric keys for two separate parties: the Bank and the Ombudsman, both of whom have to cooperate to later retrieve her anonymity. In fact, our protocol fits very well into this model. Alice still selects two fresh symmetric keys, but now encrypts not her plaintext ID, but the tuple

$$\langle \mathsf{CounterID}, \overline{\mathsf{id}}, \mathsf{sign}_{\mathsf{idp}}(\mathsf{hash}(\overline{\mathsf{id}}||\mathsf{CounterID}))\rangle,$$

obtained from idp. As idp is trusted to legitimately produce signatures on identities, the Bank and Ombudsman can trust the encrypted ID to be legitimate, and issue the coin as before. Should revocation be required, the Bank now simply contacts idp, allowing Alice to determine that this has occurred.

The advantage here is that Alice's withdrawn coins remain unlinkable—her ID is not encoded into them, and every instance of her ID stored by the Bank is not only encrypted with the key idp generated for it, but also with session keys generated by Alice. We note, of course, that [10] is now quite dated. However, it represents a class of digital cash protocol in which the spender's identity is stored encrypted in a database, and is used here for its simplicity. A range of other digital cash systems could use our protocol in the same way [4, 6, 17, 21], or by simply storing the pseudonym in the coin [7–9, 13].

5.2   Digital Cash Examples

If we take any digital cash protocol where the identity of the coin spender is in some way encrypted (whether stored on a remote server [10] or encoded into the coin itself [13]), we can envisage a situation in which a user either spends a digital coin twice, or participates in an illegal transaction. An authority will have some interest in this, and thus requests that the Bank trace the coins spent by the user, in order to identify her.

In the case of the protocols listed above, the identity of the user is simply decrypted (albeit by two separate authorities in the first case). The user has no way to know that she was traced, until she is apprehended! Now, we modify each protocol such that:

- in the case of protocols where the spender ID is encoded onto the coin, the coins instead contain the user's identity—encrypted using the wrap key made for idp—and the CounterID, with the signed hash of both;
- in the case of a database storing the spender ID, with a lookup value in each key, we proceed as discussed above, with the spender providing the idp-encrypted ID token which is then stored in the database.

This done, the coin spender knows that each coin can only be linked back to her with the cooperation of idp, who (since he is following the protocol) must increment the appropriate counter, allowing the spender to know if she is identified. Note that a protocol providing revocation auditability already exists [11], but requires knowledge *a priori* of who is to be traced, making the protocol unsuitable for other applications.

5.3   Electronic Voting Example

Voting is generally considered to be an area where anonymity of the user (voter) should be unequivocal. However, in some countries (such as the UK, and New Zealand), it is a legal requirement that a voter's ballot paper must be linkable back to them [20]. Smart and Ritter's work on revocable anonymity in electronic voting [15, 16] stores the voter's identity in an encrypted manner in the ballot. If instead we store the encrypted ID, with the CounterID and signed hash of both, we achieve the same property as above: if the authorities need to trace a voter, they contact the identity provider. If a voter is traced, they know that they will be able to determine this was the case, because the identity provider will have incremented their virtual monotonic counter.

An interesting problem is how to deal with *coercion resistance*: if Alice receives an encrypted identity from idp, and then sends it to a vote tallier who places it on the bulletin board unchanged, then a coercer can see that Alice has voted (this is undesirable if we wish to prevent forced-abstention attacks). In protocol vote2, permitting revocable anonymity [16, p. 197–9], revocation is effected by having Alice send the tuple $\langle \overline{\mathsf{id}} = \{\mathsf{id}\}_{\mathsf{Judge}}, \mathsf{Sign}_{\mathbb{R}}(\overline{\mathsf{id}})\rangle$ to the talliers. The ciphertext $\overline{\mathsf{id}}$ is produced by the registrar, $\mathbb{R}$, during registration.

This is followed by an encrypted transport session between the voter's TPM and a Tallier, in which a sealing wrap key used to encrypt designated verifier proofs of re-encryption is produced. Our change to the protocol is again quite small. In the registration phase, once the "join" stage of the protocol is complete, Alice sends her idp-encrypted $\overline{\text{id}}$ to $\mathbb{R}$, who performs an ElGamal encryption of it using the Judge's public key. Before the talliers post this ciphertext to the bulletin board, it is randomly re-encrypted. Should revocation be required, the co-operation of both the Judge and idp is required, and Alice will again be able to see that this has occurred.

6   Analysis

In this section we briefly discuss the security properties of the protocol. The main property that we achieve is that Alice is always able to determine whether her anonymity is revoked or not (non-repudiation of anonymity revocation). This property is satisfied as a result of the knowledge that, having attested to the state of his TPM (and hence, the software being run on the host), idp will either:

- act according to the protocol specification, or
- be unable to decrypt Alice's identity.

Our reasoning is as follows. If the Identity Provider adheres to the specification, he generates a counter for Alice's identity using a nonce she supplies. He encrypts her identity using a keypair which can only be used again by a TPM in the same state which Alice originally accepted.

The information that idp generates to send to Alice must be correct, otherwise idp is deviating from the protocol. It follows that, when s requests Alice's anonymity to be revoked, idp must first increment the associated counter. If idp *does* deviate from the protocol, he will not be able to use the same key k_I later on to decrypt Alice's identity, as that key is bound to his original TPM state (which would change if different, or malicious, software were used).

Thus, the most a rogue idp could achieve is suggesting Alice's anonymity has been revoked when it has not (i.e., tampering with the counter), opening up idp to further questioning (it is hence not in the identity provider's interest to lie to Alice in this way). Since the counter must always be incremented before Alice's identity is decrypted, Alice will always know when she has been identified, by querying the counter.

We next consider Alice's interaction with s. In her communication with s, Alice provides her pseudonym and the counter ID tied to it, together with a signed hash of these values (as originally provided to her by idp). This convinces s that the identity provided is genuine. This leads us to the issue of eavesdropping attacks, allowing a user to illegitimately obtain the pseudonym of another user, and thus 'frame' an innocent victim for a crime. Note that without identifying Alice immediately, s cannot be further convinced that the pseudonym is indeed *hers*. However, our protocol prevents this problem from arising: in the message *idm* sent from idp to Alice, Alice's pseudonym and counter information are encrypted using a binding wrap key, meaning that only her TPM can obtain these values. The only other message where these two values are together is in Alice's communication with s, and here, the entire message is encrypted for s.

The message containing Alice's actual identity is signed by idp before being sent back to s. Hence, providing s trusts idp, he will always obtain Alice's legitimate identity by following the protocol. We might consider that s does *not* trust idp, in which case we could request that s and idp also undergo some sort of attestation, like that between Alice and idp. In the case of the digital cash example presented earlier, we could require that the Bank and Ombudsman each force idp to attest to its state.

Trustworthiness of the Service Provider. Note that, as we have already mentioned, we do not consider how s behaves, as it is outside of the scope of this protocol. However, we now discuss a possible course of action to prevent a rogue s replaying the counter and pseudonym values sent to him by an honest user. In order to mitigate this issue, we need to force the pseudonym's actual owner to prove her ownership. We therefore alter some of the messages in the protocol (numbered according to Figure 1, where messages 10a–d come between messages 10 and 11):

   7. idp→Alice: $\{\overline{\mathsf{id}}, \mathsf{CreateCertificate}, \mathsf{sign}_{\mathsf{idp}}(\mathsf{hash}(\overline{\mathsf{id}} \parallel \mathsf{hash}(\mathsf{CounterID})))\}_{pk_{TA}}$
   8. Alice→idp: $\{\mathsf{ReadCounter}(\mathsf{CounterID}, n_a)\}_{pk_I}$
   9. idp→Alice: $\{\mathsf{ReadCertificate}\}_{pk_{TA}}$
 10. Alice→s: $\{m, \overline{\mathsf{id}}, \mathsf{hash}(\mathsf{CounterID}), \mathsf{sign}_{\mathsf{idp}}(\overline{\mathsf{id}} \parallel \mathsf{hash}(\mathsf{CounterID}))\}_s$
10a. s→Alice: c_{ctr}
10b. Alice→s: $\mathsf{hash}(\mathsf{CounterID} \parallel c_{ctr})$
10c. s→idp: $\overline{\mathsf{id}}, c_{ctr}$
10d. idp→s: $\mathsf{hash}(\mathsf{CounterID} \parallel c_{ctr})$
 11. s→idp: $\mathsf{sign}_{\mathsf{Judge}}(\overline{\mathsf{id}}, n_S)$

These changes are appropriate if we wish to prevent a rogue *s* from gaining an $\langle \overline{\mathsf{id}}, \mathsf{CounterID} \rangle$ pair with which to frame another user. We begin by altering what idp sends to Alice, such that the signed hash now itself contains a hash of CounterID. Both the request and result of reading the counter are encrypted for idp's and Alice's TPM respectively.

The messages from 10 onwards are the most important. Rather than sending her counter's ID in the clear for s, Alice sends a hash of it, which fits in with the signed hash provided by idp. s now returns a challenge c_{ctr}, which Alice hashes with CounterID and returns. In 10c and 10d, s sends the pair $\langle \overline{\mathsf{id}}, c_{ctr} \rangle$ to idp, who looks up $\overline{\mathsf{id}}$ and returns a hash of its associated CounterID concatenated with the challenge. This allows s to ensure that Alice really is the owner of the pseudonym and counter ID she provided. No further changes are necessary, as this prevents s from stealing Alice's pseudonym and counter ID: s would be unable to generate message 10b as he never sees CounterID in the clear. Note that consequently, message 11 also needs to change.

In this section, we have discussed the security properties of our work. Note that changes to mitigate against a corrupt service provider are only appropriate where untrustworthy service providers are a risk—hence we do not include these changes in the main protocol.

7   Conclusions and Future Work

In this paper, we have presented work on a protocol which allows users of a protocol providing revocable anonymity to audit whether or not their anonymity is revoked. We have shown how virtual monotonic counters can be used on an authenticated host to track anonymity revocation, for use with any other class of security protocol requiring revocable anonymity. Further, we addressed how to mitigate the actions of a corrupt service provider. This work makes significant steps in auditable anonymity revocation, a field which has not been considered in detail before.

There are factors which we would like to consider in future work. Some of those are motivated by the issues Sarmenta *et al.* discuss regarding log-based virtual monotonic counters in [14]. The counters are non-deterministic, being based on the single counter in use by the TPM in any one power cycle. This means that counter increment values are unpredictable—not a problem for our application, but potentially a cause of high overhead. Indeed, the ReadCertificate for a counter would include "the log of *all* increments of *all* counters...since the last increment". The size of such a certificate could be substantial. Power failures mid-cycle on idp could also cause the counters to become untrustworthy.

These issues are mitigated by the idea of *Merkle hash tree-based* counters [14, pp. 34–6] which would require changes to the TPM's API. It is for this reason that we did not adopt this solution, but would instead look to it for future work. We would also like to consider a formal analysis of the security properties of the protocol.

One might also consider whether the third party, idp, is required for this protocol to work: an exemplar alternative might be in which Alice and s interact only with each other, assuring trustworthiness via a protocol such as DAA [3]. Alice seals her identity using a key generated by her TPM, meaning that interaction with her TPM is again required to reveal her identity (and thereby, Alice is informed that this has happened). This solution will not work: as we mentioned earlier, a rogue Alice would rather switch her machine off than risk detection. Using a high-availability third party, which proves itself to be following the correct protocol, mitigates this problem.

We feel the protocol we have presented has wide-ranging applicability to a number of user-anonymous protocols—particularly those in digital cash and electronic voting—allowing all users subject to revocable anonymity to be assured of whether or not they can be identified.

References

1. Ables, K., Ryan, M.D.: Escrowed Data and the Digital Envelope. In: Acquisti, A., Smith, S.W., Sadeghi, A.-R. (eds.) TRUST 2010. LNCS, vol. 6101, pp. 246–256. Springer, Heidelberg (2010)
2. Blackburn, R.: The Electoral System in Britain. Macmillan, London (1995)
3. Brickell, E., Camenisch, J., Chen, L.: Direct Anonymous Attestation. In: Proceedings of the 11th ACM Conference on Computer and Communications Security, CCS 2004, pp. 132–145. ACM (2004)
4. Camenisch, J., Maurer, U., Stadler, M.: Digital Payment Systems with Passive Anonymity-Revoking Trustees. Journal of Computer Security 5(1), 69–89 (1997)
5. Challener, D., Yoder, K., Catherman, R., Safford, D., Doorn, L.V.: A Practical Guide to Trusted Computing. IBM Press, Boston (2008)
6. Chen, Y., Chou, J.S., Sun, H.M., Cho, M.H.: A Novel Electronic Cash System with Trustee-Based Anonymity Revocation From Pairing. Electronic Commerce Research and Applications (2011), doi:10.1016/j.elerap.2011.06.002
7. Fan, C.I., Liang, Y.K.: Anonymous Fair Transaction Protocols Based on Electronic Cash. International Journal of Electronic Commerce 13(1), 131–151 (2008)
8. Fuchsbauer, G., Pointcheval, D., Vergnaud, D.: Transferable Constant-Size Fair E-Cash. In: Garay, J.A., Miyaji, A., Otsuka, A. (eds.) CANS 2009. LNCS, vol. 5888, pp. 226–247. Springer, Heidelberg (2009)
9. Hou, X., Tan, C.H.: On Fair Traceable Electronic Cash. In: Proceedings, 3rd Annual Communication Networks and Services Research Conference, pp. 39–44. IEEE (2005)
10. Jakobsson, M., Yung, M.: Revokable and Versatile Electronic Money (Extended Abstract). In: CCS 1996: Proceedings of the 3rd ACM Conference on Computer and Communications Security, pp. 76–87. ACM Press, New York (1996)
11. Kügler, D., Vogt, H.: Off-line Payments with Auditable Tracing. In: Blaze, M. (ed.) FC 2002. LNCS, vol. 2357, pp. 269–281. Springer, Heidelberg (2003)
12. Moran, T., Naor, M.: Basing Cryptographic Protocols on Tamper-Evident Seals. Theoretical Computer Science 411(10) (2010)
13. Pointcheval, D.: Self-Scrambling Anonymizers. In: Frankel, Y. (ed.) FC 2000. LNCS, vol. 1962, pp. 259–275. Springer, Heidelberg (2001)
14. Sarmenta, L.F., van Dijk, M., O'Donnell, C.W., Rhodes, J., Devadas, S.: Virtual Monotonic Counters and Count-Limited Objects using a TPM without a trusted OS. In: Proceedings of the First ACM Workshop on Scalable Trusted Computing, STC 2006, pp. 27–42. ACM, New York (2006)
15. Smart, M., Ritter, E.: Remote Electronic Voting with Revocable Anonymity. In: Prakash, A., Sen Gupta, I. (eds.) ICISS 2009. LNCS, vol. 5905, pp. 39–54. Springer, Heidelberg (2009)
16. Smart, M., Ritter, E.: True Trustworthy Elections: Remote Electronic Voting Using Trusted Computing. In: Calero, J.M.A., Yang, L.T., Mármol, F.G., García Villalba, L.J., Li, A.X., Wang, Y. (eds.) ATC 2011. LNCS, vol. 6906, pp. 187–202. Springer, Heidelberg (2011)
17. Tan, Z.: An Off-line Electronic Cash Scheme Based on Proxy Blind Signature. The Computer Journal 54(4), 505–512 (2011)
18. TCG: Trusted Computing Group: TPM Main: Part 2: Structures of the TPM, Version 1.2, Revision 103 (October 2006), http://bit.ly/camUwE
19. TCG: Trusted Computing Group: TPM Main: Part 3: Commands, Version 1.2, Revision 103 (October 2006), http://bit.ly/camUwE

20. The Electoral Commission: Factsheet: Ballot Secrecy (December 2006),
    http://www.electoralcommission.org.uk/__data/assets/
    electoral_commission_pdf_file/0020/13259/Ballot-Secrecy-2006-12_
    23827-6127__E__N__S__W__.pdf
21. Wang, C., Lu, R.: An ID-based Transferable Off-Line e-Cash System with Revokable Anonymity. In: Proceedings, International Symposium on Electronic Commerce and Security, ISECS 2008, pp. 758–762. IEEE (2008)
22. Weber, S.G., Mühlhäuser, M.: Multilaterally Secure Ubiquitous Auditing. In: Caballé, S., Xhafa, F., Abraham, A. (eds.) Intelligent Networking, Collaborative Systems and Applications. SCI, vol. 329, pp. 207–233. Springer, Heidelberg (2010)

Lockdown: Towards a Safe and Practical Architecture for Security Applications on Commodity Platforms

Amit Vasudevan[1], Bryan Parno[2,*], Ning Qu[3,**], Virgil D. Gligor[1], and Adrian Perrig[1]

[1] CyLab/Carnegie Mellon University
{amitvasudevan,gligor,perrig}@cmu.edu
[2] Microsoft Research
parno@microsoft.com
[3] Google Inc.
quning@gmail.com

Abstract. We investigate a new point in the design space of red/green systems [19,30], which provide the user with a highly-protected, yet also highly-constrained trusted ("green") environment for performing security-sensitive transactions, as well as a high-performance, general-purpose environment for all other (non-security-sensitive or "red") applications. Through the design and implementation of the Lockdown architecture, we evaluate whether *partitioning*, rather than virtualizing, resources and devices can lead to better security or performance for red/green systems. We also design a simple external interface to allow the user to securely learn which environment is active and easily switch between them. We find that partitioning offers a new tradeoff between security, performance, and usability. On the one hand, partitioning can improve the security of the "green" environment and the performance of the "red" environment (as compared with a virtualized solution). On the other hand, with current systems, partitioning makes switching between environments quite slow (13-31 seconds), which may prove intolerable to users.

1 Introduction

Consumers currently use their general-purpose computers to perform many sensitive tasks; they pay bills, fill out tax forms, check account balances, trade stocks, and access medical data. Unfortunately, increasingly sophisticated and ubiquitous attacks undermine the security of these activities. Red/green systems [19,30] have been proposed as a mechanism for improving user security without abandoning the generality that has made computers so successful. They are based on the observation that users perform security-sensitive transactions infrequently, and hence enhanced security protections need only be provided *on demand* for a limited set of activities. Thus, with a red/green system, the user spends most of her time in a general-purpose, untrusted (or "red") environment which retains the full generality of her normal computer; i.e., she can install arbitrary applications that run with good performance. When the user wishes to perform a security sensitive transaction, she switches to a trusted (or "green") environment that includes stringent protections, managed code, network and services at the cost of some performance degradation.

---

* This work was done while Bryan Parno was still at CyLab/Carnegie Mellon University.
** This work was done while Ning Qu was still at CyLab/Carnegie Mellon University.

S. Katzenbeisser et al. (Eds.): TRUST 2012, LNCS 7344, pp. 34–54, 2012.

The typical approach to creating a red/green system relies on virtualization to isolate the trusted and untrusted environments [19,30]. While straightforward to implement, this approach has several drawbacks. First, it requires virtualizing all of the system resources and devices that may be shared between the two environments. From a security perspective, this introduces considerable complexity [16] into the reference monitor (i.e., the virtual machine monitor) responsible for keeping the two environments separate. In addition, even without compromising a reference monitor, actively sharing resources by allowing both environments to run simultaneously exposes side-channels that can be used to learn confidential information [36,9,31,18]. From a performance perspective, the interposition necessary to virtualize devices adds overhead to both trusted and untrusted applications [16].

Through our design and implementation of the Lockdown architecture, we investigate whether *partitioning* resources can overcome these drawbacks. In particular, Lockdown employs a light-weight hypervisor to partition system resources across time, so that only one environment (trusted or untrusted) runs at a time. When switching between the two environments, Lockdown resets the state of the system (including devices) and leverages existing support for platform power-management to save and restore device state. This approach makes Lockdown device agnostic, removes considerable complexity from the hypervisor, and yet maintains binary compatibility with existing free and commercial operating systems (e.g., Windows and Linux run unmodified). It also allows the untrusted environment to have unfettered access to devices, resulting in near native performance for most applications, although a small performance degradation is necessary to protect Lockdown from the untrusted environment. In the trusted environment, Lockdown employs more expensive mechanisms to keep the environment pristine. For example, Lockdown only permits known, trusted code to execute. Since this trusted code may still contain bugs, Lockdown ensures that trusted applications can only communicate with trusted sites. This prevents malicious sites from corrupting the applications, and ensures that even if a trusted application is corrupted, it can only leak data to sites the user already trusts with her data.

As an additional contribution, we study the design and implementation of a user interface for red/green systems that is independent of the choice of virtualization versus partitioning. Our design results in a small, external USB device that communicates the state of the system (i.e, trusted or untrusted) to the user. The security display is beyond the control of an adversary and cannot be spoofed or manipulated. Its simple interface (providing essentially one bit of input and one bit of output), makes it easy to understand and use, and overcomes the challenges in user-based attestation [26] to create a trusted communication channel between the user and the red/green system.

We have implemented and evaluated a full prototype of our user interface (which we call the Lockdown Verifier) plus Lockdown for Windows and Linux on commodity x86 platforms (AMD and Intel). To the best of our knowledge, this represents the first complete, end-to-end design, implementation and evaluation of a red/green system on commodity platforms; we discuss related work in § 8. The Lockdown hypervisor implementation has 10K lines of code, including the code on the Lockdown Verifier. The small size and simple design supports our hypothesis that partitioning (instead of virtualization) can improve security. Our evaluation also indicates that the performance of untrusted applications is the same or better with partitioning (as opposed to virtualization). Lockdown only imposes a 3% average overhead for memory and 2-7% overhead for disk operations for untrusted applications. Virtualization on the other hand imposes overhead for *all* platform hardware with the overhead ranging from 3-81% depending on the resources being virtualized (§ 7.2). The primary limitation of partitioning on current systems is the time (13–31 seconds) needed to switch between the two environments. While we describe several potential optimizations that could significantly reduce this time, whether this tradeoff between security, performance, and usability is acceptable remains an open question.

2   Problem Definition

Goals. The goal of a red/green system is to enable a set of trusted software to communicate with a set of trusted sites while preserving the secrecy and integrity of these applications and the data they handle. Protecting trusted software that does not require network access is a strict subset of this goal. Ideally, this should be achieved without modifying any hardware or software the user already employs. In other words, a user should be able to run the same OS (e.g., Windows), launch her favorite browser (e.g., Internet Explorer) and connect to her preferred site (e.g., a banking website) via the Internet in a highly secure manner while maintaining the current level of performance for applications that are not security-sensitive.

Adversary Model. We assume the adversary can execute arbitrary code within the untrusted environment and may also monitor and manipulate network traffic to and from the user's machine. However, we assume the adversary is remote and cannot perform physical attacks on the user's machine.

Assumptions. The first three assumptions below are necessary for any red/green system. The last two are particular to Lockdown's implementation. (i) **Trusted Software and Sites**: As we discuss in § 3.2, we assume certain software packages and certain websites can be trusted to not deliberately leak private data; (ii) **Reference Monitor Security**: We assume that our reference monitor code does not contain vulnerabilities. Reducing the complexity and amount of code in the reference monitor (as we do with Lockdown) allows manual audits and formal analysis to validate this assumption; (iii) **User Abilities**: We assume the user can be trained to perform security-sensitive operations in the trusted environment; (iv) **Hardware Support**: We assume the user's computer supports Hardware Virtualization Extensions (with Nested Page Table support [10]) and contains a Trusted Platform Module [44] chip. Both technologies are ubiquitous; and (v) **Trusted BIOS**: Lockdown uses the BIOS during its installation and to reset devices, so we must assume the BIOS has not been corrupted. Fortunately, most modern BIOSes require signed updates [32], preventing most forms of attack.

3   Lockdown's Architecture

At a high level (Figure 1), Lockdown splits system execution into two environments, trusted and untrusted, that execute non-concurrently. This design is based on the belief

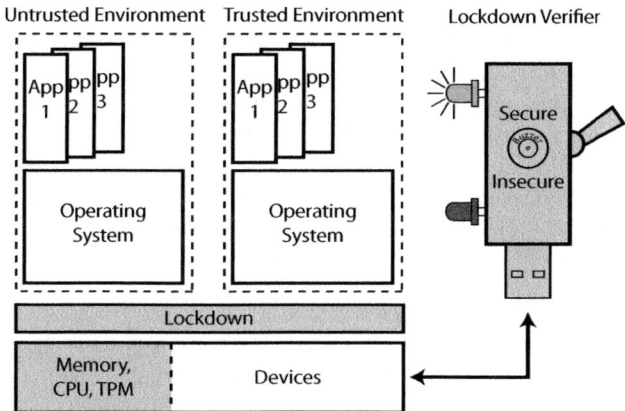

Fig. 1. Lockdown System Architecture. Lockdown partitions the platform into two environments; only one environment executes at a time. An external device (which we call the Lockdown Verifier) verifies the integrity of Lockdown, indicates which environment is active and can be used to toggle between them. The shaded portions represent components that must be trusted to maintain isolation between the environments.

that the user has a set of tasks (e.g., games, browsing for entertainment) that she wants to run with maximum performance, and that she has a set of tasks that are security sensitive (e.g., checking bank accounts, paying bills, making online purchases) which she wants to run with maximum security and which are infrequent and less performance-critical. The performance-sensitive applications run in the untrusted environment with near-native speed, while security-sensitive applications run in the trusted environment, which is kept pristine and protected by Lockdown. The Lockdown architecture is based on two core concepts: (i) **hyper-partitioning**: system resources are partitioned as opposed to being virtualized. Among other benefits, this results in greater performance, since it minimizes resource interpositioning, and it eliminates most side-channel attacks possible with virtualization; and (ii) **trusted environment protection**: Lockdown limits code execution in the trusted environment to a small set of trusted applications and ensures that network communication is only permitted with trusted sites.

3.1 Hyper-partitioning

Since the untrusted environment may be infected with malware, Lockdown must isolate the trusted environment from the untrusted environment. Further, Lockdown must isolate itself from both environments so that its functionality cannot be deliberately or inadvertently modified. One way to achieve this isolation is to rely on the platform hardware to partition resources. With platform capabilities such as Single-Root I/O Virtualization (SR-IOV) [29] and additional hardware such as an IOMMU, it is possible to assign physical devices directly to an environment (untrusted or trusted) [4,17]. This hardware capability facilitates concurrent execution of multiple partitions without virtualizing devices. Unfortunately, not all devices can be shared currently (e.g., video, audio) [5] and such platform support is not widely available today [6,17].

CPU and Memory Partitioning. Lockdown partitions the CPU in time by only allowing one environment to execute at a time. The available physical memory in the system is partitioned into three areas: the Lockdown memory region, the untrusted environment's memory region, and the trusted environment's memory region[1]. Lockdown employs Nested Page Tables (NPT)[2] [10] to restrict each environment to its own memory region. In other words, the NPT for the untrusted environment does not map physical memory pages that belong to the trusted environment and vice versa. Further, it employs hardware-based DMA-protection within each environment to prevent DMA-based access beyond each environment's memory regions.

Device Partitioning. With hyper-partitioning, both the untrusted and trusted environments use the same set of physical devices. Devices that do not store persistent data, such as video, audio, and input devices can be partitioned by saving and restoring their states across environment switches. However, storage devices may contain persistent, sensitive data from the trusted environment, or malicious data from the untrusted environment. Thus, Lockdown ensures that each environment is provided with its own set of storage devices and/or partitions. For example, Lockdown can assign a different hard disk to each environment. Alternatively, Lockdown can assign a different partition on the same hard disk to each environment. The challenge is to save and restore device state in a device agnostic manner, and to partition storage devices without virtualizing them, while providing strong isolation that cannot be bypassed by a malicious OS.

Lockdown leverages the Advanced Configuration and Power-management Interface (ACPI) [14] to save and restore device states while partitioning non-storage devices. The ACPI specification defines an ACPI subsystem (system BIOS and chipset) and an Operating System Power Management (OSPM) subsystem. With an ACPI-compatible OS, applications and device drivers interact with the OSPM code, which in turn interacts with the low-level ACPI subsystem. ACPI defines four system sleep states which an ACPI-compliant computer system can be in: S1 (power is maintained to all system components, but the CPU stops executing instructions), S2 (the CPU is powered off), S3 (standby), and S4 (hibernation: all of main memory is saved to the hard disk and the system is powered down). Figure 2a shows how an OSPM handles ACPI Sleep States S3 and S4. When a sleep command is initiated (e.g., when the user closes the lid on a laptop), the OSPM first informs all currently executing user and kernel-mode applications and drivers about the sleep signal. They, in turn, store the configuration information needed restore the system when it awakes. The device drivers use the OSPM subsystem to set desired device power levels. The OSPM then signals the ACPI subsystem, which ultimately performs chipset-specific operations to transition the system into the desired sleep state. The OSPM polls the ACPI subsystem for a wake signal to determine when it should reverse the process and wake the system. Note that with this scheme, Lockdown does not need to include any device drivers or interpose on device operations. The OS contains all the required drivers that deal directly with the devices for normal operation and for saving and restoring device states.

---

[1] An implementation using ACPI S4 state for hyper-partitioning (§ 6), requires only two memory regions, Lockdown and the current environment (untrusted or trusted) since ACPI S4 results in the current environment's memory contents being saved and restored from the disk.

[2] Also termed as Extended Page Tables on Intel platforms.

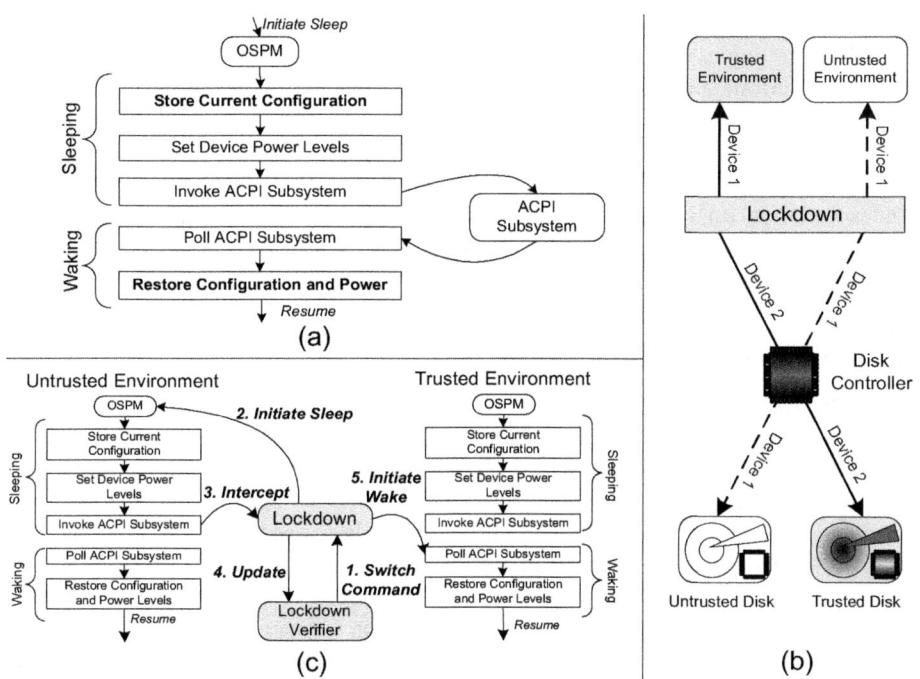

Fig. 2. Hyper-Partitioning. **(a)** Lockdown leverages the Advanced Configuration and Power-management Interface (ACPI) OS sleep mechanism to partition (by saving and restoring states) non-storage system devices while being device agnostic. **(b)** Storage devices (e.g., disk) are partitioned by intercepting the device selection requests and redirecting device operations to the appropriate device, based on the current environment. **(c)** Environment switching is performed upon receiving a command from the Lockdown Verifier. The OS ACPI sleep steps are modified by Lockdown to transition between environments (untrusted and trusted).

Lockdown efficiently partitions storage devices by interposing on device selection, rather than device usage. It takes advantage of the fact that modern storage devices rely on a controller that implements the storage protocol (e.g., ATA, SATA) and directs storage operations to the attached devices. When the operating system writes to the storage controller's I/O registers (a standard set for a given controller type), Lockdown intercepts the write and manipulates the device controller to select the appropriate device for the currently executing environment (see Figure 2b). All other device operations (e.g., reads and writes) proceed unimpeded by Lockdown. A similar scheme can be adopted for two partitions on the same hard disk by manipulating sector requests. Our evaluation (§ 7) shows that interposing on device/sector selection has a minimal effect on performance. Since we assume the BIOS is trusted (§ 2), we can be sure that Lockdown will always be started first, and hence will always maintain its protections over the trusted disk.

Environment Switching. Lockdown performs an environment switch by transitioning the current environment to sleep and waking up the other. Figure 2c shows the steps taken for an environment switch, assuming the user starts in the untrusted environment. When the user toggles the switch on the trusted Lockdown Verifier to initiate a switch to the trusted environment (Step 1), the Lockdown Verifier communicates with Lockdown which in turn instructs the OSPM in the untrusted environment to put the system to sleep (Step 2). When the OSPM in the untrusted environment issues the sleep command to the ACPI Subsystem, Lockdown intercepts the command (Step 3), resets all devices, updates the output on the Lockdown Verifier (Step 4), and issues a wake command to the OSPM in the trusted environment (Step 5). Switching back to the untrusted environment follows an analogous procedure.

3.2 Trusted Environment Protection

Lockdown's trusted environment runs a commodity OS and applications. Lockdown verifies the integrity of all the files of the trusted environment during Lockdown's installation. Further, Lockdown trusts the software in the trusted environment to not leak data deliberately. However, vulnerabilities within the OS or an application in the trusted environment can be exploited either locally or remotely to execute malicious code. Further, since the trusted environment and untrusted environment use the same devices, the untrusted environment could change a device's firmware to act maliciously. Lockdown uses approved code execution and network protection to ensure that only trusted code (including device firmware code) can be executed and only trusted sites can be visited while in the trusted environment, as explained below.

Approved Code Execution. For non-firmware code, Lockdown uses Nested Page Tables (NPT) to enforce a $W \oplus X$ policy on physical memory pages used within the trusted environment. Thus, a page within the trusted environment may be executed or written, but not both. Prior to converting a page to executable status, Lockdown checks the memory region against a list of trusted software (§ 3.2 describes how this list is established). Execution is permitted only if this check succeeds. Previous work enforces a similar policy only on the kernel [37], or uses it to determine what applications are running [21]. In contrast, Lockdown uses these page protections to restrict the OS and the applications to a limited set of trusted code. For device firmware code, Lockdown, during installation, scans all installed hardware and enumerates all system and device firmware code regions. It assumes this code has not yet been tampered with and uses NPTs to prevent either environment from writing to these regions.

Network Protection. Since users perform many security-sensitive activities online, applications executing in the trusted environment need to communicate with remote sites via the network. However, permitting network communication exposes the trusted environment to external attacks. Remote attackers may exploit flaws in the OS's network stack, or the user may inadvertently access a malicious site, or a network-based attacker may perform SSL-based attacks (e.g., tricking a user into accepting a bogus certificate). While approved code execution prevents many code-based attacks, the trusted environment may still be vulnerable to script-based attacks (e.g., Javascript) and return-oriented programming attacks [38].

To forestall such attacks, Lockdown restricts the trusted environment to communicate only with a limited set of trusted sites. It imposes these restrictions by interposing on all network traffic to or from the trusted environment. Lockdown uses hardware CPU and physical memory protections to prevent the trusted environment from seeing or accessing any physical network devices present in the system. Network communication is permitted via a proxy network driver that Lockdown installs in the guest OS. This driver forwards packets to Lockdown, which analyzes the packets and then forwards them to the physical network interface. The trusted environment can use a distinct physical network interface or reuse the same interface of the untrusted environment for network communication (since the environments run non-concurrently). In both cases the Lockdown hypervisor will need to include the network driver for the physical interface. A simpler approach is to perform network access (either wireless or wired) using the Lockdown Verifier. In this case, the Lockdown hypervisor does not need to contain any network driver but simply forwards the packets to the verifier.

Lockdown uses packet analysis to determine which network packets are permitted. One approach, with the argument that any site with sensitive data should be using SSL to protect it in transit, would be to allow only SSL and DNS network packets to pass through to trusted sites. All other packets are dropped. When an SSL session is initiated, Lockdown determines if the request is a valid SSL connection request. If it is, Lockdown validates the site's SSL certificate and checks it against the list of trusted sites (the creation and maintenance of this list is discussed in the following section). If any of these checks fail, the packet is dropped. Incoming packets are permitted only if they belong to an existing SSL session or are in response to an earlier DNS request. Note that DNS-based attacks are forestalled by SSL certificate verification. From a technical perspective, supporting other network protocols such as SSH is also possible.

Defining Trusted Entities. To keep the trusted environment safe, Lockdown restricts the software that can execute and the sites that can be visited. To define what software and sites can be trusted, we leverage the user's existing trust in the distributor of Lockdown, i.e., the organization that provided the user with a copy of Lockdown in the first place. For example, in a corporation, the IT department would play the role of Lockdown distributor. For consumers, the role might be played by a trusted company or organization, such as RedHat, Mozilla, or Microsoft. Lockdown's key insight is that by agreeing to install Lockdown, the user is expressing their trust in the Lockdown provider, since Lockdown will be operating with maximum platform privileges on their computer. Thus, we can also trust that same organization to vet trusted software and websites. The list of trusted software can be relatively small: primarily an operating system and a trusted browser. The list of trusted sites is necessarily larger, since it should include the security-sensitive companies a user interacts with. However, to limit potential leaks to entities on the list that the user does not interact with, the user can customize the list. During Lockdown's installation, the user is presented with the master list of trusted software and trusted websites and selects a subset of each list. Thus, the user can choose her favorite web browser, and select the handful of websites she actually uses from the hundreds of sites on the master list. Lockdown will then prohibit the trusted environment from contacting any site not on the user's restricted list. A small application that runs in the trusted environment allows the user to update her selection at a later time.

4   External Verification and Trusted Path

While the reference monitor (i.e., the hypervisor or virtual machine monitor) in a red/-green system always knows whether the trusted or the untrusted environment is currently operating, it must create a trusted path to the user to convey this information in a way she can easily understand and trust. Otherwise, she might be tricked into performing security-sensitive operations in the untrusted environment. Below, we show how to eliminate such attacks by using a simple, external device to control the environment switching and to display the result of the switch to the user. We also show how the external device can verify that it is interacting with a correct version of the red/green system, preventing malware from misleading the device.

The Lockdown Verifier. The user employs an external device called the Lockdown Verifier to switch between trusted and untrusted environments. To enable the user to trust the Lockdown Verifier, it must possess the following properties: (i) **Correct Operation**: Software executing on the Lockdown Verifier must be robust against compromise. By minimizing the code for the verifier, we make it amenable to formal analysis;(ii) **Minimal Input Capabilities**: To minimize complexity (and hence user confusion), we wish to minimize the number of input options; and (iii) **Minimal Output Capabilities**: To reduce confusion, the user should be able to easily learn which environment she is working in. To achieve these properties, the Lockdown Verifier consists of a single switch, two LEDs, and a buzzer (Figure 1). The switch can be toggled from secure to insecure (or vice versa). When the user is in the trusted environment, the green LED is lit. When the user is in the untrusted environment, the red LED is lit. To provide additional feedback to the user (e.g., after she toggles the switch), the verifier uses a blinking red LED to indicate processing. Thus, the user need only remember to check that the green LED is lit before performing security-sensitive tasks. The Lockdown Verifier uses the buzzer to attract the user's attention whenever the LEDs change state. The verifier can also create an alarm buzz if it is unable to verify the correctness of the reference monitor (e.g., Lockdown) or if the system encounters a fatal error.

Secure Channel. To accurately verify the state of the system (trusted or untrusted), the Lockdown Verifier must be able to communicate securely with the red/green reference monitor (i.e., the hypervisor or virtual machine monitor). More precisely, it should not be possible for an adversary to impersonate or undetectably modify the reference monitor. We can achieve this goal using a combination of CPU protections and hardware attestation via a TPM [44]. To create a secure channel for communicating with the Lockdown Verifier, the reference monitor uses CPU protections to reserve a USB controller and to prevent both environments from accessing it. We use USB as an interface as it is intuitive for users and eliminates the need for an external power source for the verifier. To convince the Lockdown Verifier that it is communicating with the correct reference monitor, we use TPM-based attestation. Initially, the reference monitor is started using a *measured launch* operation [15,7] which securely records a hash of the reference monitor's code in the TPM. When the verifier is connected to the system, it sends a challenge (a cryptographic nonce) to the reference monitor. The reference monitor uses the TPM to generate a quote (essentially a signed statement describing the software state of the system) that it securely transmits to the Lockdown Verifier using the reserved USB controller. The Lockdown Verifier then checks the attestation based on the TPM public key (setup during installation). If verification fails, the Lockdown Verifier halts, sets the LED state to blinking red and emits an alarm buzz. If it succeeds, the Lockdown Verifier emits an attention buzz and sets the LED state to solid red if the untrusted environment is running or to solid green if the trusted environment is running.

Since it is connected via USB, the Lockdown Verifier can also detect when the system is rebooted, since on a reboot, a USB controller sends all attached USB devices a reset signal. When this happens, the Lockdown Verifier emits the attention buzz and sets the LED state to blinking red, since it can no longer vouch for the state of the system. It then performs the procedure described above to verify that the reference monitor is back in control and to learn which environment is currently active. Note that the measured launch operation coupled with the TPM-based attestation and the reserved USB controller/channel eliminates the need to setup and share a secret key between the reference monitor and the Lockdown Verifier.

5   Security Analysis

Trusted Environment Isolation. Lockdown's hyper-partitioning and network protection mechanisms are designed to isolate the trusted environment from local and remote malware. Locally, Lockdown ensures that the trusted environment and untrusted environment never execute concurrently, preventing malware in the untrusted environment from directly interfering with the trusted environment's execution. Lockdown's use of Nested Page Tables ensures that software in the untrusted environment cannot even address the trusted environment's memory region, thus protecting its secrecy and integrity. To prevent device-based attacks, Lockdown uses hardware DMA protections to prevent DMA-based reads and writes to sensitive areas, and it ensures that all devices are reset during an environment switch. Storage devices are partitioned between the two environments to prevent secrets from leaking out of the trusted environment, and to prevent maliciously crafted inputs from penetrating into the trusted environment. Remotely, Lockdown's network protections prevent untrusted entities from contacting the trusted environment. To provide defense-in-depth, these protections also prevent the trusted environment from contacting untrusted sites. Thus, even if a bug in the trusted OS or applications results in a data leak, the data can only travel to sites the user already trusts with her data.

Code Integrity. Lockdown's approved execution ensures that only measured code that appears on Lockdown's list of trusted software can run within the trusted environment. Further, once the code is measured, Lockdown renders it immutable. Lockdown thus prevents a significant class of attacks that modify existing code or execute new malicious code. However, this approach does not check interpreted code (e.g., JavaScript). Hence, if a trusted site is compromised, it may allow an attacker to manipulate the trusted environment. Thus, one drawback of Lockdown's current approach is that a compromise at one of the user's trusted sites can affect the security of her transactions at other sites. Improving browser-based isolation can mitigate these concerns [46,12], but eventually, we anticipate a trusted environment for each trusted site.

Trusted Path. Lockdown is designed to create a trusted path to the user, i.e., to provide the user with the confidence that she is communicating securely with the party she intends to contact. Lockdown achieves this property by providing a simple indicator (a green LED) on the Lockdown Verifier to signal when the user is operating in the trusted environment. This indicator is only provided in response to a message received from Lockdown over the secure channel that the Lockdown Verifier establishes with Lockdown (§ 4). This channel is protected by Lockdown's exclusive access to the USB controller combined with the TPM's ability to provide a verifiable summary of the system's software and a guarantee that the hardware memory protections are in place.

5.1 Other Attacks

Denial of Service. Lockdown's hyper-switching mechanism triggers the sleep state in the OSPM of the untrusted environment in order to switch to the trusted environment. However, malware in the untrusted environment can modify the OSPM to ignore the sleep command. Thus, malware in the untrusted environment can keep the trusted environment from loading. However, it cannot do so undetectably. Before Lockdown triggers the sleep state in the OSPM of the untrusted environment, it lights up a blinking red LED on the Lockdown Verifier and sounds an attention buzz to indicate processing. If the untrusted environment ignores the sleep command, then the switch to the trusted environment will never complete, and hence the Lockdown Verifier LED will never glow green. Lockdown relies on the user to wait for a green LED before performing security-sensitive tasks.

Corrupt Lockdown Distributor. Lockdown depends on an external party to define the master list of trusted software and trusted sites. If this party were corrupted, the user might install malicious software in the trusted environment or visit malicious sites. However, users already depend on remote entities for software updates. For example, if an attacker could corrupt the Windows Update Service, then he could perform a similar attack to load malware onto millions of machines. Lockdown merely leverages this existing trust to more precisely define what can be done in the trusted environment.

Social Engineering. A clever attacker may convince the user to perform a security-sensitive task in the untrusted environment, rather than in the trusted environment. Lockdown cannot prevent such an attack; it can only rely on the user to check the system's status as displayed by the Lockdown Verifier, and to switch to the trusted environment for security-sensitive tasks. With sufficient user education, users can obtain strong assurance if they elect to participate.

6   Implementation

We implemented a complete prototype of Lockdown on both AMD and Intel x86 platforms with Windows 2003 Server as the OS in both the trusted and untrusted environments. To demonstrate that Lockdown's hyper-partitioning is a generic primitive that works with other ACPI-compliant OSes, we also developed a prototype using Linux guests. Neither prototype required changing any code in the OS kernels. Due to space constraints, we focus on describing our Windows prototype on the AMD platform.

Our Lockdown prototype consists of a Lockdown Loader and the Lockdown Runtime. The SKINIT instruction is used to perform a *late-launch* [7] operation which ensures that the Lockdown Loader runs in a hardware-protected environment and that its measurement (cryptographic hash) is stored in the TPM's Platform Configuration Register (PCR) 17. The trusted Lockdown Loader loads the Lockdown Runtime and protects the Lockdown Runtime's memory region from DMA reads and writes (using AMD's Device Exclusion Vector [7]). It then verifies the integrity of the Lockdown Runtime and extends a measurement (a cryptographic hash) of the Lockdown Runtime's code into the TPM's PCR 19. The Lockdown Loader then initializes the USB controller on the host for communication with the Lockdown Verifier, creates the Nested Page Tables [10] for the trusted and untrusted environments and transfers control to the Lockdown Runtime. When first launched, the Lockdown Runtime requests a challenge from the Lockdown Verifier. The Lockdown Runtime and the Lockdown Verifier then engage in the authentication protocol described in § 4. The Lockdown Runtime launches the environment currently indicated on the Lockdown Verifier in a hardware virtual machine, and informs the Lockdown Verifier once the environment has been launched, so that the Lockdown Verifier can sound the attention buzz and light the appropriate LED. The Lockdown Runtime's role in hyper-partitioning, and protection of the trusted environment is described below.

6.1 Hyper-partitioning

To implement hyper-partitioning for non-storage devices under the Windows OS, Lockdown makes use of the ACPI S4 (hibernate) sleep state. ACPI S3 (standby) would offer faster switching times, but Windows ACPI implementation only saves and restores device state during an S4 sleep, and hence we cannot use S3 with Windows without modifying its source code. Memory and storage device partitioning are described below.

Memory. In our current implementation (on systems with 4 GB of physical memory), Lockdown reserves 186 MB for itself and 258 MB for the system's firmware. The rest of physical memory is available to the trusted or untrusted environments. Isolation between the environments and Lockdown is maintained by using Nested Page Tables; the page-table entries which point to Lockdown's physical memory regions are marked not-present, while the entries for the system firmware are set to prohibit writes.

Storage Devices. Our prototype can assign a different hard drive to each environment (trusted and untrusted), or it can partition a single hard drive into separate regions for each environment. Lockdown assigns each environment its own hard drive by intercepting read and write accesses to the ATA/SATA drive-select and command port (e.g., 0x1F6/7). This allows Lockdown to prevent the trusted environment from accessing the untrusted disk (and vice versa). For example, if the trusted environment writes a request to port 0x1F6 to select the master drive, an exception is generated, returning control to Lockdown. Lockdown writes to the disk controller's register and selects the slave (trusted) disk instead. A similar procedure prevents the untrusted environment from selecting the trusted disk. Lockdown isolates partitions within a single disk by intercepting write accesses to the ports which are required to set the LBA (Logical Block Address) sector addresses (e.g., ports 0x1F3/4/5) and the sector count (e.g., port 0x1F2) in addition to the command port. When a sector read or write command is initiated by the environments using the command port, Lockdown verifies that the sector LBA address and count are within limits of the partition of the current environment before forwarding the command to the disk controller.

Environment Switching. Lockdown establishes control over the system's ACPI modes by intercepting the trusted and untrusted environments' attempts to access the ACPI Sleep and Status registers. The Lockdown Runtime determines the I/O location of these registers by parsing the ACPI Fixed Address Descriptor Table. When the user toggles the switch on the Lockdown Verifier, Lockdown sets an internal switch flag and signals the Lockdown Monitor inside the current environment to initiate the sleep state. The Lockdown Monitor is an untrusted application which uses the *SetSuspendState* Windows API in order to trigger an S4 Sleep. The OSPM in Windows then prepares the system for hibernation, saves the memory contents to disk, and writes to the ACPI Sleep Register. Lockdown captures this write and instead clears the switch flag and updates the Lockdown Verifier to indicate the newly active environment. Lockdown then resets the system via a soft-reset to reset the device states. Finally, Lockdown launches the target environment by waking it from hibernation. The Windows OS in the target environment loads the hibernation image from the disk, restores the device states, and transfers control to the Windows Kernel.

6.2   Protecting the Trusted Environment

Approved Code Execution. To enforce approved code execution, Lockdown uses page-level code hashing, similar to the approach used by previous work [21,37]. Prior to executing the trusted environment, Lockdown sets its Nested Page Table (NPT) entries to prevent execution of those pages. When the trusted environment attempts to execute a page, it causes a fault that returns control to Lockdown. Lockdown computes a hash of the faulting page and compares it to the hashes in its list of trusted software. If a match is found, the corresponding NPT entry is updated to allow execution but prevent writes. If the trusted environment later writes to this page, a write fault will be generated. Lockdown will re-enable writing but disable execution. Matching a code page to the list of approved software is straightforward. In Windows, an application's entire executable is mapped into memory, so the executable's header and relocation tables are always present at runtime. Lockdown uses this information to compute the inverse of the relocation operation and compare the page to hashes of the original executable.

Network Protection. To provide network protection for the trusted environment, we developed an untrusted network driver for Windows, and an SSL Protocol Analyzer within Lockdown. The analyzed network packets are sent to the Lockdown Verifier using Lockdown's USB driver, and ultimately out to the network. The Lockdown Verifier has an ethernet port and a dedicated network chipset. Our OS-level network driver sends and receives network packets to and from the SSL Protocol Analyzer via a hypercall. Our SSL Protocol Analyzer is based on `ssldump`[3]. We added support for SSL

---
[3] http://www.rtfm.com/ssldump/

session tracking and event handling depending on the SSL packet (e.g., Certificate, ServerHello). The certificate handler is used to compare a site's SSL certificate against Lockdown's list of trusted-site certificates.

6.3   External Verification and Trusted Path

We built the Lockdown Verifier using a low-cost LPC 2148 development board. The board is equipped with a 60Mhz ARM7 CPU, 512 KB flash, 42 KB RAM and an ethernet chipset/port. We attached a red and a green LED, a switch, and a buzzer to the board. The Lockdown Runtime contains USB and TPM drivers that communicate with the Lockdown Verifier and the host system TPM respectively. The verifier upon reset or power-up waits for a challenge request from Lockdown. Upon receiving the challenge request, the Lockdown Verifier transmits a cryptographic nonce and receives a TPM-generated attestation from Lockdown. The attestation contains the TPM's signature over the current values of PCRs 17 and 19, as well as the nonce that was provided. The verifier uses the TPM's public-key (installed during Lockdown's installation) to verify the attestation. If the verification succeeds, the Lockdown Verifier goes into a trusted communication mode with Lockdown and responds to commands to set LEDs and report on the switch's status, until the system is reset or turned off.

7   Evaluation

7.1   Trusted Computing Base (TCB)

Like all security systems, Lockdown must assume the correctness and security of its core components. This assumption is more likely to hold if we reduce the amount of code that must be trusted, keep the design simple and minimize the external interface. This reduces opportunities for bugs and makes the code more amenable to formal analysis. Lockdown's total TCB is only 10KLOC, placing Lockdown within the reach of formal verification and manual audit techniques. Lockdown's design is simple and greatly reduces the attack surface. Lockdown does not expose any interface while the untrusted environment is running and interposes only on memory and disk accesses. When the trusted environment is executing, Lockdown also intercepts execution on memory pages for approved code execution. These operations are handled transparently via well-defined CPU intercepts. Further, in the trusted environment, Lockdown exposes a single hypercall interface to the guest OS network driver. The arguments to this hypercall interface are the type of operation (read or write), the network packet length and the packet data which are sanity checked by the Lockdown Runtime.

Lockdown's TCB compares favorably with other popular hypervisors and VMMs (Figure 3), which tend to be orders of magnitude larger, despite not providing Lockdown's protection's for a trusted environment. Xen, KVM, and Hyper-V include an entire OS in the TCB for device access and administrative purposes, dramatically increasing their TCBs. While VMware ESXi does not require such an OS, it still includes a large TCB, since it employs full virtualization of devices and hence must include device drivers for all supported platforms. Only L4Ka-Pistachio [2] and NOVA [40]

Hypervisor/Micro-kernel	TCB	Supports *any* unmodified OS	Free from device Virtualization
Lockdown	10KLOC	✓	✓
L4Ka-Pistachio	25KLOC	✗	✗
NOVA	36KLOC	✗	✗
VMWare ESXi	200KLOC	✓	✗
Xen + Linux	400KLOC	✓	✗
KVM + Linux + QEMU	470KLOC	✓	✗
Hyper-V + Windows	5000KLOC	✓	✗

Fig. 3. Lockdown's TCB and Features. Comparison with popular, general-purpose hypervisors and micro-kernels. Note: We assume a Linux kernel with only the required device drivers for a host platform. For our test system this came up to 300KLOC. As VMWare, Hyper-V and Windows are closed-source, we rely on publicly available information to estimate their SLOC [1,20,3]. QEMU's TCB with only x86 support is around 150KLOC.

approach Lockdown's TCB size. However, the L4Ka-Pistachio requires non-trivial OS porting and cannot run OSes such as Windows. While NOVA is designed to run an unmodified OS, it currently only runs Linux due to its minimal device support; its virtualization architecture also requires device drivers to be written from scratch.

7.2 Performance Measurements

We use our prototype to determine Lockdown's performance on a recent laptop with a dual-core AMD Phenom-II N620 CPU, 4GB RAM, 250GB SATA hard disk, a v1.2 TPM and two USB controllers.

CPU and Memory Overhead. Lockdown's use of Nested Page Tables (NPT) to hyper-partition memory adds latency to memory accesses, since it adds an extra layer of indirection when resolving addresses. AMD and Intel are actively working to improve the performance of this recently-added feature [10]. Lockdown also adds overhead to code execution in the trusted environment due to its verification of approved code. To measure the CPU and memory overhead, we use benchmarks from the SPECint 2006 suite. We run the benchmarks in the trusted environment, in the untrusted environment, and on the native system We also run the benchmarks in the trusted environment with approved code protection disabled to allow us to distinguish between overhead added by these protections and overhead added by the NPTs. Figure 4a shows Lockdown's overhead as a percentage of the native system's performance. In the untrusted environment, performance is only slightly worse than native (3% average overhead). The trusted environment adds considerably more overhead (15–59%). Even without including the overhead of approved code execution, the trusted environment is still slower than the untrusted environment due to its use of smaller page size. In the untrusted environment, we use the 2 MB pages to improve performance. However, in the trusted environment, we also use NPTs to check for approved code at a page granularity, and hence the trusted environment must use the smaller 4 KB pages, making it less efficient. Nonetheless, this performance is appropriate for infrequent tasks, such as online banking, that are less performance intensive.

Storage Overhead. To partition the system's disks between the trusted and untrusted environments, Lockdown intercepts both environments' drive/sector selection

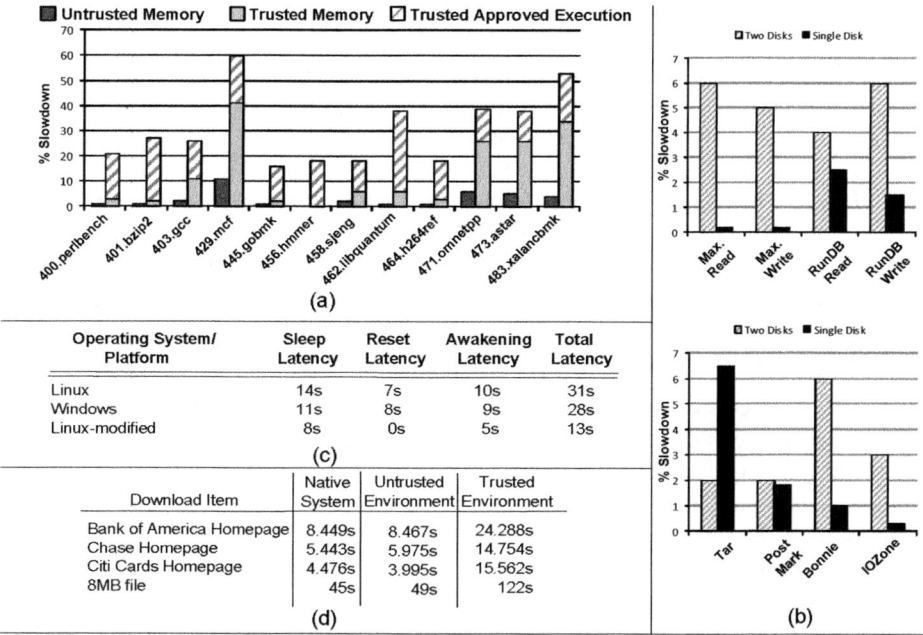

Fig. 4. Lockdown Performance Measurements. (a) CPU and memory overhead relative to native (smaller is better), (b) Storage micro- and macrobenchmarks compared to native (smaller is better), (c) Environment switch latency, (d) Network-protection latency.

commands, adding overhead to disk I/O. To measure this overhead with microbenchmarks, we employ Iometer, an industry-standard disk benchmarking tool. We use Iometer to measure Lockdown's maximum throughput for direct reads and writes, as well as reads and writes from a database workload. For macrobenchmarks, we use a variety of standard disk-bound applications, including Postmark (10000 files and 10000 transactions), IoZone (2GB file), Bonnie (2GB file), and `tar` (on the Windows installation folder). Figure 4b shows the results of these benchmarks relative to the native system's performance. As expected (since Lockdown treats both environments equally when partitioning storage devices), the two environments perform similarly. On these disk-bound tests, Lockdown imposes relatively modest overheads of 2–7%.

Environment Switch Latency. We split Lockdown's environment switch latency into three parts: (a) sleep latency: the time taken from when the user flips the switch on the Lockdown Verifier to the time the guest OS finishes preparing for sleep and invokes the ACPI subsystem, (b) reset latency: the time taken for Lockdown to reset the system's devices, and transfer control to the target environment's OSPM and, (c) awakening latency: the time taken by the OSPM in the target environment to resume normal operations. Figure 4c shows the measurements for Lockdown's environment switch latency. The switch currently requires 31 seconds on Windows and 13–28 seconds on Linux. While longer than ideal, we expect users to swap between the two environments relatively infrequently. Our results indicate that the direction of the switch has a relatively small impact on the switching time. The reset latency is largely due to Lockdown's use of the BIOS to reset the system's devices. The BIOS performs a far more extensive reset than Lockdown needs (more than 25% of the switch time), completely reinitializing the CPU, chipset, memory and devices. BIOS vendors are actively working to greatly reduce this latency with the Unified Extensible Firmware Interface (UEFI) [33]. The reset process can also be significantly accelerated as computers adopt the new PCI-Express 2.0 bus standard. With this standard, Lockdown can use a single PCI-bus command to reset each device in the system, instead of using the BIOS. Further, if OS device drivers are architected in a way that no prior state assumptions are made about the device (as in Linux), we can completely eliminate the reset latency by modifying the kernel to restart itself without issuing a platform reset.

Network Protection Overhead. Since Lockdown interposes on the trusted environment's network connections, we expect performance to be worse in the trusted environment. Since the untrusted environment has full access to the network interface, it should be comparable to native. To measure Lockdown's network overhead, we use Firefox with the YSlow add-on to measure the time necessary to load three popular banking websites, as well as the time required to download a 8 MB file. We averaged the download times over 5 runs, clearing the Firefox cache each time. Figure 4d summarizes our results. As expected, the untrusted environment's performance is equivalent to the native system (within experimental error). The trusted environment takes longer, because all network packets traverse via the SSL protocol analyzer and over USB through the Lockdown Verifier. Fortunately, most security-sensitive online transactions involve small network transmissions that makes the download times usable.

Comparison with Virtualization. Finally, we compare Lockdown's performance with traditional virtualization approaches. We choose the popular Xen (3.4.2) hypervisor for our comparison even though it does not provide the same high level of protection as Lockdown. We instantiate two virtual machines (VMs) with identical configuration for the untrusted and trusted environments within Xen. For measurement purposes, we benchmark the core platform subsystems comprising the memory, disk, network and graphics. To measure the memory overhead we use benchmarks from the SPECint 2006 suite. We use Tar, Bonnie, Postmark and IoZone (with the same parameters as discussed previously) as our disk macrobenchmarks. We use Flashget to measure the average network throughput and the PassMark 2D benchmark suite to measure the graphics performance. Figure 5 shows the performance of Lockdown and Xen as a percentage of the native system's performance, for both the untrusted and trusted environments[4]. Our results show that virtual machine monitors in general (including Xen) virtualize the underlying platform resources and therefore introduce similar performance latency in all VMs (untrusted and trusted). The slowdown is particularly high for the disk (54%), network (55%) and graphics (81%) subsystems. In contrast, Lockdown only imposes restrictions for the trusted partition and lets the untrusted partition run near native speed

---

[4] Note that we could not compare Xen with direct device assignment [4], as that requires special platform support that is not widely available today [6,29]. Futher, not all devices can be assigned currently (e.g., video, audio) [5,29].

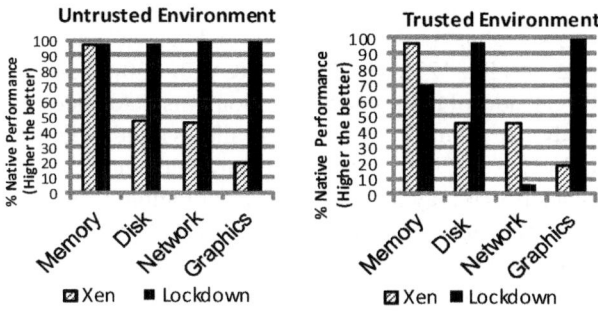

Fig. 5. Comparison of Partitioning (Lockdown) with Virtualization (Xen). Partitioning penalizes only the trusted environment while virtualization treats both environments as equal and imposes similar overheads.

(only a 3% average overhead for memory and 2-7% overhead for disk). These results demonstrate the efficiency advantage of partitioning vs virtualization. The performance degradation in the trusted partition is higher for memory and network due to Lockdown's approved execution and network protection mechanisms. However, for the disk and graphics subsystem the overhead introduced is less than Xen.

8   Related Work

Following our earlier preliminary work on hyper-partitioning [45], systems such as No-Hype and SecureSwitch, like Lockdown, advocate the use of partitioning in order to minimize TCB. However, both these systems are fairly different from Lockdown in many ways.

NoHype [17] uses static partitioning of devices leveraging specialized platform hardware capabilities such as Single-Root I/O Virtualization (SR-IOV) [29] and aims to run commodity operating systems. However, SR-IOV capabilities are only found in few high-end server platforms today. Also, NoHype does not have a particular operating model in mind and treats all VMs equally, as opposed to Lockdown which has a particular operating model in mind, i.e., trusted and untrusted, and takes steps to keep the trusted partition more secure. Furthermore, NoHype lacks the trusted path provided by Lockdown for assessing and switching between environments.

SecureSwitch [41] attempts to provide isolation between untrusted and trusted OSes with low switch times. However, unlike Lockdown, it does not provide any trusted environment protections (approved execution and trusted network access) or user-verifiable trusted path for input and output. In addition, their isolation mechanism requires changing the system BIOS and relies on specialized hardware (southbridge DIMM isolation, dual disk controllers with disk locking feature and motherboard jumpers for switching) that are not commodity.

In contrast, Lockdown represents a *complete end-to-end solution* of a red/green system on *commodity platforms* (without specialized platform hardware) and does not require changes to the system BIOS or the OSes. The Lockdown Verifier is an *external*

USB device that communicates verified system state ("red" or "green") to the user and enables trustworthy switching between the "red" and "green" environments.

Systems such as NetTop [27], HAP [28], NGSCB [30], Terra [13], Qubes [43], Virtics [34], or Overshadow [11] use virtualization to isolate code running at different security levels. As discussed in § 7, virtualization allows rapid switching (orders of magnitude faster than Lockdown) between multiple environments. However, virtualization increases side-channels that may leak sensitive information. Device virtualization also degrades performance and increases the amount of trusted code by orders of magnitude. Several proposals use virtualization to isolate one web application from another [46,12], but they do not protect the web browser from other code on the system. However, this work would be complementary to Lockdown if used within the trusted environment to prevent a compromise of one trusted site from affecting the other trusted sites.

Specialized hypervisor systems such as Proxos [42], Nizza [39], Flicker [23,25,24] and TrustVisor [22] allow a small, specially-crafted piece of code to run in isolation from the rest of the system. However, they typically do not protect general-purpose applications or provide full access to system devices.

OS level approaches such as Apiary [35] and WindowBox [8] modify the OS kernel or leverage specific OS features (e.g., FreeBSDs jails) to enforce application specific execution containers. However, as these containers share the same OS kernel, memory and system devices, any vulnerability within the OS can be exploited to subvert the protection mechanisms.

9   Conclusion

We evaluated a new point in the design space of red/green systems by using partitioning, rather than virtualization to share critical system resources and devices. Our implementation and results indicate that partitioning offers increased security (by reducing the size of the reference monitor to 10K lines of code and by reducing opportunities for side channels) and performance (by giving the untrusted environment unfettered access to system devices) at the cost of slow switching times (on current systems). Determining whether the switching times can be reduced to an acceptable level, or whether the security and performance benefits can be adopted by virtualization-based approaches, are interesting directions for future research.

Acknowledgement. This research was supported by CyLab at Carnegie Mellon under grants DAAD19-02-1-0389, W911NF-09-1-0273, W911NF10C0037, and MURI W 911 NF 0710287 from the Army Research Office, and by support from NSF under awards CCF-0424422 and CNS-0831440. The views and conclusions contained here are those of the authors and should not be interpreted as necessarily representing the official policies or endorsements, either express or implied, of ARO, CMU, NSF or the U.S. Government or any of its agencies.

References

1. Vmware esx server node evaluator's guide,
   http://www.vmware.com/pdf/esx_vin_eval.pdf
2. The l4ka project (2011), http://www.l4ka.org

3. Source lines of code (2011),
   http://en.wikipedia.com/wiki/Source_lines_of_code
4. Xen pcipassthrough (October 2011),
   http://wiki.xensource.com/xenwiki/XenPCIpassthrough
5. Xen vgapassthrough (October 2011),
   http://wiki.xensource.com/xenwiki/XenVGAPassthrough
6. Xen vtdhowto (October 2011),
   http://wiki.xensource.com/xenwiki/VTdHowTo
7. Advanced Micro Devices. AMD64 architecture programmer's manual: Volume 2: System programming. AMD Publication no. 24594 rev. 3.11 (December 2005)
8. Balfanz, D., Simon, D.R.: Windowbox: A simple security model for the connected desktop. In: Proceedings of the 4th USENIX Windows Systems Symposium (2000)
9. Bernstein, D.J.: Cache-timing attacks on aes (April 2005),
   http://cr.yp.to/papers.html
10. Bhargava, R., Serebrin, B., Spadini, F., Manne, S.: Accelerating two-dimensional page walks for virtualized systems. In: ASPLOS (March 2008)
11. Chen, X., Garfinkel, T., Lewis, E.C., Subrahmanyam, P., Waldspurger, C.A., Boneh, D., Dwoskin, J., Ports, D.R.K.: Overshadow: A virtualization-based approach to retrofitting protection in commodity operating systems. In: ASPLOS (2008)
12. Cox, R.S., Gribble, S.D., Levy, H.M., Hansen, J.G.: A safety-oriented platform for web applications. In: IEEE S&P, pp. 350–364 (May 2006)
13. Garfinkel, T., Pfaff, B., Chow, J., Rosenblum, M., Boneh, D.: Terra: A virtual machine-based platform for trusted computing. In: SOSP (October 2003)
14. Hewlett-Packard, Intel, Microsoft, Phoenix, and Toshiba. Advanced configuration and power interface specification. Revision 3.0b (October 2006)
15. Intel Corporation. Trusted execution technology – preliminary architecture specification and enabling considerations. Document number 31516803 (November 2006)
16. Karger, P., Safford, D.: I/O for virtual machine monitors: Security and performance issues. IEEE Security and Privacy 6(5), 16–23 (2008)
17. Keller, E., Szefer, J., Rexford, J., Lee, R.B.: Nohype: virtualized cloud infrastructure without the virtualization. In: International Symposium on Computer Architecture (2010)
18. Lampson, B.: A note on the confinement problem. Comm. of the ACM 16(10) (1973)
19. Lampson, B.: Usable security: How to get it. Comm. of the ACM 52(11) (2009)
20. Leinenbach, D., Santen, T.: Verifying the Microsoft Hyper-V Hypervisor with VCC. In: Cavalcanti, A., Dams, D.R. (eds.) FM 2009. LNCS, vol. 5850, pp. 806–809. Springer, Heidelberg (2009)
21. Litty, L., Lagar-Cavilla, H.A., Lie, D.: Hypervisor support for identifying covertly executing binaries. In: Proceedings of the USENIX Security Symposium (2008)
22. McCune, J.M., Li, Y., Qu, N., Zhou, Z., Datta, A., Gligor, V., Perrig, A.: TrustVisor: Efficient TCB reduction and attestation. In: IEEE S&P (May 2010)
23. McCune, J.M., Parno, B., Perrig, A., Reiter, M.K., Isozaki, H.: Flicker: An execution infrastructure for TCB minimization. In: EuroSys (April 2008)
24. McCune, J.M., Parno, B., Perrig, A., Reiter, M.K., Seshadri, A.: Minimal TCB code execution (extended abstract). In: IEEE Symposium on Security and Privacy (May 2007)
25. McCune, J.M., Parno, B., Perrig, A., Reiter, M.K., Seshadri, A.: How low can you go? Recommendations for hardware-supported minimal TCB code execution. In: ACM ASPLOS (March 2008)
26. McCune, J.M., Perrig, A., Seshadri, A., van Doorn, L.: Turtles all the way down: Research challenges in user-based attestation. In: USENIX Workshop on Hot Topics in Security (2007)
27. Meushaw, R., Simard, D.: Nettop: Commercial technology in high assurance applications. VMware Tech Trend Notes 9(4), 1–8 (2000)

28. National Security Agency. High assurance platform program (January 2009), `http://www.nsa.gov/ia/programs/h_a_p/index.shtml`
29. PCI SIG. Single Root I/O Virtualization and Sharing Specification. V. 1.1 (2010)
30. Peinado, M., Chen, Y., England, P., Manferdelli, J.L.: NGSCB: A Trusted Open System. In: Wang, H., Pieprzyk, J., Varadharajan, V. (eds.) ACISP 2004. LNCS, vol. 3108, pp. 86–97. Springer, Heidelberg (2004)
31. Percival, C.: Cache missing for fun & profit. In: BSDCan (2005)
32. Phoenix Technologies. TrustedCore: Foundation for secure CRTM and BIOS implementation (2006), `https://forms.phoenix.com/whitepaperdownload/docs/trustedcore_wp.pdf`
33. Phoenix Technologies. Transitioning the Plug-In Industry from Legacy to Unified Extensible Firmware Interface (UEFI). Intel Developer Forum (September 2009)
34. Piotrowski, M., Joseph, A.D.: Virtics: A system for privilege separation of legacy desktop applications. Technical Report UCB/EECS-2010-70, EECS Department, University of California, Berkeley (May 2010)
35. Potter, S., Nieh, J.: Apiary: Easy-to-use desktop application fault containment on commodity operating systems. In: USENIX Annual Technical Conference (2010)
36. Ristenpart, T., Tromer, E., Shacham, H., Savage, S.: Hey, you, get off of my cloud: Exploring information leakage in third-party compute clouds. In: ACM CCS (2009)
37. Seshadri, A., Luk, M., Qu, N., Perrig, A.: SecVisor: A tiny hypervisor to provide lifetime kernel code integrity for commodity OSes. In: SOSP (2007)
38. Shacham, H.: The geometry of innocent flesh on the bone: Return-into-libc without function calls (on the x86). In: ACM CCS (2007)
39. Singaravelu, L., Pu, C., Haertig, H., Helmuth, C.: Reducing TCB complexity for security-sensitive applications: Three case studies. In: EuroSys (2006)
40. Steinberg, U., Kauer, B.: Nova: A microhypervisor-based secure virtualization architecture. In: EuroSys (2010)
41. Sun, K., Wang, J., Zhang, F., Stavrou, A.: Secureswitch: Bios-assisted isolation and switch between trusted and untrusted commodity oses. In: NDSS (2012)
42. Ta-Min, R., Litty, L., Lie, D.: Splitting interfaces: Making trust between applications and operating systems configurable. In: OSDI (2006)
43. The Qubes OS, `http://qubes-os.org/Home.html`
44. Trusted Computing Group. Trusted Platform Module Main Specification. V. 1.2 (2007)
45. Vasudevan, A., Parno, B., Qu, N., Gligor, V.D., Perrig, A.: Lockdown: A safe and practical environment for security applications. Technical Report CMU-CyLab-09-011, CyLab, Carnegie Mellon University (July 2009)
46. Wang, H.J., Grier, C., Moshchuk, A., King, S.T., Choudhury, P., Venter, H.: The multi-principal OS construction of the gazelle web browser. In: USENIX Security Symposium (2009)

Experimenting with Fast Private Set Intersection

Emiliano De Cristofaro[1] and Gene Tsudik[2]

[1] PARC
[2] UC Irvine

Abstract. Private Set Intersection (PSI) is a useful cryptographic primitive that allows two parties (client and server) to interact based on their respective (private) input sets, in such a way that client obtains nothing other than the set intersection, while server learns nothing beyond client set size. This paper considers one PSI construct from [DT10] and reports on its optimized implementation and performance evaluation. Several key implementation choices that significantly impact real-life performance are identified and a comprehensive experimental analysis (including micro-benchmarking, with various input sizes) is presented. Finally, it is shown that our optimized implementation of this RSA-OPRF-based PSI protocol markedly outperforms the one presented in [HEK12].

1 Introduction

Private Set Intersection (PSI) is a primitive that allow two parties (client and server), to interact on their respective input sets, such that client only obtains the intersection of the two sets, whereas, server learns nothing beyond the size of client input set. PSI is appealing in many real-world settings: common application examples include national security/law enforcement [DT10], Intelligence Community systems [DJL+10], healthcare and genomic applications [BBD+11], collaborative botnet detection techniques [NMH+10], location sharing [NTL+11] as well as cheating prevention in online gaming [BLHB11]. Motivated by practical relevance of the problem, the research community has considered PSI quite extensively and devised a number of techniques that vary in costs, security assumptions and adversarial models, e.g., [FNP04,KS05,HL08], [JL09,DSMRY09,DT10,HN10,JL10,DKT10,ADT11]. (Notable PSI protocols are reviewed in Appendix A.)

In this paper, we focus on a specific RSA-OPRF-based PSI protocol from [DT10] that currently offers the most efficient operation. It achieves linear computational and communication complexity and improves overall efficiency (over prior work) by reducing the total cost of underlying cryptographic operations. Although [DT10] actually presents two PSI protocols, this paper focuses on the second – RSA-OPRF-based, in Figure 4 of [DT10] – which is the more efficient of the two. Hereafter, it is referred to as DT10-v4.

Objectives: We discuss our implementation of DT10-v4 and experimentally assess its performance. Our goal is twofold: (1) Identify implementation choices that impact overall protocol performance, and (2) Provide a comprehensive performance evaluation.

Organization: Next section overviews DT10-v4. Then, Section 3 and Section 4 describe, respectively, its implementation and performance evaluation. Finally, performance analysis of our optimized implementation is contrasted with that in [HEK12].

S. Katzenbeisser et al. (Eds.): TRUST 2012, LNCS 7344, pp. 55–73, 2012.

2   The DT10-v4 PSI Protocol

We now review the PSI protocol presented in Figure 4 in [DT10], from here on denoted as DT10-v4. First, we introduce some notation, present actual construction, and, finally, discuss settings where (server-side) precomputation is possible/recommended.

2.1   Notation

Notation used in the rest of this paper is reflected in Table 1 below:

Table 1. Notation

$a \leftarrow A$	variable a is chosen uniformly at random from set A
τ, τ'	security parameters
p, q	safe primes
$N = pq, e, d$	RSA modulus, public and private exponents
$H(\cdot)$	full-domain hash function $H : \{0,1\}^* \rightarrow \mathbb{Z}_N^*$
$H'(\cdot)$	cryptographic hash function $H' : \{0,1\}^{\tau_1} \rightarrow \{0,1\}^{\tau'}$
$\mathcal{C}, \mathcal{S}$	client's and server's sets, respectively
v, w	sizes of $\mathcal{C}$ and $\mathcal{S}$, respectively
$i \in [1, v],\ j \in [1, w]$	indices of elements of $\mathcal{C}$ and $\mathcal{S}$, respectively
c_i, s_j	i-th and j-th elements of $\mathcal{C}$ and $\mathcal{S}$, respectively
hc_i, hs_j	$H(c_i)$ and $H(s_j)$, respectively

2.2   Protocol Specification

Figure 1 shows the operation of DT10-v4 below.

Client,	**Server,**
on input $\mathcal{C} = \{c_1, \ldots, c_v\}$	on input $p, q, d, \mathcal{S} = \{s_1, \ldots, s_w\}$

Client	Server
$\forall_i = 1, \ldots, v :$	$\forall_j = 1, \ldots, w :$
(1) $r_i \leftarrow \mathbb{Z}_N$	(1) $ks_j = (hs_j)^d \bmod N$
(2) $\mu_i = hc_i \cdot r_i{}^e \bmod N$	(2) $ts_j = H'(ks_j)$
(3) $\xrightarrow{\{\mu_1, \ldots, \mu_v\}}$	(3)
	$\forall_i = 1, \ldots, v :$
	(4) $\mu_i' = (\mu_i)^d \bmod N$
(4) $\xleftarrow{\{\mu_1', \ldots, \mu_v'\}}$ $\{ts_1, \ldots, ts_w\}$	
$\forall_i = 1, \ldots, v :$	
(5) $kc_i = \mu_i'/r_i \bmod N$	
(6) $tc_i = H'(kc_i)$	
(7) If $\exists_j$ s.t. $tc_i = ts_j$ **output** $c_i \in \mathcal{C} \cap \mathcal{S}$	

Fig. 1. DT10-v4 executes on common input: $N, e, H(\cdot), H'(\cdot)$

Correctness: If $c_i \in \mathcal{C} \cap \mathcal{S}$, then $\exists_j$ s.t.: $kc_i = \mu'_i/r_i = (hc_i \cdot r_i{}^e)^d/r_i = hs_j{}^d = ks_j \Longrightarrow tc_i = ts_j$.

Security: DT10-v4 is proven secure in the presence of semi-honest adversaries, under the One-More-RSA assumption [BNPS03] in the Random Oracle Model (ROM) – see [DT10] for details. The proof in Appendix B of [DT10] actually achieves one-side (adaptive) simulation in the ideal-world/real-world paradigm.[1] Thus, security of DT10-v4 may actually hold in the presence of a malicious client and a semi-honest server. Further, security against a malicious server also seems easy to obtain: RSA signatures have the desirable property of verifiability, thus, client can easily verify server's adherence to the protocol with respect to the computation of $\mu'_i = (\mu_i)^d \bmod N$. Also, client's message to server (i.e., the first round) does not depend on any information from latter, which, in fact, produces no output. However, server would need to prove that its RSA parameters are generated correctly, and it could do so using, for example, techniques from [CM99] or [HMRT11]. Nonetheless, we leave as part of future work formal proofs for malicious security of DT10-v4.

Communication Complexity: DT10-v4 communication complexity amounts to $2v$ group elements and w hash outputs. Specifically, in the first round, client sends v elements in $\mathbb{Z}_N$, whereas, in the second, server transfers v elements in $\mathbb{Z}_N$ and w outputs of $H'(\cdot)$. For 80-bit security, SHA-1, which has 160-bit outputs, may suffice.

Computational Complexity: We note that server workload can be dramatically reduced if exponentiations $(\cdot)^d \bmod N$ are optimized using the ***Chinese Remainder Theorem*** (CRT)[2], since server knows factorization of N. Specifically, DT10-v4's computational complexity is as follows. *Server* computes: w full-domain hashes; $2w + 2v$ modular exponentiations with $(|N|/2)$-bit exponents and $(|N|/2)$-bit moduli (using CRT); w invocations of $H'(\cdot)$. *Client* computes: v full-domain hashes; v exponentiations with $|e|$-bit exponent and $|N|$-bit modulus (in practice, one can select $e = 3$); v modular inverses of $|N|$-bit integers modulo $|N|$ bits; $2v$ modular multiplications of $|N|$-bit integers modulo $|N|$ bits; v invocations of $H'(\cdot)$. Thus, on server side, computational complexity is dominated by $O(w + v)$ CRT exponentiations, whereas, client's computation is dominated by $O(v)$ modular multiplications and inverses. Since client does not perform *any* expensive cryptographic operation (i.e., no modular exponentiations), DT10-v4 is particularly suited for scenarios where *client runs on a resource-poor device*, e.g., a smart-phone.

2.3   Precomputation

One beneficial feature of DT10-v4, as well as some other PSI techniques in [HL08], [JL09], [JL10], is that server computation over its own input does not depend on any client input. Therefore:

---

[1] Specifically, the proof constructs of an (adaptive) ideal world simulator SIM_c from a malicious real-world client C^*, and shows that the views of C^* in the real game with the real-world server and in the interaction with SIM_c are indistinguishable.

[2] See items 14.71 and 14.75 in [MVOV97] for more details on CRT-based exponentiation.

1. Server does not need to wait for client to perform its w exponentiations to compute $ks_j = H(hs_j)^d \bmod N$ (for $j = 1, \ldots, w$). These operations can be done as soon as server set is available. In the absolute worst case, server can perform these operations in parallel with receiving client's first message.

2. Results of server computation over its own set can be re-used in multiple protocol instances. Thus, unless server's set changes frequently, the overhead is negligible.

In light of the above, [DT10] suggests to divide the protocol into two phases: *off-line* and *on-line*. This way, computational complexity of the latter is dominated by $O(v)$ CRT exponentiations, while *off-line* phase overhead amounts to $O(w)$ CRT exponentiations. This makes DT10-v4 particularly appealing for scenarios where server input set is not *"very dynamic"*.

3 Implementing DT10-v4

This section presents our implementation of DT10-v4 PSI construction from [DT10]. We discuss some design choices that may affect overall performance, present our prototype implementation, and discuss additional techniques to optimize performance.

3.1 Important Design Choices

We now identify and discuss some factors that significantly affect overall performance of DT10-v4 implementation. We begin with straightforward issues and then turn to some less trivial strategies. (*Note: for the sake of generality, we assume below that server does NOT perform precomputation.*)

1. **Small RSA public exponent:** Recall from Section 2.2, that the only modular exponentiations performed by client are those in step (2), specifically, raising random values r_i-s to the e-th power $(\bmod N)$. Therefore, the choice of RSA public exponent e directly influences client run-time. Common choices of e are: $3, 17$, and $2^{16}+1 = 65537$. The cryptography research community has often raised concerns related to possible attacks when using $e = 3$ for RSA encryption [Bon98,FKJM+06]. However, although further careful consideration is needed, such concerns do not seem to apply in this setting, since r_i-s are generated anew, at random.

2. **Chinese Remainder Theorem:** On server side, the most computation-intensive operations are exponentiations $(\cdot)^d \bmod N$ – in steps (1) and (4). As discussed in Section 2.2, these can be optimized using (CRT). Specifically, it is well known that using CRT can make exponentiations 4 times faster.

3. **Pipelining:** While we describe DT10-v4 as a sequence of steps, pipelining can be used to maximize overall efficiency by minimizing wait times. A good start is to implement computation and communication in separate *threads*, such that independent operations can be performed in parallel. (Note that this does not presume that underlying hardware has multiple cores). Specifically:

   a) Server can compute $ts_j = H'((hs_j)^d \bmod N)$, $j = 1, \ldots, w$ (i.e., steps (1)-(2)), as soon as $(s_j\text{'s})$ are available, i.e., even before starting interaction with client, or, in the worst case, as soon as client starts transmitting. This is as simple as implementing server's steps (1)-(2) in a dedicated thread.

b) Server does not need to wait for $\mu_{i+1}, \ldots, \mu_v$ to arrive in order to compute $\mu_i' = (\mu_i)^d \bmod N$. To minimize waiting, we simply need to implement exponentiations in a separate thread drawing input from a shared buffer, where the thread listening on the channel pushes received values.

c) Similarly, client can compute r_i^{-1} (needed to compute $\mu_i/r_i \bmod N$) in step (5) in parallel with steps (2)-(4).

d) Finally, client does not need to wait for $\mu_{i+1}', \ldots, \mu_v$ to arrive to compute $tc_i = H'(\mu_i'/r_i \bmod N)$, i.e., steps (5)-(6).

4. ***Threading in Multi-core Settings:*** Structuring the code in multiple threads allows us to further improve overall performance. For example, on server side, we can create two threads for step (1) and step (4), respectively. Thus, if multiple cores are available (or the computing architecture using aggressive pipelining), these operations are performed in parallel, thus, lowering overall run-time. Once again, we note that parallel thread execution is transparent to application developers and normally incurs no extra costs.

5. ***Fast Cryptographic Library:*** The choice of the cryptographic library is a crucial factor affecting overall performance. Efficiency of modular exponentiations varies widely across cryptographic libraris. For example, Table 2 shows modular exponentiations measured on a 64-bit desktop with an Intel Xeon CPU E31225 at 3.10GHz (running Ubuntu 11.10), using increasingly large exponents and moduli.

Table 2. Benchmarking of modular exponentiations with increasingly large moduli

	1024-bit	2048-bit	3072-bit
C/GMP	0.60ms	4.44ms	14.08ms
C/OpenSSL	0.81ms	6.12ms	20.89ms
Java (v1.6.0_23)	3.33ms	24.47ms	76.91ms
Ratio Java/GMP	5.55	5.51	5.46

3.2   Prototype Implementation

Due to space limitations, we refer the readers to the full version of the paper (in [DT12]) for a detailed description of our implementation of DT10-v4. The prototype is implemented in C, using the GMP library for large integer arithmetic and OpenSSL for key generation and hash function implementation.

3.3   Additional Performance-Optimizing Techniques

Besides design choices discussed in Section 3.1 above – all of which can be easily adopted – there are some less obvious aspects that can help us further optimize implementation of DT10-v4. Although we discuss them below, we defer their implementation to the next version of the prototype, since these optimizations appeal to specific settings. Whereas, this paper focuses on the general PSI scenario.

1. ***Bottleneck Identification:*** In settings where the PSI protocol is executed over the Internet and communication takes place over slow links, communication overhead is likely to become the bottleneck. For instance, consider a scenario, where server

runs on an Intel Xeon CPU at 3.10GHz. Using GMP, it takes, on average, $0.15ms$ to perform $(\cdot)^d \mod N$ exponentiations, with 1024-bit moduli, using CRT. Therefore, one can estimate the link speed at which the bottleneck becomes transmission of the $\{\mu_i\}_{i=1}^v$ and $\{ts_j\}_{j=1}^w$ values, respectively. Specifically, if network speed is lower than: $\frac{|\mu_i'|}{\text{time}} = \frac{1024 \text{ bits}}{0.15\text{ms}} = 7.31$Mbps, it takes longer to transmit μ_i' than to compute it. Whereas, if network speed is lower than: $\frac{|ts_j|}{\text{time}} = \frac{160 \text{ bits}}{0.15\text{ms}} = 1.14$Mbps then it takes longer to send ts_j than to compute it. These estimates could be useful for further protocol optimizations; see below.

2. ***Exploiting Parallelism:*** Many modern desktops and laptops have multiple cores. Thus, if the bottleneck is computation of $(\cdot)^d$ exponentiations, the server-side thread in charge of receiving $\{\mu_i\}_{i=1}^v$ will push them into the buffer faster than the thread computing $\{(\mu_i)^d\}_{i=1}^v$ can pull them. With multiple cores, exponentiations of multiple values in the buffer could be done in parallel. Similarly, computation of $\{(hs_j)^d\}_{i=j}^w$ does not depend on any other information; thus, it could be parallelized too.

3. ***Minimizing Transmission:*** If the bottleneck is transmission time, then we can optimize software by, for example, using UDP instead of TCP, or choosing socket options geared for transmission of many tiny packets.

4   Performance Evaluation

We now present a detailed performance evaluation of our DT10-v4 implementation.

Experimental Setup. Experiments are performed on the following testbed: PSI server ran on a Linux computer, equipped with an Intel Xeon E31225 CPU (running at 3.10GHz). PSI client ran on a Mid-2011 13-inch Apple Macbook Air, with an Intel Core i5 (running at 1.7GHz). Server and client are connected through a 100Mbps Ethernet LAN. The code was written in C using the GMP library for modular arithmetic operations and OpenSSL for other cryptographic operations (such as, random numbers and key generation, hash function invocations). Finally, note that we used 1024-bit, 2048-bit, or 3072-bit RSA moduli and SHA-1 to instantiate the $H'(\cdot)$ function.

4.1   Protocol Total Running Time

In Figures 2 and 3, we report total run-times for DT10-v4 protocol running on, respectively, small (100 to 1000) and medium (1000 to 10000) sets, using 1024-bit moduli.[3] Next, Figures 4, 5, 6, and 7, respectively, report total run-time for small and medium sets, using 2048-bit and 3072-bit moduli, respectively.

Time is measured as the difference between system time read when the protocol starts and time read when the protocol ends. Specifically, we consider the protocol as *started* whenever client initiates protocol execution (i.e., it opens a connection on server's

---

[3] We also ran experiments with even large sets (in the order of hundreds of thousands). We do not include them here as they simply grow linearly for increasing set sizes, thus, one can obtain an estimation of them, for essentially any input size, by looking at Figures 2–7.

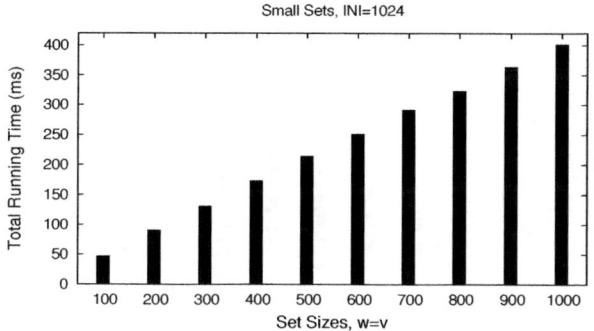

Fig. 2. DT10-v4 total run-time for small sets (100 to 1000 items), using 1024-bit moduli

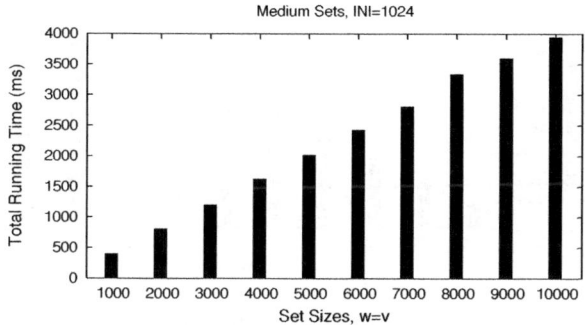

Fig. 3. DT10-v4 total run-time for medium sets (1000 to 10000 items), using 1024-bit moduli

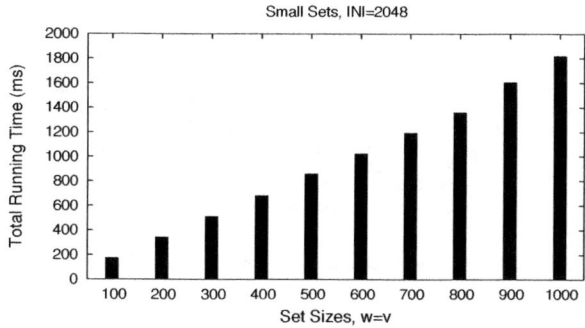

Fig. 4. DT10-v4 total run-time for small sets (100 to 1000 items), using 2048-bit moduli

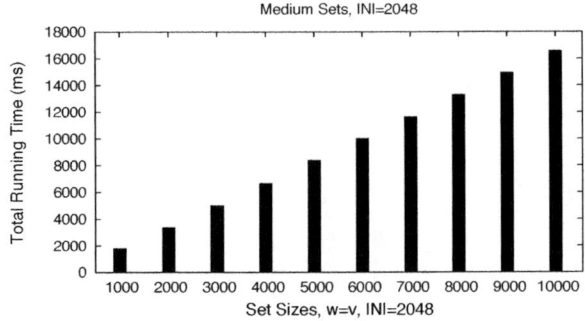

Fig. 5. DT10-v4 total run-time for medium sets (1000 to 10000 items), using 2048-bit moduli

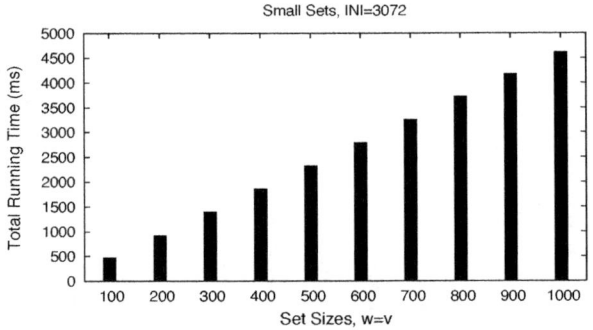

Fig. 6. DT10-v4 total run-time for small sets (100 to 1000 items), using 3072-bit moduli

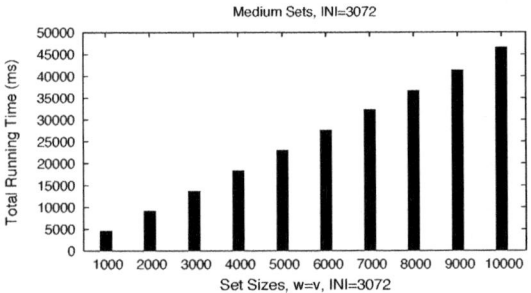

Fig. 7. DT10-v4 total run-time for medium sets (1000 to 10000 items), using 3072-bit moduli

listening socket), whereas, the protocol ends whenever client outputs the intersection (if any). In other words, *we do not perform precomputation* and, on a conservative stance, we do not allow the server to start computation of $\{(hs_j)^d \bmod N\}_{j=1}^{w}$ (its step (1)) until client establishes a connection on the listening socket.

The only cryptographic operation performed ahead of time (thus, not included in run-time) is RSA key generation, since server executes it only once for all possible clients and all executions. Finally, protocol execution time does not count time spent by server waiting for an incoming connection, since the listening socket is created only once, for all possible clients and all protocol executions.

4.2 Micro-benchmarking

We now analyze performance of specific operations performed by client and server during DT10-v4 protocol execution. We start with **Client**. In Figure 8 (resp., Figure 10), we measure the time spent by the process executing DT10-v4 client, using 1024-bit (resp., 2048-bit) moduli, for the following operations:

1. Label 'Receive' corresponds to the time spent to wait/receive the $\{\mu_i'\}_{i=1}^{v}$ and $\{ts_j\}_{j=1}^{w}$ values from server.
2. Label 'Cli-1' corresponds to the time needed to compute $\{\mu_i = hc_i \cdot r_i{}^e \bmod N\}_{i=1}^{v}$.
3. Label 'Inverse' corresponds to the time to compute $\{r_i^{-1} \bmod N\}_{i=1}^{v}$.
4. Label 'Cli-2' corresponds to the time needed to compute $\{tc_i = H'(\mu_i'/r_i \bmod N)\}_{i=1}^{v}$.

Next, we look at **Server**. In Figure 9, (resp., Figure 11)), we measure the time spent by the process executing DT10-v4 server, using 1024-bit (resp., 2048-bit) moduli, for the following operations:

1. Label 'Receive' corresponds to the time spent to wait/receive the $\{\mu_i\}_{i=1}^{v}$ values from client.
2. Label 'BlindSig' corresponds to the time to compute $\{\mu_i' = (\mu_i)^d \bmod N\}_{i=1}^{v}$.
3. Label 'Sig' corresponds to the time to compute $\{ts_j = H'((hs_j)^d \bmod N)\}_{j=1}^{w}$.

It is interesting to observe that, using 1024-bit moduli, client actually spends less time to receive all the values from server than vice versa, despite the former actually needs to receive more. This is a good opportunity to see multi-threading *in action*: client's thread responsible to send the $\{\mu_i\}$ values has to wait for them to be available, thus, causing some waiting time to server's thread that receives them. In other words, by looking at the micro-benchmarking one can identify different "bottlenecks" in the different settings.

5 Comparison to [HEK12]

In this section, we focus on the performance evaluation of the DT10-v4 PSI protocol presented in [HEK12].

The work in [HEK12] presents a few novel Private Set Intersection constructions based on garbled circuits [Yao82]: the main intuition is that, by leveraging the *Oblivious Transfer* (OT) extension [IKNP03], the complexity of such protocols is essentially tied to a number of OTs (thus, public-key operations) equal to the security parameter k. In fact, OT extension achieves an unlimited number of OTs at the cost of (essentially) k OTs. Therefore, for very large security parameters, the number of public-key

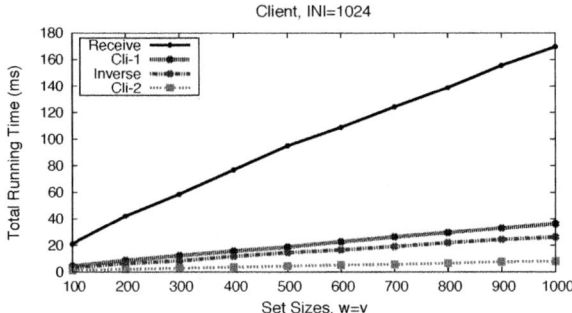

Fig. 8. Micro-benchmarking client's operations in DT10-v4 (small sets), using 1024-bit moduli

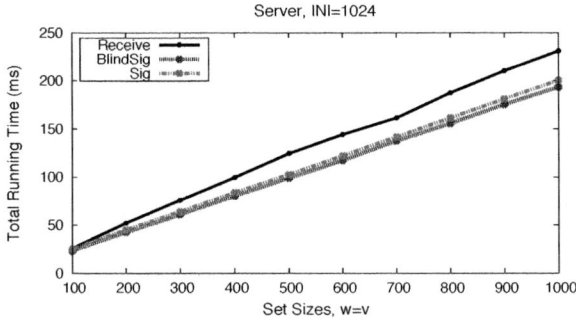

Fig. 9. Micro-benchmarking server's operations in DT10-v4 (small sets), using 1024-bit moduli

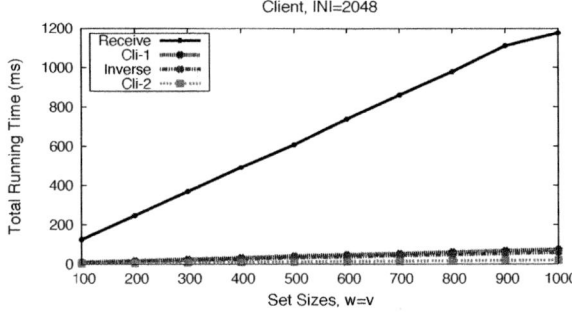

Fig. 10. Micro-benchmarking client's operations in DT10-v4 (small sets), using 2048-bit moduli

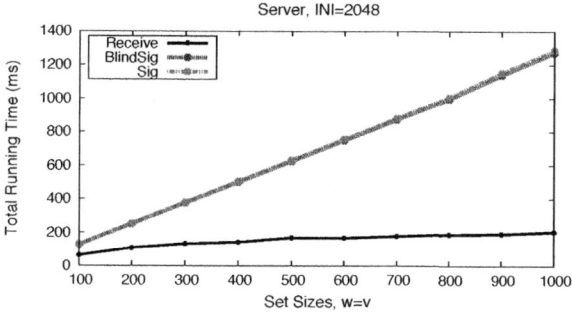

Fig. 11. Micro-benchmarking server's operations in DT10-v4 (small sets), using 2048-bit moduli

operations with this technique may grow more gracefully than with custom protocols. Finally, [HEK12] compares the efficiency of newly proposed constructions to an implementation of "custom" PSI protocols from [DT10].

Note that we do not examine the proposals and the experimental methodology of [HEK12]. Rather, we observe that the implementation of DT10-v4 presented in this paper achieves a remarkable speed up compared to performance results presented in [HEK12] for same protocols. Finally, we highlight some open questions regarding comparison between techniques in [HEK12] and those in [DT10].

5.1   Performance Comparison

We start by noticing that the run-time of the PSI protocol in [DT10] is reported to be around 10 seconds in a setting where $|\mathcal{S}| = |\mathcal{C}| = 1024$, the security parameter is 80-bit (thus, RSA moduli are 1024-bit), no precomputation is allowed at server, and communication between server and client is over a 100Mbps LAN. It is not clear whether this measure is the sum of server and client execution time or represents the time for the protocol to complete. On a conservative stance, we assume the former. On a comparable hardware,[4] and using the parameters discussed above, our measure for DT10-v4 protocol never exceeded 1 seconds (and DT10-v4 is actually not reported as the fastest protocol – see Section 5.2). Similarly, evaluation in [HEK12] reports 62 seconds (resp., 126 seconds) using 2048-bit (resp., 3072-bit) moduli; whereas, our implementation of DT10-v4 never exceeds 2 seconds (resp., 5 seconds).

In Table 3, we summarize running times for DT10-v4 as per our implementation, and compare to those for garbled-circuit based techniques presented in [HEK12] and reported in Fig. 11 of [HEK12]. We argue that our implementation of DT10-v4 markedly outperforms PSI protocols based on garbled circuits, in all the three security-parameter settings that we consider (and that are realistic today), in stark contrast to what has been claimed in [HEK12].

---

[4] In [HEK12] both server and client run on 3GHz CPU, whereas, in our experiments, server runs on a 3.1GHz CPU and client on a 1.7GHz CPU.

Table 3. Summary of PSI running times (with $|\mathcal{S}| = |\mathcal{C}| = 1024$)

	80-bit	112-bit	128-bit
DT10-v4 as per our implementation	< 1s	< 2s	< 5s
Best Custom-protocol PSI as per [HEK12]'s experiments	10.9s	62.4s	126s
Garbled-circuit based PSI in [HEK12]	51.5s	57.1s	61.5s

5.2   The Choice of Protocols from [DT10]

Authors of [HEK12] argue that the protocol in Figure 3 of [DT10], based on the One-More-DH assumption, is more efficient than that in Figure 4 (based on the One-More-RSA assumption and denoted as DT10-v4) in scenarios where server-side pre-computation is not possible. Our analysis below shows that this is wrong.

In the following, aiming at 80-bit security, we use: a 1024-bit RSA modulus N, an RSA public exponent $e = 3$, CRT-optimized exponentiations, a 1024-bit prime p, a 160-bit prime q, and SHA-1 hash function. Also recall that $w = |\mathcal{S}|$ and $v = |\mathcal{C}|$. We also use m to denote a modular multiplication of 1024-bit integers. Consequently, we say that exponentiations modulo 1024 bits require, on average, $O(1.5 \cdot |exp|) \cdot m$, where $|exp|$ denotes exponent size. Modular exponentiations with 512-bit moduli count for approximately $O(1.5 \cdot |exp|) \cdot m/4$. As we discussed earlier in the paper, the computational complexity of protocol in Figure 4 in [DT10] (DT10-v4) is clearly determined by $2w + 2v$ exponentiations with 512-bit exponents and moduli, thus, $(2w + 2v)(1.5 \cdot 512)m/4$, i.e., $(384w + 384v) \cdot m$. Whereas, the computational complexity of protocol in Figure 3 of [DT10] comes down to $w + 3v$ exponentiations with 160-bit exponents and 1024-bit moduli, thus, $(w + 3v) \cdot (1.5 \cdot 160) \cdot m$, i.e., $(240w + 720v) \cdot m$.

If one allows precomputation, then protocol in Figure 4 (DT10-v4) is straightforwardly more efficient than the Figure 3 counterpart, since online complexity goes down to $(384v) \cdot m$. But if one does not allow precomputation (as in [HEK12]), then it would seem that Figure 3 protocol would outperform DT10-v4 for settings where approximately $\frac{v}{w} < \frac{4}{10}$ — a setting that is anyway never tested in [HEK12], which always assumes $w = v$. Nonetheless, when precomputation is not possible, then the analysis of Figure 3's complexity should actually account for $w + v$ additional exponentiations needed to evaluate the $H(\cdot)$ function, which is of the *hash-into-the-group* kind, i.e., $H(x) = x^{(\frac{p-1}{q})} \bmod p$, thus, protocol in Figure 3 appears to be always slower than Figure 4 (i.e., DT10-v4.) Therefore, the protocol in [DT10]'s Figure 4 is always more computational efficient than the one in Figure 3.

5.3   Evaluation Criteria

Once again, note that it is out of the scope of this paper to provide a definite explanation as to why our implementation of DT10-v4 achieves run-times several times lower than those reported by [HEK12] (see section 7 thereof). Similarly, we do not analyze the validity of the conclusions drawn by the authors of [HEK12] regarding whether or not

DT10-v4 PSI protocol is more efficient than garbled circuits-based constructions in all settings. However, we make some observations regarding implementation of DT10-v4 by Huang et al. [HEK12] and also argue that a comprehensive comparison should take into account several settings (we sketch those below and leave the task of addressing them as an interesting open problem).

1. As discussed earlier, several design factors (e.g., pipelining, CRT, etc.) significantly impact overall performance of custom PSI protocols (see Section 3.1) and it is unclear whether they were taken into account in [HEK12].

2. [HEK12] implements techniques from [DT10] and in [HEK12] in *Java*. Java usually offers slower performance than other programming languages (such as C/C++). Nonetheless, this choice might seem irrelevant, since both techniques are implemented in Java. However, we believe it remains to be seen if the use of Java penalizes techniques from [DT10] that perform a higher number of public-key operations. For instance, as mentioned earlier, a CRT-based RSA exponentiation takes 5.55 times longer in Java than in C/GMP. Does this slowdown occur, *in the same measure* for *all* Java operations (e.g., symmetric-key)? If not, then the choice of Java might not be fair, as constructions in [HEK12] heavily rely on symmetric-key operations.[5] Also, it would also be interesting to measure memory overhead for increasing set sizes incurred by all techniques. We believe that performance and scalability could be tremendously affected by, for example, inability to keep an entire circuit in memory.

3. [HEK12] employs techniques that are fundamentally and markedly different from those used by custom protocols. Thus, a different choice of parameters can significantly favor one while penalizing the other. We mention just a few:

   a) Techniques in [HEK12] are tested in settings where $|\mathcal{S}| = |\mathcal{C}|$. As a result, we believe that a more thorough comparison would include scenarios where $|\mathcal{S}| \neq |\mathcal{C}|$. Also, comparisons in [HEK12] are given only for $|\mathcal{S}| = |\mathcal{C}| = 1024$. It remains unclear how performance of protocols in [HEK12] would scale for higher set sizes, since at least some of them involve *non-linear* complexities, as opposed to their counterparts in [DT10].

   b) Some protocols in [HEK12] incur higher communication complexity than protocols in [DT10]. Therefore, we argue that a more thorough comparison must include (realistic) settings where the subject protocol is executed on the Internet, and not only over fast 100Mbps LANs. (Complexity is not analyzed asymptotically but authors of [HEK12] report, on page 13, that the SCS-WN protocol consumes more bandwidth: 147–470MB, depending on the security level, versus 0.4–2.0MB.)

   c) Experiments in [HEK12] measure run-times as a total execution time. However, we believe that more details – ideally, a benchmark of sub-operations – should also be provided to better understand if the testing setting and implementation choices penalize one technique while favoring another.

---

[5] To encrypt 1 million 64-byte strings with AES-CBC, using C/OpenSSL, it takes, on average 0.60 and 0.83 seconds, with, respectively, 128-bit and 256-bit keys. Whereas, in Java, it takes 1.22 and 1.58 seconds. Therefore, the slowdown factor here is only 2.03 for 128-bit keys and 1.90 for 256-bit keys (versus about 5.5 for modular exponentiations).

Finally, while research on custom PSI protocols reached the point where malicious security can be achieved efficiently – at the same asymptotic complexity as semi-honest security [HN10,JL10,DKT10] – efficiency of garbled-circuit-based techniques secure in the malicious model remains unclear.

6 Conclusion

This paper presented an optimized implementation and performance evaluation of the currently fastes PSI protocol from [DT10]. We analyzed implementation choices that impact overall performance and presented an experimental analysis, including micro-benchmarking, with different set sizes. We showed that resulting run-times appreciably outperform those reported in [HEK12]. Achieved speed up is significantly higher than what one would obtain by simply porting [HEK12] implementation of DT10-v4 from Java to C. Finally, we identified some open questions with respect to comparisons of custom PSI protocols with generic garbled-circuit based constructions.

Acknowledgments. We gratefully acknowledge Yanbin Lu, Paolo Gasti, Simon Barber, and Xavier Boyen for their help and suggestions. We would also like to thank the authors of [HEK12] for their valuable feedback.

References

ADT11.   Ateniese, G., De Cristofaro, E., Tsudik, G. (If) Size Matters: Size-Hiding Private Set Intersection. In: Catalano, D., Fazio, N., Gennaro, R., Nicolosi, A. (eds.) PKC 2011. LNCS, vol. 6571, pp. 156–173. Springer, Heidelberg (2011)

AL07.   Aumann, Y., Lindell, Y.: Security Against Covert Adversaries: Efficient Protocols for Realistic Adversaries. In: Vadhan, S.P. (ed.) TCC 2007. LNCS, vol. 4392, pp. 137–156. Springer, Heidelberg (2007)

BBD$^+$11.   Baldi, P., Baronio, R., De Cristofaro, E., Gasti, P., Tsudik, G.: Countering gattaca: efficient and secure testing of fully-sequenced human genomes. In: CCS (2011), http://arxiv.org/abs/1110.2478

BCC$^+$09.   Belenkiy, M., Camenisch, J., Chase, M., Kohlweiss, M., Lysyanskaya, A., Shacham, H.: Randomizable Proofs and Delegatable Anonymous Credentials. In: Halevi, S. (ed.) CRYPTO 2009. LNCS, vol. 5677, pp. 108–125. Springer, Heidelberg (2009)

BLHB11.   Bursztein, E., Lagarenne, J., Hamburg, M., Boneh, D.: OpenConflict: Preventing Real Time Map Hacks in Online Games. In: IEEE Security and Privacy (2011)

BNPS03.   Bellare, M., Namprempre, C., Pointcheval, D., Semanko, M.: The one-more-RSA-inversion problems and the security of Chaum's blind signature scheme. Journal of Cryptology 16(3) (2003)

Bon98.   Boneh, D.: Twenty years of attacks on the RSA cryptosystem. Notices of the AMS 46(2) (1998)

CM99.   Camenisch, J.L., Michels, M.: Proving in Zero-Knowledge that a Number Is the Product of Two Safe Primes. In: Stern, J. (ed.) EUROCRYPT 1999. LNCS, vol. 1592, pp. 107–122. Springer, Heidelberg (1999)

CS03.   Camenisch, J.L., Shoup, V.: Practical Verifiable Encryption and Decryption of Discrete Logarithms. In: Boneh, D. (ed.) CRYPTO 2003. LNCS, vol. 2729, pp. 126–144. Springer, Heidelberg (2003)

DJL$^+$10.   De Cristofaro, E., Jarecki, S., Liu, X., Lu, Y., Tsudik, G.: Automatic Privacy Protection Program – UC Irvine Team Web Site (2010),
http://sprout.ics.uci.edu/projects/iarpa-app

DKT10.   De Cristofaro, E., Kim, J., Tsudik, G.: Linear-Complexity Private Set Intersection Protocols Secure in Malicious Model. In: Abe, M. (ed.) ASIACRYPT 2010. LNCS, vol. 6477, pp. 213–231. Springer, Heidelberg (2010)

DSMRY09.   Dachman-Soled, D., Malkin, T., Raykova, M., Yung, M.: Efficient Robust Private Set Intersection. In: Abdalla, M., Pointcheval, D., Fouque, P.-A., Vergnaud, D. (eds.) ACNS 2009. LNCS, vol. 5536, pp. 125–142. Springer, Heidelberg (2009)

DT10.   De Cristofaro, E., Tsudik, G.: Practical Private Set Intersection Protocols with Linear Complexity. In: Sion, R. (ed.) FC 2010. LNCS, vol. 6052, pp. 143–159. Springer, Heidelberg (2010), http://eprint.iacr.org/2009/491

DT12.   De Cristofaro, E., Tsudik, G.: On the Performance of certain Private Set Intersection Protocols. Cryptology ePrint Archive (2012),
http://eprint.iacr.org/2012/054

ElG85.   ElGamal, T.: A public key cryptosystem and a signature scheme based on discrete logarithms. IEEE Transactions on Information Theory 31(4) (1985)

FIPR05.   Freedman, M.J., Ishai, Y., Pinkas, B., Reingold, O.: Keyword Search and Oblivious Pseudorandom Functions. In: Kilian, J. (ed.) TCC 2005. LNCS, vol. 3378, pp. 303–324. Springer, Heidelberg (2005)

FKJM$^+$06.   Fouque, P.-A., Kunz-Jacques, S., Martinet, G., Muller, F., Valette, F.: Power Attack on Small RSA Public Exponent. In: Goubin, L., Matsui, M. (eds.) CHES 2006. LNCS, vol. 4249, pp. 339–353. Springer, Heidelberg (2006)

FNP04.   Freedman, M.J., Nissim, K., Pinkas, B.: Efficient Private Matching and Set Intersection. In: Cachin, C., Camenisch, J.L. (eds.) EUROCRYPT 2004. LNCS, vol. 3027, pp. 1–19. Springer, Heidelberg (2004)

GGM86.   Goldreich, O., Goldwasser, S., Micali, S.: How to construct random functions. Journal of the ACM 33(4) (1986)

HEK12.   Huang, Y., Evans, D., Katz, J.: Private Set Intersection: Are Garbled Circuits Better than Custom Protocols. In: NDSS (2012)

HL08.   Hazay, C., Lindell, Y.: Efficient Protocols for Set Intersection and Pattern Matching with Security Against Malicious and Covert Adversaries. In: Canetti, R. (ed.) TCC 2008. LNCS, vol. 4948, pp. 155–175. Springer, Heidelberg (2008)

HMRT11.   Hazay, C., Mikkelsen, G.L., Rabin, T., Toft, T.: Efficient rsa key generation and threshold paillier in the two-party setting. Cryptology ePrint Archive (2011),
http://eprint.iacr.org/2011/494

HN10.   Hazay, C., Nissim, K.: Efficient Set Operations in the Presence of Malicious Adversaries. In: Nguyen, P.Q., Pointcheval, D. (eds.) PKC 2010. LNCS, vol. 6056, pp. 312–331. Springer, Heidelberg (2010)

IKNP03.   Ishai, Y., Kilian, J., Nissim, K., Petrank, E.: Extending Oblivious Transfers Efficiently. In: Boneh, D. (ed.) CRYPTO 2003. LNCS, vol. 2729, pp. 145–161. Springer, Heidelberg (2003)

JL09.   Jarecki, S., Liu, X.: Efficient Oblivious Pseudorandom Function with Applications to Adaptive OT and Secure Computation of Set Intersection. In: Reingold, O. (ed.) TCC 2009. LNCS, vol. 5444, pp. 577–594. Springer, Heidelberg (2009)

JL10.   Jarecki, S., Liu, X.: Fast Secure Computation of Set Intersection. In: Garay, J.A., De Prisco, R. (eds.) SCN 2010. LNCS, vol. 6280, pp. 418–435. Springer, Heidelberg (2010)

KL08.   Katz, J., Lindell, Y.: Introduction to modern cryptography. Chapman & Hall/CRC (2008)

KS05.   Kissner, L., Song, D.: Privacy-Preserving Set Operations. In: Shoup, V. (ed.)
            CRYPTO 2005. LNCS, vol. 3621, pp. 241–257. Springer, Heidelberg (2005)
MVOV97.   Menezes, A., Oorschot, P.V., Vanstone, S.: Handbook of Applied Cryptography.
            CRC (1997)
NMH$^+$10. Nagaraja, S., Mittal, P., Hong, C.Y., Caesar, M., Borisov, N.: BotGrep: Finding
            Bots with Structured Graph Analysis. In: Usenix Security (2010)
NP06.   Naor, M., Pinkas, B.: Oblivious polynomial evaluation. SIAM Journal on Comput-
            ing, 1–35(5) (2006)
NTL$^+$11. Narayanan, A., Thiagarajan, N., Lakhani, M., Hamburg, M., Boneh, D.: Location
            Privacy via Private Proximity Testing. In: NDSS (2011)
Pai99.   Paillier, P.: Public-Key Cryptosystems Based on Composite Degree Residuosity
            Classes. In: Stern, J. (ed.) EUROCRYPT 1999. LNCS, vol. 1592, pp. 223–238.
            Springer, Heidelberg (1999)
RS60.   Reed, S., Solomon, G.: Polynomial codes over certain finite fields. Journal of the
            Society for Industrial and Applied Mathematics 8(2) (1960)
Sha79.   Shamir, A.: How to Share a Secret. Communications of ACM 22(11) (1979)
Yao82.   Yao, A.C.: Protocols for secure computations. In: FOCS (1982)

A   Survey of PSI Techniques

In this appendix, we survey research work on Private Set Intersection (PSI). This appendix is organized in chronological order: we first overview work prior to [DT10], then, after discussing the work in [DT10], we present recent results.

A.1   Work Prior to [DT10]

Once again, recall that PSI is a protocol involving a server and a client, on inputs $S = \{s_1, \ldots, s_w\}$ and $C = \{c_1, \ldots, c_v\}$, respectively, that results in client obtaining $S \cap C$. As a result of running PSI, set sizes are reciprocally disclosed to both server and client. In the variant called *PSI with Data Transfer* (PSI-DT), each item in server set has an associated data record, i.e., server's input is $S = \{(s_1, data_1), \cdots, (s_w, data_w)\}$, and client's output is defined as $\{(s_j, data_j) \in S \mid \exists c_i \in C \ s.t. \ c_i = s_j\}$.

We distinguish between two classes of PSI protocols: one based on Oblivious Polynomial Evaluations (OPE) [NP06], and the other based on Oblivious Pseudo-Random Functions (OPRF-s) [FIPR05].

Freedman, Nissim, and Pinkas [FNP04] introduce the concept of Private Set Intersection and and propose a protocol based on OPE. They represent a set as a polynomial, and elements of the set as its roots. A client encodes elements in its private set C as the roots of a v-degree polynomial over a ring R, i.e., $f = \prod_{i=1}^{v}(x - c_i) = \sum_{i=0}^{k} \alpha_i x^i$. Then, assuming pk_C is client's public key for any additively homomorphic cryptosystem (such as Paillier's [Pai99]), client encrypts the coefficients with pk_C, and sends them to server. The latter homomorphically evaluates f at each $s_j \in S$. Note that $f(s_j) = 0$ if and only if $s_j \in C \cap S$. For each $s_j \in S$, returns $u_j = E(r_j f(s_j) + s_j)$ to client (where r_j is chosen at random and $E(\cdot)$ denotes additively homomorphic encryption under pk_C). If $s_j \in C \cap S$ then client learns s_j upon decrypting. If $s_j \notin C \cap S$ then u_j decrypts to a random value. To enable data transfer, server can return $E(r_j f(s_j) + (s_j || data_j))$, for each s_j in its private set $\mathcal{S}$. The protocol in [FNP04] incurs the following complexities: The number of server operations depends on the evaluation of client's encrypted polynomial with v coefficients on w points (in $\mathcal{S}$). Using Paillier cryptosystem [Pai99] and a 1024-bit modulus, this costs $O(vw)$ of 1024-bit mod 2048-bit exponentiations.[6] On the other hand, client computes $O(v + w)$ of 1024-bit mod 2048-bit exponentiations. However, server computation can be reduced to $O(w \log \log v)$ using: (1) Horner's rule for polynomial evaluations, and (2) a hashing-to-bins method (see [FNP04] for more details). If one does not need *data transfer*, it is more efficient to use the Exponential ElGamal cryptosystem [ElG85] (i.e., an ElGamal variant that provides additively homomorphism).[7] Such a cryptosystem does not provide efficient decryption, however, it allows client to test whether a ciphertext is an encryption of "0", thus, to learn that the corresponding element belongs to the set intersection. As a result, efficiency is improved, since in ElGamal the computation may make use of: (1) very short random exponents (e.g., 160-bit) and (2) shorter moduli in exponentiations (1024-bit). The PSI protocol in [FNP04] is secure against honest-but-curious adversaries in the standard model, and can be extended to malicious in the Random Oracle Model (ROM), at an increased cost.

Hazay and Nissim [HN10] present an improved construction of [FNP04], in the presence of malicious adversaries without ROM, using zero-knowledge proofs to let client demonstrate that encrypted polynomials are correctly produced. Perfectly hiding commitments, along with an Oblivious Pseudo-Random Function evaluation protocol, are used to prevent server from deviating from the protocol. The protocol in [HN10] incurs $O(v + w(\log \log v + m))$ computational and $O(v + w \cdot m)$ communication complexity, where m is the number of bits needed to represent a set element.

Kissner and Song [KS05] also propose OPE-based protocols involving (potentially) more than two players. They present one technique secure in the standard model against semi-honest and one – against malicious adversaries. The former incurs quadratic – $O(vw)$ – computation (but linear communication) overhead. The latter uses expensive generic zero-knowledge proofs to prevent parties from deviating to the protocol. Also, it is not clear how to enable *data transfer*.

Dachman-Soled, et al. [DSMRY09] also present an OPE-based PSI construction, improving on [KS05]. Their protocol incorporates a secret sharing of polynomial inputs: specifically, as Shamir's secret sharing [Sha79] implies Reed-Solomon codes [RS60], generic (i.e., expensive) zero-knowledge proofs can be avoided. Complexity of resulting protocol amounts to $O(wk^2 \log^2(v))$ in communication and $O(wvk \log(v) + wk^2 \log^2(v))$ in computation, where k is a security parameter.

Other techniques rely on *Oblivious Pseudo-Random Functions* (OPRF-s), introduced in [FIPR05]. An OPRF is a two-party protocol that securely computes a pseudo-random function $f_k(\cdot)$ on key k contributed by the sender and input x contributed by the receiver, such that the former learns nothing from the interaction and the latter learns

---

[6] Encryption and decryption in the Paillier cryptosystem [Pai99] involve exponentiations mod n^2: if $|n| = 1024$ bits, then $|n^2| = 2048$ bits (where n is the public modulus).

[7] In the Exponential ElGamal variant, encryption of message m is computed as $E_{g,y}(m) = (g^r, y^r \cdot g^m)$ instead of $(g^r, m \cdot y^r)$, for random r and public key y.

only the value $f_k(x)$. Most prominent OPRF-based protocols are presented below. The intuition behind OPRF-based PSI protocols is as follows: server and client interact in v parallel execution of the OPRF $f_k(\cdot)$, on input k and $c_i, \forall\, c_i \in \mathcal{C}$, respectively. As server transfers $T_{s:j} = f_k(s_j), \forall\, s_j \in \mathcal{S}$ and client obtains $T_{c:i} = f_k(c_i), \forall\, c_i \in \mathcal{C}$, client learns the set intersection by finding matching $(T_{s:j}, T_{c:i})$ pairs, while it learns nothing about values $s_l \in \mathcal{S} \setminus \mathcal{S} \cap \mathcal{C}$, since $f_k(s_l)$ is indistinguishable from random, if $f_k(\cdot)$ is a pseudo-random function.[8]

Hazay and Lindell [HL08] propose the first PSI construction based on OPRF-s. In it, server generates a secret random key k, then, for each $s_j \in \mathcal{S}$, computes $u_j = f_k(s_j)$, and sends client the set $\mathcal{U} = \{u_1, \cdots, u_w\}$. Next, client and server engage in an OPRF computation of $f_k(c_i)$ for each $c_i \in \mathcal{C}$. Finally, client learns that $c_i \in \mathcal{C} \cap \mathcal{S}$ if (and only if) $f_k(c_i) \in \mathcal{U}$. [HL08] introduces two constructions: one secure in the presence of malicious adversaries with one-sided simulatability, the other – in the presence of covert adversaries [AL07].

Jarecki and Liu [JL09] improve on [HL08] by constructing a protocol secure in the standard model against both malicious parties, based on the Decisional q-Diffie-Hellman Inversion assumption, in the Common Reference String (CRS) model, where a safe RSA modulus must be pre-generated by a trusted party. The OPRF in [JL09] is built using the Camenisch-Shoup additively homomorphic cryptosystem [CS03] (CS for short). However, this technique can be optimized, leading to the work by Belenkiy, et al. [BCC+09]. In fact, the OPRF construction could work in groups of 160-bit prime order, unrelated to the RSA modulus, instead of (more expensive) composite order groups [JL09]. Thus improved, the protocol in [JL09] incurs the following computational complexity: server needs to perform $O(w)$ PRF evaluations, specifically, $O(w)$ modular exponentiations of m-bit exponents mod n^2, where m the number of bits needed to represent set items and n^2 is typically 2048-bit long. The client needs to compute $O(v)$ CS encryptions, i.e., $O(v)$ m-bit exponentiations mod 2048 bits, plus $O(v)$ 1024-bit exponentiations mod 1024 bits. The server also computes $O(v)$ 1024-bit exponentiations mod 1024 bits and $O(v)$ CS decryptions – i.e., $O(v)$ 1024-bit exponentiations mod 2048 bits. Complexity in malicious model grows by a factor of 2. The input domain size of the pseudo-random function in [JL09] is limited to be polynomial in the security parameter, since the security proof requires the ability to exhaustively search over input domain.

A.2   Protocols in [DT10]

The work in [DT10] presented two linear-complexity PSI protocols, both secure in the Random Oracle Model in the presence of semi-honest adversaries. Specifically, in [DT10], they present:

1. One protocol (Figure 3) secure under the *One-More-Gap-DH* assumption [BNPS03]. It imposes $O(w + v)$ *short* exponentiations on server, and $O(v)$ – on client. Note that the term "short" exponentiation refers to the fact that exponentiations can be of 160-bit exponents modulo 1024 bits (for 80-bit security).

---

[8] For more details on pseudo-random functions, we refer to [KL08,GGM86].

2. Another protocol (Figure 4) secure under the *One-More-RSA* assumption [BNPS03], whose implementation we have presented and analyzed in this paper. Recall that, in this protocol, server computational overhead amounts to $O(w + v)$ RSA signatures using CRT optimization (i.e., 512 bits modulo 512 bits exponentiations for 80-bit security). Whereas, client complexity is dominated by $O(v)$ RSA encryptions, i.e., in practice, $O(v)$ modular multiplications if a short RSA public exponent is selected.

Both protocols incur the following communication overhead: client and server need to send and receive $O(v)$ group elements (i.e., 1024-bit); additionally, server sends client $O(w)$ hash outputs (e.g., 160-bit using SHA-1).

A.3 Recent Results

Shortly after [DT10], Jarecki and Liu [JL10] also propose a PSI protocol with linear complexity and fast exponentiations. (Remark that some of the proofs in [DT10] are based on that of Jarecki and Liu.) This protocol is based on a concept related to OPRFs, i.e., *Unpredictable Functions* (UPFs). One specific UPF, $f_k(x) = H(x)^k$, is used as a basis for two-party computation (in ROM), with server contributing the key k and client – the argument x. The client picks a random exponent α and sends $y = H(x)^\alpha$ to server, that replies with $z = y^k$, such that client recovers $f_k(x) = z^{1/\alpha}$. By using a zero-knowledge discrete-log proofs of knowledge, the protocol in [JL10] can obtain *malicious security* and implement secure computation of (Adaptive) Set Intersection, under the *One-More-Gap-DH* assumption in ROM [BNPS03]. Therefore, the computational complexity of the UPF-based PSI in [JL10] also amounts to $O(w + v)$ exponentiations with short exponents at server side and $O(v)$ at client side (e.g., 160-bit mod 1024-bit). Communication complexity is also linear is input set size, i.e., $O(w + v)$.

De Cristofaro, et al. [DKT10] present another linear-complexity short-exponent PSI construction secure in ROM in the presence of *malicious* adversaries. However, compared to [JL10], its security relies on a weaker assumption – DDH vs One-More-Gap-DH. Then, Ateniese, et al. [ADT11] introduce the concept of *Size-Hiding* Private Set Intersection (SHI-PSI). Besides the standard privacy features guaranteed by the PSI primitive, SHI-PSI additionally provides *unconditional* (i.e., not padding-based) hiding of client's set size. The security of this novel protocol is under the RSA assumption in ROM, in the presence of semi-honest adversaries. Server's computational complexity amounts to only $O(w)$ exponentiations in the RSA setting, thus, it is independent of size of client's input. Whereas, client's overhead is in the order of $O(v \cdot \log v)$ exponentiations. Communication complexity is limited to $O(w)$, i.e., it is also independent of size of client's input.

Finally, Huang, et al. [HEK12] present novel PSI constructions based on garbled circuits [Yao82]. The main intuition is that, by leveraging the *Oblivious Transfer* (OT) extension [IKNP03], the complexity of such protocols is tied to a number of OTs (thus, public-key operations) equal to the security parameter k. In fact, OT extension achieves an unlimited number of OTs at the cost of (essentially) k OTs. Therefore, for increasing security parameters, the number of public-key operations with their technique grows more gracefully than with custom protocols.

Reliable Device Sharing Mechanisms for Dual-OS Embedded Trusted Computing

Daniel Sangorrín, Shinya Honda, and Hiroaki Takada

Graduate School of Information Science, Nagoya University,
Furo-cho, Chikusa-ku, 464-8601, Nagoya, Japan
{dsl,honda,hiro}@ertl.jp

Abstract. Dual-OS virtualization techniques allow consolidating a trusted real-time operating system (RTOS) and an untrusted general-purpose operating system (GPOS) onto the same embedded platform. In order to protect the reliability and real-time performance of the RTOS, platform devices are usually duplicated and assigned exclusively to each operating system causing an increase in the total hardware cost. This paper investigates and compares several mechanisms for sharing devices reliably in a dual-OS system. In particular, we observe that device sharing mechanisms currently used for cloud virtualization are not necessarily appropriate for dual-OS systems. We propose two new mechanisms based on the dynamic re-partition of devices; and evaluate them on a physical platform to show the advantages and drawbacks of each approach.

Keywords: Device sharing, Virtualization, TrustZone, Real-time.

1   Introduction

A dual-OS system[1–4] is a method for consolidating a real-time operating system (RTOS) and a general-purpose operating system (GPOS) onto the same embedded platform—to reduce the hardware cost—thanks to the use of a virtualization layer (VL). The RTOS provides support for applications with strict reliability, security and real-time requirements. Both the RTOS and the VL are small scale and considered to belong to the trusted computing base (TCB). In contrast, the GPOS provides support for applications with high functionality requirements, and is considered to belong to the untrusted computing base (UCB) due to its large scale. The most fundamental requirement of a dual-OS system is protecting the *reliability* of the TCB against any misbehavior or malicious attack coming from the UCB[5]. For that reason, in dual-OS systems devices are usually duplicated and assigned exclusively to each guest OS: devices that are critical for the reliability of the system are assigned to the RTOS; and the remainder devices are assigned to the GPOS. The dual-OS VL must guarantee that neither the GPOS nor GPOS devices—particularly devices with Direct Memory Access (DMA)—are allowed to access the memory and devices assigned to the RTOS.

Device duplication is useful for ensuring the reliability of the RTOS, and maximizing the system performance. However, it also adds a significant increase in

S. Katzenbeisser et al. (Eds.): TRUST 2012, LNCS 7344, pp. 74–91, 2012.

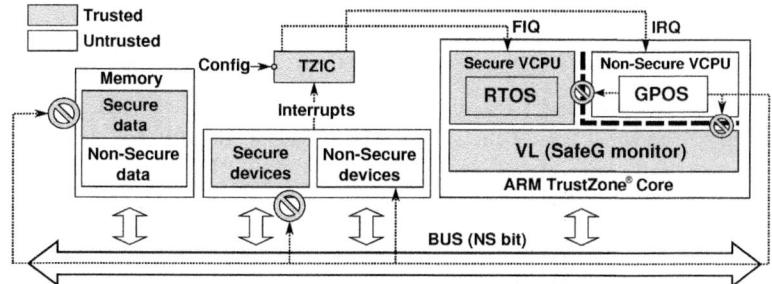

Fig. 1. Architecture of the SafeG dual-OS system

the total hardware cost. Several device sharing mechanisms have been proposed in the context of cloud virtualization[6, 7] to reduce this cost. Most of them use a model in which device drivers are paravirtualized, splitting them between a front-end driver in the guest OSs, and the real back-end driver running on a trusted domain. The most typical application is sharing high-bandwidth network and storage devices that are concurrently accessed by numerous guest OSs. Despite its benefits, this approach is not suitable for dual-OS systems because of its rather high overhead; issues on the real-time performance of the trusted domain; and a significant increase in the complexity of the TCB.

This paper investigates and compares several mechanisms for sharing devices reliably and efficiently in a dual-OS system. The main contributions are:

- A study on the suitability of existing device sharing mechanisms for dual-OS systems. We observe that—in contrast to cloud virtualization—highly concurrent device sharing is not usually required in dual-OS systems. Instead, a more common pattern is to use devices in turns, where the GPOS usage percentage greatly exceeds the RTOS usage percentage.
- We propose two new mechanisms based on the dynamic re-partition of devices to operating systems at run time. The difference is a trade-off between execution overhead and the latency to access a shared device.

We implemented both mechanisms and the paravirtualization approach on a physical platform using SafeG[3], an open source reliable dual-OS system based on ARM TrustZone[8]. From the results of the evaluation, we observed that each mechanism is best suited to a particular set of conditions and assumptions. In particular, our two new mechanisms seem more suitable for device sharing patterns commonly found in dual-OS systems than the paravirtualization approach.

The paper is organized as follows. Section 2 reviews knowledge about SafeG and presents a motivational example. Section 3 is the core of this paper and explains several device sharing mechanisms for dual-OS systems. Section 4 details the implementation of our two new mechanisms and the paravirtualization approach on SafeG. Section 5 evaluates the overhead, latency and code modifications of each implementation. Section 6 compares this research with previous work. Finally, the paper is concluded in Section 7.

2   Background

2.1   SafeG: A Dual-OS System Based on ARM TrustZone

Fig. 1 depicts the architecture of SafeG[3, 9] (*Safety Gate*), a reliable open-source dual-OS system based on ARM TrustZone[8] hardware. Here, we briefly introduce some concepts about SafeG and TrustZone. For details, refer to [3, 8].

- *Virtual CPUs*: a processor core contains two Virtual CPUs (VCPUs), the Secure and the Non-Secure VCPU, that are executed in a time-sliced fashion. Each VCPU is equipped with its own memory management unit (MMU) and exception vectors; and supports all ARM operation modes. SafeG assigns the RTOS and GPOS to the Secure and Non-Secure VCPUs respectively.
- *SafeG monitor*: the Secure VCPU has an additional mode — called the monitor mode—which is used by the SafeG monitor to context switch between both OSs. The entry to SafeG monitor can only be triggered by software executing the Secure Monitor Call (SMC) instruction or the occurrence of an FIQ (Fast Interrupt Request) while the Non-Secure VCPU is active. The SafeG monitor is small—around 2KB[3]—and executes with all interrupts disabled, which simplifies its verification. A VCPU context switch on an ARM1176[10] processor requires around 200 cycles[3] and involves saving and restoring all ARM general-purpose registers.
- *Address space partitioning*: when a bus master accesses memory or devices, the NS bit (Non-Secure bit) is propagated through the system bus indicating the privilege of that access (i.e., secure or non-secure). This allows partitioning the address space into two virtual worlds: the Secure and the Non-Secure world. The Secure VCPU can access memory and devices from both worlds. However, hardware logic makes sure that Secure world memory and devices cannot be accessed by the Non-Secure VCPU or Non-Secure DMA devices. At initialization, SafeG configures RTOS memory and devices as Secure world resources; and GPOS memory and devices as Non-Secure world resources. For that reason, the RTOS address space is protected against malicious accesses from the untrusted GPOS.
- *Interrupts partitioning*: ARM processors have two types of interrupt known as FIQ and IRQ. The main difference is that FIQs have higher priority and more banked registers. SafeG configures RTOS devices to generate FIQs; and GPOS devices to generate IRQs. This configuration is done through a TrustZone interrupt controller (e.g., TZIC[11]), only accessible from the Secure VCPU. FIQ and IRQ interrupts can be disabled in privileged mode by setting the F and I flags of the Current Program Status Register (CPSR) respectively. To prevent the GPOS from masking RTOS device interrupts, SafeG takes advantage of the FW (F flag Writable) bit, which is only accessible by the Secure VCPU. This allows the RTOS to ensure that hard real-time tasks always meet their deadlines.

The execution flow is controlled by two principles that ensure the real-time performance of the RTOS: the GPOS is scheduled as the RTOS idle task; and the RTOS can recover the control of the processor at any time through an FIQ.

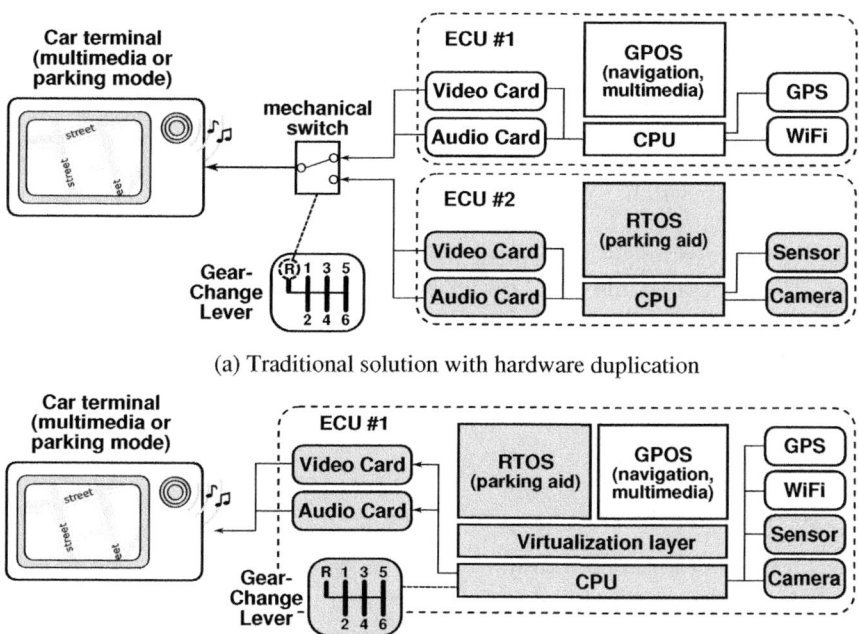

(a) Traditional solution with hardware duplication

(b) Solution based on a dual-OS system with shared devices

Fig. 2. Motivational example for device sharing applied to an in-vehicle system

2.2 Motivational Example

Fig. 2 illustrates a motivational example for reliable device sharing inside an in-vehicle car terminal[12] that operates in two modes: multimedia and parking mode. In *multimedia mode*, the terminal is used for GPS navigation, video playback or Internet access. This mode requires highly functional libraries such as video codecs or network stacks. For that reason, the most suitable way to implement it is by using a GPOS. In *parking mode*, the system fetches data from a camera and a distance sensor placed on the rear of the car. The camera data is displayed on the terminal to assist the driver during parking maneuver, and the distance to nearby obstacles is indicated through a repetitive sound. This mode requires high reliability and time determinism to avoid a potential car accident. For that reason, the most suitable way to implement it is by using an RTOS.

The traditional approach to implement this system is illustrated by Fig. 2(a) and consists of two separated computing units (ECUs). One computer contains a GPOS with rich libraries to handle the multimedia mode; and the other one contains a reliable RTOS to handle the parking mode. Parking mode is activated through a mechanical switch (i.e., the gear-change lever) whenever the car is driven backwards. Although this approach can satisfy the main requirements of the system, it requires duplicated hardware that increases the total cost.

In contrast, Fig. 2(b) illustrates a solution based on a dual-OS system with device sharing capabilities. Thanks to the use of a virtualization layer and device

sharing, it is possible to consolidate both operating systems onto the same platform and avoid duplicating hardware. An important difference with device sharing in enterprise cloud virtualization is that devices (e.g., the video and sound
card) are shared with low concurrency or rather in turns. For example, the
car terminal is expected to operate in multimedia mode during most of the
time; and only switch to parking mode occasionally. For that reason, existing device sharing mechanisms designed for highly concurrent systems—such
as paravirtualization[6]—are not suited to this situation. Ideally, in a dual-OS
system the GPOS should have direct access to devices for maximizing performance; and use its own feature-rich drivers instead of relying on a more complex
TCB. Additionally, the worst-case amount of time that the RTOS has to wait for
a shared device to be usable with reliability guarantees must be upper-bounded.

3   Reliable Device Sharing

3.1   Requirements and Assumptions

Based on the motivational example above, we define the following set of requirements for the design of a reliable device sharing mechanism.

(a) *Completion*: device sharing mechanisms must guarantee that the TCB has
    full control over the successful completion of operations on shared devices.
(b) *Memory isolation*: TCB resources must be protected against any access—
    accidental or malicious—coming from UCB (including devices with DMA).
(c) *Real-time*: the timeliness of the RTOS must be guaranteed. In particular,
    malicious GPOS software must not be able to prevent or delay further use
    of a shared device (i.e., *device latency*) for an unbounded amount of time.
(d) *Software-only*: device sharing must be implemented in software. Customized
    hardware implementations are out of the scope of this paper.
(e) *Performance*: the overhead caused by a device sharing mechanism (e.g., due
    to unnecessary data copies or context switches) must be minimized. Ideally,
    a device should be operated with native performance.
(f) *Code modifications*: modifications to the TCB software must be minimized.
    In particular, complex modifications to the VL must be avoided because
    they can increase the latency of RTOS interrupts. In contrast, the GPOS
    kernel can be extended with drivers. Nonetheless, GPOS applications and
    libraries should not require modifications for the sake of reusability.

We also make the following assumptions: software that belongs to the UCB does
not have deffects; the RTOS and GPOS drivers can be modified; the hardware
reset time of a shared device is upper-bounded; the processor has a single core;
and finally, we assume that the GPOS cannot damage a shared device.

3.2   Suitability of Existing Device Sharing Approaches

Fig. 3(a)–(d) illustrate several existing approaches to device sharing, adapted to
the context of a dual-OS system. Bellow we analyze each approach.

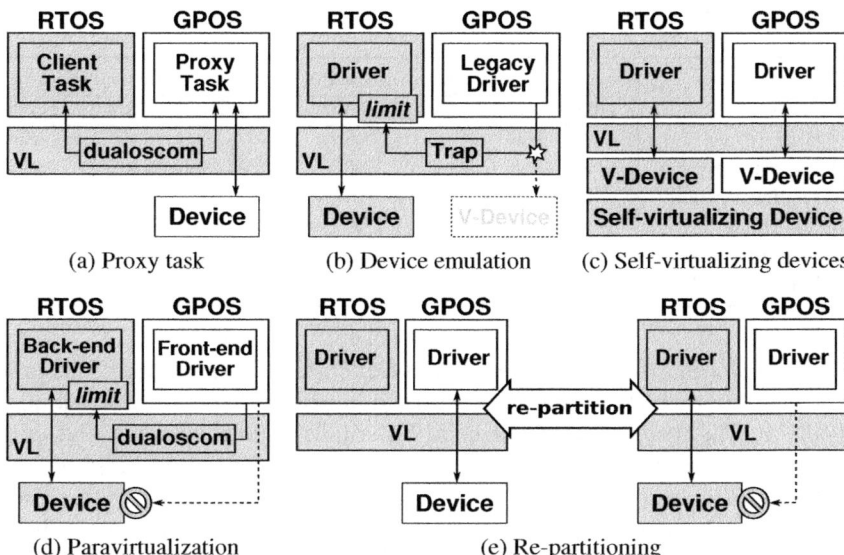

Fig. 3. Device sharing approaches (VL=Virtualization Layer, dualoscom=Dual-OS communications, V-Device=Virtual Device)

(a) *Proxy task*: in this approach, RTOS client tasks send requests to a proxy task in the GPOS—through a dual-OS communications system[13] usually provided by the VL—with the intention of leveraging the richness of GPOS libraries and drivers. Requests can be sent with a high level of abstraction (e.g., play this sound), and therefore the overhead incurred is rather low. Despite all these benefits, the proxy task approach cannot be used for *reliable* device sharing because GPOS software is untrusted and it may misbehave or ignore RTOS requests which goes against requirement 3.1(a).

(b) *Device emulation*: this approach follows the classical Popek and Goldberg's trap-and-emulate model for machine virtualization[14]. The GPOS is tricked to think that there is a legacy device in the board. GPOS accesses to this virtual device are trapped by the VL and forwarded to the RTOS, where a driver handles the real device. This approach brings platform independence and flexibility to the GPOS. However, it has a significant execution overhead, and requires complex extensions to the TCB (see requirement 3.1(f)) in order to implement the trap mechanism. Additionally, traps are typically delivered to the RTOS as software interrupts. To guarantee the real-time performance of the RTOS (see requirement 3.1(c)), the TCB must limit the rate of these software interrupts, which may become a performance bottleneck if the GPOS needs to access device registers very frequently.

(c) *Self-virtualizing devices*: A self-virtualizing device with built-in support for real-time reservations could be shared seamlessly by the RTOS and the GPOS through separated interfaces, achieving near-native performance. Hardware virtualization support was recently introduced to some devices[15].

Table 1. Qualitative comparison of device sharing approaches

	Existing approaches				Re-partitioning	
Property	Proxy	Emulation	Self-virt	Paravirt.	Pure	Hybrid
(1) Real-time	✗	✓	✓	✓	✓	✓
(2) Functionality	✓	✗	✓	✗	✓	✓
(3) Device Latency	✗	✓	✓	✓	✗	✓
(4) Overhead	✓	✗	✓	✗	✓	✗
(5) Concurrency	✓	✓	✓	✓	✗	✗
(6) Hardware Cost	✓	✓	✗	✓	✓	✓

Unfortunately, the current availability of such devices is limited in practice to high bandwidth network and storage interfaces for enterprise cloud computing. The design of customized self-virtualizing hardware with support for real-time reservations is out of the scope of this paper (see 3.1(d)).

(d) *Paravirtualization*: in this approach, the GPOS is extended with a paravirtual driver—typically known as the front-end driver in XEN[6] split-driver terminology—that uses dual-OS communications for sending requests to the RTOS back-end driver. Paravirtualization helps raising the level of abstraction from bus operations to device-level operations in order to reduce the overhead, though its performance is still far from native. Similar to the emulation approach, the rate of device operation requests must be limited not to affect the real-time performance of the RTOS. The major drawback of this approach is the fact that the GPOS is limited to the functionality supported by the RTOS driver. RTOS drivers do not necessarily provide support for all of the functionality available in a certain device. For instance, a sound card may have audio capture features that are not needed by the RTOS. Implementing this extra functionality on the RTOS would complicate unnecessarily the TCB (see requirement 3.1(f)).

The left part of Table 1 summarizes qualitatively the properties of each approach. Property (1) refers to the ability to guarantee the timeliness of the RTOS. Property (2) indicates whether the GPOS uses its own fully functional drivers or not. Property (3) shows the adequacy of each approach to minimize the device latency. Property (4) refers to the overhead introduced by each approach. Property (5) expresses the suitability of each approach for a highly concurrent scenario. Finally, property (6) refers to the hardware cost of each approach.

We discard the proxy, device emulation and self-virtualizing approaches (i.e., approaches (a), (b) and (c)) because they cannot satisfy requirements 3.1(a), 3.1(f) and 3.1(d) respectively. Paravirtualization (approach (d)) can satisfy all of the requirements enumerated in Sec. 3.1, at the cost of reduced functionality and moderate overhead. However, it is not suitable for the type of device sharing patterns described in Sec. 2.2, where the GPOS usage percentage of the shared device greatly exceeds the RTOS usage percentage. For that reason, in Sect. 3.3 we explore a new approach based on dynamically re-partitioning devices between the RTOS and the GPOS at run time.

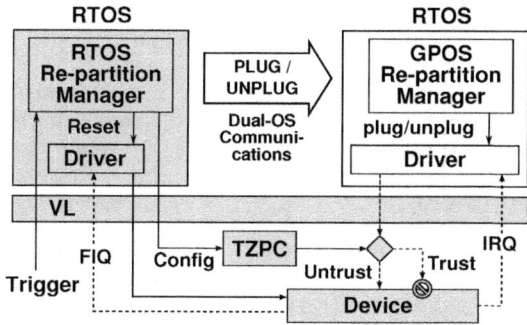

Fig. 4. Architecture of the pure re-partitioning mechanism

3.3   Reliable Device Sharing through Re-partitioning

The re-partitioning approach—depicted in Fig. 3(e)—consists of dynamically modifying the assignment of devices to each OS at run time. Re-partitioning is always initiated by the RTOS after a trigger condition (e.g., car going into backwards mode) and has several benefits:

- Devices can be accessed directly by both OSs which minimizes overhead.
- If a device is assigned to the GPOS, its interrupts (IRQ) are handled by the GPOS itself, which runs with the lowest RTOS priority. For that reason, the timeliness of RTOS tasks and interrupt handlers can be guaranteed.
- The VL does not require complex or any modifications at all.
- Any device can be used (e.g., not restricted to self-virtualizing devices).
- The GPOS can leverage its own feature-rich drivers, while the RTOS restricts itself to offer the minimum support in order to keep the TCB small.

We propose two mechanisms for implementing device sharing using the re-partitioning approach: a *pure* re-partitioning mechanism and a *hybrid* one. The main difference between them is a trade-off between the higher performance of pure re-partitioning; and the lower device latency of the hybrid mechanism.

Pure Re-partitioning is illustrated by Fig. 4. The architecture uses the concept of *hotplugging*—typically found in buses such as USB—and applies it to the dynamic re-partitioning of a device between the RTOS and the GPOS. Device sharing is managed by the so-called *Re-partition Manager* agents at each OS. The pseudo code of both agents is shown in Fig. 5. When a condition triggers the re-partitioning process, the RTOS re-partition manager is activated. The RTOS re-partition manager needs to handle two scenarios:

- If the device must be re-partitioned to the TCB, the RTOS re-partition manager will send an UNPLUG event to the GPOS counterpart. The RTOS re-partition manager is not dependent on the state of its GPOS counterpart. This is necessary for ensuring that even if the GPOS misbehaved, the RTOS

```
1 task RTOS_Repartition_Manager is        1 task GPOS_Repartition_Manager is
2 begin                                    2 begin
3   loop                                   3   loop
4     accept Repartition(Device, Trigger) do   4     Wait(Event, Device)
5       case Trigger is:                   5       case Event is:
6         when 'Set_Trust' =>              6         when 'UNPLUG' =>
7           Send_Event(UNPLUG)             7           Unplug(Device)
8           Reset(Device)                  8         when 'PLUG' =>
9           Config(Device, TRUST)          9           Plug(Device)
10        when 'Set_Untrust' =>           10      end case
11          Flush(Device)                 11    end loop
12          Config(Device, UNTRUST)       12 end task
13          Send_Event(PLUG)
14      end case
15    end Repartition
16  end loop
17 end task
```

Fig. 5. Pseudo code of the pure re-partitioning mechanism

would still be able to use the shared device with reliability guarantees. For that reason, once the hotplug event is sent, the RTOS re-partition manager needs to fully reset the device into a predefined state. This operation may involve disabling the device's interrupt, canceling current operations or waking the device from low-power mode. Immediately after resetting the device—and without the GPOS being able to execute—the RTOS re-partition manager configures the device as part of the TCB. Note that the opposite order would be insecure if the device was in the middle of a DMA operation. The method to configure a shared device as part of the TCB is dependent on the VL implementation. Once the re-partition process finishes, the RTOS can respond to the trigger condition and use the device reliably. When the GPOS is scheduled to execute by the VL (e.g., when the RTOS becomes idle) the GPOS re-partition manager must handle the UNPLUG event. The way to handle it may differ depending on the implementation but typically requires killing or suspending tasks that were using the device; and unloading or disabling the corresponding device driver.

– If the device must be re-partitioned to the UCB (e.g., because the RTOS does not longer need it), the RTOS re-partition manager must flush any sensitive data from the shared device; configure it as part of the UCB; and send a PLUG event to the GPOS. The GPOS re-partition manager will handle the PLUG event, which typically involves re-enabling or loading the corresponding device driver; and sending a notification to user space for registered processes to resume applications that were previously stopped.

The pure re-partitioning mechanism provides both OSs with direct access to devices for maximizing performance. However, fully resetting devices before re-partitioning can boost device latency to tens of milliseconds (see Sect. 5), which depending on the real-time application may be considered excessive.

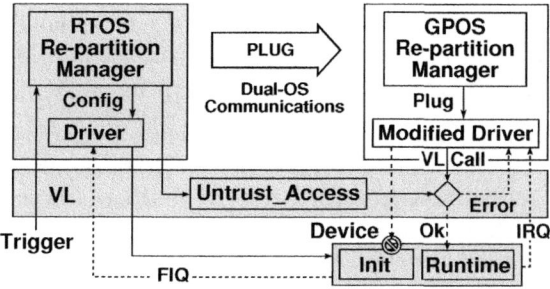

Fig. 6. Architecture of the hybrid re-partitioning mechanism

```
1  task RTOS_Repartition_Manager is
2  begin
3    Init(Device)
4    loop
5      accept Repartition(Device, Trigger) do
6        case Trigger is:
7          when 'Set_Trust' =>
8            Reset_Runtime(Device)
9            Config(Device, TRUST)
10         when 'Set_Untrust' =>
11           Flush(Device)
12           Config(Device, UNTRUST)
13           Send_Event(PLUG)
14       end case
15     end Repartition
16   end loop
17 end task
```

```
1  task GPOS_Repartition_Manager is
2  begin
3    loop
4      Wait_Event(PLUG, Device)
5      Plug(Device)
6    end loop
7  end task

1  procedure Write(Reg : in, Value : in) is
2  begin
3    Ret = VL_call(Reg,Value)
4    if Ret == Error then
5      Unplug(This)
6      Exit
7    end if
8  end procedure
```

Fig. 7. Pseudo code of the hybrid re-partitioning mechanism

Hybrid Re-partitioning is depicted in Fig. 6. In order to reduce the device latency, we modified the pure re-partitioning mechanism with some concepts inspired by the paravirtualization approach, ergo the name of hybrid re-partitioning. The mechanism is derived from the observation that most part of the time spent on resetting a device is consumed on operations that are only performed at initialization (e.g., setting the clock rate) but not at run time. In the hybrid mechanism, the interface of a shared device is logically divided between bits that are required at initialization (*Init* interface); and those required during run time (*Runtime* interface). The Init interface can only be accessed by the RTOS. For that reason, the RTOS can guarantee that certain conditions (e.g., that the device is powered on) are satisfied at all times, and thus reduce the time for resetting a device. In contrast, the Runtime interface can be re-partitioned to the RTOS or the GPOS. A software-only method to implement the hybrid approach consists of configuring the device as part of the TCB, and extending the VL with a simple VL call for the GPOS to access the Runtime interface. Access permissions to the Runtime interface are controlled by the RTOS re-partition manager and the VL through a boolean variable (Untrust_Access) in trusted memory. Fig. 7 shows the pseudo code of the hybrid mechanism which differs from the one in Fig. 5 in the following aspects:

- Devices do not require a complete reset when re-partitioned to the TCB because only the Runtime interface could have been altered by the UCB.
- In a software-only implementation, RTOS UNPLUG events can be replaced by a *lazy* algorithm. If the GPOS attempts calling the VL while the Runtime interface is assigned to the TCB, the VL will return an error code. The GPOS device driver is modified to handle this error code as an UNPLUG event. Note that the handling of PLUG and UNPLUG events must be serialized to avoid race conditions.

The right part of Table 1 summarizes the properties of each re-partitioning mechanism. The hybrid mechanism has the major benefit of a shorter device latency, compared to the pure re-partitioning mechanism, because it ensures that time-consuming device initialization operations are not available to the GPOS. However, a software-only implementation of the hybrid mechanism requires small modifications to the VL and introduces overhead on each register access. Also, if the shared device has DMA capabilities, the VL may require further modifications in order to check that DMA memory addresses belong to the UCB.

4   Implementation

We implemented both re-partitioning mechanisms (pure and hybrid) and the paravirtualization approach—suitable for highly concurrent shared devices—on a physical platform for comparison. We used TOPPERS/SafeG v0.3, TOPPERS/ASP v1.6[9] and Linux v2.6.33 with buildroot[16] as the VL, RTOS and GPOS respectively. The hardware platform consisted of a PB1176JZF-S board[17] equipped with an ARM1176JZF-S[10] running at 210MHz with 32 KB of cache, 128 MB of Non-Secure dynamic memory and 8 MB of Secure static memory. The following device peripherals were used for the implementation:

- *Sound device*: an ARM PrimeCell Advanced Audio CODEC Interface connected to an LM4549 audio CODEC that is compatible with AC'97 Rev 2.1. The device in the board provides an audio channel with 512-depth transmit and receive FIFOs for audio playback and audio capture respectively.
- *Display device*: an ARM PrimeCell Color LCD controller (CLCDC) that provides a display interface with outputs to a DVI digital/analog connector for connecting to a CLCD monitor. The controller has dual 16-deep programmable 64-bit wide FIFOs for buffering incoming display data through a DMA master interface. The controller is configured through a slave interface, and has a color palette memory for low-resolution configurations.

Both devices can be configured to be part of the TrustZone Secure or Non-Secure worlds through the TrustZone Protection Controller (TZPC[18]). In particular, the master and slave interfaces of the CLCDC can be selectively configured as Secure and Non-Secure.

For the implementation of the paravirtualization approach, the GPOS was extended with a new ALSA[19] sound driver that acts as the front-end driver; and a simplified back-end sound driver—without capturing features—was added to the RTOS. GPOS operations on the sound card are forwarded to the RTOS back-end driver through the SafeG dual-OS communications system[13]. The GPOS video driver was also splitted in two parts. The GPOS front-end driver implements the Linux framebuffer interface by sending requests to a simplified RTOS back-end driver which uses a low-resolution configuration. After that, pixel operations are performed directly on a region of Non-Secure memory accessed by DMA. The RTOS back-end driver validates that DMA addresses sent by the GPOS front-end driver belong to the UCB.

For the implementation of the two re-partitioning mechanisms, we used the baseline feature-rich (e.g., with audio capturing or high resolution video) GPOS sound and video drivers; and simplified drivers for the RTOS. The GPOS re-partition manager executes with a high SCHED_FIFO priority and handles hotplug events by killing/restarting tasks associated to a device; and removing/installing the corresponding device driver modules. The hybrid mechanism was implemented in software (i.e., through VL calls) because the TrustZone controller currently does not support bit granularity for the configuration of a device interface as Secure or Non-Secure. Therefore, the SafeG monitor was extended with a lightweight system call—implemented with a few assembly instructions—for the GPOS to access the Runtime interface. This system call involves a secure monitor call (SMC) instruction; a branch that depends on the value of the Untrust_Access variable (placed in Secure memory); validating the bits being accessed (including DMA addresses); and returning back to the GPOS.

5 Evaluation

This section presents the results of the evaluation of the device sharing implementations described above. The evaluation environment is the same as the one used for the implementation in Sect. 4. All time measurements represent worst-case values among a total of 10,000 measurements.

5.1 Overhead

In this section we evaluate the overhead that each mechanism causes on the handling of shared devices. The RTOS has direct device access (i.e., no overhead) in all mechanisms, and therefore we only evaluate the overhead on the GPOS.

First, we configured a system in which the RTOS is always idle and the GPOS is used either to play a 16bits/48Khz OGG Vorbis music file; or to show an MP4 video with 1024x768 pixels and 16 bpp resolution streamed from a network server. Both applications are executed with lower priority than the GPOS re-partition manager. Table 2 shows the measured execution time overhead per register access for each mechanism. In the pure re-partitioning mechanism, the GPOS can access shared devices directly, and therefore no overhead appears.

Table 2. Execution time overhead per register access

	Paravirtual			Pure			Hybrid		
	min	avg	max	min	avg	max	min	avg	max
Sound	$61\mu s$	$122\mu s$	$182\mu s$	0	0	0	$30\mu s$	$41\mu s$	$52\mu s$
Video	$47\mu s$	$117\mu s$	$187\mu s$	0	0	0	$30\mu s$	$42\mu s$	$53\mu s$

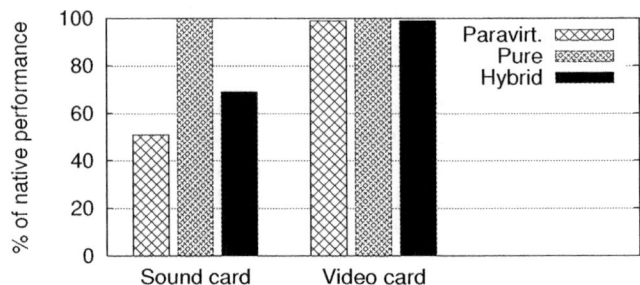

Fig. 8. CPU performance for each mechanism

The overhead incurred by the paravirtualization mechanism is caused by the communications between the back- and front-end drivers. Note that we measured the overhead as per-register access because a single paravirtual operation may involve the reading or writing of several registers at once. Finally, the hybrid mechanism has lower overhead because register accesses do not cause a full context switch to the RTOS as in the paravirtualization approach.

Then, we repeated the same experiment but this time we also executed the *Dhrystone*[16] benchmark on the GPOS (with a lower priority) for quantifying the performance decrease caused by each mechanism. Fig. 8 shows the performance of each mechanism as a percentage of the native performance. As expected, pure re-partitioning achieves 100% of native performance for both devices. The overhead of the paravirtualization and the hybrid mechanisms is considerably more pronounced for the sound card than for the video card. The reason is that the sound card is completely handled through registers; while the video card—once initialized through its slave interface registers—is managed simply by modifying a block of RAM memory that the master interface accesses through DMA. Currently, the overhead of the hybrid mechanism is higher than what we had expected because we found a cache coherence problem between the Secure and Non-Secure worlds. We have temporarily solved this problem by flushing the data cache for each register access, which introduces significant overhead. We also observed that the overhead of the paravirtualization approach in the handling of the sound card can be reduced by increasing the size of the buffer used to store music samples inside the ALSA front-end driver in the GPOS.

Table 3. Device latency of each mechanism

	Paravirtual	Pure	Hybrid
Sound	$83\mu s$	10.53ms	$113\mu s$
Video	$3\mu s$	20.22ms	$10\mu s$

Table 4. Number of source lines of code modified

	Paravirtual	Pure	Hybrid
GPOS(user)	0	153	113
GPOS(kernel)	297	0	54
RTOS	38	43	32
VL	0	0	37

5.2   Device Latency

Device latency is the worst-case amount of time that the RTOS may have to wait until a shared device can be used reliably. We modified the system described in Sect. 5.1 (without the Dhrystone benchmark) so that every 10 seconds the GPOS audio or video playback application is interrupted by the RTOS, in order to emit a short beep sound (a raw PCM linked to the RTOS binary) or display a black and white alert message on the screen.

Table 3 shows the worst-case measurements for the device latency of each mechanism. The measurements for the paravirtualization and hybrid mechanisms are an order of magnitude smaller than the ones observed for pure re-partitioning. The reason for that is the fact that both the paravirtualization and the hybrid approach can limit GPOS access to critical bits of the device interface. For example, the GPOS is not allowed to set the AC'97 CODEC or the LCD in low power mode. In contrast, the pure re-partitioning approach allows the GPOS to access the device directly, and therefore shared devices must be fully reset every time the RTOS needs to use them. This must be taken into account during the real-time scheduling analysis of the system. The device latency of the hybrid mechanism is slightly longer than the latency observed for the paravirtualization approach. This can be explained by the fact that in the paravirtualization approach the usable functionality of a device is limited by the support included in the simplified RTOS driver. In contrast, in the hybrid approach the GPOS uses its own feature-rich drivers (e.g., with support for audio capturing and high video resolutions), and therefore there are a few more registers that need to be reconfigured.

5.3   Code Modifications

Table 4 displays the number of source lines of code (C code, except the VL which is written in assembly) modified for each implementation. The paravirtualization mechanism required a new GPOS sound driver and modifications to the GPOS video driver in order to communicate with the RTOS drivers, which also required modifications. In the pure re-partitioning mechanism, most modifications occurred at user level where the re-partition managers execute. Finally, the hybrid approach required modifications both in user and kernel level. In particular, GPOS drivers were modified to perform calls to the VL, which was extended to handle this new paravirtual call.

6   Related Work

While techniques for virtualizing processing time and memory resources have usually a rather low overhead, it is challenging to efficiently virtualize I/O devices. There exists a substantial amount of literature describing methods to virtualize hardware devices. In particular, virtualization of high-bandwidth network interface devices in the context of enterprise virtualization for data centers has been the subject of extensive research.

– *Full device emulation* is used by fully virtualized systems[20]. In this approach, guest OS accesses to a virtual legacy device interface are trapped by a hypervisor, which converts them into operations on a real device. The main benefits of this approach are the fact that guest OSs do not require modifications; and the ability to migrate them between heterogeneous hardware. However, this approach incurs a significant performance degradation due to frequent context switches between the guest OS and the hypervisor.

– *Paravirtualization* is the de-facto approach to device sharing in most popular enterprise hypervisors[6, 7]. In this approach, guest OSs contain device drivers that are hypervisor-aware. A paravirtualized device driver operates by communicating with the real device driver which runs outside the guest. The real device driver that actually acccesses the hardware can reside in the hypervisor or in a separate device driver domain with privileged access. The level of abstraction is raised from low-level bus operations to device-level operations. For that reason, paravirtualized devices achieve better performance than emulated ones. Nonetheless, paravirtualization introduces a rather high CPU overhead compared to a non-virtualized environment which also leads to throughput degradation in high bandwidth networks[21]. Several techniques to improve the performance of paravirtualized drivers have been presented. In [22] the authors report a 56% reduction of execution overhead on the receive path for conventional network interfaces through improvements on the driver domain model. [23] introduces improvements to the memory sharing mechanism used by paravirtualized drivers to communicate with the real device driver, reporting a reduction of up to 31% in the per-packet overhead. [24] proposes a software architecture which runs middleware modules at the hypervisor level. Their approach reduces I/O virtualization overhead by increasing the level of abstraction which allows to cut down the number of guest-hypervisor context switches. Despite the numerous performance improvements, paravirtual solutions are still far from native performance.

– *Direct device assignment*—also known as pass-through access—provides guest OSs with direct access to the real device, maximizing performance. With direct device assignment, an untrusted guest OS could potentially program a DMA device to overwritte the memory of another guest or the hypervisor itself. [25] presents a study on available protection strategies. The most extended strategy involves the use of I/O memory management units (IOMMUs)[26]. Software-based approaches have also been presented[27, 28]. Recently, in [29] the authors report up to 97%-100% of bare-metal performance for I/O virtualization in a system that combines the usage of IOMMU and a software-only approach for handling interrupts within guest virtual machines. Despite its benefits, direct device assignment does not allow guest OSs to share the same device and makes live migration difficult[30, 31].

– *Self-virtualizing devices* have been introduced[15, 28, 32, 33] to avoid the high performance overhead of software-based device virtualization. This approach allows guest OSs to access devices directly, through separate interfaces that can be assigned independently to each guest OS. The main drawbacks of this approach are its increased hardware cost and limited availability.

Micro-kernels use a technique close to paravirtualization. Device drivers are implemented as user-space processes and applications communicate with them through inter-process communication[5]. Finally, direct device assignment is not easy to implement in embedded systems because they are not usually equipped with an IOMMU to provide the necessary isolation. Fortunately, recent ARM high-end embedded processors include TrustZone hardware security extensions[8] which provide similar functionality for up to two domains.

7   Conclusions and Future Work

In this paper, we investigated several device sharing mechanisms for dual-OS systems, where the most fundamental requirement is protecting the reliability of the RTOS. We observed that previous approaches are not well suited to device sharing patterns where the GPOS share greatly exceeds that of the RTOS. For that reason, we proposed two new approaches (pure and hybrid) that are based on dynamically re-partitioning devices between the RTOS and the GPOS at run time. The reliability of the RTOS is ensured by the fact that before a device is re-partitioned to the RTOS, the device (or its run-time interface) is reset and configured as a TCB resource, which prevents further accesses by malicious GPOS applications. Additionally, when a device is re-partitioned back to the GPOS, its buffers are flushed to avoid leaking sensitive data. We evaluated both approaches and compared them with the paravirtualization approach, popular in cloud virtualization. We observed a trade-off between the lower overhead and higher functionality of the re-partitioning approaches; and the shorter device latency of the paravirtualization approach. We suggest that TrustZone hardware could be extended to allow configuring device interfaces with finer granularity for the hybrid approach to be implemented with near-native performance.

In Sec. 3.1, we assumed a dual-OS system that runs on a single-core processor. On a multi-core implementation, both re-partitioning algorithms need to address a race condition that may occur if the GPOS accesses a device just after being reset by the RTOS, and before being configured as a TCB resource (e.g., lines 8 and 9 of the RTOS re-partition manager in Fig. 5). To solve this problem, a mechanism for the RTOS to block UCB accesses to the shared device, while still configured as an UCB resource, is needed. The implementation could be done in software by extending the VL with support for TCB critical sections; or in hardware by adding a new flag for blocking UCB accesses to the shared device.

Acknowledgments. Part of this work is supported by the KAKENHI (23700035) and the Monbukagakusho scholarship.

References

1. Wilson, P., Frey, A., Mihm, T., Kershaw, D., Alves, T.: Implementing Embedded Security on Dual-Virtual-CPU Systems. IEEE Design & Test of Computers 24(6), 582–591 (2007)
2. Heiser, G.: The Role of Virtualization in Embedded Systems. In: Proceedings of the 1st Workshop on Isolation and Integration in Embedded Systems, Glasgow, UK, pp. 11–16 (2008)
3. Sangorrin, D., Honda, S., Takada, H.: Dual Operating System Architecture for Real-Time Embedded Systems. In: Proceedings of the 6th International Workshop on Operating Systems Platforms for Embedded Real-Time Applications (OSPERT), Brussels, Belgium, pp. 6–15 (2010)
4. Beltrame, G., Fossati, L., Zulianello, M., Braga, P., Henriques, L.: xLuna: a Real-Time, Dependable Kernel for Embedded Systems. In: Proceedings of the 19th IP Based Electronics System Conference and Exhibition (IP-SoC), Grenoble, France (2010)
5. Armand, F., Gien, M.: A practical look at micro-kernels and virtual machine monitors. In: Proceedings of the 6th IEEE Conference on Consumer Communications and Networking Conference, Piscataway, USA, pp. 395–401 (2009)
6. Chisnall, D.: The Definitive Guide to the Xen Hypervisor, 1st edn. Prentice Hall Press (2007)
7. Kivity, A., Kamay, Y., Laor, D., Lublin, U., Liguori, A.: kvm: the Linux Virtual Machine Monitor. In: Proceedings of the Ottawa Linux Symposium (OLS 2007), Ottawa, Canada, pp. 225–230 (2007)
8. ARM Ltd.: ARM Security Technology. Building a Secure System using TrustZone Technology, PRD29-GENC-009492C (2009)
9. TOPPERS project: Official website, http://www.toppers.jp/
10. ARM Ltd.: ARM1176JZF-S TRM, DDI 0301G (2008)
11. ARM Ltd.: AMBA3 TrustZone Interrupt Controller TRM, DTO 0013B (2008)
12. Hergenhan, A., Heiser, G.: Operating Systems Technology for Converged ECUs. In: Proceedings of the 6th Embedded Security in Cars Conference (ESCAR), Hamburg, Germany (2008)
13. Sangorrin, D., Honda, S., Takada, H.: Reliable and Efficient Dual-OS Communications for Real-Time Embedded Virtualization, Internal Report, Nagoya University, Japan (2012)

14. Popek, G., Goldberg, R.: Formal requirements for virtualizable third generation architectures. Communications of the ACM 17(7), 412–421 (1974)
15. PCI-SIG: I/O Virtualization, http://www.pcisig.com/specifications/iov/
16. Buildroot: Official website, http://buildroot.uclibc.org/
17. ARM Ltd.: RealView Platform Baseboard for ARM1176JZF-S User Guide (2011)
18. ARM Ltd.: AMBA3 TrustZone Protection Controller TRM, DTO 0015A (2004)
19. ALSA project: Official website, http://www.alsa-project.org/
20. Sugerman, J., Venkitachalam, G., Lim, B.: Virtualizing I/O Devices on VMware Workstation's Hosted Virtual Machine Monitor. In: Proceedings of the USENIX 2001 Annual Technical Conference, Boston, USA, pp. 1–14 (2001)
21. Menon, A., Santos, J., Turner, Y., Janakiraman, G., Zwaenepoel, W.: Diagnosing performance overheads in the XEN virtual machine environment. In: Proceedings of the 1st ACM/USENIX International Conference on Virtual Execution Environments (VEE 2005), Chicago, USA, pp. 13–23 (2005)
22. Santos, J., Turner, Y., Janakiraman, G., Pratt, I.: Bridging the gap between software and hardware techniques for I/O virtualization. In: Proceedings of the USENIX 2008 Annual Technical Conference, Boston, USA, pp. 29–42 (2008)
23. Ram, K., Santos, J., Turner, Y.: Redesigning Xens Memory Sharing Mechanism for Safe and Efficient I/O Virtualization. In: Proceedings of the 2nd conference on I/O virtualization (WIOV 2010), Pittsburgh, USA (2010)
24. Gordon, A., Ben-Yehuda, M., Filimonov, D., Dahan, M.: VAMOS, Virtualization Aware Middleware. In: Proceedings of the 3rd Conference on I/O Virtualization (WIOV 2011), Portland, USA (2011)
25. Willmann, P., Rixner, S., Cox, A.: Protection strategies for direct access to virtualized I/O devices. In: Proceedings of the USENIX 2008 Annual Technical Conference, Boston, USA, pp. 15–28 (2008)
26. Ben-Yehuda, M., Xenidis, J., Ostrowski, M., Rister, K., Bruemmer, A., Doorn, L.: The Price of Safety: Evaluating IOMMU Performance. In: Proceedings of the Ottawa Linux Symposium (OLS 2007), Ottawa, Canada, pp. 9–20 (2007)
27. Xia, L., Lange, J., Dinda, P., Bae, C.: Investigating Virtual Passthrough I/O on Commodity Devices. Operating Systems Review 43(3), 83–94 (2009)
28. Willmann, P., Shafer, J., Carr, D., Menon, A., Rixner, S., Cox, A., Zwaenepoel, W.: Concurrent Direct Network Access for Virtual Machine Monitors. In: Proceedings of the 13th IEEE International Symposium on High-Performance Computer Architecture (HPCA-13), Phoenix, USA, pp. 306–317 (2007)
29. Gordon, A., Amit, N., HarEl, N., Ben-Yehuda, M., Landau, A., Schuster, A., Tsafrir, D.: ELI: Bare-Metal Performance for I/O Virtualization. In: Proceedings of the 17th ACM International Conference on Architectural Support for Programming Languages and Operating Systems (ASPLOS 2012), London, UK (2012)
30. Zhai, E., Cummings, G., Dong, Y.: Live Migration with Pass-through Device for Linux VM. In: Proceedings of the Ottawa Linux Symposium (OLS 2008), Ottawa, Canada, pp. 261–268 (2008)
31. Kadav, A., Swift, M.: Live migration of direct-access devices. Operating Systems Review 43(3), 95–104 (2009)
32. Raj, H., Schwan, K.: High performance and scalable I/O virtualization via self-virtualized devices. In: Proceedings of the 16th International Symposium on High Performance Distributed Computing, California, USA, pp. 179–188 (2007)
33. Rauchfuss, H., Wild, T., Herkersdorf, A.: A network interface card architecture for I/O virtualization in embedded systems. In: Proceedings of the 2nd Conference on I/O Virtualization (WIOV 2010), Pittsburgh, USA (2010)

Modelling User-Centered-Trust (UCT) in Software Systems: Interplay of Trust, Affect and Acceptance Model

Zahid Hasan, Alina Krischkowsky, and Manfred Tscheligi

Christian Doppler Laboratory for Contextual Interfaces
HCI & Usability Unit, ICT&S Center, University of Salzburg
Sigmund-Haffner-Gasse 18, 5020 Salzburg, Austria
`firstname.lastname@sbg.ac.at`

Abstract. Even though trust is a frequently articulated topic in software technology literatures, yet the user centered point of view of trust is hardly discussed. How users perceive the trustworthiness of software systems is not trivial, in fact, if a user cannot trust a program to execute on his behalf, then he should not run it [36]. This paper identifies a potential lack in examination of trust in software systems from user's perspective and aims to develop a conceptual User-Centered-Trust (UCT) framework to model it. This model integrates both Technology Acceptance Model (TAM) and trust under Theory of Reasoned Action (TRA) nomological network. In order to integrate them, trust has been conceptualized as an attitude towards the usage of the systems having two distinct dimensions: cognitive and affective.

Keywords: Trust, Acceptance model, Technology.

1 Introduction

The advent of World Wide Web (WWW) and the emergence of e-commerce during the 90s [23] introduced new types of buying-selling behaviors over the Internet which differ from traditional 'face-to-face' interaction. In this new paradigm trust is considered as an essential component [2]. A considerable number of trust models and frameworks have been proposed during past decades. However, the trust targets in most of these studies are humans (e-vendor or organizations), and the nature as well as the role of trust in technological artifacts remains unclear [71]. What has been generally absent from these investigations is a focus on the effects of trust placed in the information technology (IT) artifacts-hardware and software systems [69].

Trust in IT is an important concept because people today rely on IT more than ever before [48], although, the nature of trust in technological artifacts is still an under-investigated and not well understood topic [71]. Researchers debate whether or not technological artifacts can be an object of trust [71], and if it is valid to ascribe human characteristics to technological artifacts [71]; [10]; [48]; [49]; [13].

S. Katzenbeisser et al. (Eds.): TRUST 2012, LNCS 7344, pp. 92–109, 2012.

In parallel to trust aspect, another stream of research surfaced during the 80's which is Technology Acceptance Model (TAM) - TAM assumes that how individuals accept a new technology is based on an internal cost-benefit analysis. Users assess a technology's usefulness and evaluate whether that usefulness exceeds the costs associated with gaining access to it or learning to use it [54].

Each of these two models explains different aspects of usages. While TAM focuses on technological interface, trust focuses on user's perceptions of the e-vendor [5]. A number of attempts have been undertaken to combine these two essential theories to predict user behavior in e-commerce environment. However, since there is no commonly-agreed definition of trust model, these attempts generally yield diverse interpretations (for details see [5]).

Both TAM and trust model can be explained through the Theory of Reasoned Action (TRA), which essentially posits that behaviour is driven by intentions where intentions are a function of an individual's attitude and these attitudes are derived from beliefs. However, most often in TAM and trust literatures these attitudes are dropped out. This exclusion of attitude poses two problems, first it has created inconsistencies between trusting beliefs and technology beliefs[5]. Second, It reduced the scope of exploring the role of affect (as a dimension of attitude) in technology acceptance.

Considering the points mentioned above, this paper provides a conceptual framework for understanding trust related phenomena in software systems from users' perspective. This hypothetical model incorporates both TAM and trust under TRA nomological network.

2   Concept of Trust

Sociologist Diego Gambetta says:

> "Trust is one of the most important social concepts that helps human agents to cope with their social environment and is present in all human interaction"[24].

In fact, trust helps us to make rational decisions in the real world based on the mixture of bounded rational calculation and trust [33]. The meaning of trust is so diverse that articulating a precise definition of trust is not a simple matter. Some define trust as people's behavior in a situation of vulnerability or simply their attitude or the degree of confidence [32]. Even at worst, when researchers tried to come up with a common definition of trust by surveying a massive number of empirical studies, ultimately, it produced a 'conceptual confusion' regarding the meaning of trust [40]. The meaning of trust in the OXFORD dictionary is defined as 'confidence in or reliance on some quality or attribute of a person or thing, or the truth of a statement'. However this simplistic view of trust is not often sufficient to describe the complex interaction of trust-relationship. Researchers do not have a common consensus on what exactly trust is, disagreeing even on basic definitions [72]. Moreover, trust has been studied by different disciplines - sociology, psychology, management, marketing, ergonomics, industrial psychology, electronic commerce (e-commerce) where it has been defined according to specific disciplinary jargon and conceptualized by own understanding and findings. For example, Psychologists consider trust as an important element for personality development. Philosophers define trust in terms of social values and benefits. In management and business trust is related to organizational benefit and believed to increase business productivity. Researchers from Marketing field often define trust within buyer-seller relationship, branding and services. Trust plays a central role in helping consumers overcome perceptions of risk and insecurity.

2.1   Trust as Belief, Attitude, Intention and Psychological State

Trust has been conceptualized as belief, attitude, intention across different fields. The following section provides a short description of each concepts.

Belief: According to Pavlou (2003) [56], trust in e-commerce is defined as the belief that allows consumers to willingly become vulnerable to Web retailers after having taken the retailers' characteristics into consideration.

Attitude: Jones (1996)[37] defines trust as an attitude of optimism about the goodwill and competence of another. The attitude of optimism is based on both beliefs about the other's trustworthiness and emotions.

Intention: Mayer, Davis, and Schoorman (1995) [47] define trust as the intention (willingness) of a party to be vulnerable to the actions of another party based on the expectation that the other will perform a particular action important to the trustor, irrespective of the ability to monitor or control that other party. Hoy and Tschannen-Moran (1999) [32] states: *Trust is an individuals or groups willingness to be vulnerable to another party based on the confidence that the later party is benevolent, reliable, competent honest and open.* Doney, Cannon, and Mullen (1998) [19] define trust as a willingness to rely on another party and to take action in circumstances where such action makes one vulnerable to the other party.

Psychological State: According to Rousseau, Sitkin, et al. (1998) [58], trust is a psychological state comprising the intention to accept vulnerability based upon positive expectations of the intentions or behavior of another. Trust can be defined as a state involving confident positive expectations about anothers motives with respect to oneself in situations entailing risk ([8], appeared in [73])

Although there is no common agreement about the definition of trust, most researchers acknowledge the importance of trust in human life. For instance, one can decrease complexity by adopting trust since it helps reducing the number of options one has to consider in a given situation, which enables people to live in risky and uncertain situations [13].

2.2   Confusion about Trust and Trustworthiness

Russell Hardin (1996) [29] argued that when philosophers attempt to consider trust, often they inadvertently consider trustworthiness, mistaking it for trust.

Mayer, Davis, and Schoorman (1995) [47] separated the notion of 'trust' (the general beliefs) from 'trustworthiness' (the set of specific beliefs). Colquitt, Scott, et al. (2007) [12] distinguished trustworthiness (the ability, benevolence, and integrity of a trustee) and trust propensity (a dispositional willingness to rely on others) from trust (the intention to accept vulnerability to a trustee based on positive expectations of his or her actions). Slemrod and Katuscak (2002) [60] assert the flip side of trust is trustworthiness.

2.3   Anomalies in Trust Measures

Not surprisingly being a vague notion, trust does not provide any coherent way of measurement. Different authors adopted different models of trust and also tend to measure it from different conceptualizations.

Geyskens, et al. (1998)[28] noted that although there exists conceptual agreement on trust in marketing channel field, however, studies differ in their operational measurement of trust. They criticized that most studies include one or both aspects of trust in a single or global and uni-dimensional measure of trust.

Gefen (2002) [26] found that previous researches on trust had mostly used a single dimensional scale that combines many aspects of trustworthiness into one factor [34], or measured consumers' assessment of their overall trust in the online vendor[25]. The data from his experiment showed that trustworthiness and trust should not be regarded as a single construct. According to him [26], overall trust is a distinct construct that is the product of three trustworthiness-beliefs

McKnight, et al. (1998) [51] raised the question: *'If one researcher defines trust in a widely different way from another researcher, how can the theoretical formulations and the empirical results of researchers build on each other?'*

3   TAM: Technology Acceptance Model

TAM is one of the most influential extensions of Ajzen and Fishbeins theory of reasoned action (TRA) which was originated in 1975 [20]. TRA theorizes that the relationship between beliefs and intentions is indirect and mediated by attitudes. TRA posits that beliefs lead to attitudes, which lead to behavioral intentions, which results in behavior itself. Ten years later, in 1985, Davis (1985)[15] adopted this model into his Technology Acceptance Model (TAM). The goal of TAM is to provide an explanation of the determinants of computer acceptance that is general, capable of explaining user behavior across a broad range of end-user computing technologies and user populations [17]. This model uses a response that can be explained or predicted by user motivation, which is directly influenced by an external stimulus comprising of the actual system's features and capabilities [9]. Relevant beliefs are perceived usefulness (U) and perceived ease of use (EOU). Perceived usefulness has a causal effect on perceived usefulness.

Perceived usefulness is defined as: *The degree to which an individual believes that using a particular system would enhance his or her job performance.*

Perceived ease of use is defined as: *The degree to which an individual believes that using a particular system would be free of physical and mental effort.*

However, Venkatesh and Davis (1996) [70] found that both perceived usefulness and perceived ease of use have a direct effect on behavioral intentions, thus
eliminating the need for attitude construct from the TAM model.

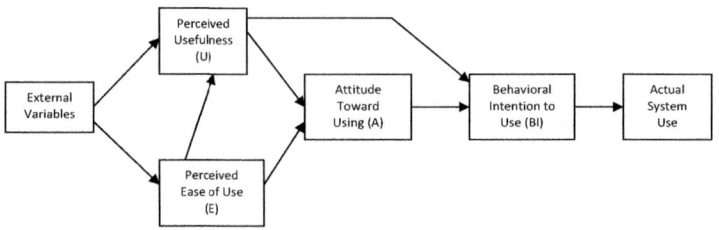

Fig. 1. Technology Acceptance Model (TAM) by [17]

3.1 Trust and TAM

These two theories Trust and TAM, are complement each other. Each model
explains a different aspect of the consumer's relationship with an online retailer
[5]. TAM explains the effects of consumers' technology beliefs on use, on the
other hand, trust focuses less on the technology interface and more on the users
perceptions of the e-vendor. Benamati, et al. (2010)[5] argued that in order to
explain consumers' intentions and behaviors in a more complete way, we need
to combine these two theories (see figure 2).

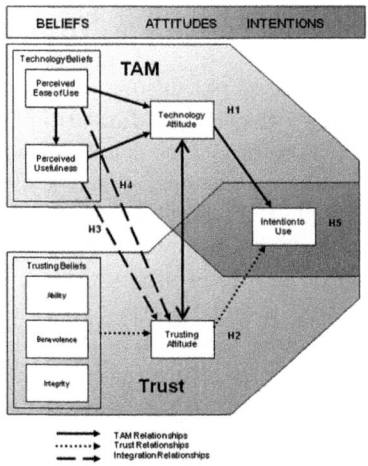

Fig. 2. Trust with TAM proposed by Benamati, et al. (2010) [5]

Since e-commerce is heavily technology-driven and at the same time it entails high perceived risk, it is justifiable to combine both trust, risk and TAM into a single model [56]. Suh and Han (2002)[63] found trust has a more direct effect on a customer's attitude than on perceived ease of use in the Internet banking context.

Benamati, et al. (2010) [5] noted that past studies which tried to integrate TAM with trust posit very different relationships between model constructs. For example, Pavlou (2003)[56] found that trust affects technology beliefs, Suh and Han (2002)[63] observed that technology beliefs affect trust, whereas Gefen, et al. (2003)[27] found trust and technology beliefs affect each other.

4   Trust in Technology vs. Trust in People

Even if some scholars argue that trust in technology is inappropriate, because technology lacks the requisite properties of a social actor, for example, according to Friedman, et al. (2000)[22], trust requires both parties to be able to extend good will, be vulnerable and experience betrayal. However, It appears that there is sufficient evidence to indicate that people are capable of instilling trust in an artifact of technology, such as an information document or a computer system [10].

Recent trust research in the information systems (IS) field has described trust as not only a primary predictor of technology usage but also as a fundamental construct for understanding user perceptions of technology [41]. However, trust in IS is defined in terms of trust in people (how trust in people affects IT-acceptance) without regard for trust in the technology itself [49]. Most IS trust research has focused on a web vendor or virtual team members and thus the trustee has been human, or an organization of humans [41]. Trust-in-technology is defined as the extent to which one is willing to depend on a technology because one believes the technology itself exhibits desirable attributes [48]. There are two approaches adopted to measure trust in technology: 1) measuring trust using **interpersonal-trust variables** including ability, benevolence, and integrity [41], [71]. and 2) measuring trust using **system-like trust variables** including functionality, helpfulness, and reliability [48], [65], [42]. According to Tripp, McKnight, et al. (2011)[68], even if both of these two measures work well, it is unclear when researchers should use interpersonal versus system-like trust in technology. They found that in human like technology (e.g. facebook) interpersonal trust is more appropriate measure and for less human-like system (e.g. Microsoft Access) system-like trust measure is more suitable.

McKnight (2005)[48] distinguished between trust in people and trust in technology. They proposed a set of system-like trust variables (functionality, helpfulness, and reliability) which is counterpart of interpersonal-trust variables (ability, benevolence, and integrity). According to him [48], since technology lacks moral agency, it is difficult to ascribe to IT without reverting to unwarranted anthropomorphisms, for example, one cannot say an IT cares (related to trusting belief-benevolence) or tells the truth (related to trusting belief-integrity). Based on this assumption McKnight, et al. (2011)[49] differentiated trusting beliefs in people and technology in the following way:

Competence vs. Functionality: With trust in people, one assesses the efficacy of the trustee to fulfill a promise in terms of their ability or power to do something for us. With technology, users consider whether the technology delivers on the functionality promised by providing features needed to complete a task.

Benevolence vs. Helpfulness: With people, one hopes they care enough to offer help when needed. With technology, users sense no caring emotions because technology itself has no moral agency. However, users do hope that a technology"s help function will provide advice necessary to complete a task.

Integrity vs. Reliability: In both cases, we hope trustees are consistent, predictable or reliable. With people, predictability refers to the degree to which an individual can be relied upon to act in a predictable manner. Although technology has no volition, it still may not function consistently due to built-in flaws or situational events that cause failures.

Li, et al. (2009)[42] hold similar arguments. Since attributes requiring moral capability and volitional control may not be easily ascribed to all IT artifacts, they [42] argued that beliefs about benevolence and integrity are not essential dimensions of technology trust. They [42] proposed that that technology trust is a function of beliefs regarding two generalizable attributes of all technologies belief in capability and belief in reliability.

5   Trust in Software Systems

5.1   Trust in ISO Definition

The growing number of research regarding trust related issues indicates that trust is an important factor in human computer interaction. Realizing this fact the notion of Trust has been included in the new ISO standard ISO/IEC 25010 [6]. Trust has been included in 'Satisfaction in use' and defined as the extent to which the user is satisfied that the product will behave as intended. According to Bevan (2010)[7], *'Trust is the stakeholders satisfaction with the perceived pragmatic do-goal of using a system that is secure. This is satisfaction with security.'*

5.2   Trust in Software Development Process

In Trusted Software Methodology (TSM) (which was held by America government and business organizations), trusted software is defined as: *'the degree of confidence that exists that the software will be acceptable for one's needs'.* According to Amoroso, et al. (1991)[3], the above definition suffers from the problem of subjectivity, that is the degree to which software is trusted will be dependent on users past experience, education, background and so on. Amoroso, et al (1991)[3] argued that one way to remove this subjectivity is to define a set of specific detailed guidelines.

5.3 Trustworthy Software

According to Hasselbring and Reussner (2006)[30], software trustworthiness consists of five attributes, such as, correctness, safety, quality of service, security and privacy. Zhao, et al. (2010)[75] identified five disjoint attributes: availability, reliability, maintainability, safety and security. Trustworthiness is a new concept based on such attributes of software as such the accuracy, reliability, safety, timeliness, integrity, availability, predictability, survival, controllability, and many other concepts [64].

Becker, et al. (2006)[4] considered trustworthy systems should have the following attributes: Correctness, Safety, Quality of Services (Availability, Reliability, Performance), Security and Privacy. Sommerville, et al. (2006)[61] consider trustworthiness of a system corresponds to the technical notion of dependability, that is, trustworthiness reflects the systems availability, reliability, safety, confidentiality, integrity and maintainability.

6 User-Centered-Trust (UCT) in Software Systems

As we have seen, in software engineering trust has been discussed mainly in software security and software development process. It is assumed that if a software is secured and reliable then it would be more trustworthy [38] even though security is one of the features of trustworthiness. In software development process, there are several development guidelines or heuristics (auditing, testing etc.) which are thought to make the software trusted to the developers [3]. Some others [30] proposed software quality attributes (reliability, performance, privacy etc.) necessary for trustworthy software systems. The new ISO standard ISO/IEC 25010 also defines trust as satisfaction with security [6] .

If a user cannot trust a program to execute on his behalf, then he should not run it [36]. However, it is clear that trust has been studied in software systems without taking into account the end-users perspective. We only deal with software attributes. It seems that software built according to the specifications of trustworthiness (e.g., [3]) will be more trustworthy from the point of view of software designers, vendors and the software industry, but it will not have any effects on users. Jiang, Li and Xu (2010) [35] mentioned that researchers focused on developing new technologies to build the trust, however, users' perspective of trust has been hardly discussed. According to them [35] 'The researchers are busy in dealing with sending message in a secure way, but rarely concern about how to send message to users friendly'. So, it can be argued that there is a strong need to have a proper trust model in software systems that incorporates both technical and end-user perspective.

6.1 Conceptualization of Trust in Software Systems

Following Mayer, et al. (1995) [47], we would like to explain trust phenomenon under TRA's (Theory of Reasoned Action) nomological network. TRA-based model of trust implies that trusting beliefs (competence/functionality, benevolence/helpfulness, integrity/reliability) affect trusting attitude (overall judgement), which, in turn, influences behavioral intentions. However unlike [47], we incorporated attitude in our model followed by Benamati, et al. (2010) [5].

Trust in software system can be categorized in the following ways :

1. **Dimensions of Trust:** Two dimensions of trust exist in software systems. Trusting attitude is composed of two elements, one is cognitive and another one is affective or emotional [37] dimension.

    (a) *Affective trust* is rooted in a person's emotional attitude toward software and/or vendors. Bonding occurs through emotionally charged experiences with technology; for example, if a systems failure leads to a catastrophic loss, it is likely to have a strong emotional impact on the user[10]. On the other, a beautiful, attractive interface may provide positive impression.

    (b) *Cognitive trust* is provided by signals of system state (e.g., a program is running rather than freezing or crashing, a network is operating at normal speed) [10].

2. **Levels of Trust:** Three levels of trust can be identified in software technology.

    (a) *Dispositional trust* is the general tendency to be willing to depend on software technology across a broad spectrum of situations and technologies [49]. Dispositional trust to software system corresponds to technology bias, the attitude a person holds toward computing technology in general.

    (b) *Interpersonal trust* is invoked with respect to the developer or vendor of the system. According to Jin, et al. (2009)[36], how to obtain trust in a program is two fold: 1. User must trust the author of the program, and 2. he must trust that the program he is executing is the same as the program written by the author.

    (c) *Societal or Institutional trust* applies to underlying technology (might be network architecture, hardware, software licenses and so on).

3. **Dimensions of Trustworthiness of Vendors (trusting beliefs in vendors):** In accordance with TRA, we follow the model of Mayer, et al. (1995)[47] where a clear distinction between trust and trustworthiness was drawn. According to Serva, et al. (2005)[76], trustworthiness is not the same as trust, but rather it forms the basis for trust and downstream trust-related actions. The three dimensions have been taken from [50].

    (a) *Benevolence* is the belief that the developer/vendor is interested in the well being of the user without intention of opportunistic behavior and motivated by a search for a mutually beneficial relationship.

    (b) *Competence* is the degree with which user perceives that developer/vendor is in possession of the necessary knowledge and skills to complete an agreement or exchange.

    (c) *Integrity* refers that user believes the developer makes good- faith agreements, tells the truth, acts ethically, and fulfils promises.

4. **Dimensions of Trustworthiness of Technology (Trusting beliefs in technology):** These dimensions are taken from [49].

   (a) *Functionality* represent users' expectations about the trustee's capability.

   (b) *Helpfulness* represent users' beliefs that the technology provides adequate, effective, and responsive help.

   (c) *Reliability* assume trustees are consistent, predictable or reliable in performance.

5. **Preconditions:** The followings are met in order to establish trust relationship.

   (a) *Uncertainty or risk*: Risk is present because there is the potential for systems failure, in which case the user may lose valuable information [10].

   (b) *Goal/Dependability*: arises when user needs to perform operations on the systems.

The following diagram illustrates the conceptions of trust:

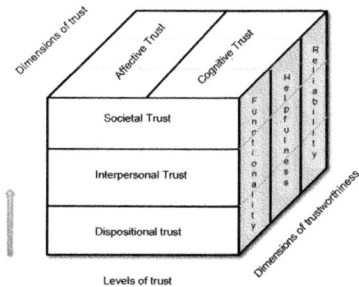

Fig. 3. Conceptualization of Trust in software systems

7   Proposition 1: Attitude, Acceptance and Affect

Technology attitude is frequently omitted from TAM studies, even though TRA deems it a necessary mediator and empirical justification for the exclusion is lacking [5]. Yang and Yoo (2004)[74] noted that attitude was given little value in predicting IS use, because Davis (1989)[17] had observed no influence of attitude on IS use when PU was considered to predict IS use. However, Yang and Yoo (2004) [74] argued that since attitude has both affective and cognitive components and since Davis (1989) [17] did not take affect into account, so he (Davis) failed to observe it. According to Yang and Yoo (2004) [74]: *'Therefore, one can argue that one of the reasons that Davis et al. did not find a significant influence of attitude in their study was because the potentially significant influence of cognition was offset by the insignificant influence of affect.'*

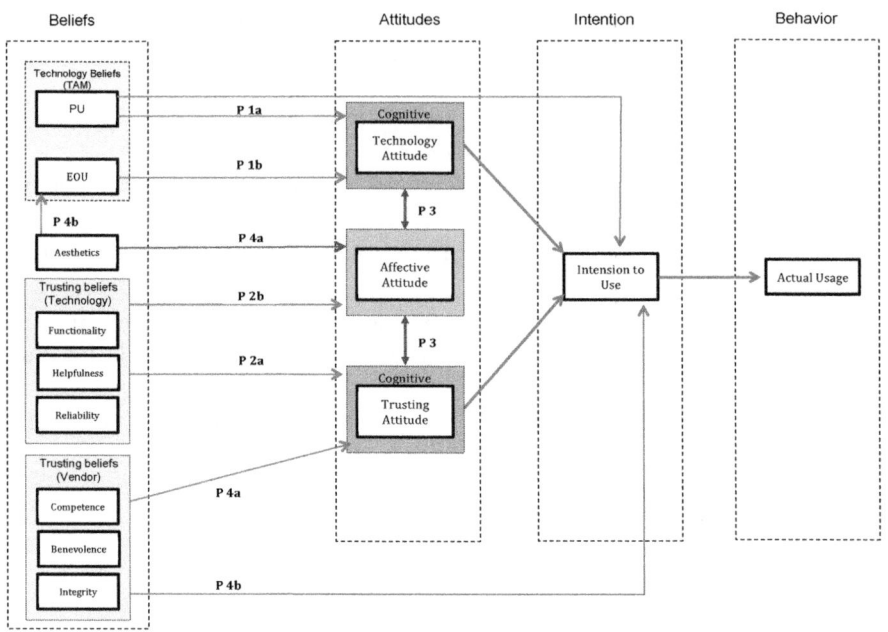

Fig. 4. User Centered Trust (UCT) model in software system

In the context of e-commerce, Benamati, et al. (2010)[5] argued that beliefs can only affect intentions when the user forms an attitude toward using the online vendor. Hence, the formation of the behavioral intention becomes contingent on the formation of an attitude toward the action.

The concept of attitude has a long history as a research topic, and definitions and measures have varied [5]. According to Ajzen and Fishbein (1972) [1], attitude refers solely to a person's location on a bipolar evaluative or affective dimension with respect to some object, action, or event. The meaning of attitude is based on both evaluative (cognitive) and affective (emotional) response [5].

Affective dimension of attitude is based on emotion which describes the feelings toward an object and focuses on how much the person likes the object of thought. Thus affective attitude measures the degree of emotional attraction toward the object. On the other hand, the cognitive dimension of attitude is based on an objective appraisal of the properties of an object and consists of the evaluation, judgment, reception, or perception of the object of thought based on values (adapted from [74])

Proposition 1a: Technology attitude mediates the relationship between perceived usefulness (PU) and intention to use.

Proposition 1b: Technology attitude mediates the relationship between perceived ease of use (PEU) and intention to use.

8   Proposition 2: Attitude, Trust and Affect

We discussed earlier that trust was conceptualized as beliefs, as attitude, as intentions or hybrid-combination of both belief and intentions [51]. Since TRA has been successfully applied in consumer behavior, technology acceptance and system use, and a variety of instances of human behavior [56], we would like to explain trust within TRA nomological network and for this it would be rational to conceptualize trust as attitude, instead of beliefs or intentions. Even though McKnight, et al. (1998)[51] explained trust in TRA model, however he excluded attitude from trust. McKnight, et al. (2002)[50] argued that *.....since[16] found that attitudes fell out of the model empirically, making their model more parsimonious..... Applying this more parsimonious version of TRA, we posit that trusting beliefs lead to trusting intentions, which in turn result in trust-related behaviors.*

However, as we stated earlier that this is because of not considering affect as a distinct dimension of attitude. So following Benamati, et al. (2010) [5] who operationalized trust as intention and conceptualized trust as an attitude, we define trust as the *attitude based on cognitive and affective judgements of trustworthiness that lead the trustor to be vulnerable to the actions of trustee in risky situation.*

According to this definition trust as attitude should mediate beliefs and intentions. Based on this fact we formulate the following:

Proposition 2a: Trusting attitude mediates the relationship between trusting beliefs and intention to use.

Proposition 2b: Trusting belief (trustworthiness) has positive impact on affective attitude.

9   Proposition 3: Cognitive and Affective Attitude

Trust in everyday life is a mix of feeling and rational thinking. Excluding one one of these two dimensions of trust would lead to misconceptions that conflate trust with faith or prediction[40], for example if all cognitive content was removed from emotional trust, we would be left with blind faith, on the other hand, if all emotional content was removed from cognitive trust, we would be left with only rational prediction or rationally calculated risk. Sonnenwald (2003)[62] argued that cognitive trust and distrust may exist in conjunction with affective trust and distrust. Claro, et al. (2008)[11] developed a trust model for distribution channel comprising six mechanisms (Calculative, Affective, Belief, Embeddedness, Continuity and Capability) to build up trust on performance. While the literature of transaction cost economics solely acknowledges the calculative mechanism, they found evidence for the importance of the social aspects of trust (affective, belief) in relationships.

Yang and Yoo (2004)[74] posit that upon the use of the tool, users form cognitive beliefs about the usefulness and ease of use of the tool. These evaluative beliefs (i.e., the cognitive attitude) in turn develop into users' affective attitudes (like or hate). However, Lindgaard (2006)[45] points out that emotional response occurs before cognitive response. There are two major perspectives of dealing with emotion in human computer interaction. One perspective refers emotions as consequences of product use [18], [31]. Emotions are seen as the result of cognitive appraisal processes of the product and the usage situation. The other perspective on emotions in HCI sees emotions as antecedents of product use and evaluative judgments [53], [66], [46]. It has been demonstrated that emotions influence people's attitude towards their current and next action and there is evidence that they play an essential role in rational decision making, perception, learning, and other cognitive functions [57]. Based on these facts we except the following:

Proposition 3: There is a correlation between affective attitude and cognitive attitude.

10   Proposition 4: From Aesthetics to Emotions and Cognition

When assessing websites regarding trustworthiness, Fogg (2002)[21] found that instead of paying attention to the rigorous criteria (e.g., privacy policy) people pay more attention to the superficial aspects of a site, such as visual cues. In a cross-cultural study, Cyr (2008) [14] investigated the impact of website design (information design, navigation design, and visual design) on trust level. Their results suggest that perceptions of visual design leading to trust vary by culture. Moreover, Sillence, et al. (2006) [59] present a framework for understanding trust factors in web based health advice. They found that if the websites are visually unattractive people instantly reject them. Lindgaard et al. (2011) [44] noted that visual appeal dominates first impression judgements of other characteristics such as perceived usability and trustworthiness. To the extent that aesthetics is a pleasant experience or an experience that leads to pleasure, it implies a relationship to emotion [43].

In 1995, Kurosu and Kashimura (1995)[39] conducted one of the first experiments ever to study the relationship between users' aesthetic perceptions and their a priori perceptions of a system's usability. The results found that apparent usability has a greater correlation with beauty than inherent usability. Basically indicating that people expect things that they think look good to actually work better. Further studies conducted by Tractinsky (1997)[66] and Tractinsky, et al. (2000) [67] were able to replicate these results across cultures. These results led them to propose the existence of a 'what is beautiful is usable' stereotype.

According to Norman (2002)[52], positive emotion causes people to be more creative in thinking and brainstorming which lead to find an alternate solution. Products designed for more relaxed, pleasant occasions can enhance their usability through pleasant, aesthetic design. A positive emotional response to a product increases positive attitude toward the brand, and the likelihood of purchase.

Proposition 4a: Aesthetics is an antecedent of affective attitude.

Proposition 4b: Perception of aesthetics has positive influence on perceived ease of use (EOU).

11   Proposition 4: Trust in Vendor

Interpersonal trust exist between user and vendor (e.g. developer). It refers to user's beliefs regarding the trustworthiness of the vendor. Trustworthiness of a vendor is composed of user's perceptions of a vendor's competence, integrity and benevolence [47]. If a user does not trust the developer or vendor of the system, it is unlikely that she/he is going to use the system. In the case of e-commerce, empirical studies found that trusting beliefs in competence, benevolence and integrity of a merchant affect customers' attitude, purchase intention and actual purchase behavior towards this merchant [42].

Proposition 4a: Trust in vendor positively affects trusting attitude.

Proposition 4b: Trust in vendor positively affects purchase intention.

12   Conclusions, Limitations and Future Directions

This paper pointed out that the users' perspective of trust was largely neglected in traditional software technology research. We present a trust model form users' point of view that incorporates both technology acceptance model and trust. This model also address users' trust on vendor/developer perspective. It might be the case that If the user do not trust the developer or vendor of the system, he or she might not use it. When we talk about trust in technology, generally we perceive two types of trust; trust in technology itself and traditional interpersonal trust between user and vendor or developer of the systems. Our assumption is based on the model of [42] who found that technology trust complements interpersonal trust as a predictor of intention and behavior. Following [5], We conceptualize trust as an attitude which has two distinct dimensions: cognitive and affective.

This paper focused on the interplay of trust, TAM and affect along with a discussion on how these influence the users to accept technology artifacts like software systems. Therefore the research model did not consider other beliefs and the precedents (such as, reputation, personality, disposition to trust, familiarity, security/privacy and so on) of trust.

We believe that a common shared understanding of trust in software systems from users' point of view can benefit us to develop an effective measure of trust and the trust model presented in this paper is the initial step toward achieving that goal. This model will be evaluated and applied in two of our on going research projects.

Acknowledgements. The financial support by the Federal Ministry of Economy, Family and Youth and the National Foundation for Research, Technology and Development is gratefully acknowledged (Christian Doppler Laboratory for Contextual Interfaces). The research was also supported by the European Union Seventh Framework Programme (FP7/2007-2013) under grant no 257930 (Aniketos).

References

1. Ajzen, I., Fishbein, M.: Attitudes and normative beliefs as factors influencing behavioral intentions. Journal of Personality and Social Psychology 21(1), 1 (1972)
2. Ambrose, P., Johnson, G.: A trust based model of buying behavior in electronic retailing (1998)
3. Amoroso, E., Nguyen, T., Weiss, J., Watson, J., Lapiska, P., Starr, T.: Toward an approach to measuring software trust. In: Proceedings of IEEE Computer Society Symposium on Research in Security and Privacy, pp. 198–218. IEEE (1991)
4. Becker, S., Hasselbring, W., Paul, A., Boskovic, M., Koziolek, H., Ploski, J.: Trustworthy software systems: a discussion of basic concepts and terminology. ACM SIGSOFT Software Engineering Notes 31(6), 1–18 (2006)
5. Benamati, J., Fuller, M., Serva, M., Baroudi, J.: Clarifying the integration of trust and tam in e-commerce environments: implications for systems design and management. IEEE Transactions on Engineering Management 57(3), 380–393 (2010)
6. Bevan, N.: Classifying and selecting ux and usability measures. In: International Workshop on Meaningful Measures: Valid Useful User Experience Measurement, pp. 13–18 (2008)
7. Bevan, N.: Extending the concept of satisfaction in iso standards. In: Proceedings of the KEER 2010 International Conference on Kansei Engineering and Emotion Research (2010)
8. Boon, S., Holmes, J.: The dynamics of interpersonal trust: Resolving uncertainty in the face of risk. Cooperation and Prosocial Behavior, 190–211 (1991)
9. Calantone, R., Di Benedetto, C.: Clustering product launches by price and launch strategy. Journal of Business & Industrial Marketing 22(1), 4–19 (2007)
10. Chopra, K., Wallace, W.: Trust in electronic environments. In: Proceedings of the 36th Annual Hawaii International Conference on System Sciences, p. 10. IEEE (2003)
11. Claro, D.P., Claro, P.B.O.: Managing trust relationships: calculative, affective, belief and performance. BAR. Brazilian Administration Review 5, 289–303 (2008)
12. Colquitt, J., Scott, B., LePine, J.: Trust, trustworthiness, and trust propensity: A meta-analytic test of their unique relationships with risk taking and job performance. Journal of Applied Psychology 92(4), 909 (2007)
13. Corritore, C., Kracher, B., Wiedenbeck, S.: On-line trust: concepts, evolving themes, a model. International Journal of Human-Computer Studies 58(6), 737–758 (2003)
14. Cyr, D.: Modeling web site design across cultures: Relationships to trust, satisfaction, and e-loyalty. Journal of Management Information Systems 24(4), 47–72 (2008)
15. Davis, F.: A technology acceptance model for empirically testing new end-user information systems: Theory and results. Ph.D. thesis, Massachusetts Institute of Technology, Sloan School of Management (1985)

16. Davis, F.: Perceived usefulness, perceived ease of use, and user acceptance of information technology. MIS Quarterly, 319–340 (1989)
17. Davis, F., Bagozzi, R., Warshaw, P.: User acceptance of computer technology: a comparison of two theoretical models. Management Science, 982–1003 (1989)
18. Desmet, P., Hekkert, P.: Framework of product experience. International Journal of Design 1(1), 57–66 (2007)
19. Doney, P., Cannon, J., Mullen, M.: Understanding the influence of national culture on the development of trust. Academy of Management Review 601–620 (1998)
20. Fishbein, M., Ajzen, I.: Belief, attitude, intention and behaviour: An introduction to theory and research. Addison-Wesley (1975)
21. Fogg, B., Soohoo, C., Danielson, D., Marable, L., Stanford, J., Tauber, E.: How do people evaluate a web site's credibility? results from a large study. Consumer WebWatch (2002)
22. Friedman, B., Khan Jr., P., Howe, D.: Trust online. Communications of the ACM 43(12), 34–40 (2000)
23. Fung, R., Lee, M.: Ec-trust (trust in electronic commerce): Exploring the antecedent factors (1999)
24. Gambetta, D.: Can we trust trust. Trust: Making and Breaking Cooperative Relations 213–237 (2000)
25. Gefen, D.: E-commerce: the role of familiarity and trust. Omega-Oxford-Pergamon Press 28, 725–737 (2000)
26. Gefen, D.: Reflections on the dimensions of trust and trustworthiness among online consumers. ACM SIGMIS Database 33(3), 38–53 (2002)
27. Gefen, D., Karahanna, E., Straub, D.: Trust and tam in online shopping: An integrated model. MIS Quarterly, 51–90 (2003)
28. Geyskens, I., Steenkamp, J., Kumar, N.: Generalizations about trust in marketing channel relationships using meta-analysis1. International Journal of Research in Marketing 15(3), 223–248 (1998)
29. Hardin, R.: Trustworthiness. Ethics 107(1), 26–42 (1996)
30. Hasselbring, W., Reussner, R.: Toward trustworthy software systems. Computer 39(4), 91–92 (2006)
31. Hassenzahl, M.: The effect of perceived hedonic quality on product appealingness. International Journal of Human-Computer Interaction 13(4), 481–499 (2001)
32. Hoy, W., Tschannen-Moran, M.: Five faces of trust: An empirical confirmation in urban elementary schools. Journal of School Leadership 9, 184–208 (1999)
33. Huang, J., Fox, M.S.: An ontology of trust: formal semantics and transitivity. In: Proceedings of the 8th International Conference on Electronic Commerce (2006)
34. Jarvenpaa, S., Tractinsky, N., Saarinen, L.: Consumer trust in an internet store: A cross-cultural validation. Journal of Computer-Mediated Communication 5(2) (1999)
35. Jiang, H., Li, Y., Xu, Y.: User-centered trust model visibility of trust technologies. In: 2010 7th International Conference on Ubiquitous Intelligence & Computing and 7th International Conference on Autonomic & Trusted Computing (UIC/ATC), pp. 456–459 (2010)
36. Jin, W., Yongjian, L., Xuyun, N., Mengjuan, L.: The trust management model of trusted software. In: International Forum on Information Technology and Applications, IFITA 2009, vol. 3, pp. 534–537. IEEE (2009)
37. Jones, K.: Trust as an affective attitude. Ethics 107(1), 4–25 (1996)
38. Josang, A., Ismail, R., Boyd, C.: A survey of trust and reputation systems for online service provision. Decision Support Systems 43(2), 618–644 (2007)

39. Kurosu, M., Kashimura, K.: Apparent usability vs. inherent usability: experimental analysis on the determinants of the apparent usability. In: Conference Companion on Human factors in Computing Systems, pp. 292–293 (1995)
40. Lewis, J., Weigert, A.: Trust as a social reality. Social Forces 63(4), 967–985 (1985)
41. Li, X., Hess, T., Valacich, J.: Why do we trust new technology? a study of initial trust formation with organizational information systems. The Journal of Strategic Information Systems 17(1), 39–71 (2008)
42. Li, X., Rong, G., Thatcher, J.: Do we trust the technology? people? or both? ruminations on technology trust (2009)
43. Lindgaard, G.: Aesthetics, visual appeal, usability, and user satisfaction: What do the user's eyes tell the user's brain. Australian Journal of Emerging Technologies and Society 5(1), 1–14 (2007)
44. Lindgaard, G., Dudek, C., Sen, D., Sumegi, L., Noonan, P.: An exploration of relations between visual appeal, trustworthiness and perceived usability of homepages. ACM Transactions on Computer-Human Interaction (TOCHI) 18(1), 1 (2011)
45. Lindgaard, G., Fernandes, G., Dudek, C., Brown, J.: Attention web designers: You have 50 milliseconds to make a good first impression! Behaviour & Information Technology 25(2), 115–126 (2006)
46. Mahlke, S., Thüring, M.: Studying antecedents of emotional experiences in interactive contexts. In: Proceedings of the SIGCHI Conference on Human Factors in Computing Systems, pp. 915–918. ACM (2007)
47. Mayer, R., Davis, J., Schoorman, F.: An integrative model of organizational trust. Academy of Management Review, 709–734 (1995)
48. McKnight, D.: Trust in information technology. The Blackwell Encyclopedia of Management 7, 329–331 (2005)
49. Mcknight, D., Carter, M., Thatcher, J., Clay, P.: Trust in a specific technology: An investigation of its components and measures. ACM Transactions on Management Information Systems (TMIS) 2(2), 12 (2011)
50. McKnight, D., Choudhury, V., Kacmar, C.: Developing and validating trust measures for e-commerce: An integrative typology. Information Systems Research 13(3), 334–359 (2002)
51. McKnight, D., Cummings, L., Chervany, N.: Initial trust formation in new organizational relationships. Academy of Management Review, 473–490 (1998)
52. Norman, D.: Emotion and design: attractive things work better. Interactions 9(4), 36–42 (2002)
53. Norman, D.: Emotional design: Why we love (or hate) everyday things. Basic Civitas Books (2004)
54. Orlikowski, W., Iacono, C.: Research commentary: desperately seeking the" it" in it research-a call to theorizing the it artifact. Information Systems Research 12(2), 121–134 (2001)
55. Papachristos, E., Avouris, N.: Are first impressions about websites only related to visual appeal? In: Human-Computer Interaction INTERACT 2011, pp. 489–496 (2011)
56. Pavlou, P.: Consumer acceptance of electronic commerce: Integrating trust and risk with the technology acceptance model. International Journal of Electronic Commerce 7(3), 101–134 (2003)
57. Picard, R.: Affective computing. MIT press (1997)
58. Rousseau, D., Sitkin, S., Burt, R., Camerer, C., et al.: Not so different after all: A cross-discipline view of trust. Academy of Management Review 23(3), 393–404 (1998)

59. Sillence, E., Briggs, P., Harris, P., Fishwick, L.: A framework for understanding trust factors in web-based health advice. International Journal of Human-Computer Studies 64(8), 697–713 (2006)
60. Slemrod, J., Katuscak, P.: Do trust and trustworthiness pay off? National Bureau of Economic Research (2002)
61. Sommerville, I., Dewsbury, G., Clarke, K., Rouncefield, M.: Dependability and trust in organisational and domestic computer systems. Trust in Technology: A Socio-Technical Perspective, 169–193 (2006)
62. Sonnenwald, D.: Managing cognitive and affective trust in the conceptual r&d organization. Trust in Knowledge Management and Systems in Organizations, 82–106 (2003)
63. Suh, B., Han, I.: Effect of trust on customer acceptance of internet banking. Electronic Commerce Research and Applications 1(3-4), 247–263 (2002)
64. Tao, H., Chen, Y.: A new metric model for trustworthiness of softwares. In: International Conference on Information Science and Applications (ICISA), pp. 1–8 (2010)
65. Thatcher, J., McKnight, D., Baker, E., Arsal, R., Roberts, N.: The role of trust in postadoption it exploration: An empirical examination of knowledge management systems. IEEE Transactions on Engineering Management, (99), 1–15 (2010)
66. Tractinsky, N.: Aesthetics and apparent usability: empirically assessing cultural and methodological issues. In: Proceedings of the SIGCHI Conference on Human Factors in Computing Systems, pp. 115–122 (1997)
67. Tractinsky, N., Katz, A., Ikar, D.: What is beautiful is usable. Interacting with Computers 13(2), 127–145 (2000)
68. Tripp, J., McKnight, H., Lankton, N.: Degrees of humanness in technology: What type of trust matters? (2011)
69. Vance, A., Elie-Dit-Cosaque, C., Straub, D.: Examining trust in information technology artifacts: The effects of system quality and culture. Journal of Management Information Systems 24(4), 73–100 (2008)
70. Venkatesh, V., Davis, F.: A model of the antecedents of perceived ease of use: Development and test*. Decision Sciences 27(3), 451–481 (1996)
71. Wang, W., Benbasat, I.: Trust in and adoption of online recommendation agents. Journal of the Association for Information Systems 6(3), 72–101 (2005)
72. Wang, Y., Emurian, H.: An overview of online trust: Concepts, elements, and implications. Computers in Human Behavior 21(1), 105–125 (2005)
73. Yan, Z., Holtmanns, S.: Trust modeling and management: from social trust to digital trust. In: Computer Security, Privacy and Politics: Current Issues, Challenges and Solutions pp. 290–323 (2008)
74. Yang, H., Yoo, Y.: It's all about attitude: revisiting the technology acceptance model. Decision Support Systems 38(1), 19–31 (2004)
75. Zhao, X., Shi, Y., Liu, Y., Zhang, L.: An empirical study of the influence of software trustworthy attributes to software trustworthiness. In: 2010 2nd International Conference on Software Engineering and Data Mining (SEDM), pp. 603–606. IEEE (2010)
76. Serva, M.A., Benamati, J.S., Fuller, M.A.: Trustworthiness in B2C e-commerce: An examination of alternative models. ACM SIGMIS (2005)

Clockless Physical Unclonable Functions

Julian Murphy

Centre for Secure Information Technologies,
Queens University Belfast,
Belfast, BT3 9DT,
United Kingdom
j.p.murphy@qub.ac.uk

Abstract. Physically Unclonable Functions (PUFs) exploit the physical characteristics of silicon and provide an alternative to storing digital encryption keys
in non-volatile memory. A PUF maps a unique set of digital inputs to a corresponding set of digital outputs. In this paper, the use of asynchronous logic and
design techniques to implement PUFs is advocated for Asynchronous Physically Unclonable Functions (APUFs). A new method of using asynchronous
rings to implement PUFs is described called AsyncPUF which features inherent
field programmability. It is a novel and holistic PUF design compared to the existing state-of-the-art as it naturally addresses the two challenges facing PUFs
to-date that prevent wide-spread adoption: robustness and entropy. Results of
electrical simulation in a 90 nano-metre lithography process are presented and
discussed.

Keywords: Cryptography, Physically Unclonable Functions, PUFs, Asynchronous Physically Unclonable Functions, Clockless Physically Unclonable
Functions.

1   Introduction

Many security mechanisms are based upon the concept of a secret. Classic cryptography applications contain a secret key as input to encryption algorithms in order to
scramble and decipher data. While they are secure against attack at the algorithm and
mathematical level, it is commonly known that digitally-stored secret keys can be
attacked or cloned relatively easily. In security tokens, such as smartcards, keys are
stored on-chip in non-volatile memory. While field-programmable gate arrays
(FPGAs) instead store keys in off-chip memory. This is because FPGA technology
cannot easily integrate non-volatile memory, and besides read latency issues, it only
acts to further increase vulnerability to attack.

  Physical Unclonable Functions (PUFs) offer an efficient alternative to storing
digital keys in on or off-chip memory. They exploit the physical lithography manufacturing variations of silicon integrated circuits (ICs). A PUF maps a unique set of digital inputs, known as challenges, to a corresponding set of digital outputs, known as
responses, for use in challenge-response security protocols. Almost every year since
2000 there has been a new PUF design proposed as highlighted in Table 1.

S. Katzenbeisser et al. (Eds.): TRUST 2012, LNCS 7344, pp. 110–121, 2012.
© Springer-Verlag Berlin Heidelberg 2012

Table 1. Different types of PUF

Year	PUF Type
2000-2004	Device mismatch [9], One-way function [10], Physical Random Function [11], Arbiter PUF [12]
2005-2008	Coating PUF [13], Ring Oscillator PUF [2], SRAM PUF [14], Butterfly PUF [15]
2009-2011	Power distribution PUF [16], Glitch PUF [17], Mecca PUF [18]
2012	**AsyncPUF (this paper)**

A typical challenge-response identity authentication scenario is illustrated in Fig. 1. Here, a challenge is given to an IC to authenticate its identity via the on-chip PUF. If the received response is not equal to the known challenge which has been recorded during manufacturing it is identified as fake.

Sadly, the unique benefits of silicon PUFs come with inherent stability design issues. In addition, in their basic configuration PUFs lack enough entropy to prevent modeling attacks [1]. However, it can be observed that PUFs are naturally asynchronous in nature. Insomuch as that they attempt to exploit asynchronous effects such as metastability, propagation delay or binary signal glitches. Therefore, it follows that asynchronous techniques may deliver much better PUF designs or provide an alternative to the existing state-of-the-art.

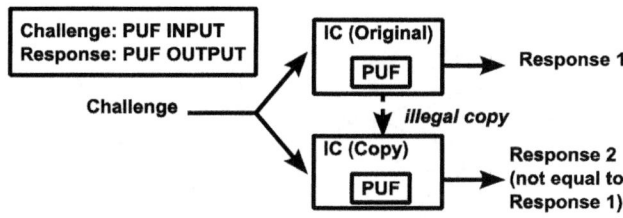

Fig. 1. Challenge-response authentication of chip identity using a PUF

In this paper, we present AsyncPUF which uses asynchronous rings for robust operation and to replace inverter chain ring oscillators used in ring oscillator PUFs [2] (RO-PUFs). It is fully digital and features inherent field programmability which naturally addresses the two challenges facing PUFs that prevents wide-spread adoption: robustness and entropy. Results of electrical simulation using a 90 nano-metre UMC lithography are discussed.

1.1   Contributions and Paper Organization

Our research, technical and scientific contributions are as follows:

- We propose Asynchronous Physically Unclonable Functions (APUFs).
- We advocate the use of asynchronous logic and techniques to implement PUFs.

- We propose ASYNCPUF, which is inherently field-programmable to address robustness and entropy challenges. It uses asynchronous rings to replace inverter ring oscillators (IROs) used in ring oscillator PUFs [2] (RO-PUFs).

The remainder of the paper is organised as follows: Section 2 gives an overview of asynchronous logic. Section 3 discusses asynchronous rings. Section 4 describes ASYNCPUF. Section 5 presents results from electrical simulation. Section 6 draws conclusions.

2   Asynchronous Logic

The design of synchronous digital circuitry is based upon the discretisation of time, where a synchronous system changes from one state to the next at transitions of a system clock. The state is held in a set of registers and the next state outputs are derived from Boolean logic acting on the old state and present inputs. While the next state is copied through the registers on every rising and falling edge of a global clock signal. As such, the system exhibits deterministic behaviour as long as certain timing constraints on the inputs are met.

On the other hand, asynchronous designs do not follow this regime. In general, there is no global clock to govern the timing of state changes. Subsystems and components exchange information at mutually negotiated times. Therefore, certain parts of a design are always quiescent when they are not in use and hardware runs as faster as computational dependencies, input rate and the lithography device switching times.

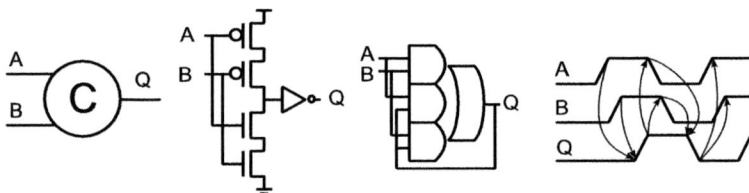

Fig. 2. The Muller C-element

As a field, it is historically seen as niche due to the profound understanding of concurrency, hardware, and semiconductors it takes to implement functionally correct designs. However, interest in the field has grown linearly in recent years in terms of applications as the fringes of Moore's Law have been reached and hardware data security issues have become main-stream.

A plethora of design paradigms and techniques are known in literature. These range from high performance transistor level pipelines for processor design [3] and application to physical security [4]. The common denominator in all of which is the hysteresis capable Muller-C element [5] shown in Fig. 2. Both inputs must be equal to set or reset its output otherwise it holds its original state.

3   Asynchronous Rings

One of the most widely-used structures that use Muller-C elements are asynchronous rings (ARs) [7], which are purposely used here to implement ASYNCPUF. That is, as an alternative to inverter ring oscillators (IROs) in RO-PUFs for increased PUF stability and entropy.

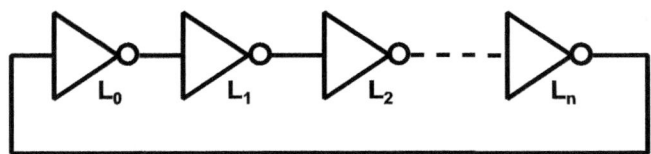

Fig. 3. L stage inverter ring oscillator

To illustrate how ARs operate an IRO structure is shown in Fig. 3. Here, L inverter stages are connected to form a ring. The oscillation time is the propagation delay of one logical transition all around the ring.

While an AR structure of L stages is shown in Fig. 4 and corresponds to the control path of a micro-pipeline [7]. Each stage is composed of a Muller C-element and an inverter, where for stage i: F_i is the forward input, R_i is the reverse input, and C_i is the output. The forward input value is written to the output if the forward and reverse input values are different otherwise the previous output is maintained.

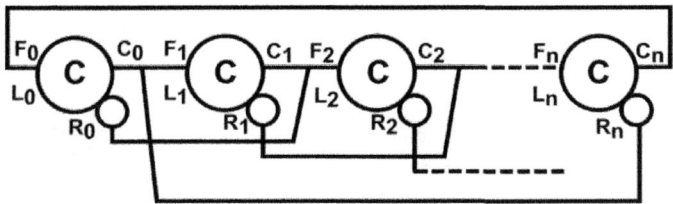

Fig. 4. Asynchronous Ring

3.1   Bubbles and Tokens

With reference to Fig. 4 the *bubbles and tokens* concept is as follows:

- Stage i contains a bubble if its output C_i is equal to the output of the previous stage C_{i-1}: $C_i = C_{i-1}$.
- Stage i contains a token if its output C_i is different from the output of the previous stage C_{i-1}: $C_i \neq C_{i-1}$.

Hence, for a 5 stage AR an initial state could be the token-bubble tuple:

$$\{Bubble_0, Token_0, Token_1, Bubble_1, Bubble_2\} \tag{1}$$

Which would correspond to the initial binary state:

$$\{S_0, S_1, S_2, S_3, S_4\} = \{1,0,1,1,1\} \tag{2}$$

As each stage i has a value of token or bubble determined by its output C_i and the output of the previous stage C_{i-1} the mapping from (1) to (2) is: $Token_0 = \{C_0, C_1\} = \{1,0\}$, $Token_1 = \{C_1, C_2\} = \{0,1\}$ $Bubble_1 = \{C_2, C_3\} = \{1,1\}$ etc.

Since it is possible to configure an AR with respect to bubbles and tokens, as explained above, they are naturally field-programmable and will increase the available entropy in an AR based PUF design such as ASYNCPUF.

3.2   Token and Bubble Propagation

Based on the token and bubbles concept, a token propagates from the stage i to the stage $i + 1$, if, and only if, the next stage $i + 1$ contains a bubble as shown in **Fig. 5**. In the same way, a bubble propagates from the stage i+1 to the previous stage i, if and only if, the previous stage i contains a token. Hence, ARs will have an oscillatory behaviour if the following conditions hold:

- $L \geq 3$ and $L = N_t + N_b$.
- $N_b > 1$, where N_b is the number of bubbles.
- N_t is a positive even number of tokens.

The oscillation depends on the stage timing parameters determined by process variability and the ratio N_t/N_b. It should be understood, while it is possible to maintain high frequencies in ARs, frequency decreases linearly with the number of stages in IROs. That is, different AR ring configurations will result in different frequencies for the same ring lengths.

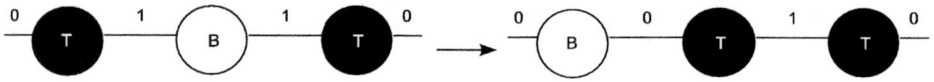

Fig. 5. Token and bubble propagation

3.3   Noise

Both ARs and IROs exhibit thermal noise (known as jitter in the time-domain and phase noise in the frequency domain) such that the propagation delay will resemble a Gaussian distribution. Fig. 6. illustrates the effect of jitter on an IRO in a 90 nanometre SPICE transient noise analysis simulation using thermal noise with a bandwidth of 100KHz to 10GHz. A clear 71 pico-second variance is observable.

Where ARs and IROs differ is through how jitter accumulates. An IRO's period is defined by two loops of one token around the ring, and accumulates jitter from the number of crossed stages. But, in an AR, several tokens propagate in the ring simultaneously indicating the period is governed by the time between successive tokens. As such, each token crossing a stage experiences a variation in its propagation delay due to the jitter contribution of that particular stage. This is contrary to the IRO effect of jitter accumulation. This naturally provides improved robustness against noise insta-bilities caused by jitter in PUF designs, that is, by use of ARs instead of IROs.

In addition to Gaussian jitter, deterministic jitter occurs from non-random varia-tions in propagation delays due to external global influences. The main difference is again in that in an AR several events propagate simultaneously, so deterministic jitter affects each event in the same way rather than the whole structure. This again leads to increased robustness in ARs versus IROs, and a more stable PUF design if ARs are used instead of IROs.

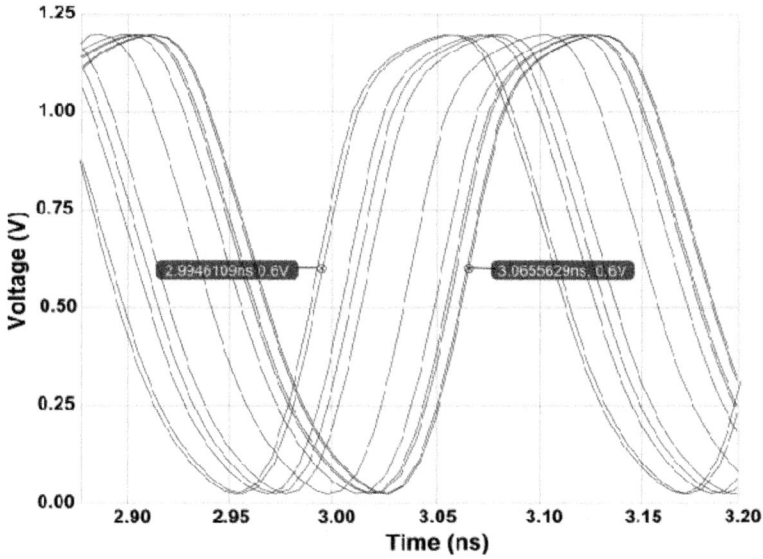

Fig. 6. Effect of jitter

4   ASYNCPUF

We present in this section how to build AsyncPUF using asynchronous rings by replacing IROs in RO-PUFs.

A 1-bit RO-PUF is composed of 2 identically laid-out RO's, RO_1 and RO_2 with frequencies f_1 to f_2. They are selected using a pair of multiplexers that takes a bit of the PUF challenge as the select bit. Due to process variation, f_1 and f_2 will differ generating one response bit, R, of the PUF from comparison of the two frequencies measured by their respective counters. When enabled, R will be 1 if $f_1 > f_2$ other-wise 0, hence producing a single bit of a PUF response signature. The exemplary design in Fig. 7 produces a single PUF bit - n-bit PUF configurations are built by cascading these 1-bit RO-PUF structures.

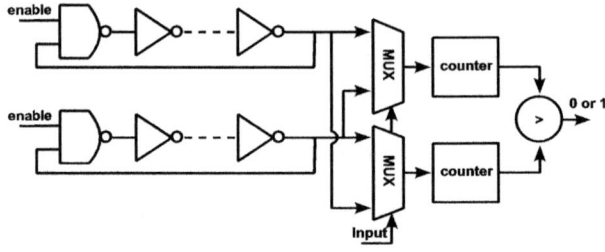

Fig. 7. Ring-oscillator based PUF design

Since IRO frequencies are closely matched, environmental effects can cause the oscillators to switch their outputs, for increasing temperature and/or decreasing voltage resulting in incorrect responses. It can be also observed large arrays of ring oscillators can cause a change in local chip temperature. These temperature stability issues are depicted on the left in Fig. 8. The ideal scenario is that the frequency difference should be sufficient to ensure consistent operation over temperature and voltage as shown on the right in Fig. 8. The approach to this problem in PUFs to-date has been to use error-correcting methods, which are expensive in terms of silicon area and add additional complexity to the challenge-response protocol. The other disadvantage of RO-PUFs is that they can be easily modelled to break the underlying security [1] to permit cloning.

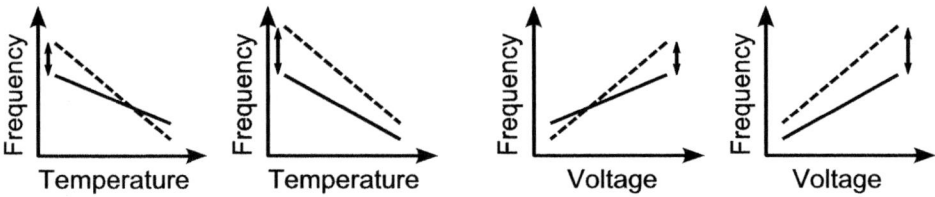

Fig. 8. Temperature and voltage effects on RO-PUFs

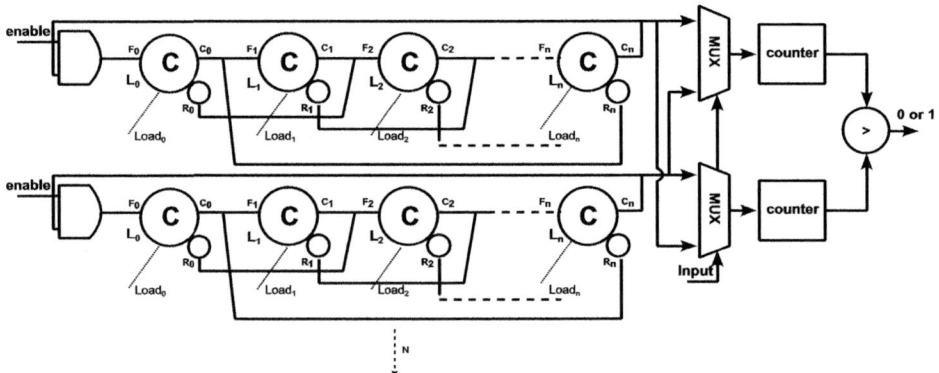

Fig. 9. AsyncPUF

ASYNCPUF is an AR based PUF, as shown in Fig. 9, and gives the opportunity to address the above issues as well as noise. By configuring N_t and N_b, that is, by purposely controlling L, the number of stages, and their initial value by setting or resetting the Muller-C elements (This can be accomplished, for example, through the load inputs as shown in the figure and extra internal pull-up or pull-down transistors). By determining the configuration of the ARs with the maximum frequencies differences maximum reliability can be attained. This inherent configurable permits extremely low error rates by tending towards the ideal scenario. A further opportunity is to calibrate the ASYNCPUF configurability according to different operating conditions. For example, the entire operating range of temperature and voltage could be divided into regions and have different AR load bit patterns.

Furthermore, AsyncPUF offers the opportunity to not only increase robustness through tolerance to environmental effects, but also the fact they can be re-configured increases entropy to address modelling attacks. This is because, as discussed, ARs can be easily configured to change their frequency by controlling N_t and N_b. Thus varying N_t and the load bit patterns in-field will result in completely new PUF designs, therefore thwarting modelling as no two PUFs are the same. Another alternative is to allocate different values randomly during manufacture and store in on-chip non-volatile memory.

It should be noted, for correct operation the AR run-time has to be low enough so that the counters do not overflow as is the case with all oscillator based PUFs. This can be ensured by controlling the enable signal duty cycle accordingly. It is worth noting also, other methods are perfectly plausible to convert the varying AR frequencies to a binary bit, rather than using a pure multiplexer approach. How RO-PUFs are cascaded for n-bit PUFs may also differ (e.g. AR re-use). Extensive works exist on this topic for RO-PUFs which the author is aware of and appreciates can be similarly adopted here a fully parallel ASYNCPUF architecture is presented merely to correctly and clearly convey this work.

5   Results

Experiments were performed using Monte Carlo SPICE analysis on the highest accuracy setting with a 90 nano-metre UMC lithography process and thermal noise with a bandwidth of 100KHz to 10GHz. Firstly, ARs were characterized to quantify how their oscillation frequency is affected by intra-die and inter-die process variation i.e. to understand their response to the lithography effects PUFs exploit. Simulations were conducted for a 6-stage AR using a 20 nano-second window and 1000 iterations for the two types of process variation (die-to-die and within-die). They took approximately 8 hours to complete on a high-end multi-core Linux server under the Cadence Design Framework. Fig. 10 shows the results from each of the 1000 simulations.

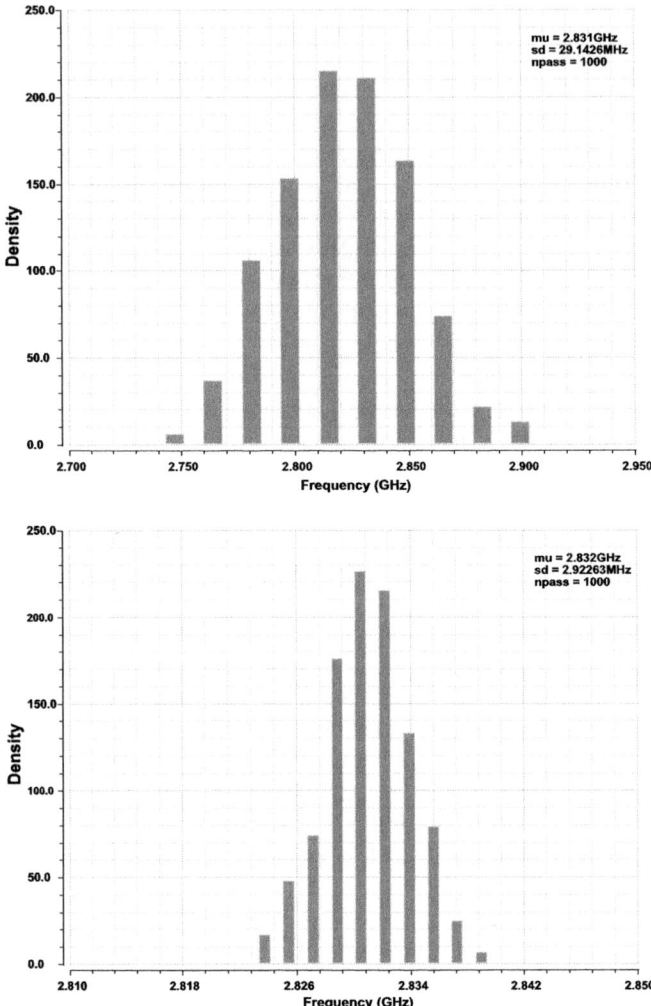

Fig. 10. Die-to-die (top) and within-die (bottom) variation

The ARs exhibit clear frequency deviations confirming their suitability for use as PUFs. For die-to-die variation an average frequency of 2.83GHz is obtained and a standard deviation of 29.14MHz, which indicates a die-to-die variation of 1.03%. And for within-die variation an average frequency of 2.83GHz is obtained and a standard deviation of 2.92MHz, which indicates a within-die variation of 0.10%. Clearly, the variation in AR frequency is greater between silicon wafers than on the same wafer for this particular lithography process; while both results exhibit a bell-curve Gaussian distribution.

Next 20 ASYNCPUFs of length 6, 12 and 18 each able to generate 32-bits of a response (i.e. 64 rings) were constructed, which was found in the setup phase to allow practical SPICE simulation. Note, using four different AR configurations a 128-bit response output can be generated, which highlights the trade-offs that are possible with ASYNCPUF due to its inherent field-programmability.

This time both die-to-die and within-die process variation SPICE simulation switches were activated together for analogous electrical simulation of 20 ASYNCPUF silicon chips. Matlab was used to parse and process the simulation data obtained and to generate random input challenges. Using two well-known PUF metrics, uniqueness and reliability (defined below), ASYNCPUF was evaluated. Both uniqueness and reliability results were captured at supply voltages between 0.4 V and 1.1 V, and temperatures ranging from -30C to 100C. Note, these result graphs were produced by Matlab rather than exported directly from Cadence as in **Fig. 11**. And to fit within the paper length, the presented results highlight the effect of temperature effects only. This is also because temperature affects PUFs silicon chips more than regulated voltage that can be viewed as a constant variable.

- Uniqueness is a measure of how easily an individual PUF can be differentiated; and quantifies the hamming distance between the responses of different ICs implementing the same PUF design that have been challenged with the same input. It is characterized by the probability density distribution (PDF) of the hamming distances, where PUFs with PDF curves centred at half the number of response bits and tall are more easily identifiable (unique) than PUFs with flatter curves.
- Reliability is a measure of how easily a given PUF can reproduce the same output response for the same input challenge. This is measured by the bits that remain unchanged under varying environmental conditions with the same input challenge. The PDF representing hamming distance of the response characterizes reliability of the same PUF subject to different environmental conditions i.e. changes in temperature and supply voltage. PUFs with PDF curves centred at 0 and tall are more stable than PUFs with flatter curves.

It was observed with increasing length of the ring, uniqueness is consistent, with a slight tendency for a stronger PDF the longer the length, shown on the left in **Fig. 11**. This result was consistent across all ASYNCPUF lengths initialized with arbitrary token patterns that satisfy the requirements in Section 2.

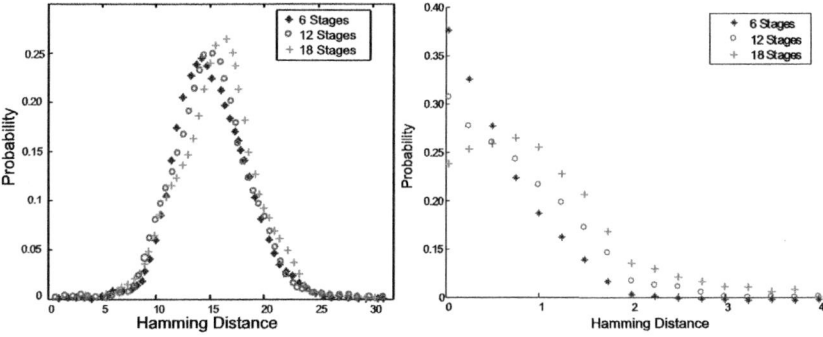

Fig. 11. Uniqueness and reliability of ASYNCPUF with respect to temperature

Fig. 11 on the right shows the effect of the stage length for ASYNCPUF for reliability. It was observed for ASYNCPUF that 6 stages are most stable followed by 12 and 18 stages. Therefore, it can be concluded that shorter stages leads to better stability and can be exploited for area efficient PUF implementations.

6   Conclusions

We have proposed using asynchronous logic to address the inherent issues with physically unclonable functions. We have presented and described a method of using asynchronous rings to implement a novel APUF architecture design, ASYNCPUF to enable increased robustness and entropy. We presented Monte Carlo SPICE analysis results of uniqueness and reliability. The results represent as close as possible to physical silicon chip results.

Our future work is to consider application of asynchronous techniques to further PUF technologies and tape-out of a silicon chip. For instance, it would be possible to build PUF designs using elements from asynchronous elastic controllers [4] or eager monotonic logic [5]. Or alternative structures could be used instead of C-elements to implement ASYNCPUF ring stages that are widely published in literature e.g. GasP.

References

1. Rührmair, U., Sehnke, F., Sölter, J., Dror, G.: Modeling Attacks on Physical Unclonable Functions. In: Proceedings of 17th ACM Conference on Computer and Communications Security, pp. 237–249 (2010)
2. Suh, G.E., Devadas, S.: Physical Unclonable Functions for Device Authentication and Secret Key Generation. In: Proceedings of the 44th annual Design Automation Conference, DAC 2007, New York, NY, USA, pp. 9–14 (2007)
3. Sutherland, I., Fairbanks, S.: GasP: A Minimal FIFO Control. In: Seventh International Symposium on Asynchronous Circuits and Systems, pp. 46–53 (2001)
4. Murphy, J., Yakovlev, A.: An Alternating Spacer AES Crypto-processor. In: Proceedings of the 32nd European Solid-State Circuits Conference, pp. 126–129 (2006)
5. Muller, D.E., Bartky, W.S.: A Theory of Asynchronous Circuits. In: Proceedings of the International Symposium on Theory of Switching, Part 1, pp. 204–243. Harvard University Press (1959)
6. Williams, T.E., Horowitz, M.A.: A Zero-Overhead Self-Timed 160-ns 54-b CMOS Divider. IEEE Journal of Solid-State Circuits 26(11), 1651–1661 (1991)
7. Sutherland, I.E.: Micropipelines. Communications of ACM 32(6), 720–738 (1998)
8. Ebergen, J.C., Fairbanks, S., Sutherland, I.E.: Predicting Performance of Micropipelines Using Charlie Diagrams. In: Proceedings of Fourth International Conference on Asynchronous Circuits and Systems, pp. 238–246 (1998)
9. Lofstrom, K., Daasch, W., Taylor, D.: IC Identication Circuit Using Device Mismatch. In: Digest of Technical Papers, IEEE International Conference in Solid-State Circuits (ISSCC), pp. 372–373 (2000)
10. Pappu, R.S., Recht, B., Taylor, J., Gershenfeld, N.: Physical One-way Functions. Science 297, 2026–2030 (2002)

11. Gassend, B., Clarke, D., van Dijk, M., Devadas, S.: Silicon Physical Random Functions. In: Proceedings of the 9th ACM Conference on Computer and Communications Security (CCS), New York, USA, pp. 148–160 (2002)
12. Lim, D., Lee, J., Gassend, B., Suh, G., van Dijk, M., Devadas, S.: Extracting Secret Keys from Integrated Circuits. IEEE Transactions on Very Large Scale Integration Systems 13(10), 1200–1205 (2005)
13. Tuyls, P., Schrijen, G.-J., Škorić, B., van Geloven, J., Verhaegh, N., Wolters, R.: Read-Proof Hardware from Protective Coatings. In: Goubin, L., Matsui, M. (eds.) CHES 2006. LNCS, vol. 4249, pp. 369–383. Springer, Heidelberg (2006)
14. Guajardo, J., Kumar, S.S., Schrijen, G.-J., Tuyls, P.: FPGA Intrinsic PUFs and Their Use for IP Protection. In: Paillier, P., Verbauwhede, I. (eds.) CHES 2007. LNCS, vol. 4727, pp. 63–80. Springer, Heidelberg (2007)
15. Kumar, S., Guajardo, J., Maes, R., Schrijen, G.-J., Tuyls, P.: "Extended abstract: The butterfly PUF Protecting IP on Every FPGA. In: IEEE International Workshop on Hardware-Oriented Security and Trust (HOST), pp. 67–70 (2008)
16. Helinski, R., Acharyya, D., Plusquellic, J.: A Physical Unclonable Function Defined Using Power Distribution System Equivalent Resistance Variations. In: Proceedings of the 46th Annual Design Automation Conference (DAC), New York, USA, pp. 676–681 (2009)
17. Suzuki, D., Shimizu, K.: The Glitch PUF: A New Delay-PUF Architecture Exploiting Glitch Shapes. In: Mangard, S., Standaert, F.-X. (eds.) CHES 2010. LNCS, vol. 6225, pp. 366–382. Springer, Heidelberg (2010)
18. Krishna, A.R., Narasimhan, S., Wang, X., Bhunia, S.: MECCA: A Robust Low-Overhead PUF Using Embedded Memory Array. In: Preneel, B., Takagi, T. (eds.) CHES 2011. LNCS, vol. 6917, pp. 407–420. Springer, Heidelberg (2011)

Lightweight Distributed Heterogeneous Attested Android Clouds

Martin Pirker, Johannes Winter, and Ronald Toegl

Institute for Applied Information Processing and Communications (IAIK),
Graz University of Technology, Inffeldgasse 16a, 8010 Graz, Austria
{mpirker,jwinter,rtoegl}@iaik.tugraz.at

Abstract. Moving local services into a network of Cloud nodes raises
security concerns as this affects control over data and code execution. The
Trusted Platform Module can help detect Cloud nodes running unknown
software configurations. To achieve this, we propose a node join protocol
that enforces remote attestation. We prototype our approach on both
current x86 systems with Intel Trusted Execution Technology and on
ARM hardware platforms. We use Android as common system software,
and show that it is well suited to build a chain-of-trust.

1 Introduction

The rapid advancement of virtualisation and multi-core technologies in conjunction with cheap storage and fast Internet connections has created a market for
providing computing resources as a commodity. Large, high-density data centers
can take advantage of the economics of scale and dynamically lease computing
power or storage capacities to clients on demand. This promises to more efficiently utilize IT resources and reduce costs. Naturally, more and more services
are migrated to such *Cloud Computing* providers.

Consequently, a going-into-the-Cloud strategy should consider the effect on
all properties of a service and resist being dominated by the economic moti-
vation(s) alone. A central issue is the problem of the security of data storage
and secure data processing in a remote Cloud. For instance, leakage of customer
sensitive data may prove fatal for a business, or a least cause intervention by
data protection authorities.

A common sense property of running conventional, local IT services is that
this *modus operandi* implicitly offers full control over the hardware as well as
the software setup. In contrast, handing off computing and storage to a remote
Cloud facility leaves one with nothing but the service level contractually agreed
with the Cloud provider.

Such a provider can implement data center security in many different ways,
for instance with automated 24x7 network monitoring, intrusion detection technologies, a defined life-cycle for storage media, physical access restrictions with
multi-factor identification, or armed guards. Still, Cloud datacenter security may
fail eventually and expose clients' data. This may happen e.g. through human
error, mailicious intent, or law enforcement compelled-assistance scenarios.

S. Katzenbeisser et al. (Eds.): TRUST 2012, LNCS 7344, pp. 122–141, 2012.

Contribution. In this paper, we address aspects of the loss of control on remote data and code execution in the Cloud. First, we assume a generic Cloud architecture which distributes processing nodes widely, possibly over diverse sets of physical sites, operators and hardware platforms. This raises the challenge for focused physical manipulation attacks compared to centralized datacenters. Second, our design integrates Trusted Computing technologies into the Cloud formation phase, which enables us to remotely assess and report the security state of the connecting and running Cloud nodes. This enables enforcement of nodes to only known-good configurations. Third, we investigate not just commercial off-the-shelf x86 servers which currently ship with Trusted Computing extensions. We also investigate the potential of near-future[1] ARM-based integrated server designs, which promise a higher CPUs per rack density and high power efficiency. Our contribution therefore considers heterogeneous hardware platforms together with the hardware-abstractions offered by the more-and-more popular Android environment.

More precisely, we improve the cloud join protocol and scenario previously sketched in the short paper [25]. With practical prototyping we demonstrate that secure Clouds can be assembled from heterogeneous platform architectures. Our implementation results on both x86 and ARM-based platforms support the viability of the approach. We use Android as the common software environment and show that it is highly suitable for forming an effective and efficient chain-of-trust. Also, we take a higher-level view and survey surrounding platform security properties, trade-offs and technologies.

While there is never absolute security, we believe our proposal offers an interesting trade-off between physical control and security properties for local versus distributed data processing.

Outline. The remainder of the paper is structured into the following major sections. Section 2 offers a brief background summary of the capabilities of Trusted Computing technologies. We then continue in Section 3 to present our architecture, along with the core Cloud join protocol. Portions of our approach were implemented in prototypes, our results are reported in Section 4. Based on the previous sections we discuss the security implications and trade-offs achieved in Section 5. In Section 6 we present links to related work. Finally, Section 7 concludes the paper.

2   Security Enhanced Mass-Market Platforms

Over the last years, mass-market consumer computer platforms and devices were enhanced with dedicated functions to support advanced security concepts. In the following we give a short introduction on Trusted Computing features available,

---

[1] First ARM based server prototypes have been announced by commercial vendors for the first half of 2012.

which can be put to good use in the implementation of trustworthy infrastructures, meaning that every processing node in the network is based on a modern security enhanced hardware platform.

2.1 Trusted Platform Module

The concept of Trusted Computing as promoted by the Trusted Computing Group (TCG) extends the industry standard PC architecture with a specialised hardware component, the Trusted Platform Module (TPM) [33].

A TPM features cryptographic primitives similar to a smartcard, but is physically bound to its host platform. The tamper-resilient chip provides functions for public-key cryptography, key generation, cryptographic hashing, random-number generation, and others. With these hardware crypto support, and being a chip operating independently from other devices, the TPM can provide certain trusted functions.

An important concept of Trusted Computing is the measurement logging and reporting of the platform state. Upon platform hardware reset a special set of platform configuration registers (PCRs) in the TPM are reset to a well defined start value. PCRs cannot be directly written to. Rather, a PCR with index i, $i \geq 0$ in state t is extended with input x by setting $PCR_i^{t+1} = \text{SHA-1}(PCR_i^t||x)$. This enables the construction of a *chain-of-trust*. From the BIOS onwards, every block of code is measured into a PCR before execution control is passed to it. Thus, the current values in the set of PCRs represent a log of what happend since system reboot, up to the current state of the system.

The TPM can *bind* data to a platform by encrypting it with a *non-migratable* key, which never leaves the TPM protection. An extension to this is *sealing*, where a key may only be used with a specific (trusted) PCR configuration. Thus, decryption of sealed data can be restricted to an expected state – running software and configuration – of the computer. The current state may also be TPM signed with the TPM *Quote* operation and reported in a so-called *remote attestation* protocol.

TPMs also provide a limited amount of non-volatile memory (NV-RAM) to store user- or owner-supplied information. One specific piece in NV is the TPM Endorsement Key (EK). It is a unique asymmetric RSA keypair of which the private part never leaves the TPM in clear. An accompanying certificate – typically signed by the manufacturer – documents the fact that the key belongs to a real hardware TPM on a trusted computing platform. It can also serve as a unique identification of a platform.

2.2 Trusted Execution Technology

In the last years PC hardware manufacturers have added hardware features which allow to realise enhanced security for specific scenarios. Recent platforms from Intel[2] extend the basic TCG model of a *static* chain-of-trust from hardware reboot and trust rooted in early BIOS. They provide the option of a *dynamic* switch to a well-defined, measured system state [14] at any point of execution after platform reboot. This is called a *dynamic root of trust for measurements (DRTM)*. Consequently, this capability significantly cuts down the complexity of the chain-of-trust measurements to assess the platform state by excluding the early, messy bootup operations.

Further, the initialisation code executed upon switching to a measured system state is capable of enforcing a Launch Control Policy (LCP). The administrator of the TPM may store a LCP in the TPM non-volatile memory which specifies which piece of TXT mode startup code is allowed to execute on this platform. This capability ensures that a certain PCR state can only be reached by executing code explicitly specified by the system administrator. However, by default all TXT platforms are shipped with a default *ANY* policy, which allows everyone to startup TXT.

2.3   ARM Platforms

The ARM family of microprocessors is widely used in a wide variety of systems, from small embedded devices, to power-efficient mobile phones and specialized server System on Chips with high processing density.

Many of those hardware platforms include TrustZone security extensions and native secure-boot features. Unfortunately, the actual capabilities and details of these secure-boot features vary between vendors and are considered as confidential information by the manufacturers. Thus little documentation is available publicly.

Typical realizations of such native secure-boot capabilities are likely to be realized using a mask-programmed on-chip ROM which uses symmetric cryptography (HMACs) to authenticate an asymmetric boot-loader verification key (RSA), which then is employed to authenticate the external boot-code before launching it.

3   Architecture

We now outline our secure Cloud formation architecture. First we identify the core assumptions and properties we want to achieve, then we show how they can be implemented with the use of Trusted Computing features, data structures and protocols.

3.1   Cloud Node Properties

We assume a generic distributed computing scenario, oblivious to the details of the specific middleware used. Still, we consider a Cloud setting with distributed

---

[2] We restrict our discussion to Intel's Trusted Execution Technology (TXT) as this is currently the dominant technology provider – comparable features are also available on e.g. AMD platforms.

nodes that process the computation workload. In order to allow different services and technologies to be deployed atop of the architecture we propose, we strive for the following properties.

Distributed. We assume that the individual nodes in the Cloud may be distributed both geographically and organizationally. Nodes could be placed in different countries and continents, and could be owned and operated by diverse sets of operators.

Attested. Due to node distribution it is consequently more difficult to enforce conventional security oversight on the nodes. Instead of absolute physical and organizational control we use the Trusted Computing technique of *remote attestation* to enforce an assessment process. The result of this protocol is the decision whether a remote node is in a trusted state and therefore allowed to become part of the Cloud, or not.

Lightweight. In order to enable a diverse set of distributed stakeholders to be able to participate in the Cloud, the installation of a Cloud node and joining the Cloud network should be a simple setup and maintenance task that does not add significant organizational overhead.

Heterogeneous. The larger the Cloud network, the more resources may be shared among participants. Consequently, this allows to process larger tasks and improves the economics of scale which reduces costs. Thus, as many nodes as possible should be able to join the Cloud. Consequently, the Cloud node software should build on a base or primitives which are easily portable to different platforms.

3.2   Entities

A Cloud infrastructure connects many computing nodes. Still, for being part of one specific Cloud (network) there must be a central responsible entity for commisioning nodes and performing accounting and control tasks. We call this Cloud management service the *Cloud control*.

In our architecture the role of the Cloud control is served by the Cloud provider as legal and commercial real-world entitiy. The provider's always-online, professionally run 24x7 datacenter manages client profiles and is responsible for accounting, authentication and authorization. It provides an information service on available Cloud nodes and service capacities. Our generic scenario is not restricted to the potentially few processing nodes operated locally by the Cloud provider. The vast majority of nodes is expected to be run distributed, at remote sites, with their operators not necessarily under direct provider supervision.

We assume that essentially anyone can offer nodes to join the Cloud and thus provide computing capacities[3] and yet provide a certain level of security assurance. In our scenario, trust is not only based on repution and contracts, but

---

[3] And may then be compensated for doing so under some contract.

an additonal barrier protects against fraud and abuse. Cloud nodes must apply and run system software that is well-known to and trusted by the provider. Trusted Computing security features guarantee this. In practice this will mean that a Cloud node software image can be downloaded from central Cloud control and then booted at a node. If and only if the new node's security is successfully attested, a connection to Cloud control can be established and the node becomes available to the Cloud.

3.3   Core Operations

Our approach focuses on the security of the Cloud formation process of distributed remote nodes joining the Cloud network via central Cloud control. We expect every node to host a TPM as specified by the TCG (see Section 2). The Cloud node software image is booted by a trusted boot process, meaning a mechanism exists which enforces measurement of system states into the TPM PCRs, starting from a well-defined initial platform state. Our join protocol uses an extension of a modified AIK certification exchange. For space reasons we cannot explain every detail of the TCG-specified AIK exchange and refer to [24] for an extensive presentation.

Cloud Node Joining to Cloud Control. Assume a new Cloud node wants to join the Cloud. The Cloud software image is booted on the node. The image which was booted is recorded into the TPM's PCRs. Further, the image contains the unique asymmetric RSA public key CC_{pub} and the network address of Cloud control. Immediately after boot the node automatically attempts to join the Cloud.

The *join protocol* is depicted in Figure 1. Four messages are required to be exchanged between the joining node and central Cloud control:

1. The first objective is to establish a secure connection to Cloud control. The first data blob sent to CC is symmetrically encrypted with a fresh symmetric key K, while K itself is encrypted asymmetrically with CC_{pub}. The data blob contains the EK certificate (EK_{cert}) of the TPM, along with AIK_{pub} of a newly created AIK keypair in the TPM. The standard PCA *label* field is used to give an indication what hardware platform the node is running.
   Cloud control receives the blob and decrypts the payload with its secret CC_{priv}. A certificate validation process for EK_{cert}, determining a valid hardware TPM, is run.
2. On successful validation, Cloud control generates a fresh nonce, and other supplemental data for challenging of the remote node platform state, depending on the reported platform included in *label*. The return blob is again encrypted using the hybrid scheme similar to step 1, with the asymmetric encryption key being used the EK_{pub} contained in the certificate presented by the node.

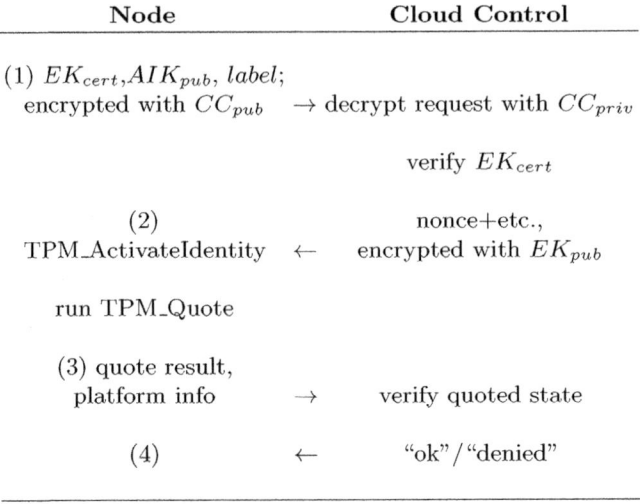

Fig. 1. Join Protocol (notation simplified for clarity)

The node uses the standard TPM_ActiveIdentity command for decrypting the package. With the received nonce the current system state is quoted using the AIK previously generated. The symmetric key created by Cloud control is used for encrypting all further message exchanges with Cloud control.

3. The signed system state obtained from the TPM, along with additional node or platform specifications (e.g. available storage or processing power) is sent back.

   Cloud control is now able to validate the included TPM signed platform state. The quote must be signed with the AIK presented in step 1, the nonce must be equal to the one sent back in step 2. The reported platform state of the node must be well-known to Cloud control, i.e. a trusted Cloud node software image must have booted.

4. Cloud control now either welcomes the node to the Cloud or denies access.

The first two steps follow the standard TCG design for AIK certification and use Trusted Computing primitives to establish a secure point to point connection from Cloud control to the hardware TPM without man-in-the-middle. For compliance with the TCG standards, we choose 2048-RSA as asymmetric, 128-bit AES as symmetric and SHA-1 as hash cryptographic primitives.

Cloud control verifies that the remote platform hosts a real hardware TPM with the non-migratable EK and a non-migratable AIK was created in it. Note that we deliberately deviate from the TCG-proposed AIK protocol that was designed to provide anonymity for platforms by issuing an unlimited number of unlinkable identities. The reason for this is that cloud providers need a proof that they actually get what they pay for, i.e. a real hardware platform with real processing power.

The next two steps convince through the Trusted Computing quote operation that an up-to-date PCR state is signed by the AIK. Thus, to Cloud control that the node is in a trusted state and can subsequently join the Cloud.

After this initial join protocol the desired Cloud software platform is run and jobs are assigned to this processing node.

Node Update / Cloud Rejoin. The joining of a new node represents the basic step to construct a Cloud network. Yet, there are two more basic operations to consider.

Eventually the Cloud's requirements for the node software image will change. Consequently, Cloud control will refuse an obsolete version, now untrusted, in step 4 of the join protocol. The Cloud node operator must obtain an updated software image and then try again.

If a Cloud node is rebooted and wants to *rejoin* the Cloud with the identical Cloud node software image, this brings up the question of persistent node data. It may be very inefficient to resychronize gigabytes of working data with the Cloud over the Internet.

In order for the Trusted Computing attestation process to produce the same measurement result every time, one can only measure read-only data in always strictly the same input order. Naturally, any data processed and code executed may affect a platforms's security state. Consequently, only after successful execution of the Cloud join protocol any user related code and data may be processed or executed. The security of data storage containing user data persisting over reboots must be ensured.

Node Local Storage. Unencrypted temporary storage on node local mass-media (e.g. harddisc) may cause serious security implications. Consequently, any node-local temporary data storage should be fully encrypted, e.g. with a transparently encrypted file system under a symmetric key. Thus, to re-access the node storage after service interruption (e.g. reboot) the key for the local temporary storage must only be made available to the identical Cloud node software image running at the identical Cloud node.

This problem can be solved by encrypting the storage key with an asymmetric TPM key *sealed* to a specific Cloud node software image.

For a full automatically (re-)bootable Cloud node we identify three data items to enable persistent, secure local Cloud node user data storage.

TPM Ownership Password

For creation of the AIK keypair in the Cloud join protocol the TPM ownership password must be available. Consequently, for a new software image version to be booted at a Cloud node the TPM owner must enter the TPM ownership password at least once. It is a sensible policy that a platform owner consents to what software is to be run on his machine. The ownership password can then be hashed into the TCG-compliant format and TPM-sealed to the specific software version booted, so reboots and Cloud joins can be automated while restricting access to the trusted environment. Again, this is a deviation from standard TCG assumptions, but it enables the automation of Cloud operations.

Bulk Storage Encryption Key

If a Cloud node is booted the first time the local storage does not exist yet. Upon first successful completion of the Cloud join protocol local encrypted storage is created and initialised, and the encryption key sealed to the current state.

If the identical Cloud node software image is rebooted at the identical platform, in step 3 of the join process the node is able to reopen the local storage, if available. This can yield a proof of previous state of work performed to Cloud control and significantly speed up reintegration into the Cloud.

Storage – Image File or Partition

The encrypted storage itself.

In our architecture a Cloud node will build a chain-of-trust consisting of a read-only, attestable Cloud software image which is booted and measured with Trusted Computing, and three pieces of data which together enable to keep persistent data over automated node reboots. As the three data pieces belong together we suggest to integrate them into one image (file or partition) for ease of maintenance.

4   Implementation

As a proof-of-concept of our approach we implemented the core chain-of-trust measurements and the four steps in the Cloud join protocol of our architecture.

We assume that every Cloud node hosts a TPM[4]. Also, every platform must provide a trusted boot feature, meaning there exists a hardware enforced chain-of-trust root which measures what software is executed, starting from a well-defined initial state.

We use Infineon TPMs, which come with an on-chip EK certificate by the manufacturer. As operating system we use Android, as it is by design split into a read-only base system image and temporary read/write areas for runtime. This property greatly simplifies[5] the modifications needed for adding the required measurement hooks for a chain-of-trust into the platform startup process.

On our two testplatforms, on x86 and ARM, Android runs with a Linux kernel, which provides a `/dev/tpm0` device as interface to the Infineon TPM. As software environment on top we use Java as programming language, a natural fit to the Android environment. jTSS [22] provides the Trusted Computing library support to access the TPM's functions. We implemented our Cloud join protocol by extending the AIK cycle code in jTpmTools.

---

[4] The Trusted Platform Module is now shipping in volume for more than 5 years and is already included in estimated 500 million PCs [34] worldwide. This is expected to rise.

[5] For a prototype on how to implement this with a regular Linux system see e.g. [23].

The following sections describe implementation details for each Cloud node platform prototype. The Cloud control server simulation runs on a generic PC.

4.1   x86 PC Platform

As hardware platform we choose an HP Elitebook 8440p, which is Intel QM57 chipset based and fully supports Intel Trusted Execution Technology. The TPM is an Infineon 1.2 TPM, firmware rev 3.17.

On the PC the BIOS controls the primary master switch to enable or disable Trusted Computing features. So setup requires going into the BIOS and enabling TXT. The default *ANY* TXT launch policy preloaded into every TPM by the PC platform manufacturer suffices and does not need to be modified. The platform owner needs to take TPM ownership once to create the storage root key (SRK) in the TPM. We assume the common well-known secret is used as SRK password – which is all zeros. The take ownership function may be done with the installed OS or come as a separate utility function on the Cloud node software image.

In our proof-of-concept prototype, we use USB-connected flash memory as medium for persistent storage as it is very simple to handle, reasonable cheap and allows for experimentation with various software images and configurations with little overhead.

The contents of the drive is a single VFAT formatted partition and the file system structure is quite simple. The bootloader used is Syslinux[6], which sits in the bootsector and requires *ldlinux.sys* and *syslinux.cfg* as support files. For display of a menu and multiboot kernel chainbooting *mboot.c32* and *menu.c32* are needed. A TXT boot requires *tboot.gz*, the trusted boot reference implementation provided by Intel [15] and a set of SINIT ACM modules, the chipset specific initialisation code, also provided by Intel. As Android base OS software we modified the image Android-x86 2.3 RC1 eeepc (Test build 20110828) of the Android x86 porting effort [1]. The Android system consists of the *kernel*, *initrd.img*, *ramdisk.img* and *system.sfs*.

The *syslinux.cfg* file connects all pieces together. *Menu.c32* specifies as primary kernel *mboot.c32*, which runs *tboot*, which starts up TXT with the proper *SINIT ACM* module. Control comes back to *tboot*, which executes the Android *kernel*, who with help of the *initrd* and *ramdisk* starts the full system from the *system.sfs*. To summarize the chain-of-trust: *SINIT* measures *tboot*, which measures *kernel*, *initrd* and *ramdisk*, while the script in the *initrd* measures the *system.sfs* image.

The modifications to the Android system to implement a trusted boot process are as follows: The default eeepc optimized kernel is replaced by a generic kernel supporting all common x86 hardware, including the TPM and TXT drivers. This increases the *systems.sfs* from 79MB to 97MB. The *init* script of the *initrd* is modified to load the TPM *tpm_tis* kernel driver and measure the *system.sfs* Android base system into a PCR. This measurement operation needs to load the full system image once, however to due the small size (see above) and modern

---

[6] http://www.syslinux.org/

USB flash drives read speeds of 10 to 20MB/s this delays the boot process only by a few seconds. Then the system partition is mounted and chroot-ed into. The support *TPM_extend* utility binaries increase the *initrd* size by about 700kb. Consequently, we assess the impact on boot process performance and binaries size as negligible.

For this prototype the Android *cloud_node.apk* is then installed immediately after bootup via *adb* remote instrumentation and executed. This Java-based client accesses the TPM and runs the Cloud join protocol with the Cloud control server simulation. Any Java-based Cloud middleware could be extended with this functionality.

4.2   ARM Platform

Our primary hardware reference platform for the ARM implementation of our proof of concept approach is a Freescale iMX51 evaluation kit [13]. A picture of our setup is shown in Figure 2. The Freescale MX515D application processor found on this board is based on ARM's Cortex-A8 core and would offer advanced security features, which include ARM's TrustZone security extensions and a set of secure boot facilities.

Unfortunately, most parts of the documentation describing the MX515D processor is only available under NDA from Freescale. For this reason we do not apply these advanced hardware security features in the prototype implementation we report, but focus on the TPM-based chain-of-trust instead.

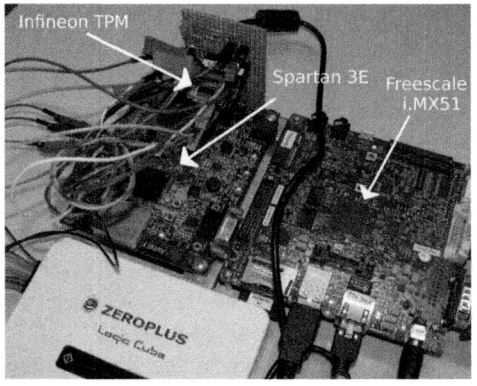

Fig. 2. Experimental hardware setup (Freescale i.MX51 EVK)

As software we use Android in a similar configuration as on the x86 platform. The open-source U-boot [9] bootloader is used to load and boot the Android kernel, initial ramdisk and file-system images from a removeable SD card. With the iMX51 board we use the built-in SD card boot facilities of the processor's integrated boot ROM to start our U-boot bootloader, without having to modify any of the board's flash memory chips.

TPM Support on ARM Platforms. The ARM platform used in our experiment does not natively include a Trusted Platform Module. Moreover, this platform does not provide a Low-Pin-Count (LPC) bus, which could be used to connect a standard TPM intended for integration on desktop platforms.

Consequently, for the purpose of our distributed Cloud node prototype we decided to implement a simple LPC bus adapter, to be able to attach a TPM to our ARM platform. The adapter is based on a common off-the shelf FPGA development board. The FPGA board used as interface adapter contains a Cypress-FX2 microcontroller with USB interface as well as a small Xilinx Spartan 3E FPGA. The block diagram in figure 3 gives a high-level overview of our hardware setup.

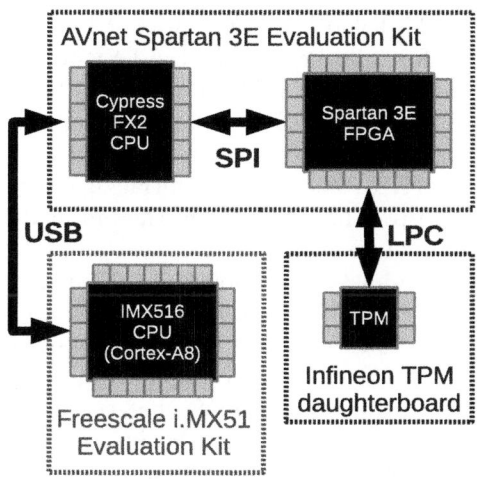

Fig. 3. Hardware setup for the ARM implementation

The LPC bus controller is implemented inside the FPGA. An external control interface is exposed via a serial peripheral interface (SPI) bus. This design allows the FPGA-based LPC bus controller, and consequently any TPM attached to it, to be connected to virtually any microcontroller or microprocessor system – just like the iMX51 evaluation board we use. The FX2 microcontroller hides the low-level details of the LPC bus protocol and offers a convenient USB interface instead.

TPM-Based Chain of Trust on the ARM Platform. On PC platforms TXT depends on a series of modifications to platform hardware, firmware and CPU microcode in order to enable establishment of a fully measured, well-defined system state. Common ARM platforms do not provide a direct functional equivalent to Intel's Trusted Execution Technology out of the box. They do, however, provide the required building blocks to construct a system with comparable security capabilities.

The PC version of our Android Cloud node uses TXT to construct a trusted boot chain for the base system loaded from a removable USB thumb drive. The ARM implementation of the Cloud node software is booted from a removable SD card. This SD card contains the actual bootloader (u-boot), the Android Linux kernel, an initial RAM-disk and the actual Android root filesystem. The mechanism used to load the boot-loader from the removable SD card depends on the hardware platform being used. In case of our prototype's iMX51 evaluation kit we rely on the processor's fixed on-chip boot ROM to perform a direct boot from the SD card.

Once the u-boot boot-loader has been loaded from the SD card, we are in full control of all details of the remaining platform boot process. The modifications to realize a TXT-style trusted boot process on the ARM platform are as follows: The initial RAM-disk of the Android boot image is extended to include a system-level service for interfacing with the USB-to-TPM adapter discussed in the previous section. This Android TPM Access Service (ATAS) is implemented as native application, to allow its inclusion at a very early stage of the platform startup phase, before the standard Android runtime environment has been fully initialized. ATAS takes care of initializing the TPM interface hardware. Moreover, it is responsible to perform the initial PCR extend operations for constructing a chain of trust.

The outlined approach for bootstrapping the chain of trust on an ARM platform suffers from one obvious problem: From a Trusted Computing perspective ATAS takes the role of the core root of trust for measurement (CRTM). Without additional support from the underlying hardware and on-chip boot ROM there is, however, no (hardware) guarantee that the initial measurements were actually performed by the (intended) CRTM. In order to fix the deficiencies in the bootstrapping process of the simple chain of trust some support from the boot-ROM of the platform would be required. The Freescale i.MX51 platform includes native secure-boot features that could accomplish a strong binding between the device and the CRTM, thus making the simple chain of trust approach viable again.

Emulation of Trusted Execution on an ARM Platform. The preceding section focussed on constructing a chain of trust on an ARM platform in precisely the same way as a static root of trust (S-RTM) works on a PC platform. In case of the relatively simple and deterministic software configuration of the mobile Cloud node client, this will be sufficient for most practical uses.

We were able to demonstrate a working TPM integration on the ARM platform as described. Once the Android base system successfully started the identical *cloud_node.apk* was installed and ran as described with the x86 based prototype. The Cloud join process was successful.

5   Platform Security Survey

Our approach presented in this paper offers attested (and attestable at a later time by any client) Cloud nodes through use of Trusted Computing technologies.

The security properties of the Cloud join protocol were discussed immediately following its presentation (see Section 3.3). In the following we reflect on the security properties and trade-offs of the surrounding components, platforms and technologies.

5.1   Trust Perimeter

Trust into something can be established when one can inspect it and attain an informed opinion of its inner working. Unfortunately, the sheer size of source code in modern operating systems makes it impossible to inspect it personally. Consequently, it is often required that one trusts the opinion, certification or competence of some third party. With Trusted Computing we can identify the following components where our own inspection capabilities end.

Intel TXT initialisation of a PC platform into a well-defined state relies on an opaque binary initialisation code blob called *SINIT ACM* supplied by Intel. While it is possible to disassemble and reverse-engineer its function, it is forbidden by the code license to do so. Further, obviously only Intel engineers know how their chipsets work internally.

The singular proof that a trusted platform hosts a real hardware TPM is embodied by the EK certificate for the TPM. To our knowledge to date only Infineon includes an EK certificate with their TPM chip. We have to trust Infineon that during manufacturing the EK (certificate) creation is secured and no one gets the opportunity to see the private part of the EK injected into the TPM.

5.2   Distributed Nodes

The motivation to allow for distribution of Cloud nodes to geographically distributed operators is the value for physical platform security. While Trusted Computing can provide a robust attestation of the booted node software, with full physical access to a node one can defeat a state-of-the-art TXT implementation, as demonstrated by [37].

We are optimistic that not all Cloud node operators are malicious. Instead, under the assumption that the majority of node operators is honest and/or not technically capable of sophisticated hardware attacks, consequently malicious forces would have to force their way. They would have to break down many real-world doors – noisily and committing intrusion crimes – in order to gain physical access to the Cloud nodes. Naturally, this significantly raises the resources needed to accomplish surveillance or manipulations via physical attacks on a large number of distributed Cloud nodes.

Obviously, a distributed structure with a potential share of compromised nodes is not best suited for all tasks. Sensitive computations do not tolerate loss of nodes, containing sensitive code and data, at all. However, other not-so-sensitive computations may just compensate with techniques such as secret splitting, redundancy or cross-checking approaches.

5.3   Node Diversity

The distribution of Cloud nodes to a diverse mixture of parties assists the hetero-genity of the Cloud node hardware population. Trusted Computing technology is still a young technology and exploits are still found. If, for example, one TXT system firmware implementation is buggy (e.g. for a SMM Bios [38]) it would be fatal to run on a monoculture of computers. Instead, a diverse set of platform manufactures encourages resilience. For security issues only specific models in a platforms series should be affected and not the whole Cloud.

5.4   Attack Surface

Under the assumption that the physical platform is safe, this leaves software attacks as primary attack surface. Runtime operating system bugs may always exist. If e.g. the network exposed TCP/IP stack of the Linux kernel contains a bug so that one can obtain control via remote access – well, then many servers in the world can be compromised also.

The primary exposure of a platform to the Internet is the network card. Modern (server) network interface cards are no longer just "dumb" network packet transfer devices. Instead, they also contain a small processor with firmware, which allows to do remote management functions. Consequently, for these functions to work the network card needs main memory access through DMA and other powerful platform primitives. Thus, if the card firmware can be exploited then security may be compromised remotely. A proof of concept work of this problem was demonstrated by [11] and the problem of attesting a network card firmware in [12].

Thus, the Internet exposed network card should be as dumb as possible to provide a minimal attack surface. The same security argument applies to any other "intelligent" devices or interfaces on a modern PC.

5.5   Open Source Cloud Node Platform

A Cloud node can attest what specific software image was booted and is currently running during the Cloud join protocol. Naturally, who testifies that the software image was engineered in a proper way?

As our prototype implementation demonstrates, a Cloud node can be assembled almost solely from open-source software components, with the main component in our prototype implementation being Android. The use of public, well-known sources, for example a major Linux distribution, to base the Cloud node software platform on, ensures the possibility for thorough inspection. This raises confidence that the Cloud node base software is not maliciously manipulated.

5.6   Future Trusted Platforms

On the PC platform the current TPM v1.2 has been the Trusted Computing basic building block for almost a decade. Its design does not accomodate for all of the demands of modern platforms today, e.g. with virtualization scenarios. Also, the current generation of TPM chips and Trusted Execution Technology have been demonstrated to be compromisable [38,39,31,37]. However, we expect many of these attacks to be fixed as the technology matures. Also, an updated TPM revision has been announced for the near future.

With our ARM prototype we attached a dedicated hardware TPM to our platform. However, any additional component increases the cost of a platform. An alternative approach would be to take advantage of ARM TrustZone [2] technology. This ARM processor security extension provides two virtual domains, which are the so-called *secure-world* and *normal-world*. This design allows the placement of a software TPM emulation into the *secure* world domain, which is strictly isolated from rest of the system running in the *normal* world. Its functions can be exported via /dev/tpm0 to applications and they would not be able to notice a difference to a hardware TPM. Consequently, this alternative approach also provides TPM functions, but the security implications, advantages and disadvantages need to be studied carefully for each scenario, as the platform boot process is obviously different.

6   Related Work

The Trusted Computing TPM is now becoming mainstream enough for systems integration research and actual prototypes. For the Cloud the TPM promises the possibility to strongly identify a single platform in the Cloud, to measure and report the exact software configuration and to protect the integrity of data and code stored in the Cloud.

Deployment and enrollment scenarios for trusted platforms have also been considered by Schiffman et al. [28] and Danner and Hein [8]. A number of security challenges occur in distributed systems. A recent report of ENISA [7] lists several security risks, many of those are still not solved. A very promising line of research [30,6,17,35,18] to overcome the security limitations of distributed computation networks is to incorporate Trusted Computing based on the widely available TPM. A pragmatic way to integrate attestation into legacy software, that is not aware of being trusted, is to establish attested communication tunnels [19,10].

Often, virtualization platforms are used to leverage trust and security specifically for the Cloud. Krishna et al. [27] propose a basic security architecture involving trusted virtualization and present a few security protocols. No practical implementation was reported. Also, Krautheim et al. propose in [16] the Trusted Virtual Environment Module, a software appliance that serves as virtual security module for IaaS Cloud applications on virtualization platforms. As a cryptographic module the proposal shows a potential way to allow platform owner and Cloud user to share responsibility and control over data in the Cloud. Brown and Chase [5] propose to use remote attestation so that users can gain insights and trust into SaaS service applications by leveraging trust in a neutral third party. They assume the Cloud platform and provider to be trustworthy, without actually relying on hardware security mechanisms. SICE [3] is a novel framework to provide hardware-level isolation and protection for sensitive workloads running on x86 platforms in compute Clouds. It is not based on a traditional hypervisor, but it utilizes the System Management Mode (SMM) to isolate different CPU cores. The presented prototype therefore requires a customized platform firmware and currently does not integrate further trust mechanism such as the TPM. The IBM Trusted Virtual Data center (TVDc) [4] is designed to offer security guarantees in hosted data centers. It provides containment and trust guarantees based on virtualization. Isolation and TPM-based integrity are managed. It builds upon a Hypervisor derived from Xen and performs TPM-based measurements of software. The UK myTrustedCloud [36] project studies the integration of an IaaS Cloud platform with KVM-based virtualization and hypervisor trust mechanisms built upon IBM IMA. Different levels of attestation are provided for the different layers in the software architecture. In paper [29] Schiffman et al. propose a centralized cloud verifier (CV) service which aids customers in verifying the integrity of a Cloud platform running the customer's VMs in IaaS Clouds.

Use of Intel Trusted Execution Technology for enforcement of a certain platform state is still a new technology and has been used only in a few prototype efforts. Flicker [21] isolates security sensitive code by halting the main OS, switching into a defined system state using the DRTM switch, and executing short-lived pieces of application logics (PALs). PALs may use the TPM to document their execution and handle their results. As a trusted hypervisor, TrustVisor [20] is initiated via the DRTM process, assumes full control and allows managing, running and attesting multiple PALs in its protection mode, without the switch costs incurred by the Flicker approach. The acTvSM [32] project demonstrates TXT integration into an off-the-shelf Debian Linux system. Starting from a DRTM initiated by Tboot, a measurement chain spans from the kernel over the initial ramdisk (initrd) into the read-only base system. On top of the base system virtualized application images can be run with a consistent chain-of-trust. Based on the acTvSM platform, Podesser and Toegl [26] studied the Cloud scenario. They demonstrate seamless integration of remote attestation in a SaaS Cloud for Java applications. The architecture enables developers to annotate code with security requirements that are automatically enforced throughout the attested Cloud.

7 Outlook and Conclusion

We have shown a feasible approach to join Cloud nodes that are in a specific, trusted state, into a Cloud computing network. We prototyped a joining protocol which uses low-level Trusted Computing processes. An automatic start of a Cloud middle-ware software package is beyond our prototype and the decision which specific package is best suited to run the Cloud infrastructure on top of our trusted Android Cloud nodes needs to be investigated separately. In future work we will study whether it is more beneficial to keep Trusted Computing things strictly separate, or integrate them directly into the Cloud framework operations.

In our approach we propose Cloud nodes which are attested with Trusted Computing methods. A geographical distribution of Cloud nodes raises the effort required for physical manipulation of Trusted Computing components on a large number of nodes. Based on Trusted Computing technologies we presented a protocol which ensures that nodes joining the Cloud can only do this if they can attest that they are in a trusted state. Our implementation prototypes demonstrate a lightweight setup and update procedure, which offers easy deployability. Overcoming the limits of available hardware our ARM based prototype of a potential future TPM enhanced ARM platform demonstrates security qualities similar to x86-based systems. This supports the vision of future heterogeneous networked Cloud nodes. The use of Android as a Open-Source base platform provides the common software ground and maintains the link to the highly dynamic developments in this area.

Acknowledgements. We thank the anonymous reviewers for their feedback on the paper. This work has been supported by the European Commission through project FP7-SEPIA, grant agreement number 257433.

References

1. Android x86 Team: Android-x86 - porting android to x86 (2011),
   http://www.android-x86.org/
2. ARM Ltd.: TrustZone Technology Overview (2011),
   http://www.arm.com/products/esd/trustzone_home.html
3. Azab, A.M., Ning, P., Zhang, X.: Sice: a hardware-level strongly isolated computing environment for x86 multi-core platforms. In: Proceedings of the 18th ACM Conference on Computer and Communications Security, CCS 2011, pp. 375–388. ACM, New York (2011), http://doi.acm.org/10.1145/2046707.2046752
4. Berger, S., Cáceres, R., Pendarakis, D., Sailer, R., Valdez, E., Perez, R., Schildhauer, W., Srinivasan, D.: Tvdc: managing security in the trusted virtual datacenter. SIGOPS Oper. Syst. Rev. 42, 40–47 (2008),
   http://doi.acm.org/10.1145/1341312.1341321
5. Brown, A., Chase, J.S.: Trusted platform-as-a-service: a foundation for trustworthy cloud-hosted applications. In: Proceedings of the 3rd ACM Workshop on Cloud Computing Security Workshop, CCSW 2011, pp. 15–20. ACM, New York (2011), http://doi.acm.org/10.1145/2046660.2046665
6. Cooper, A., Martin, A.: Towards a secure, tamper-proof grid platform. In: Sixth IEEE International Symposium on Cluster Computing and the Grid, CCGRID 2006, vol. 1, p. 8 (2006), doi:10.1109/CCGRID.2006.103
7. Daniele Catteddu, G.H.: Cloud Computing benefits, risks and recommendations for information security. Tech. rep., European Network and Information Security Agency, ENISA (2009)
8. Danner, P., Hein, D.: A trusted computing identity collation protocol to simplify deployment of new disaster response devices. Journal of Universal Computer Science 16(9), 1139–1151 (2010)
9. Denk, W., et al.: Das u-boot – the universal boot loader (2010),
   http://www.denx.de/wiki/U-Boot

10. Dietrich, K., Pirker, M., Vejda, T., Toegl, R., Winkler, T., Lipp, P.: A Practical Approach for Establishing Trust Relationships between Remote Platforms Using Trusted Computing. In: Barthe, G., Fournet, C. (eds.) TGC 2007. LNCS, vol. 4912, pp. 156–168. Springer, Heidelberg (2008)

11. Duflot, L., Perez, Y.A.: Can you still trust your network card. CanSecWest 2010 (2010), http://www.ssi.gouv.fr/IMG/pdf/csw-trustnetworkcard.pdf

12. Duflot, L., Perez, Y.A.: Run-time firmware integrity verification: what if you can't trust your network card? CanSecWest 2011 (2011),
http://www.ssi.gouv.fr/IMG/pdf/Duflot-Perez_runtime-firmware-integrity-verification.pdf

13. Freescale Semiconductor Inc.: i.mx51 evaluation kit (2010),
http://www.freescale.com/webapp/sps/site/
prod_summary.jsp?code=MCIMX51EVKJ

14. Grawrock, D.: Dynamics of a Trusted Platform: A Building Block Approach. Intel Press (February 2009)

15. Intel Corporation: Tboot - Trusted Boot (2008),
http://sourceforge.net/projects/tboot/

16. Krautheim, F.J., Phatak, D.S., Sherman, A.T.: Introducing the Trusted Virtual Environment Module: A New Mechanism for Rooting Trust in Cloud Computing. In: Acquisti, A., Smith, S.W., Sadeghi, A.-R. (eds.) TRUST 2010. LNCS, vol. 6101, pp. 211–227. Springer, Heidelberg (2010),
http://dl.acm.org/citation.cfm?id=1875652.1875667

17. Löhr, H., Ramasamy, H.V., Sadeghi, A.-R., Schulz, S., Schunter, M., Stüble, C.: Enhancing Grid Security Using Trusted Virtualization. In: Xiao, B., Yang, L.T., Ma, J., Muller-Schloer, C., Hua, Y. (eds.) ATC 2007. LNCS, vol. 4610, pp. 372–384. Springer, Heidelberg (2007)

18. Mao, W., Martin, A., Jin, H., Zhang, H.: Innovations for grid security from trusted computing (2009), http://dx.doi.org/10.1007/978-3-642-04904-0_18

19. McCune, J.M., Jaeger, T., Berger, S., Caceres, R., Sailer, R.: Shamon: A system for distributed mandatory access control. In: 22nd Annual Computer Security Applications Conference, ACSAC 2006, pp. 23–32 (2006)

20. McCune, J.M., Li, Y., Qu, N., Zhou, Z., Datta, A., Gligor, V., Perrig, A.: TrustVisor: Efficient TCB reduction and attestation. In: Proceedings of the IEEE Symposium on Security and Privacy (May 2010)

21. McCune, J.M., Parno, B.J., Perrig, A., Reiter, M.K., Isozaki, H.: Flicker: an execution infrastructure for tcb minimization. In: Proc. of the 3rd ACM SIGOPS/EuroSys European Conference on Computer Systems, pp. 315–328. ACM (2008)

22. Pirker, M., Toegl, R.: Trusted computing for the Java^{TM} platform (2011),
http://trustedjava.sourceforge.net/

23. Pirker, M., Toegl, R., Gissing, M.: Dynamic Enforcement of Platform Integrity. In: Acquisti, A., Smith, S.W., Sadeghi, A.-R. (eds.) TRUST 2010. LNCS, vol. 6101, pp. 265–272. Springer, Heidelberg (2010)

24. Pirker, M., Toegl, R., Hein, D., Danner, P.: A PrivacyCA for Anonymity and Trust. In: Chen, L., Mitchell, C.J., Martin, A. (eds.) Trust 2009. LNCS, vol. 5471, pp. 101–119. Springer, Heidelberg (2009)

25. Pirker, M., Winter, J., Toegl, R.: Lightweight distributed attestation for the cloud. In: Proceedings of the 2nd International Conference on Cloud Computing and Services Science, CLOSER (2012)

26. Podesser, S., Toegl, R.: A Software Architecture for Introducing Trust in Java-Based Clouds. In: Park, J.J., Lopez, J., Yeo, S.-S., Shon, T., Taniar, D. (eds.) STA 2011. CCIS, vol. 186, pp. 45–53. Springer, Heidelberg (2011),
http://dx.doi.org/10.1007/978-3-642-22339-6_6
27. Santos, N., Gummadi, K.P., Rodrigues, R.: Towards trusted cloud computing. In: Proceedings of the 2009 Conference on Hot Topics in Cloud Computing. USENIX Association, Berkeley, CA, USA (2009),
http://dl.acm.org/citation.cfm?id=1855533.1855536
28. Schiffman, J., Moyer, T., Shal, C., Jaeger, T., McDaniel, P.: Justifying integrity using a virtual machine verifier. In: ACSAC 2009: Proceedings of the 2009 Annual Computer Security Applications Conference, pp. 83–92. IEEE Computer Society Press, Washington, DC (2009)
29. Schiffman, J., Moyer, T., Vijayakumar, H., Jaeger, T., McDaniel, P.: Seeding clouds with trust anchors. In: Proceedings of the 2010 ACM Workshop on Cloud Computing Security Workshop, CCSW 2010, pp. 43–46. ACM, New York (2010),
http://doi.acm.org/10.1145/1866835.1866843
30. Smith, M., Friese, T., Engel, M., Freisleben, B.: Countering security threats in service-oriented on-demand grid computing using sandboxing and trusted computing techniques. J. Parallel Distrib. Comput. 66(9), 1189–1204 (2006)
31. Tarnovsky, C.: Hacking the Smartcard Chip. In: Blackhat DC (2010),
http://www.blackhat.com/html/bh-dc-10/bh-dc-10-briefings.html#Tarnovsky
32. Toegl, R., Pirker, M., Gissing, M.: acTvSM: A Dynamic Virtualization Platform for Enforcement of Application Integrity. In: Chen, L., Yung, M. (eds.) INTRUST 2010. LNCS, vol. 6802, pp. 326–345. Springer, Heidelberg (2011)
33. Trusted Computing Group: TCG TPM Specification Version 1.2 (2007),
https://www.trustedcomputinggroup.org/developers/
34. Trusted Computing Group: Do You Know? A Few Notes on Trusted Computing Out in the World (2011),
http://www.trustedcomputinggroup.org/community/2011/03/
do_you_know_a_few_notes_on_trusted_computing_out_in_the_world
35. Vejda, T., Toegl, R., Pirker, M., Winkler, T.: Towards Trust Services for Language-Based Virtual Machines for Grid Computing. In: Lipp, P., Sadeghi, A.-R., Koch, K.-M. (eds.) Trust 2008. LNCS, vol. 4968, pp. 48–59. Springer, Heidelberg (2008)
36. Wallom, D., Turilli, M., Taylor, G., Hargreaves, N., Martin, A., Raun, A., McMoran, A.: mytrustedcloud: Trusted cloud infrastructure for security-critical computation and data managment. In: Proeedings of Cloudcom (2011) (in print)
37. Winter, J., Dietrich, K.: A Hijacker's Guide to the LPC Bus. In: EuroPKI 2011 Proceedings (2011) (in print)
38. Wojtczuk, R., Rutkowska, J.: Attacking Intel Trusted Execution Technology. Tech. rep., Invisible Things Lab (2009),
http://invisiblethingslab.com/resources/bh09dc/Attacking
%20Intel%20TXT%20-%20paper.pdf
39. Wojtczuk, R., Rutkowska, J., Tereshkin, A.: Another Way to Circumvent Intel Trusted Execution Technology. Tech. rep., Invisible Things Lab (2009),
http://invisiblethingslab.com/resources/misc09/
Another%20TXT%20Attack.pdf

Converse PUF-Based Authentication

Ünal Kocabaş[1], Andreas Peter[1],
Stefan Katzenbeisser[1], and Ahmad-Reza Sadeghi[2]

[1] Technische Universität Darmstadt (CASED), Germany
[2] Technische Universität Darmstadt & Fraunhofer SIT Darmstadt, Germany
{unal.kocabas,ahmad.sadeghi}@trust.cased.de, andreas.peter@cantab.net,
skatzenbeisser@acm.org

Abstract. Physically Unclonable Functions (PUFs) are key tools in the construction of lightweight authentication and key exchange protocols. So far, all existing PUF-based authentication protocols follow the same paradigm: A resource-constrained prover, holding a PUF, wants to authenticate to a resource-rich verifier, who has access to a database of pre-measured PUF challenge-response pairs (CRPs). In this paper we consider application scenarios where all previous PUF-based authentication schemes fail to work: The verifier is resource-constrained (and holds a PUF), while the prover is resource-rich (and holds a CRP-database). We construct the first and efficient PUF-based authentication protocol for this setting, which we call *converse* PUF-based authentication. We provide an extensive security analysis against passive adversaries, show that a minor modification also allows for authenticated key exchange and propose a concrete instantiation using controlled Arbiter PUFs.

Keywords: Physically Unclonable Functions (PUFs), Authentication, Key Exchange.

1 Introduction

With rapid improvements in communication technologies, networks have become widespread, connecting both low-cost devices and high-end systems. Low-cost devices, such as RFID-tags, sensor nodes, and smart cards are likely to form the next generation pervasive and ubiquitous networks. Such networks are designed to store sensitive information and transmit this information to participants over a potentially insecure communication channel. Due to the potentially sensitive data they handle, security features such as authentication and encrypted data transfer and required. At the same time, the deployed security features must be extremely lightweight to fit the application scenario.

Physically Unclonable Functions [12], security primitives that extract noisy secrets from physical characteristics of integrated circuits (ICs), have emerged as trust anchors for lightweight embedded devices. Instead of relying on heavyweight public-key primitives or secure storage for secret symmetric keys, PUFs can directly be integrated in cryptographic protocols. PUFs have successfully

S. Katzenbeisser et al. (Eds.): TRUST 2012, LNCS 7344, pp. 142–158, 2012.
© Springer-Verlag Berlin Heidelberg 2012

been used in the context of anti-counterfeiting solutions that prevent cloning of products, and in the construction of various cryptographic protocols, involving identification and authentication.

In this paper we are merely concerned with PUF-based authentication protocols. All previous approaches, including [24,15,9], considered the problem of authenticating a lightweight device (called prover) containing a PUF to a remote entity (called verifier), which has more storage and processing capabilities. In particular, the verifier is required to store a database of measured PUF *challenge-response pairs* (CRPs). In order to perform the authentication, the verifier sends a random challenge to the prover, who has to measure the PUF on the challenge and respond with the measured PUF response. If the obtained response matches the one stored in the CRP, the prover is authenticated. Note that CRPs cannot be re-used since this would enable an adversary to mount replay attacks; furthermore, it would allow tracing of the tag. Besides this issue, some PUFs are subject to model-building attacks [25], which allow to obtain a model of the PUF in use by observing the PUF challenge-response pairs contained in the protocol messages.

In this work we consider PUF-based authentication protocols tailored towards a different scenario in which the verifier V is a very resource-constrained (yet PUF-enabled) device, while the prover P has comparably rich computational resources. For example, one can consider the scenario in which a sensor node (acting as verifier) wants to authenticate a sink (prover) in order to transmit sensitive sensor readings. In this setting, all currently available PUF-based authentication protocols are not applicable, since the roles of prover and verifier are reversed (simply swapping the roles of verifier and prover in traditional protocols does not work either, since a resource-constrained device is not able to keep a CRP database). In this paper we therefore propose a novel PUF-based authentication protocol that works in this situation: The prover P holds a CRP-database, while the lightweight verifier V has access to the PUF. Due to this converse approach of using the PUF in authentication, we call protocols that follow this new paradigm *converse PUF-based authentication protocols*. As a second feature of our protocol, which is in contrast to all previous approaches, our construction *never* needs to transmit PUF responses (or hashes thereof) over the channel, which effectively prevents passive model-building attacks as well as replay attacks. Since in this work, we deal with passive adversaries only, we see our solution as the first step in this converse approach and hope to see more work on this matter in the future.

1.1   Contributions

In summary, the paper makes the following contributions:

Introduction of a New Paradigm for PUF-Based Authentication. We introduce the paradigm of converse PUF-based authentication: In this setting a prover P holds a CRP-database, while a lightweight verifier V has access to a PUF.

First Construction. Based on an idea introduced in [5], we construct the first converse PUF-based authentication protocol, which is at the same time very efficient. It uses a controlled PUF at the verifier and a CRP database at the prover. A key feature is that during the protocol only a random tag and two PUF-challenges are exchanged over the communication channel; this effectively prevents model building attacks.

Security Analysis. We provide an extensive security analysis of the new protocol and show that it is secure against passive adversaries. We deduce precise formulae that upper bound the success probability of a worst-case adversary after having seen a certain number of protocol transcripts.

Authenticated Key Exchange. Finally, we show that a minor modification of our authentication protocol allows the two participants to agree on a common secret key. This basically comes for free, since this modification only amounts to the evaluation of one additional hash function at both sides.

1.2 Outline

After presenting a brief summary of PUFs and their properties, fuzzy extractors, and controlled PUFs in Section 2, we introduce our converse PUF-based authentication protocol including a proof of correctness in Section 3. Then, in Section 4 we discuss the security model we consider and prove our protocol secure against passive adversaries. Finally, implementation details are given in Section 5. We conclude with a summary and some possible directions for future work in Section 6.

2 Background and Related Work

PUFs exploit physical characteristics of a device, which are easy to measure but hard to characterize, model or reproduce. Typically, a stimulus, called challenge C, is applied to a PUF, which reacts with a response R. The response depends on both the challenge and the unique intrinsic randomness contained in the device. A challenge and its corresponding response are called a *challenge-response pair* (CRP). Typical security assumptions on PUFs include [21]:

- *Unpredictability:* An adversary A cannot predict the response to a specific PUF challenge without modeling its intrinsic properties. Moreover, the response R_i of one CRP (C_i, R_i) gives only a small amount of information on the response R_j of another CRP (C_j, R_j) with $i \neq j$.
- *Unclonability:* An adversary A cannot emulate the behavior of a PUF on another device or in software, since the behavior is fully dependent on the physical properties of the original device.
- *Robustness:* The outputs of a PUF are stable over time; thus, when queried with the same challenge several times, the corresponding responses are similar (which opens the possibility to apply an error correcting code in order to obtain a stable response).

PUFs meeting these assumptions provide secure, robust and low cost mechanisms for device identification and authentication [24,30,23,26], hardware-software binding [13,16,14,7] or secure storage of cryptographic secrets [8,33,18,4]. Furthermore, they can be directly integrated into cryptographic algorithms [1] and remote attestation protocols [27].

Among different PUF architectures, we focus on electronic PUFs, which can be easily integrated into ICs. They essentially come in three flavors: *Delay-based PUFs* are based on digital race conditions or frequency variations and include arbiter PUFs [17,23,19] and ring oscillator PUFs [12,29,22]. *Memory-based PUFs* exploit the instability of volatile memory cells after power-up, like SRAM cells [13,15], flip-flops [20,32] and latches [28,16]. Finally, *Coating PUFs* [31] use capacitances of a special dielectric coating applied to the chip housing the PUF.

Arbiter PUFs. In this paper we use *Arbiter PUFs* (APUF) [17], which consist of two logical paths, controlled by a challenge. Both paths get triggered at the same time. Due to the inherently different propagation delays induced by manufacturing variations, one of the two paths will deliver the signal faster than the other; a digital arbiter finally determines which of the two signals was faster and produces a one-bit response. The number of challenge-response pairs is typically exponentially large in the dimensions of the APUF, which makes them a good candidate to be used in authentication mechanisms.

However, it was claimed in [25] that APUFs are subject to model building attacks that allow predicting responses with non-negligible probability, once an attacker has full physical access to the APUF or can record sufficiently many challenge-response pairs. Further, the response of an APUF cannot be used directly as a cryptographic key in an authentication mechanism without postprocessing, since two queries of the same challenge may give slightly different responses due to noise. In order to counter these problems, additional primitives must be used: *Fuzzy Extractors* (FE) [6] and *Controlled PUFs* [9].

Fuzzy Extractors. The standard approach to make the PUF responses stable, is to use Fuzzy Extractors [6] consisting of a *setup phase*, an *enrolment phase* and a *reconstruction phase*.

In the setup phase, an error-correcting binary[1] linear $[\mu, k, d]$-code $\mathcal{C}$ of bit length μ, cardinality 2^k, and minimum distance d is chosen. Due to the choice of parameters, the code can correct up to $\lfloor \frac{d-1}{2} \rfloor$ errors. There are many known ways to construct such codes for given parameters [6], and we just mention here that we need to set the parameter μ to be the bit length of the output of the used PUF (some care has to be taken when choosing the amount of errors the code needs to correct, see [3]).

In the enrolment phase, denoted by FE.Gen, which is carried out before the deployment of the chip in a device in a trusted environment, for any given PUF response R, we choose a random codeword $\gamma \xleftarrow{U} \mathcal{C}$ and compute the *helper data* $h := \gamma \oplus R$. Later, during the reconstruction phase (denoted by FE.Rep), for

---

[1] We restrict our attention to binary codes (i.e., codes over the binary Galois field $\mathbb{F}_2$), although the same discussion can be done for non-binary codes as well.

any given PUF response R and corresponding helper data h, we first compute $W := R \oplus h$, and then use the decoding algorithm of the error correcting code C on W, which outputs the same codeword γ that we randomly picked in the enrolment phase.

Controlled PUFs. If one requires a uniformly distributed output (which a PUF usually does not provide), one can apply a cryptographic hash function $H : \{0,1\}^* \longrightarrow \{0,1\}^n$ to the output γ of the FE [3]. Here, we will always treat such a hash function H as a random oracle [2] which ensures that the output is uniformly distributed in $\{0,1\}^n$. Usually, an LFSR-based Toeplitz Hash function is used in order to implement this *privacy amplification phase* because of its low cost. The resulting combined primitive, i.e., applying the hash function H to the output of the FE, which itself was applied to the PUF, is called a *controlled PUF*.

3   Converse PUF-Based Authentication

All currently existing PUF-based (unilateral, two-party) authentication protocols (e.g., [24,15,9]) follow the same paradigm: A prover $\mathcal{P}$, who has access to a PUF, wants to authenticate himself to a verifier $\mathcal{V}$ who holds a database of challenge-response pairs (CRP) of $\mathcal{P}$'s PUF. In this section, we propose a new PUF-based authentication protocol that actually works the other way around: The prover $\mathcal{P}$ holds a (modified and reduced) CRP-database, while the verifier $\mathcal{V}$ has access to a PUF. Due to this converse approach of using the PUF in the authentication, we call protocols that follow this new paradigm *Converse PUF-based Authentication Protocols*.

3.1   Protocol Description

We consider a controlled PUF consisting of an underlying physical PUF (denoted by **PUF**), the two procedures FE.Gen and FE.Rep of the underlying Fuzzy Extractor (FE), and a cryptographic hash function $H : \{0,1\}^* \longrightarrow \{0,1\}^n$.

Now, as in usual PUF-based authentication, our protocol needs to run an *enrolment phase* in order to create a CRP-database on the prover's side. We note that this database will not consist of the actual CRPs of **PUF** but of responses of the controlled PUF (i.e., the PUF challenges C, some helper data h and hash values $H(\gamma)$ for FE outputs γ). More precisely, in the enrolment phase the prover $\mathcal{P}$ sends some random PUF challenge C to the verifier $\mathcal{V}$, who runs the enrolment phase of the FE on **PUF**(C), which outputs a value γ and some helper data h. Then, $\mathcal{V}$ returns the values $R(C, h) = H(\gamma)$ and h to $\mathcal{P}$. The prover $\mathcal{P}$ stores this data together with the PUF challenge in a database $\mathcal{D}$. These steps are repeated ρ times in order to generate a database $\mathcal{D}$ of size ρ. The described procedure is summarised in Fig. 1.

Now, whenever $\mathcal{P}$ needs to authenticate himself to $\mathcal{V}$, the following *authentication phase* is run: First $\mathcal{V}$ sends a random $0^n \neq \Delta \xleftarrow{U} \{0,1\}^n$ to $\mathcal{P}$. Then, $\mathcal{P}$

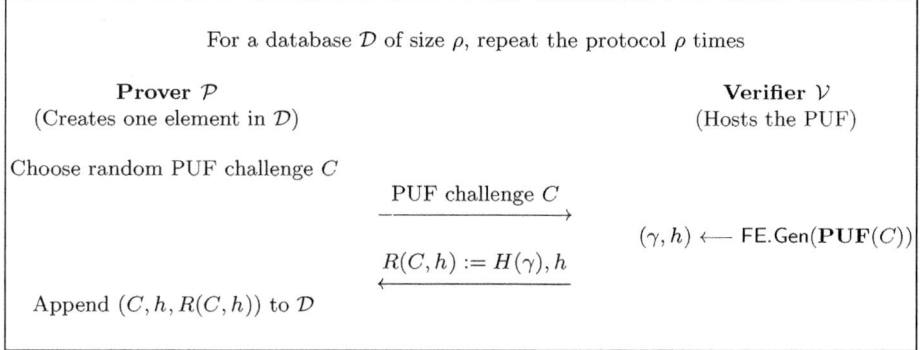

Fig. 1. Enrolment phase: Creating $\mathcal{P}$'s database $\mathcal{D}$

searches through his database $\mathcal{D}$ in order to find two elements $(C_1, h_1, R(C_1, h_1))$ and $(C_2, h_2, R(C_2, h_2))$ such that $\Delta = R(C_1, h_1) \oplus R(C_2, h_2)$, and sends the pairs (C_1, h_1) and (C_2, h_2) to $\mathcal{V}$. In other words, he is looking for two controlled PUF outputs whose XOR is Δ. If no such elements exist in $\mathcal{D}$, $\mathcal{P}$ just sends $(C_1, h_1) = (C_2, h_2)$ to $\mathcal{V}$, where both the PUF challenge C_1 and the helper data h_1 are chosen at random. In this case the authentication fails; we will choose the protocol parameters in a way that this happens only with small probability. Now, $\mathcal{V}$ uses the reconstruction phase of the FE twice – once on input $\mathbf{PUF}(C_1)$ and h_1, and once on input $\mathbf{PUF}(C_2)$ and h_2 which output two code words γ_1 and γ_2, respectively. After applying the hash function H to this (yielding values $R(C_1, h_1) = H(\gamma_1)$ and $R(C_2, h_2) = H(\gamma_2)$, respectively), $\mathcal{V}$ checks whether $R(C_1, h_1) \oplus R(C_2, h_2) = \Delta$. If equality holds, $\mathcal{V}$ sends the message $M = \top$ back to $\mathcal{P}$ in order to indicate that $\mathcal{P}$ successfully authenticated himself to $\mathcal{V}$; else it returns $M = \bot$, signaling that the authentication failed. In a subsequent step, the responses may optionally be used to exchange a shared secret key (see Section 3.3). The complete authentication phase is summarised in Fig. 2.

3.2   Correctness of the Protocol

We recall that in the enrolment phase, the prover $\mathcal{P}$ gets a database $\mathcal{D}$ of size ρ containing pairs of *PUF-challenges* C, *helper data* h and corresponding *responses* $R(C, h)$ from the verifier $\mathcal{V}$. Furthermore, we recall that after applying the Fuzzy Extractor, we input the resulting output into a cryptographic hash function H. So if we require the FE's outputs to have $\kappa \geq n$ bits of entropy, we can think of the responses $R(C, h)$ as bitstrings taken *uniformly at random* from the set $\{0, 1\}^n$ (cf. the Random Oracle Paradigm [2]). Here, we bear in mind that κ and n are public parameters of our authentication protocol that are being fixed in some setup phase.

   In this section, we consider how the probability of a successful authentication of $\mathcal{P}$ is affected by the size ρ of $\mathcal{P}$'s database $\mathcal{D}$. In other words, we will give a

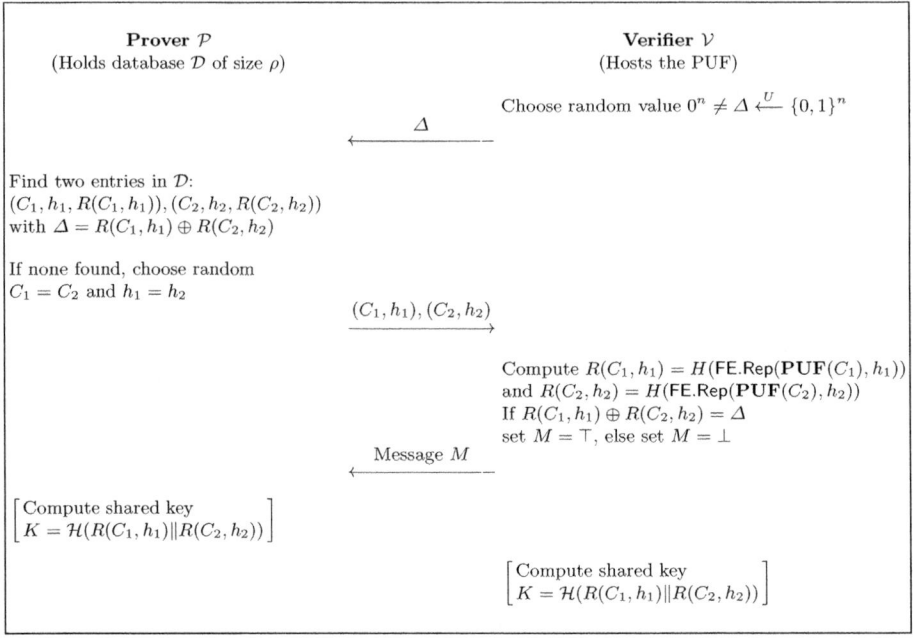

Fig. 2. Authentication phase: $\mathcal{P}$ authenticates himself to $\mathcal{V}$. As an optional step, both participants can compute a shared key K after the authentication.

lower bound on the size ρ of the database $\mathcal{D}$ in order for an authentication to be successful with a prescribed probability (assuming that both participants $\mathcal{P}$ and $\mathcal{V}$ honestly perform each step of the protocol). Here, *successful authentication* means that given a random $0^n \neq \Delta \xleftarrow{U} \{0,1\}^n$ there exist

$$(C_1, h_1, R(C_1, h_1)), (C_2, h_2, R(C_2, h_2)) \in \mathcal{D}$$

in $\mathcal{P}$'s database such that $R(C_1, h_1) \oplus R(C_2, h_2) = \Delta$.

Theorem 1. *If ρ denotes the size of $\mathcal{P}$'s database $\mathcal{D}$, then the probability of a successful authentication is*

$$\mathsf{Succ}_{\mathcal{P},n}^{\mathrm{Auth}}(\rho) := 1 - \left(1 - \frac{2}{2^n - 1}\right)^{\frac{\rho^2 - \rho}{2}}.$$

Proof. First of all, it is easy to see that only the responses $R(C, h)$ that are stored in the database $\mathcal{D}$ have an influence on the probability of a successful authentication, and so we think of $\mathcal{D}$ containing only responses $R = R(C, h)$ and forget about the PUF-challenges C and helper data h. Now, since the ρ different values $R(C, h)$ in $\mathcal{D}$ and the value Δ are uniformly distributed and independent in $\{0,1\}^n$, the probability of having a successful authentication amounts to the following:

For a set M, let $\binom{M}{2}$ denote the set of all subsets of cardinality 2 of M, whereas we denote elements of this set by pairs (R_1, R_2); so basically, this set consists of all *unordered* pairs (R_1, R_2), excluding self-pairs (R_1, R_1). Here, we consider the set $\binom{\{0,1\}^n}{2}$ which has precisely $\binom{2^n}{2}$ many elements. For the authentication, we are only interested in the XOR of two values in $\mathcal{D}$, so we want to look at the set $\binom{\mathcal{D}}{2}$ which has exactly $\binom{\rho}{2}$ many elements taken uniformly at random from $\binom{\{0,1\}^n}{2}$. We denote the set of all XOR's of any two elements in $\mathcal{D}$ by $\mathcal{D}^\oplus$, i.e., $\mathcal{D}^\oplus = \{R_1 \oplus R_2 \mid (R_1, R_2) \in \binom{\mathcal{D}}{2}\}$. Therefore, the probability of a successful authentication is the probability that $\Delta \in \mathcal{D}^\oplus$. Summing up, we have:

1. $\Delta \xleftarrow{U} \{0,1\}^n$ is sampled uniformly at random.[2]
2. The prover $\mathcal{P}$ has a database $\binom{\mathcal{D}}{2}$ of $\binom{\rho}{2}$ many elements taken uniformly at random from $\binom{\{0,1\}^n}{2}$.
3. For a random $(R_1, R_2) \xleftarrow{U} \binom{\{0,1\}^n}{2}$, the probability that we hit on Δ when XOR-ing R_1 and R_2 is $q := \frac{2^n}{\binom{2^n}{2}} = \frac{2}{2^n - 1}$.
4. We are interested in the probability of a successful authentication, i.e., in the probability $\mathrm{Succ}_{\mathcal{P},n}^{\mathrm{Auth}}(\rho) = \Pr[\Delta \in \mathcal{D}^\oplus]$, where $\mathcal{D}^\oplus = \{R_1 \oplus R_2 \mid (R_1, R_2) \in \binom{\mathcal{D}}{2}\}$ and the latter probability is taken over all random $\Delta \xleftarrow{U} \{0,1\}^n$ and random $\binom{\mathcal{D}}{2} \subset \binom{\{0,1\}^n}{2}$.

In other words, we sample $\binom{\rho}{2}$ many times from $\binom{\{0,1\}^n}{2}$ with probability $q = \frac{2}{2^n - 1}$ of success (i.e., hitting on Δ) on each trial, and ask for the probability of having *at least* $s = 1$ successes (i.e., hits on Δ). The probability of having exactly s successes is given by the *binomial probability formula*:

$$\Pr\left[s \text{ successes in } \binom{\rho}{2} \text{ trials}\right] = \binom{\binom{\rho}{2}}{s} q^s (1 - q)^{\binom{\rho}{2} - s}.$$

Therefore, the probability of having $s = 0$ successes is $(1 - q)^{\frac{\rho^2 - \rho}{2}}$. Finally, this gives us the probability of having *at least* $s = 1$ successes, i.e., a successful authentication:

$$\mathrm{Succ}_{\mathcal{P},n}^{\mathrm{Auth}}(\rho) = 1 - \Pr\left[0 \text{ successes in } \binom{\rho}{2} \text{ trials}\right] = 1 - \left(1 - \frac{2}{2^n - 1}\right)^{\frac{\rho^2 - \rho}{2}}.$$

This proves the theorem. □

Note that this success probability is 0 for $\rho = 0$ and is monotonically increasing. As a function of ρ it presents itself as an S-shaped curve with a steep slope at approximately $\rho = 2^{\frac{n}{2}}$ (see Figure 3(a) for an example). Thus, for the authentication to be successful with an overwhelming probability, the size ρ of $\mathcal{P}$'s

---

[2] To simplify the discussion, we sample from the whole set $\{0,1\}^n$ instead of $\{0,1\}^n \setminus \{0^n\}$. This does not affect the overall analysis, since the value 0^n occurs with a negligible probability.

database $\mathcal{D}$ should be chosen right after this steep slope, ensuring a probability close to 1. To give the reader an idea on how the database size ρ behaves in practice, we state that sizes of about $\rho \approx 2^{17}$ or $\rho \approx 2^{25}$ are realistic in most real-world applications. Details on this and other numerical examples can be found in Section 5.[3]

3.3   Authenticated Key Exchange

A minor modification of our authentication protocol yields an authenticated key exchange between the prover $\mathcal{P}$ and the verifier $\mathcal{V}$ (here, "authenticated" refers to the verifier $\mathcal{V}$ only, since the authentication in our protocol is unilateral). More precisely we will achieve that, if the authentication of $\mathcal{P}$ is successful, both $\mathcal{V}$ and $\mathcal{P}$ compute the same shared secret key K. If the authentication fails, $\mathcal{P}$ computes a random key, while $\mathcal{V}$ computes the "correct" key K. These two keys will be the same with a probability that is negligible in n.

Next, we describe the modification of our protocol: Let $\mathcal{H} : \{0,1\}^* \longrightarrow \{0,1\}^{2n}$ be a (publicly known) cryptographic hash function. Now, the only modifications we make to our authentication protocol are (see key computation in square brackets in Fig. 2):

1. After the prover $\mathcal{P}$ created the two PUF-challenges C_1 and C_2 together with the corresponding helper data h_1 and h_2, respectively, he computes the *key* $K = \mathcal{H}(R(C_1, h_1) \| R(C_2, h_2))$.
2. After the verifier $\mathcal{V}$ checked the authenticity of $\mathcal{P}$ and computed the message M, he computes the *key* $K = \mathcal{H}(R(C_1, h_1) \| R(C_2, h_2))$.

It can be seen immediately (when $\mathcal{H}$ is again modelled as a random oracle) that if the authentication of $\mathcal{P}$ fails, $\mathcal{P}$ will compute a key K that is uniformly distributed in $\{0,1\}^{2n}$. Therefore, the probability that $\mathcal{P}$'s key and $\mathcal{V}$'s key coincide is 2^{-2n} which is negligible in n. Otherwise, both parties have exchanged a secret key.

4   Security Model and Analysis

The security model for our authentication protocol considers a *passive* adversary $\mathcal{A}$ only.[4] This means that the adversary $\mathcal{A}$ is only able to passively listen on the communication channel, and does neither have access to the underlying PUF,

---

[3] We stress that the generation of a database of size 2^{25} in the enrolment phase is *not* impractical. The reason for this is that the enrolment phase is not carried out with the actual resource-constrained verifier but in a trusted environment. In particular, this means that the database is generated before the Controlled-PUF is engineered into the verifier-device.

[4] Our authentication protocol does not rely on a confidential communication channel. All messages are being sent in the clear. It is easy to see that, when considering an *active* adversary $\mathcal{A}$ that can for instance manipulate these messages, the authentication will fail with overwhelming probability.

nor can do any invasive analysis on the used components. More precisely, $\mathcal{A}$ is allowed to see a bounded number of protocol transcripts (a transcript is a copy of all messages sent by the prover $\mathcal{P}$ and the verifier $\mathcal{V}$ after a complete run of the authentication protocol), and then tries to break the protocol. Here, breaking the protocol means that $\mathcal{A}$ can successfully authenticate herself to the verifier $\mathcal{V}$. We briefly recall that a successful authentication amounts to finding two PUF-challenges C_1, C_2 with helper data h_1, h_2 such that for a given $\Delta \xleftarrow{U} \{0,1\}^n$,[5] the corresponding responses (after applying the hash function H and the reconstruction phase of the FE to the PUF's outputs) satisfy that $R(C_1, h_1) \oplus R(C_2, h_2) = \Delta$. Formally, the security of our protocol is modelled as follows:

Definition 1. *Let κ denote the (bit-) entropy of the output of the reconstruction phase of the FE in our authentication protocol. Then, our authentication protocol is called (t, κ, ε)-secure (against passive adversaries), if for any probabilistic polynomial time (PPT) adversary $\mathcal{A}$ who gets to see t transcripts $\tau_i = (\Delta_i, (C_i, C_i'), (h_i, h_i'))$, where $\Delta_i = R(C_i, h_i) \oplus R(C_i', h_i')$, for $i = 1, \dots, t$, successfully authenticates herself with probability at most ε, i.e.,*

$$\Pr\left[\mathcal{A}(\tau_1, \dots, \tau_t) = ((C, C'), (h, h')) \mid \Delta = R(C, h) \oplus R(C', h')\right] \leq \varepsilon,$$

where the probability is taken over the random coin tosses of $\mathcal{A}$ and random $\Delta \xleftarrow{U} \{0,1\}^n$. We denote this success probability of $\mathcal{A}$ by $\mathsf{Succ}_{\mathcal{A},n,\kappa}(t)$.

This section deals with the question of how many protocol transcripts τ the adversary $\mathcal{A}$ has to see *at least* in order to successfully authenticate herself with some prescribed probability p. In other words, we will derive a formula that computes the success probability $\mathsf{Succ}^{wc}_{\mathcal{A},n,\kappa}(t)$ of a *worst-case* adversary $\mathcal{A}$ that gets to see t transcripts. Before we do so, we need to clarify what the worst-case scenario is. To this end, we first show that since an adversary $\mathcal{A}$ never sees neither the PUF-responses nor the actual outputs of the complete construction (i.e., after applying the hash function and the FE to the PUF's outputs), the helper data h that is included in each transcript τ is completely independent of the PUF-challenges C and hence is of *no* use to $\mathcal{A}$.

On the Inutility of Helper Data. We assume that the underlying PUF produces at least 2^κ many different responses. The only relation of the helper data to the PUF-challenges is the value Δ and the PUF-responses (which the adversary $\mathcal{A}$ never sees): By construction, we have that $R(C, h) = H(\gamma)$ and $R(C', h') = H(\gamma')$ (with $H(\gamma) \oplus H(\gamma') = \Delta$) where γ, γ' are outputs of the reconstruction phase of the FE each having κ bits of entropy. Since we assume that the adversary $\mathcal{A}$ does not know the behaviour of the used PUF, she does not have any information about the PUF-responses R and R' of C and C', respectively. But for each helper data h, there are at least 2^κ different PUF-responses R that,

---

[5] We include the zero element 0^n as possible Δ-value, since it occurs with negligble probability but simplifies the discussion in this section.

together with the helper data h, will lead to a valid γ in the reconstruction phase of the FE. Then in turn, checking which γ is the correct one, the adversary $\mathcal{A}$ first needs to compute $H(\gamma)$ (and analogously $H(\gamma')$) and then check whether $H(\gamma) \oplus H(\gamma') = \Delta$. Since the hash function H is modelled as a random oracle, the best $\mathcal{A}$ can do is to fix the first hash value $H(\gamma)$ and then try all 2^{κ} many γ' (brute-force) or to guess this value, which is successful with probability 2^{κ}. Obviously, we can do the same discussion with randomly chosen helper data, which shows that the helper data is indistinguishable (in the parameter κ) from random to $\mathcal{A}$.

The Worst-Case Scenario. After seeing t transcripts, the adversary $\mathcal{A}$ has a database of t (not necessarily different) tuples of the form $(\Delta, (C, C'), (h, h'))$ such that $R(C, h) \oplus R(C', h') = \Delta$. We emphasize that $\mathcal{A}$ does not know the actual values $R(C, h)$. Now, the previous discussion allows us to forget about the helper data part in $\mathcal{A}$'s database, as it does not give the adversary any additional information (from now on, we will write $R(C)$ instead of $R(C, h)$). Then in turn, we can think of $\mathcal{A}$'s database as being a list of $2t$ PUF-challenges $C_1, \ldots, C_{2t}$ where $\mathcal{A}$ knows for at least t pairs the value $R(C_i) \oplus R(C_j) = \Delta_{i,j}$.

We consider the following example and assume that one of the PUF-challenges is always fixed, say to C_1. Then, after seeing t transcripts, the adversary $\mathcal{A}$ gets the following system of t equations:

$$R(C_1) \oplus R(C_j) = \Delta_{1,j} \text{ for all } j = 2, \ldots, t+1.$$

Adding any two of these yields a new equation of the form $R(C_i) \oplus R(C_j) = \Delta_{i,j}$ for $2 \le i < j \le t+1$. This means that the adversary can construct up to $\binom{t}{2} - t$ additional Δ-values that she has not seen before in any of the transcripts. Note that this is all an adversary can do, since the challenges and the values Δ are chosen uniformly at random and the PUF is unpredictable. Moreover, if one of these Δ's is challenged in an authentication, the adversary can check whether she can construct it from her known PUF-challenges in her database. We therefore call such Δ-values $\mathcal{A}$-*checkable*.

With this example in mind, we see that the *worst-case scenario* (which is the best case for the adversary) occurs, when there are exactly $\binom{t}{2}$ $\mathcal{A}$-checkable Δ-values. On the other hand, there are only 2^n different Δ-values in total, so if $\binom{t}{2} = \frac{t^2 - t}{2} = 2^n$, all Δ-values are $\mathcal{A}$-checkable and the adversary can successfully authenticate with probability 1. This equation, however, is satisfied if and only if t is a positive root of the degree 2 polynomial $X^2 - X - 2^{n+1}$, which in turn is satisfied if and only if $t = \frac{1}{2} + \frac{1}{2}\sqrt{1 + 2^{n+3}}$ by using the "quadratic formula". This means that once the adversary $\mathcal{A}$ has seen more than $t = \lfloor \frac{1}{2} + \frac{1}{2}\sqrt{1 + 2^{n+3}} \rfloor$ transcripts, she can successfully authenticate herself with probability 1 in the worst-case scenario.

Security Analysis. Having clarified what the worst-case scenario is, considering a passive adversary $\mathcal{A}$, we can finally prove the main theorem of this section:

Theorem 2. *Our authentication protocol is* $(t, \kappa, \mathsf{Succ}^{\mathrm{wc}}_{\mathcal{A},n,\kappa}(t))$-*secure, where*

$$\mathsf{Succ}^{\mathrm{wc}}_{\mathcal{A},n,\kappa}(t) = \begin{cases} 1 & \text{, if } t > \left\lfloor \frac{1}{2} + \frac{1}{2}\sqrt{1 + 2^{n+3}} \right\rfloor \\ \frac{(2^{\kappa}-1)t^2 - (2^{\kappa}-1)t + 2^{n+1}}{2^{n+\kappa+1}} & \text{, else} \end{cases}$$

is the probability of a worst-case adversary $\mathcal{A}$ successesfully authenticating herself after having seen t transcripts, and κ is the (bit-) entropy of the FE's output.

Proof. Let $\mathcal{B}$ be an arbitrary PPT adversary on our authentication protocol. Since $\mathcal{A}$ is a worst-case adversary, we have that $\mathsf{Succ}_{\mathcal{B},n,\kappa}(t) \leq \mathsf{Succ}^{\mathrm{wc}}_{\mathcal{A},n,\kappa}(t)$. So by Definition 1, it suffices to compute $\mathsf{Succ}^{\mathrm{wc}}_{\mathcal{A},n,\kappa}(t)$. Right above the Theorem, we have already shown that $\mathsf{Succ}^{\mathrm{wc}}_{\mathcal{A},n,\kappa}(t) = 1$, if $t > \left\lfloor \frac{1}{2} + \frac{1}{2}\sqrt{1 + 2^{n+3}} \right\rfloor$ by using the "quadratic formula" to find a positive root of $X^2 - X - 2^{n+1}$.

On the other hand, if $t \leq \left\lfloor \frac{1}{2} + \frac{1}{2}\sqrt{1 + 2^{n+3}} \right\rfloor$, i.e., $\binom{t}{2} \leq 2^n$, we know that there are precisely $\binom{t}{2}$ $\mathcal{A}$-checkable Δ-values, by definition of the worst-case scenario. So for a given random challenge $\Delta \xleftarrow{U} \{0,1\}^n$ (when $\mathcal{A}$ is trying to authenticate herself), the probability that we hit on one of these $\mathcal{A}$-checkable Δ-values is $\frac{\binom{t}{2}}{2^n} = \frac{t^2 - t}{2^{n+1}}$, i.e.,

$$\Pr_{\Delta \xleftarrow{U} \{0,1\}^n} [\Delta \text{ is } \mathcal{A}\text{-checkable}] = \frac{t^2 - t}{2^{n+1}}.$$

Then again, if we hit on a Δ that is not $\mathcal{A}$-checkable, we know by definition of the worst case that it cannot be the XOR of two responses to values in $\mathcal{A}$'s database at all. This is because if there are precisely $\binom{t}{2}$ many $\mathcal{A}$-checkable Δ-values, the adversary $\mathcal{A}$ can only construct precisely t linearly dependent equations from the t transcripts she has seen. However, this means that there are $\binom{t}{2}$ many Δ-values that can be constructed as the XOR of two responses to values in $\mathcal{A}$'s database. But since there are precisely $\binom{t}{2}$ many $\mathcal{A}$-checkable Δ-values, these must have been all such values.

Now that we know the probability of hitting on an $\mathcal{A}$-checkable Δ-value, we also know the probability of not hitting on one, namely:

$$\Pr_{\Delta \xleftarrow{U} \{0,1\}^n} [\Delta \text{ is not } \mathcal{A}\text{-checkable}] = 1 - \frac{t^2 - t}{2^{n+1}} = \frac{2^{n+1} - t^2 + t}{2^{n+1}}.$$

In such a case though, the adversary $\mathcal{A}$ cannot do better than guessing two PUF-challenges C_1, C_2 (and actually some random helper data that we neglect here, although it would actually reduce the success probability of $\mathcal{A}$ even more). But the probability of guessing correctly (meaning that $R(C_1) \oplus R(C_2) = \Delta$) is upper bounded by the probability of guessing two outputs γ_1, γ_2 of the FE such that $H(\gamma_1) \oplus H(\gamma_2) = \Delta$, which is $\frac{1}{2^{\kappa}}$ where κ is the (bit-) entropy of the outputs of the FE. So if Δ is not $\mathcal{A}$-checkable, the success probability of $\mathcal{A}$ is less or equal to $\frac{2^{n+1} - t^2 + t}{2^{n+1}} \cdot \frac{1}{2^{\kappa}}$.

In total, this shows that if $t \leq \lfloor \frac{1}{2} + \frac{1}{2}\sqrt{1 + 2^{n+3}} \rfloor$, $\mathcal{A}$'s probability of successfully authenticating herself is upper bounded by

$$\frac{(2^\kappa - 1)t^2 - (2^\kappa - 1)t + 2^{n+1}}{2^{n+\kappa+1}}.$$

This completes the proof.   □

We stress that by considering a worst-case adversary, the probability in Theorem 2 is overly pessimistic since the described worst-case scenario does happen with a very small probability only. Furthermore, we want to mention that in many existing authentication schemes, a passive adversary can perform model-building attacks on the used PUF [25]. This is done by collecting a subset of all CRPs, and then trying to create a mathematical model that allows emulating the PUF in software. However, for this attack to work, the adversary needs to have access to the PUF's responses. We counter this problem in our protocol by using a controlled PUF which hides the actual PUF responses from the adversary. This way of protecting protocols against model-building attacks is well-known and also mentioned in [25].

Replay Attacks. We stress that our above worst-case analysis captures replay attacks as well. In fact, by the birthday paradox, the probability of a successful replay attack (after having seen t transcripts) equals $1 - e^{-\frac{t^2}{2^{n+1}}}$. But this term grows more slowly than $\mathsf{Succ}^{\mathrm{wc}}_{\mathcal{A},n,\kappa}(t)$ and is always smaller than this for relevant sizes of t. For realistic values, such as $n = 32$ and $\kappa = 48$ (cf. Section 5), the probability of a successful replay attack is *always* smaller than $\mathsf{Succ}^{\mathrm{wc}}_{\mathcal{A},n,\kappa}(t)$ when the adversary has seen more than $t = 2581$ transcripts. But even if the adversary sees $t = 9268$ transcripts, this probability is still to small to raise any realistic security concerns.

5   Instantiation of the Protocol

In this section, we give a concrete instantiation of our authentication protocol which involves choosing appropriate PUFs, Fuzzy Extractors, Random Number Generators, and hash functions. Starting with the first of these, we note that we will use Arbiter PUFs which, according to [17], have a bit error rate ℓ of 3%. We stress again that our authentication protocol hides the PUF-responses, so the existing model-building attacks [25] do not work. Based on the PUF's error rate, we choose a binary linear $[\mu, k, d]$-code that can correct at least the errors that the PUF produces, for the Fuzzy Extractor. In practice, we use a certain Golay code from [3] for this implementation. An example step-by-step implementation is as follows:

1. Fix a desired output length n of the controlled PUF and the desired entropy κ we want the FE to have – these lengths basically are the security parameters as they determines the amount of protocol transcripts a worst-case adversary is allowed to see before she can break the protocol with a prescribed success

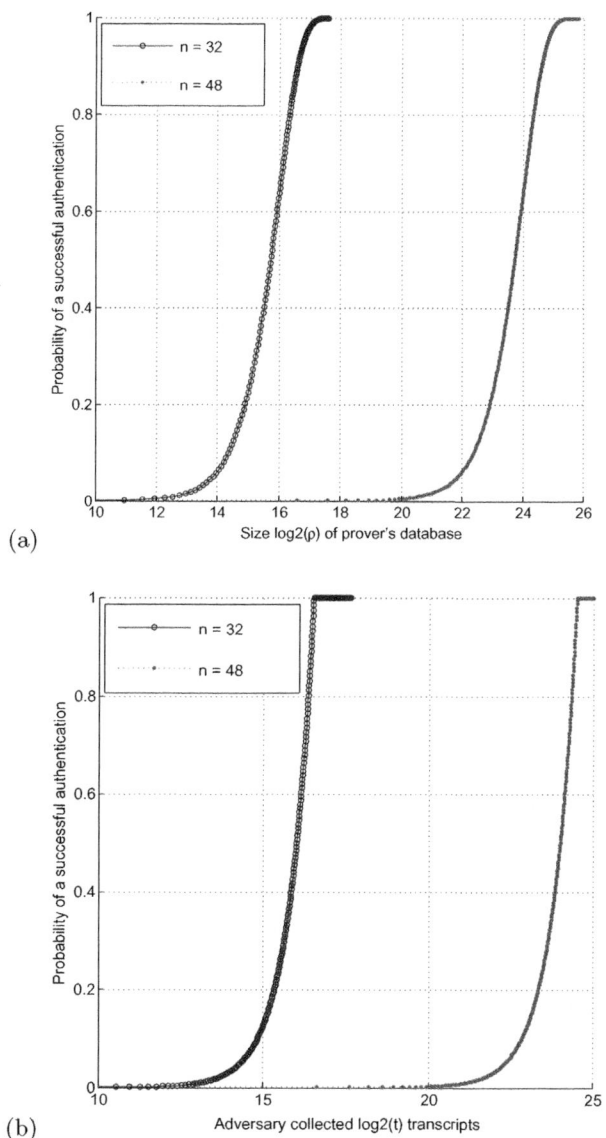

(a)

(b)

Fig. 3. (a) Probability $\mathsf{Succ}_{\mathcal{P},n}^{\mathrm{Auth}}(\rho)$ of a successful authentication for varying sizes ρ of $\mathcal{P}$'s database $\mathcal{D}$ and fixed values $n = 32$ and $n = 48$. (b) Success probability $\mathsf{Succ}_{\mathcal{A},n,\kappa}^{\mathrm{wc}}(t)$ of a worst-case adversary $\mathcal{A}$ for a growing number of protocol transcripts t she has seen and fixed values $n = 32$ and $n = 48$, while $\kappa = 48$. Note the logarithmic x-axis.

probability (cf. Theorem 2). Here, we fix $n = 32$, $\kappa = 48$ and want to bound the success probability by 0.01. As an alternative, we also provide the case where $n = 48$ for the same $\kappa = 48$.

2. Choose a cryptographic hash function $H : \{0,1\}^* \longrightarrow \{0,1\}^n$. Here, we use an LFSR-based Toeplitz Hash function of output length 32 (cf. [9]). In our alternative parameter setting, we need an output length of 48 bits.

3. Choose κ Arbiter PUFs – this ensures precisely 2^κ many PUF-responses.

4. Choose a binary linear $[\mu, k, d]$-code $\mathcal{C}$ which can correct at least $\frac{\ell \cdot \kappa}{100}$ errors. Here, we choose a $[23, 12, 7]$-Golay code (from [3]) which can correct up to $3 \geq \frac{3 \cdot 48}{100} \approx 2$ errors. In order to get an entropy of $\kappa = 48$ bits in the FE's output, we divide an output of the PUF into 4 parts containing 12 bits each. Then, we append 11 zeros to each part to ensure a length of 23. After this we continue with the usual protocol, which means that we have to use the reconstruction phase of the FE 4 times and create 4 helper data. In each authentication round, the prover then needs to send 4 helper data instead of just 1. As we have shown in Section 4, this does not affect the security of our scheme. The reconstruction phase of the FE also needs to run 4 times which creates 4 code words $\gamma_1, \ldots, \gamma_4$ of length 23 containing 12 bits of entropy each. The final evaluation of the hash function H will then be on the concatenation of these 4 code words, i.e., $H(\gamma_1 \| \ldots \| \gamma_4)$. We notice that the input $\gamma_1 \| \ldots \| \gamma_4$ to H has 48 bits of entropy which means that in Theorem 2, we can use the paramater $\kappa = 48$ as we desired.

According to Theorem 1, when our protocol is instatiated with these parameters where $n = 32$, $\kappa = 48$ (or $n = 48$), the prover $\mathcal{P}$'s database $\mathcal{D}$ can be constructed to have size $\rho = 140639$ (or $\rho = 36003337$) which ensures a successful authentication with probability $\mathsf{Succ}_{\mathcal{P},n}^{\mathrm{Auth}}(\rho) \geq 0.99$ (or $\mathsf{Succ}_{\mathcal{P},n}^{\mathrm{Auth}}(\rho) \geq 0.99$), cf. Fig. 3(a). Concerning the security of our protocol in this instantiation, Fig. 3(b) tells us that a worst-case adversary is allowed to see at most $t = 9268$ (or $t = 2372657$) protocol transcripts to ensure a success probability $\mathsf{Succ}_{\mathcal{A},n,\kappa}^{\mathrm{wc}}(t) < 0.01$ (or $\mathsf{Succ}_{\mathcal{A},n,\kappa}^{\mathrm{wc}}(t) < 0.01$), cf. Theorem 2.

Depending on the application scenario, we can arbitrarily vary the above parameters in order to get a higher level of security but on the cost of efficiency.

6   Conclusion

Motivated by the fact that previous PUF-based authentication protocols fail to work in some application scenarios, we introduced the new notion of *converse* PUF-based authentication: opposed to previous solutions, in our approach the verifier holds a PUF while the prover does not. We presented the first such protocol, gave an extensive security analysis, and showed that it can also be used for authenticated key exchange. Besides the mentioned application examples in the present paper, future work includes the employment of our new protocol to other applications. Additionally, we consider an actual implementation on resource-constraint devices (such as sensor nodes) as an interesting work to pursue.

Acknowledgement. This work has been supported in part by the European Commission through the FP7 programme under contract 238811 UNIQUE.

References

1. Armknecht, F., Maes, R., Sadeghi, A.-R., Sunar, B., Tuyls, P.: Memory Leakage-Resilient Encryption Based on Physically Unclonable Functions. In: Matsui, M. (ed.) ASIACRYPT 2009. LNCS, vol. 5912, pp. 685–702. Springer, Heidelberg (2009)

2. Bellare, M., Rogaway, P.: Random oracles are practical: A paradigm for designing efficient protocols. In: ACM CCS 1993, pp. 62–73. ACM (1993)

3. Bösch, C., Guajardo, J., Sadeghi, A.-R., Shokrollahi, J., Tuyls, P.: Efficient Helper Data Key Extractor on FPGAs. In: Oswald, E., Rohatgi, P. (eds.) CHES 2008. LNCS, vol. 5154, pp. 181–197. Springer, Heidelberg (2008)

4. Bringer, J., Chabanne, H., Icart, T.: On Physical Obfuscation of Cryptographic Algorithms. In: Roy, B., Sendrier, N. (eds.) INDOCRYPT 2009. LNCS, vol. 5922, pp. 88–103. Springer, Heidelberg (2009)

5. Das, A., Kocabaş, Ü., Sadeghi, A.-R., Verbauwhede, I.: PUF-based Secure Test Wrapper Design for Cryptographic SoC Testing. In: Design, Automation and Test in Europe (DATE). IEEE (2012)

6. Dodis, Y., Reyzin, L., Smith, A.: Fuzzy Extractors: How to Generate Strong Keys from Biometrics and Other Noisy Data. In: Cachin, C., Camenisch, J.L. (eds.) EUROCRYPT 2004. LNCS, vol. 3027, pp. 523–540. Springer, Heidelberg (2004)

7. Eichhorn, I., Koeberl, P., van der Leest, V.: Logically reconfigurable PUFs: Memory-based secure key storage. In: ACM Workshop on Scalable Trusted Computing (ACM STC), pp. 59–64. ACM, New York (2011)

8. Gassend, B.: Physical Random Functions. Master's thesis, MIT, MA, USA (January 2003)

9. Gassend, B., Clarke, D., van Dijk, M., Devadas, S.: Controlled physical random functions. In: Computer Security Applications Conference (ACSAC), pp. 149–160. IEEE (2002)

10. Gassend, B., Clarke, D., van Dijk, M., Devadas, S.: Controlled physical random functions. In: Computer Security Applications Conference (ACSAC), pp. 149–160. IEEE (2002)

11. Gassend, B., Clarke, D., van Dijk, M., Devadas, S.: Silicon physical random functions. In: Proceedings of the 9th ACM Conference on Computer and Communications Security (CCS 2002), pp. 148–160. ACM (2002)

12. Gassend, B., Clarke, D., van Dijk, M., Devadas, S.: Silicon physical random functions. In: ACM Conference on Computer and Communications Security (ACM CCS), pp. 148–160. ACM, New York (2002)

13. Guajardo, J., Kumar, S.S., Schrijen, G.-J., Tuyls, P.: FPGA Intrinsic PUFs and Their Use for IP Protection. In: Paillier, P., Verbauwhede, I. (eds.) CHES 2007. LNCS, vol. 4727, pp. 63–80. Springer, Heidelberg (2007)

14. Guajardo, J., Kumar, S.S., Schrijen, G.-J., Tuyls, P.: Brand and IP protection with physical unclonable functions. In: IEEE International Symposium on Circuits and Systems (ISCAS) 2008, pp. 3186–3189. IEEE (May 2008)

15. Holcomb, D.E., Burleson, W.P., Fu, K.: Initial SRAM state as a fingerprint and source of true random numbers for RFID tags. In: Conference on RFID Security 2007, Malaga, Spain, July 11-13 (2007)

16. Kumar, S.S., Guajardo, J., Maes, R., Schrijen, G.-J., Tuyls, P.: Extended abstract: The butterfly PUF protecting IP on every FPGA. In: Workshop on Hardware-Oriented Security (HOST), pp. 67–70. IEEE (June 2008)

17. Lee, J.W., Lim, D., Gassend, B., Suh, E.G., van Dijk, M., Devadas, S.: A technique to build a secret key in integrated circuits for identification and authentication applications. In: Symposium on VLSI Circuits, pp. 176–179. IEEE (June 2004)
18. Lim, D., Lee, J.W., Gassend, B., Suh, E.G., van Dijk, M., Devadas, S.: Extracting secret keys from integrated circuits. IEEE Transactions on Very Large Scale Integration (VLSI) Systems 13(10), 1200–1205 (2005)
19. Lin, L., Holcomb, D., Krishnappa, D.K., Shabadi, P., Burleson, W.: Low-power sub-threshold design of secure physical unclonable functions. In: International Symposium on Low-Power Electronics and Design (ISLPED), pp. 43–48. IEEE (August 2010)
20. Maes, R., Tuyls, P., Verbauwhede, I.: Intrinsic PUFs from flip-flops on reconfigurable devices (November 2008)
21. Maes, R., Verbauwhede, I.: Physically unclonable functions: A study on the state of the art and future research directions. In: Towards Hardware-Intrinsic Security (2010)
22. Maiti, A., Casarona, J., McHale, L., Schaumont, P.: A large scale characterization of RO-PUF. In: International Symposium on Hardware-Oriented Security and Trust (HOST), pp. 94–99. IEEE (June 2010)
23. Öztürk, E., Hammouri, G., Sunar, B.: Towards robust low cost authentication for pervasive devices. In: International Conference on Pervasive Computing and Communications (PerCom), pp. 170–178. IEEE, Washington, DC (2008)
24. Ranasinghe, D.C., Engels, D.W., Cole, P.H.: Security and privacy: Modest proposals for Low-Cost RFID systems. In: Auto-ID Labs Research Workshop (September 2004)
25. Rührmair, U., Sehnke, F., Sölter, J., Dror, G., Devadas, S., Schmidhuber, J.: Modeling attacks on physical unclonable functions. In: ACM Conference on Computer and Communications Security (ACM CCS), pp. 237–249. ACM, New York (2010)
26. Sadeghi, A.-R., Visconti, I., Wachsmann, C.: Enhancing RFID security and privacy by physically unclonable functions. In: Towards Hardware-Intrinsic Security. Information Security and Cryptography, pp. 281–305. Springer, Heidelberg (2010)
27. Schulz, S., Sadeghi, A.-R., Wachsmann, C.: Short paper: Lightweight remote attestation using physical functions. In: Proceedings of the Fourth ACM Conference on Wireless Network Security (ACM WiSec), pp. 109–114. ACM, New York (2011)
28. Su, Y., Holleman, J., Otis, B.P.: A digital 1.6 pJ/bit chip identification circuit using process variations. IEEE Journal of Solid-State Circuits 43(1), 69–77 (2008)
29. Suh, E.G., Devadas, S.: Physical unclonable functions for device authentication and secret key generation. In: ACM/IEEE Design Automation Conference (DAC), pp. 9–14. IEEE (June 2007)
30. Tuyls, P., Batina, L.: RFID-Tags for Anti-counterfeiting. In: Pointcheval, D. (ed.) CT-RSA 2006. LNCS, vol. 3860, pp. 115–131. Springer, Heidelberg (2006)
31. Tuyls, P., Schrijen, G.-J., Škorić, B., van Geloven, J., Verhaegh, N., Wolters, R.: Read-Proof Hardware from Protective Coatings. In: Goubin, L., Matsui, M. (eds.) CHES 2006. LNCS, vol. 4249, pp. 369–383. Springer, Heidelberg (2006)
32. van der Leest, V., Schrijen, G.-J., Handschuh, H., Tuyls, P.: Hardware intrinsic security from D flip-flops. In: ACM Workshop on Scalable Trusted Computing (ACM STC), pp. 53–62. ACM, New York (2010)
33. Škorić, B., Tuyls, P., Ophey, W.: Robust Key Extraction from Physical Uncloneable Functions. In: Ioannidis, J., Keromytis, A.D., Yung, M. (eds.) ACNS 2005. LNCS, vol. 3531, pp. 407–422. Springer, Heidelberg (2005)

Trustworthy Execution on Mobile Devices: What Security Properties Can My Mobile Platform Give *Me*?

Amit Vasudevan, Emmanuel Owusu, Zongwei Zhou,
James Newsome, and Jonathan M. McCune

CyLab/Carnegie Mellon University
{amitvasudevan,eowusu,stephenzhou,jnewsome,jonmccune}@cmu.edu

Abstract. We are now in the post-PC era, yet our mobile devices are insecure. We consider the different stake-holders in today's mobile device ecosystem, and analyze why widely-deployed hardware security primitives on mobile device platforms are inaccessible to application developers and end-users. We systematize existing proposals for leveraging such primitives, and show that they can indeed strengthen the security properties available to applications and users, all without reducing the properties currently enjoyed by OEMs and network carriers. We also highlight shortcomings of existing proposals and make recommendations for future research that may yield practical, deployable results.

1 Introduction

We are putting ever more trust in mobile devices. We use them for e-commerce and banking, whether through a web browser or specialized *apps*. Such apps hold high-value credentials and process sensitive data that need to be protected. Meanwhile, mobile phone OSes are untrustworthy. While in principle they attempt to be more secure than desktop OSes (e.g., by preventing modified OSes from booting, by using safer languages, or by sandboxing mechanisms for third-party apps such as capabilities), in practice they are still fraught with vulnerabilities.

Mobile OSes are as complex as desktop OSes. Isolation and sandboxing provided by the OS is routinely broken, c.f. Apple iOS jail-breaking by *clicking a button on a web page* [11, 42]. Mobile OSes often share code with open-source OSes such as GNU/Linux, but often lag behind in applying security fixes, meaning that attackers need only look at recent patches to the open-source code to find vulnerabilities in the mobile device's code. Therefore, there is a need for isolation and security primitives exposed to application developers in such a way that they need not trust the host OS.

We argue that this problem is severe enough to have garnered significant attention outside of the security community. Demand for mobile applications with stronger security requirements has given rise to add-on hardware with stronger security properties (§2). However, many current mobile devices already have hardware support for isolated execution environments and other security features. Unfortunately, these features are not made available to all parties who may benefit from their presence.

Today's mobile device hardware and software ecosystem consists of multiple *stake-holders*, primarily comprising the OEM (handset manufacturer), telecommunications

S. Katzenbeisser et al. (Eds.): TRUST 2012, LNCS 7344, pp. 159–178, 2012.

provider or carrier, application developers, and the device's owner (the human user). Carriers typically also serve in the role of platform integrator, customizing an OEM's handset with additional features and branding (typically via firmware or custom apps). To date, security properties desirable from the perspectives of application developers and users have been secondary concerns to the OEMs and carriers [10, 33, 45]. The historically closed partnerships between OEMs and carriers have lead to a monolithic trust model within today's fielded hardware security primitives. Everything "inside" is assumed to be trustworthy, i.e., the software modules executing in the isolated environment often reside in each other's trusted computing base (TCB). As long as this situation persists, OEMs and carriers will not allow third-party code to leverage these features. Only in a few cases, where the OEM has partnered with a third party, are these features used to protect the *user's* data (c.f. §2, Google Wallet).

We approach this scenario optimistically, and argue that there is room to meet the needs of application developers and users while adding negligible cost. We thus define the principal challenge for the technical community: **to present sound technical evidence that application developers and users can simultaneously benefit from hardware security features without detracting from the security properties required for the OEMs and carriers.**[1] Our goal in this paper is to systematize deployed (or readily available) hardware security features, and to provide an extensive and realistic evaluation of existing (largely academic) proposals for multiplexing these features amongst *all* stake-holders.

We proceed in §3 by defining a set of security features that may be useful for application developers that need to process sensitive data. Our focus is on protecting secrets belonging to the *user*, such as credentials used to authenticate to online services and locally cached data.

We next provide an overview of hardware security features available on today's mobile platforms (§4). We show that hardware security features that can provide the desired properties to application developers are prevalent, but they are typically not accessible in COTS devices' default configurations.

We then move on to evaluate existing proposals (given the hardware security features available on mobile devices) for creating a trustworthy execution environment that is able to safely run sensitive applications that are potentially considered untrustworthy by other stake-holders (§5). We show that multiplexing these secure execution environments for mutually-distrusting sensitive applications is quite possible if the threat model for application developers and users is primarily software-based attacks (§6).

Finally (§7), we provide an end-to-end analysis and recommendations for the current best practices for making the most of mobile hardware-based security features, from the points of view of each stake-holder. Unfortunately, without firmware or software changes by OEMs and carriers, individual application developers today have little opportunity to leverage the hardware security primitives in today's mobile platforms. The only real options are either to partner with a mobile platform integrator, to distribute

---

[1] We wish to distinguish this challenge from proposals that OEMs increase their hardware costs by including additional hardware security features that are exclusively of interest to application developers and users. Our intention in this paper is to emphasize practicality, and thus define such proposals to be out of scope.

a customized peripheral (e.g., a smart-card-like device that can integrate with a phone, such as a storage card with additional functionality), or to purchase unlocked development hardware. We provide recommendations for OEMs and carriers for how they can make hardware-based security capabilities more readily accessible to application developers without compromising the security of their existing uses.

2 Demand for Applications Requiring Hardware Security

Does providing third-party developers with access to hardware-supported security features make sense for the OEMs or carriers? This is an important consideration for an industry where a few cents in cost savings can be the deciding factor for features. We show that there are many applications on mobile devices that require strong security features, and that must currently work around the lack of those features. Being forced to deal with these work-arounds stifles the market for security-sensitive mobile applications, and endangers the security of the applications that are deployed anyways.

Google Wallet[2] allows consumers to use their mobile phones as a virtual wallet. The application stores users' payment credentials locally, which are then used to make transactions via near field communication (NFC) with point-of-sale (POS) devices. To store the users' credentials securely, Wallet relies on a co-processor called a Secure Element (SE) which provides isolated execution (§3), secure storage (§3), and a trusted path (§3) to the on-board NFC radio. Unfortunately, the SE only runs code that is signed by the device manufacturer. This may be because the SE lacks the ability to isolate authorized modules from each-other, or it may simply be considered a waste of time. As a result, developers without Google's clout will not be able to leverage these capabilities for their own applications. There is evidence that Apple has similar plans for its products; they recently published a patent for an embedded SE with space allocated for both a Universal Subscriber Identity Module (USIM) application and "other" applications [41].

Services such as Square and GoPay allow merchants to complete credit card transactions with their mobile device using an application and a magnetic stripe reader [34]. While Square's security policies[3] indicate that they do not store credit card data on the mobile device, the data does not appear to be adequately protected when it passes through the mobile device. Researchers have verified that the stripe reader does not protect the secrecy or integrity of the read-data [37]. This implies that malware on the mobile device could likely eavesdrop on credit-card data for swiped cards or inject stolen credit-card information to make a purchase [37].

These applications could benefit greatly from the hardware-backed security features we describe in §3. A trusted path (§3) could enforce that the intended client application has exclusive access to the audio port (with which the card readers interface), thus protecting the secrecy and integrity of that data from malware. They could also benefit greatly from a remote attestation mechanism (§3), which the servers could use to ensure that received-data is actually from the authorized client-application, and that it used a trusted-path to the reader, thus helping to ensure that the physical credit card was

---

[2] http://www.google.com/wallet/how-it-works-security.html
[3] https://squareup.com/security

actually present. OEMs could provide a more tightly integrated experience for developers, and avoid potential security vulnerabilities by opening up pre-existing hardware security primitives to application developers.

3   Desired Security Features

Here we describe a set of features intended to enable secure execution on mobile devices. This can be interpreted as the wish-list for a security-conscious application developer. The strength of these features can typically be measured by the size, complexity, and attack surface of the components that must be relied upon for a given security property to hold. This is often referred to as the *trusted computing base* (TCB). On many systems, the OS provides security-relevant APIs for application developers. However, this places the OS in the TCB, meaning that a compromised OS voids the relevant security properties. We briefly discuss whether and how the security features below are provided on today's mobile platforms, and some strategies for providing these properties to applications without including the OS in the TCB.

Isolated Execution. Isolated execution gives the application developer the ability to run a software module in complete isolation from other code. It provides secrecy and integrity of that module's code and data at *run-time*. Today's mobile OSes provide process-based isolation to protect applications' address spaces and other system resources. However, these mechanisms are circumventable when the OS itself is compromised. To provide isolated execution that does not depend on the operating system, some alternative execution environment not under control of the OS is required. Such an environment could be provided by a layer running under the OS on the same hardware (i.e., a hypervisor), or in a parallel environment (such as a separate coprocessor). We examine some candidate isolated execution environments and their suitability for mobile platforms in §5. Regarding today's mobile platforms, the Meego Linux distribution for mobile devices does include provisions for isolated execution. Meego's Mobile Simplified Security Framework (MSSF) implements a trusted execution environment (TrEE) that is protected from the OS [29]. However, this environment is not open to third party developers.

Secure Storage. Secure storage provides secrecy, integrity, and/or freshness for a software module's data *at rest* (primarily when the device is powered off, but also under certain conditions based upon which software has loaded). The most common example demonstrating the need for secure storage is access credentials, such as a cached password or a private asymmetric key. Most mobile OSes provide this property at least using file system permissions, which are enforced by the operating system. However, this can be circumvented by compromising the OS or by removing the storage media and accessing it directly.

A stronger form of secure storage can be built using a storage location that is physically protected, and with access control implemented independently of the OS – called a *root of trust for storage*, or RTS. A RTS can be used to bootstrap a larger secure storage mechanism, using *sealed storage*. The sealed storage primitive uses a key protected by the RTS to encrypt the given data, and to protect the authenticity of that data and of attached meta-data. The metadata includes an access-control-policy for which code is authorized to request decryption (e.g., represented as a hash over the code), and potentially other data such as which software module sealed the data in the first place. Sealed data (ciphertext) can then be stored on an unprotected storage device.

Symbian and Meego make use of protected memory and sealed storage [29]. MSSF uses keys kept in its Trusted Execution Environment (TrEE) (§3) to protect the integrity of application binaries, and to provide a sealed storage facility, which *is* available to third party developers [29]. While this offers protection against offline attacks, since third party applications are not allowed to execute in the TrEE, data protected by this mechanism is vulnerable to online attacks via a compromised OS. Recent versions of iOS combine a user-secret with a protected device-key to implement secure storage [3]. However, the device-key does not appear to be access-controlled by code identity, meaning that an attacker can defeat this mechanism if he is able to obtain the user secret, e.g., via malware, or via performing an online brute-force attack [17, 25]. Android offers an AccountManager API [2]. The model used by this API supports code modules that perform operations on the stored credential rather than releasing them directly, which would make it amenable to a model with sealed storage and isolated execution. Unfortunately, it appears that the data is currently stored in plaintext, and can be retrieved via direct access to the storage device or by compromising the operating system [1, 50].

Remote Attestation. Remote attestation allows remote parties to verify that a particular message originated from a particular software module. For an application running on a normal OS, the attestation would necessarily include a measurement of the OS kernel, which is part of that TCB, and of the application itself. A remote party, such as an online banking service, could use this information, if it knew a list of valid OS kernel identities and a list of valid client banking-app identities, to ensure that the system had booted a known-good kernel, and that the OS had launched a known-good version of the client banking app. Remote attestations are more meaningful when the TCB is relatively small and stable. In the example of a banking application, if a critical component of the app ran as a module in an isolated execution environment with a remote-attestation capability, then the attestation would only need to include a measurement of the smaller isolated execution environment code, and of the given module. Not only would it be easier to keep track of a list of known-good images but the attestation would be more meaningful because the isolated execution environment is presumed to be less susceptible to run-time compromise. This is important because the attestation only tells the verifier what code was *loaded*; it would not detect if a run-time exploit overwrote that code with unauthorized code.

Attestation mechanisms are typically built using a private key that is only accessible by a small TCB (§3) and kept in secure storage (§3). A certificate issued by a trusted party, such as the device manufacturer, certifies that the corresponding public key belongs to the device. One or more platform configuration registers store measurements of loaded code. The private key can then be used to generate signed attestations about its state or the state of the rest of the system. Some forms of remote attestation are implemented and used on today's mobile platforms [29]. However, as far as we know, no such mechanisms are made available to arbitrary third-party developers.

Secure Provisioning. Secure provisioning is a mechanism to send data to a *specific software module*, running on a *specific device*, while protecting that data's secrecy and integrity. This is useful for migrating data between a user's devices. For example, a user may have a credential database that he wishes to migrate or synchronize across devices while ensuring that only the corresponding credential-application running on the intended destination device will be able to access that data. One way to build a secure provisioning mechanism is to use remote attestation (§3) to attest that a public encryption key belongs to a particular software module running on a particular device. The sender can then use that key to protect data to be sent to the target software module on the target device. Some of today's mobile platforms implement mechanisms to authenticate external information from the hardware stake-holders (e.g., software updates), with the hash of the public portion of the signing key stored immutably on the device [29]. Other secure provisioning mechanisms are likely implemented and used by device manufacturers to implement features such as digital rights management. As far as we know, however, secure provisioning mechanisms are not available for direct use by arbitrary third-party developers on mobile platforms.

Trusted Path. Trusted path protects authenticity, and optionally secrecy and availability, of communication between a software module and a peripheral (e.g., keyboard or touchscreen) [18,24,32,46,52]. When used with human-interface devices, this property allows a human user to ascertain precisely the application with which she is currently interacting. With full trusted path support, malicious applications that attempt to spoof legitimate applications by creating identical-looking user interfaces will conceivably become ineffective. Building secure trusted paths is a challenging problem. Zhou et. al. propose a trusted path on commodity x86 computers with a minimal TCB [52]. Their system enables users to verify the states and configurations of one or more trusted-paths using a simple, secret-less, hand-held device. In principle, many mobile platforms also support a form of trusted path, but the TCB is relatively large and untrustworthy. For example, the *Home* button on iOS and Android devices constitutes a *secure attention sequence* that by design uncircumventably transfers control of the user interface to the OS's "Home" screen. Once there, the user can transfer control to the desired application. However, the TCB for such mechanisms includes the entire OS and third-party apps. The OS can be removed from the TCB of such trusted paths by preventing the OS from communicating directly with the device and running the device driver in an isolated environment. This requires the platform to support a low-level access-control policy for access to peripherals. ARM's TrustZone extensions facilitate this type of isolation (§4.1).

4   Available Hardware Primitives

In this section we discuss currently-available hardware security primitives with a focus on existing smartphone and tablet platforms. As the vast majority of these platforms are

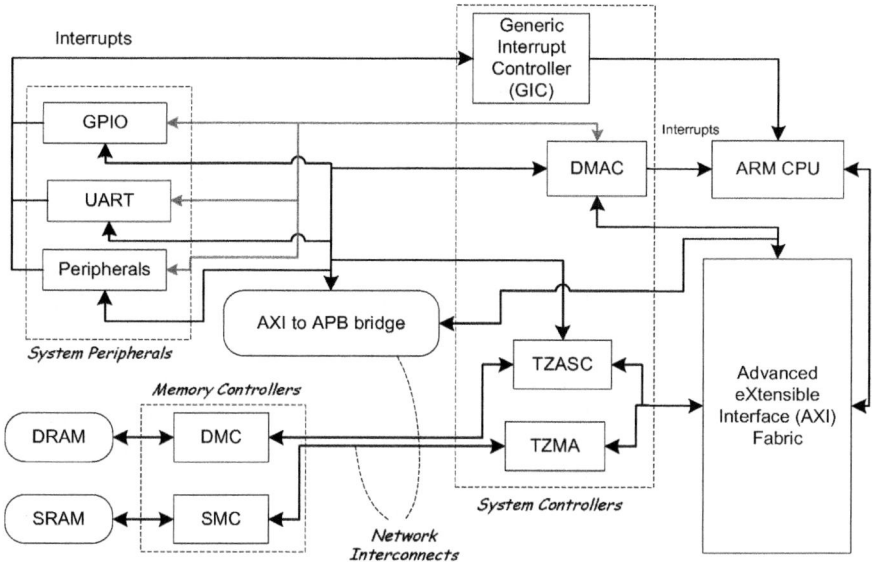

Fig. 1. Generic ARM platform hardware and security architecture

built for the ARM architecture[4], we first present a generic ARM platform hardware and security architecture, focusing our discussion on platform hardware components that help realize the features discussed in §3. We then identify design gaps and implementation challenges in off-the-shelf mobile devices that prevent third-party application developers from fully realizing the desired security properties. Finally, we provide details of inexpensive mobile *development* platforms with myriad security features, to serve as references against which to compare mass-market devices.

ARM's platform architecture comprises the Advanced Microcontroller Bus Architecture (AMBA) and different types of interconnects, controllers and peripherals. ARM calls these the "CoreLink", which has four major components (Figure 1). *Network interconnects* are the low-level physical on-chip interconnection primitives that bind various system components together. AMBA defines two basic types of interconnects: (i) the Advanced eXtensible Interface (AXI) – a high performance master and slave interconnect interface, and (ii) the Advanced Peripheral Bus (APB)—a low-bandwidth interface to peripherals. *Memory controllers* correspond to the predominant memory types: (i) static memory controllers (SMC) interfaced with SRAM, and (ii) dynamic memory controllers (DMC) interfaced with DRAM. *System controllers* include the: (i) Generic interrupt controller (GIC)—for managing device interrupts, (ii) DMA controllers (DMAC)—for direct memory access by peripheral devices, and (iii) TrustZone

---

[4] Intel ATOM [26] line of embedded processors are based on commodity x86 architecture and are also targetted towards smartphone and tablet platforms. While a few models contain security features such as hardware virtualization, the ATOM System-on-Chip (SoC) that is targetted at smartphone platforms currently does not seem to include such support [27]. We therefore focus our attention on the more widely spread ARM architecture and its security extensions.

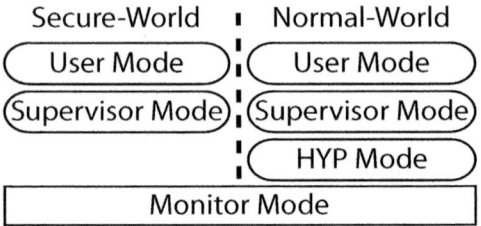

Fig. 2. ARM Isolated Execution Hardware Primitives. Split-world-based isolation enables both secure and normal processor worlds. Virtualization-based isolation adds a higher-privileged layer for a hypervisor in the normal world.

Address Space Controller (TZASC) and TrustZone Memory Adapter (TZMA)—for partitioning memory between multiple "worlds" in a split-world architecture (§4.1). *System peripherals* include LCDs, timers, UARTs, GPIO pins, etc. These peripherals can be further assigned to specific "worlds"). We now proceed to discuss the above components in the context of each of the security features described in §3.

4.1 Isolated Execution

Multiple hardware primitives exist for isolated execution on ARM architecture devices today. ARM first introduced their TrustZone Security Extensions in 2003 [4], enabling a "two-world" model, whereby both secure and non-secure software can coexist on the same processor. ARM recently announced hardware support for virtualization for their Cortex A15 CPU family [8]. These extensions enable more traditional virtualization solutions in the form of hypervisors or virtual machine monitors [39].

Split-World-Based Isolated Execution. ARM's TrustZone Security Extensions [5] enable a single physical processor core to safely and efficiently execute code in two "worlds"—the *secure world* for security sensitive application code and the *normal world* for non-secure applications (Figure 2). CPU state is banked between both worlds; the secure-world can access all normal-world state, but not vice-versa. A new processor mode, called the *monitor mode*, supports context switching between the secure-world and the normal-world. The monitor mode software is responsible for context-switching CPU state that is not automatically banked.

Memory Isolation. ARM's TrustZone Security Extensions split CPU state into two distinct worlds, but they alone cannot partition memory between the two worlds. Memory isolation is achieved using a combination of TrustZone-aware Memory Management Units (MMU), TrustZone Address Space Controllers (TZASC), TrustZone Memory Adapters (TZMA), and Tightly Coupled Memory (TCM).

A TrustZone-aware MMU provides a distinct MMU interface for each processor world, enabling each world to have a local set of virtual-to-physical memory address translation tables. The translation tables have protection mechanisms which prevent the normal-world from accessing secure-world memory. The TZASC interfaces devices such as Dynamic Memory Controllers (DMC) to partition DRAM into distinct memory regions. The TZASC has a secure-world-only programming interface that can be used to designate a given memory region as secure or normal. The TZMA provides similar functionality for off-chip ROM or SRAM. With a TZMA, ROM or SRAM can be partitioned between the two worlds. Tightly Coupled Memory (TCM) is memory that is in the same physical package as the CPU, so that physical tampering with the external pins of an integrated-based circuit will be ineffective in trying to learn the information stored in TCM. Secure-world software is responsible for configuring access permissions (secure vs. normal) for a given TCM block.

Peripheral Isolation. Peripherals in the ARM platform architecture can be designated as *secure* or *normal*. ARM's "CoreLink" architecture connects high-speed system devices such as the CPU and memory controllers using the Advanced eXtensible Interface (AXI) bus [7]. The rest of the system peripherals are typically connected using the Advanced Peripheral Bus (APB). The AXI-to-APB bridge device is responsible for interfacing the APB interconnects with the AXI fabric and contains address decode logic that selects the desired peripheral based on the security state of the incoming AXI transaction; the bridge rejects normal-world transactions to peripherals designated to be used by the secure-world. A TrustZone AXI-to-APB bridge can include an optional software programming interface that allows dynamic switching of the security state of a given peripheral. This can be used for sharing a peripheral between both the secure and normal worlds.

DMA Protection. Certain peripherals (e.g., LCD controllers and storage controllers) can transfer data to and from memory using Direct Memory Access (DMA), which is not access-controlled by the AXI-to-APB bridge. A TrustZone-aware DMA controller (DMAC) supports concurrent secure and normal peripheral DMA accesses, each with independent interrupt events. Together with the TZASC, TZMA, GIC, and the AXI-to-APB bridge, the DMAC can prevent a peripheral assigned to the normal-world from performing a DMA transfer to or from secure-world memory regions.

Hardware Interrupt Isolation. As peripherals can be assigned to either the secure or normal world, there is a need to provide basic interrupt isolation so that interrupts from secure peripherals are always handled in secure world. Hardware interrupts on the current ARM platforms can be categorized into: IRQ (normal interrupt request) and FIQ (fast interrupt request). The Generic Interrupt Controller (GIC) can configure interrupt lines as secure or normal and enables secure-world software (in monitor mode) to selectively trap such system hardware interrupts. This enables flexible interrupt partitioning models. For example, IRQs can be assigned for normal-world operations and FIQs for secure-world operations. The GIC hardware also includes logic to prevent normal-world software from modifying secure interrupt line configurations. Thus, secure world code and data can be protected from potentially malicious normal-world interrupt handlers, but TrustZone by itself is not sufficient to implement device virtualization.

Virtualization-Based Isolated Execution. ARM's Virtualization Extensions provide hardware virtualization support to normal-world software starting with the Cortex A15 CPU family [8]. The basic model for a virtualized system involves a hypervisor, that runs in a new normal-world mode called Hyp mode (Figure 2). The hypervisor is responsible for multiplexing guest OSes, which run in the normal world's traditional OS and user modes. Note that software using the secure world is unchanged by this model, as the hypervisor has no access to secure world state. The hypervisor can optionally trap any calls from a guest OS to the secure world. As hardware-supported virtualization architectures have been studied for over four decades [39], we elide further detail on the ARM specifics.

4.2 Secure Storage

Current ARM platform specifications do not include a root of trust for long-term secure storage. Platform hardware vendors are free to choose and implement a proprietary mechanism if desired. The Secure Element (SE) is one such proprietary solution for establishing a root of trust for mobile devices. SEs provide storage and processing of digital credentials and sensitive data in a physically separate protected module such as a smart-card, thereby reducing the physical attack surface. Embedded SEs are commonly used to provide security for near field communication (NFC) applications such as automated access control, ticketing, and mobile payment systems. For example, Google Wallet uses embedded secure elements to store and manage encrypted payment card credentials,[5] so that they are never available to a compromised mobile device OS. Development platforms such as the FreeScale i.MX53 (§4.7) and Texas Instruments M-Shield (§4.7), employ an embedded SE to provide a tamper-resistant secure execution and storage environment. Giesecke & Devrient and Tyfone are notable vendors currently selling removable SEs. Using these, third-party developers can develop applications against a single platform-independent interface. However, removable SEs are readily physically separated from the mobile device (e.g., the SE may be independently lost or stolen).

4.3 Remote Attestation

A remote attestation primitive relies on a private key that is exclusively accessible by a small TCB, and the presence of one or more registers to store measurements (cryptographic hashes) of the loaded code (§3). A vast majority of off-the-shelf mobile devices include support for secure or authenticated boot. The boot-ROM is a small immutable piece of code which has access to a public key (or its hash) and authenticates boot components that are signed by the device authority's private key. Platforms such as the FreeScale i.MX53 (§4.7) and Texas Instruments' M-Shield (§4.7) contain secure on-chip keys (implemented using e-fuses) that are one-time-programmable keys accessible only from inside a designated secure environment for such authentication purposes. However, none of the hardware platforms, to the best of our knowledge, support platform registers to accumulate measurements of the loaded code. In principle, this support could be added in software by leveraging the hardware isolation primitives and secure storage described previously.

4.4 Secure Provisioning

Current mobile platforms implement mechanisms to authenticate external information, with the hash of the public portion of the signing key stored immutably on the

---
[5] http://www.google.com/wallet/faq.html

device [29]. However, such capabilities are currently restricted to OEMs or carriers (e.g., software updates, assigning different identities to the device) and remain unavailable for use by arbitrary third-party developers.

4.5 Trusted Path

Platforms such as M-Shield (§4.7) provide basic hardware primitives to realize a trusted path. A special chip interconnect allows peripheral and memory accesses only by the designated secure environment, and secure DMA channels to guarantee data confidentiality from origin to destination. Such capabilities are being used for DRM (video streaming) on certain off-the-shelf mobile devices [22], but it remains unclear if they are available to third-party developers.

4.6 Design Gaps and Challenges

Having described the ARM hardware platform and security architecture and how the different components interplay to provide various hardware security features, we now identify design gaps and implementation challenges in off-the-shelf mobile devices that prevent third-party application developers from fully realizing the desired security features.

ARM's hardware platform architecture is only a specification, leaving the OEMs free to customize a specific implementation to suit their business needs. This means that OEMs could leave out components whose absence can severely constrain some security features and in some cases even break feature correctness. For example, the absence of a TZASC (and/or TZMA) leaves main memory (DRAM/SRAM) accessible to both the secure and normal worlds. The only way to enforce memory isolation between the worlds is to use TCM (§ 4.1), which has a very limited size (typically 16-32 KB). Similarly, DMA protection requires a TrustZone-aware DMA controller, GIC, TZASC (and/or TZMA), and a TrustZone-aware AXI-to-APB bridge. The absence of one of these components will result in the DMA protection being ineffective.

Unfortunately, most of today's off-the-shelf mobile devices include a single set of devices shared between the secure and normal worlds and do not include all the required components to fully realize the hardware security primitives described previously. This results in a huge gap between functional specification and device implementation. OEMs and carriers are generally not concerned with DMA-style attacks or including a TZASC (and/or TZMA) because their physical security requirements already force them to process sensitive data in TCM or other device-specific isolated environments unreachable via DMA.

Many OEMs explicitly lock-out platform security features. For example, TrustZone secure-world is enabled or disabled by a single bit in the system configuration register [5]. Once this bit is set to 1 (disabling secure-world), it can no longer be cleared until a device reset. In many off-the-shelf mobile devices such as the Droid, Droid-X, BeagleBoard, and some Gumstix platforms, this bit is set to 1 by the boot-ROM code, in essence allowing only normal-world operations.

From a developer's perspective, an abundance of documentation and open-source (or low-cost) development tools are two key factors that facilitate device and platform adoption. While ARM offers decent documentation and development tools (Fast-Model/RVDS/RTSM) to leverage the hardware security primitives, the cost of the tools (outside of academia) is greater than cost of a typical device. We believe this to be a significant reason why the open-source and hobbyist community has not rallied around ARM's tools.

4.7 Platform Case Studies

We now describe readily available, inexpensive development platforms that come with a host of interesting security features. These examples serve to show that there is no shortage of *security potential* in mobile device platforms.

The FreeScale i.MX53 is a $149 MSRP development board with an ARM Cortex A8 CPU and many security features. The i.MX53 supports a High Assurance Boot (HAB) process where the system boot-ROM prevents the platform from executing unauthorized software during the boot sequence. The i.MX53 Security Controller provides a small Secure RAM (self-clearing on tamper detection or software deallocation) area for secure cryptographic key storage. The i.MX53 Security Accelerator (SAHARA) provides a dedicated cryptographic engine for importing data to or exporting data from Secure RAM. The SAHARA has a dedicated TrustZone-aware DMA controller and accelerates several cryptographic functions such as AES, DES, HMAC, SHA-256 etc.

Texas Instruments M-Shield mobile security technology [9] is a system-level security solution with hardware and software components. The M-Shield secure environment has a secure state machine (SSM) as well as secure ROM and RAM. The SSM enforces *isolation* by enforcing the system's security policy rules during secure environment entry, execution, and exit. M-Shield provides one-time programmable on-chip keys (using e-fuses) that are accessible only from inside the secure environment, and are typically used for authentication and encryption. M-Shield also provides hardware cryptographic accelerators, and hardware primitives for *trusted path*. The platform exposes the Trust-Zone API (§6) for managing secure services. According to the white-paper [9], there are associated middleware and developer APIs for developing such secure services.

5   Isolated Execution Environments

An execution environment that is isolated from the device operating system (§3) is perhaps the most critical security feature described in §3. Such an environment can be used to run secure services that multiplex hardware-backed security features, such as secure storage (§3), amongst the various stake-holders, including third party application developers. Greater flexibility can be offered to third-party developers by allowing them to run modules inside that environment. While this increases the size and complexity of the isolated environment's trusted-computing-base, such an environment remains smaller and more trustworthy than a full-featured OS. The available isolated-execution hardware primitives (§4.1) offer several options for implementing isolated execution environments. We consider two high-level approaches: either using a parallel execution environment, or multiplexing a single execution environment using a hypervisor.

5.1   Parallel Isolated Execution

One strategy for isolated execution is to put sensitive code in a distinct, parallel environment. As described in §4.1, current ARM platforms that support TrustZone offer a mechanism by which secure software can execute in isolation within a special processor world. Several research proposals [14–16, 30, 48, 51] employ TrustZone to achieve isolation and provide a subset of the security properties discussed in §3. Other approaches make use of a physically separate protected module such as a smart-card to achieve isolation [12, 13, 43]. We provide a detailed discussion of the above frameworks in §6.

5.2   Hypervisors

A *hypervisor* is a microkernel that can run other OSes as deprivileged processes. OSes can run unmodified if the environment provided by the hypervisor (optionally with help from some of its deprivileged services) matches the physical hardware expected by that OS. Otherwise we say that the OS must be *para-virtualized*—modified to run in the environment that is provided by the hypervisor. A hypervisor can be used to implement an execution environment that is isolated from the main OS by running the operating system as one process (a virtual machine), and by running the modules to-be-isolated as separate processes.

We now briefly summarize some noteworthy existing ARM hypervisor projects. Current closed-source hypervisors include Winter [48], seL4 [28], OKL4 [35], and INTEGRITY [23]. Winter outlines an approach to merge TCG-style Trusted Computing concepts with ARM TrustZone technology in order to build an open Linux-based embedded trusted computing platform. The seL4 project gained notoriety in 2009 when they announced a formally verified microkernel for the ARM architecture. OKL4 is a microkernel-based embedded hypervisor with a small footprint and CPU support to target mobile telephony. The INTEGRITY multivisor uses a security kernel to provide domain isolation and is targeted at in-vehicle infotainment and next-generation mobile devices. Codezero[6], XenARM [49], and KVMARM[7] are some noteworthy open-source hypervisor initiatives. The CodeZero project proposes a hypervisor based on the L4 microkernel, written in C/C++ in under 10K SLOC. Samsung has supported the Xen hypervisor project to produce an open-source variant of the Xen hypervisor for the ARM architecture. A port is underway of the popular Linux KVM (Kernel Virtual Machine) to the ARM architecture.

Hypervisor frameworks potentially hold value for all stake-holders (OEMs, carriers developers, and users). From an OEM perspective, secure hypervisor frameworks allow multiplexing security-critical baseband functionality on the same processor as popular unmodified OSes and user-facing applications, thereby reducing the cost of materials in a smartphone [35, 38]. From a developer stand-point, hypervisor frameworks allow creation of custom security applications that can benefit from improved isolation (e.g., mobile banking and payments or anti-malware). From a user's perspective, a hypervisor framework may enable simultaneous execution of different OSes, offering a rich set of

---

[6] http://www.l4dev.org
[7] http://wiki.ncl.cs.columbia.edu/wiki/KVMARM:MainPage

security features and execution environments on a single mobile device. Hypervisors are deployed in custom (OEM- and carrier-specific) environments on roughly 1 billion off-the-shelf mobile devices [35, 38]. These can be, and likely already are, used to run security-critical services in isolation from a fully-featured OS running on the same CPU. Unfortunately, we observe that this is done transparently to the user and to third-party developers. These devices do not provide an open API to third-party developers to run *their own modules* in an isolated execution environment provided by the hypervisor.

6   API Architectures

Having discussed the hardware primitives available on today's mobile platforms in §4, and how those can be used to implement reduced-TCB isolated execution environments in §5, we now discuss potential application programmer interfaces (APIs) that those isolated execution environments may expose to developers. We distinguish between two types of APIs: *App-IEE* APIs and *Module-IEE* APIs. *App-IEE* APIs specify how normal applications running on the main OS interact with the isolated execution environment. *Module-IEE* APIs specify how to develop modules running inside the isolated execution environment.

A minimal way to make hardware security features available to application developers is for OEMs or network carriers to provide security-relevant services running inside the isolated execution environment, and expose them via App-IEE APIs. This approach may be attractive to OEMs and carriers, who may not want to bear the risk of allowing third-party code to run in the device's isolated environment, or the cost of implementing strong isolation between modules in that environment. We now summarize the benefits to application developers that arise from OEM- or carrier-provided security services exposed through an App-IEE interface. Secure storage (§3) can be implemented by allowing direct access to a secure storage location, or by implementing a sealed-data API. Data sealed in this way would be protected from offline attacks, and attacks where a different OS is booted (since the sealed-data-service would refuse to unseal for the modified OS). Remote attestation (§3) implemented in the App-IEE-only model can attest that a known OS image booted. This can provide some assurance to remote parties that they are communicating with a client that started in a known configuration. However, such mechanisms cannot detect if the OS has been compromised after it was booted. Similarly, a secure provisioning (§3) service built in the App-IEE-only model can ensure that exported data can only be accessed by a known device that booted a known OS. However, it would have to trust that OS to not compromise the data itself or to allow unauthorized applications to access that data. A trusted-path service (§3) implemented in the App-IEE-only model can ensure to the user that an authorized OS booted, but not that the OS remains uncompromised after it has booted.

Module-IEE API for running custom code in the isolated execution environment mitigates some of the concerns above. We summarize the desirable properties that arise when a Module-IEE API for running custom code in the isolated execution environment *is* available to application developers. Module-IEE APIs for secure storage enable developers to ensure that only their module can access sealed data, even if the OS is compromised. Module-IEE APIs for remote attestation can run code isolated from the OS, and need not include the OS's measurements in their remote attestations. Module-IEE APIs for secure provisioning can ensure that only the intended module running in the isolated execution environment will be able to access provisioned data. A trusted path implemented via Module-IEE APIs can provide assurance to the user that he is communicating with the intended module running in the isolated execution environment. We now discuss several published APIs. All of these specify App-IEE APIs; some of them additionally specify Module-IEE APIs.

Mobile Trusted Module. The Mobile Trusted Module (MTM) is a specification by the Trusted Computing Group (TCG) for a set of trusted computing primitives [44]. Like the Trusted Platform Module on PCs, the MTM provides APIs for secure storage and for attestation, but does not by itself provide an isolated execution environment for third-party code or facilities for trusted path. Unlike the TPM, the MTM is explicitly designed to be implemented in *software*. In particular, it is amenable to being implemented as a module running inside an isolated execution environment on a mobile platform. Also unlike the TPM, the MTM explicitly supports the instantiation of several parallel instances. This feature is intended to support an instance for each of a few stake-holders on a mobile platform. Adding an MTM alone to a mobile platform and allowing third-party developers to access it via App-IEE APIs would serve to expose the underlying hardware security features in a uniform way across hardware platforms. The MTM could also be used in architectures where third-party code is allowed to execute in an isolated execution environment by instantiating a fresh, private, MTM instance for each module that runs. This is similar to the approach taken by previous research on x86 platforms, with the MTM taking the place of the TPM [36, 40]. Another, orthogonal, way to use an MTM is for the isolated execution environment itself to use the MTM as a back-end. This strategy could provide a uniform interface for implementing the isolated execution environment itself across multiple hardware platforms. While several researchers have implemented the MTM [13, 16, 31, 48, 51], it is not to our knowledge implemented on any off-the-shelf mobile platforms.

OnBoard Credentials. OnBoard Credentials (ObC) [14, 30] is an architecture to provide an isolated execution environment to third-party software modules written in the Lua scripting language [14]. It includes both App-IEE and Module-IEE APIs. ObC provides most of the features described in §3: an isolated execution environment, secure (sealed) storage, and secure provisioning. It also provides a form of trusted path, implemented using a management application with a customizable interface. Unfortunately it does not provide a remote attestation API, though adding one would be straightforward.

ObC's key provisioning design seems to be optimized for DRM use-cases, where it is undesirable to have to re-encrypt media for each individual device, As a result, it relies heavily on the physical security of all participating devices. Secured data is provisioned or migrated between devices by encrypting it under a global program-family symmetric key. In this model, compromising the program-family key from any participating device is sufficient to compromise the confidentiality and integrity of data migrated by that program-family on any device—a break-once, run-anywhere attack. It may be possible to extend ObC to support a user-centric trust model, by replacing program-family-keys with user-keys, and putting the user in charge of provisioning those keys to the devices that the user owns or otherwise trusts. Such a provisioning mechanism could be built using a remote-attestation mechanism; while ObC assumes the existence of such a mechanism (using device-keys), its API does not expose a remote attestation feature to secure software modules. However, adding such an API would be straightforward. While multiple commodity smartphones are equipped with the necessary hardware support for ObC, enabling it requires a specially signed device firmware image from the OEM or carrier, and is outside the reach of third-party developers and device owners.

TrustZone API. The TrustZone API (not to be confused with the TrustZone hardware features) is an App-IEE API for managing and invoking modules in an isolated execution environment [6]. The TrustZone API model is fairly abstract and provides interfaces for selecting *which* secure "device" or "world" to communicate with (§4.1). Hence, the TrustZone API could conceivably be implemented to communicate with secure services backed with other protection mechanisms, or even services running on a remote device. The (publicly available) TrustZone API does *not* include Module-IEE APIs. Hence, while it could be a useful set of APIs to expose to app developers, allowing them to communicate with services running in an isolated execution environment, by itself it does not fully specify the APIs needed for *developing* such service modules. We are not aware of any mobile platforms where the TrustZone API is open to third-party developers.

GP Trusted Execution Environment (TEE). The GlobalPlatform consortium is developing a set of standards for a Trusted Execution Environment (TEE) [21]. It includes both App-IEE APIs for applications to interact with isolated modules [19], and Module-IEE APIs for developing such modules [20]. While the system architecture specifically suggests options where the environment is created by multiplexing resources with an untrusted OS, to our knowledge the only implementations of the TEE use a dedicated device such as a Secure Element (§4.2) or smartcard, and only run applications in the secure environment that are pre-approved by the entity deploying that device. The TEE client specification [19] includes APIs for connecting to and invoking a secure application. The TEE internal specification [20] defines the runtime support available to secure applications running inside the TEE. Of the security features from §3, those missing are remote attestation, secure provisioning, and trusted path. In principle remote attestation can be added, which, as discussed in (§3), can be used to build secure provisioning.

7   Analysis and Recommendations

We now give our analysis of the security properties that today's mobile devices can provide, and offer recommendations to the research community, to app developers, to platform integrators, and to hardware vendors. The set of primary stake-holders today includes only the OEMs and telecommunications carriers (and their immediate business partners). Thus, the hardware security primitives that are actually included in mass-market mobile devices are only those of interest to the OEMs and telecommunications providers. It is our primary recommendation that application developers and device owners be considered first-class *stake-holders* by OEMs and telecommunications service providers. While economics may prevent the inclusion of additional hardware security primitives in mass-market devices without a compelling business reason, those primitives which are present should be leveraged to offer additional security features to application developers and devices owners.

Research Community Recommendations. It is our recommendation to the research community to continue to investigate viable architectures for multiplexing mutually-distrusting stake-holders on resource-constrained hardware security primitives (§6). This is especially important as virtualization extensions make their way to the ARM architecture (§4.1), opening up the possibility for two divergent approaches (split-world vs. virtualization). Special attention should be paid to the possibility for a heterogeneous threat model: OEMs and carriers are concerned about defenses against physical attacks, whereas many use-cases for protecting the end-user's data are primarily concerned with software-based attacks that arrive via a network connection. Development hardware with a multitude of unlocked security features is now readily available and inexpensive (§4.7). Though hardware with virtualization extensions remains unavailable at the time of this writing, ARM's toolkit enables emulation of Cortex A15 platforms today. The fear of fragmentation of security APIs can be addressed by developing consistent interfaces. We recommend the adoption of consistent Module-IEE and App-IEE APIs, so that application developers that endeavor to privilege-separate their programs today can continue to reap the security benefits into the future without significant risk of incompatibility or maintenance / support nightmares.

Application Developer Recommendations. It is our recommendation to application developers to continue to demand improved security APIs and primitives in the development environment for popular mobile device platforms. We encourage application developers to learn about existing proposals for Module-IEE and App-IEE APIs, and to consider their implications for the architecture of their applications. Especially those developers with an interest in open-source can produce reference implementations that we expect may be rapidly adopted by other developers.

Platform Integrator Recommendations. We recommend that platform integrators (typically network carriers) take an interest in the security of applications on their devices. We argue that they should adopt a realistic perspective regarding the robustness of the OS APIs for security. Existing Module-IEE and App-IEE proposals should be adopted, to avoid fragmentation and a lack of developer buy-in. These security features will enable application developers to add new value to the mobile device platforms as a whole, resulting in an overall increase in the utility of mobile devices. We strongly urge platform integrators to make hardware security features available that are otherwise included in the silicon but disabled immediately during every boot. As a viable first step, we recommend an implementation of the TCG's Mobile Trusted Module (MTM) in devices with TrustZone capabilities that are otherwise unused (§6). This suggestion is consistent with the App-IEE-only approach discussed in §6, and offers new security features to application developers. Note that it does not give application developers the ability to directly execute their own code inside of an isolated execution environment (§3 and §6). Thus, it is a reasonable compromise between conservative, risk-averse OEMs and carriers, and a useful set of APIs for application developers.

Hardware Vendor Recommendations. Unconstrained memory isolation and improved protection against DMA-based attacks (§4.6) are significant needs in current device hardware. It is more difficult for us to justify the added expense in device hardware at the present time. If the market does indeed parallel our recommendations in the preceding sections, and existing hardware security features begin to enable new applications, then the logical next step is to offer additional hardware security features. To this end, our recommendation is to address the DMA insecurity problem (§4.6). This will not only add protection against currently prevalent attacks from malicious peripherals [47], but will also result in the automatic inclusion of memory address-space controllers such as a TZASC and/or TZMA (§4.1), so that security-sensitive modules that execute in isolation need not grapple with today's dearth of Tightly Coupled Memory.

Acknowledgement. This research was supported by CyLab at Carnegie Mellon University (CMU), Northrup Grumman Corp. and Google Inc. The views and conclusions contained here are those of the authors and should not be interpreted as necessarily representing the official policies or endorsements, either express or implied, of CyLab, CMU, Northrup Grumman Corp., Google Inc., or the U.S. Government or any of its agencies.

References

1. Android – An Open Handset Alliance Project. Issue 10809: Password is stored on disk in plain text (August 2010), http://code.google.com
2. Android Developers. Android API: AccountManager, developer.android.com (accessed November 2011)
3. Apple. iOS: Understanding data protection. Article HT4175 (October 2011)
4. ARM Limited. ARM builds security foundation for future wireless and consumer devices. ARM Press Release (May 2003)
5. ARM Limited. ARM security technology: Building a secure system using TrustZone technology. WhitePaper PRD29-GENC-009492C (April 2009)
6. ARM Limited. TrustZone API specification 3.0. Technical Report PRD29-USGC-000089 3.1, ARM (February 2009)
7. ARM Limited. AMBA 4 AXI4-Stream protocol version 1.0 specification (March 2010)
8. ARM Limited. Virtualization extensions architecture specification (October 2010), http://infocenter.arm.com
9. Azema, J., Fayad, G.: M-Shield mobile security: Making wireless secure. Texas Instruments WhitePaper (June 2008)
10. Becher, M., Freiling, F.C., Hoffman, J., Holz, T., Uellenbeck, S., Wolf, C.: Mobile security catching up? revealing the nuts and bolts of the security of mobile devices. In: Proceedings of the IEEE Symposium on Security and Privacy (2011)
11. comex. JailbreakMe, jailbreakme.com (accessed, November 2011)
12. Costan, V., Sarmenta, L.F.G., van Dijk, M., Devadas, S.: The Trusted Execution Module: Commodity General-Purpose Trusted Computing. In: Grimaud, G., Standaert, F.-X. (eds.) CARDIS 2008. LNCS, vol. 5189, pp. 133–148. Springer, Heidelberg (2008)
13. Dietrich, K., Winter, J.: Towards customizable, application specific mobile trusted modules. In: Proceedings of the ACM Workshop on Scalable Trusted Computing (2010)

14. Ekberg, J.E., Asokan, N., Kostiainen, K., Rantala, A.: Scheduling execution of credentials in constrained secure environments. In: Proceedings of the ACM Workshop on Scalable Trusted Computing (2008)
15. Ekberg, J.-E., Kylänpää, M.: Mobile trusted module (mtm) – an introduction. Technical Report NRC-TR-2007-015, Nokia Research Center (November 2007)
16. Ekberg, J.-E., Kylänpää, M.: MTM implementation on the TPM emulator. Source code (February 2008), http://mtm.nrsec.com
17. ElcomSoft: Proactive Software. iOS forensic toolkit (November 2011)
18. Gligor, V.D., Chandersekaran, C.S., Chapman, R.S., Dotterer, L.J., Hecht, M.S., Jiang, W.-D., Johri, A., Luckenbaugh, G.L., Vasudevan, N.: Design and implementation of Secure Xenix. IEEE Transactions on Software Engineering 13, 208–221 (1986)
19. Global Platform Device Technology. TEE client API specification version 1.0. Technical Report GPD_SPE_007 (July 2010), http://globalplatform.org
20. Global Platform Device Technology. TEE internal API specification version 0.27. Technical Report GPD_SPE_010 (September 2011), http://globalplatform.org
21. Global Platform Device Technology. TEE system architecture version 0.4. Technical Report GPD_SPE_009 (October 2011), http://globalplatform.org
22. GottaBeMobile. Texas Instruments ARM OMAP4 becomes first mobile CPU to get Netflix certification for Android HD streaming (2011), http://gottabemobile.com
23. Green Hills Software. Emergence of the mobile multivisor (2011), http://ghs.com
24. Hecht, M.S., Carson, M.E., Chandersekaran, C.S., Chapman, R.S., Dotterrer, L.J., Gligor, V.D., Jiang, W.D., Johri, A., Luckenbaugh, G.L., Vasudevan, N.: UNIX without the superuser. In: Proceedings of USENIX Technical Conference, pp. 243–256 (1987)
25. Heider, J., Boll, M.: Lost iPhone? Lost passwords! Practical consideration of iOS device encryption security. Technical report, Fraunhofer SIT (February 2011)
26. Intel Corp. Intel atom processor, http://www.intel.com/content/www/us/en/processors/atom/atom-processor.html (accessed, March 2012)
27. Intel Corp. Intel atom processor z2460 (March 2012)
28. Klein, G., Elphinstone, K., Heiser, G., Andronick, J., Cock, D., Derrin, P., Elkaduwe, D., Engelhardt, K., Kolanski, R., Norrish, M., Sewell, T., Tuch, H., Winwood, S.: seL4: formal verification of an OS kernel. In: Proceedings of the ACM Symposium on Operating Systems Principles, SOSP (2009)
29. Koistiainen, K., Reshetova, E., Ekberg, J.-E., Asokan, N.: Old, new, borrowed, blue—a perspective on the evolution of mobile platform security architectures. In: Proceedings of the First ACM Conference on Data and Application Security and Privacy, CODASPY (2011)
30. Kostiainen, K., Ekberg, J.E., Asokan, N., Rantala, A.: On-board credentials with open provisioning. In: Proceedings of ASIACCS (2009)
31. Kursawe, K., Schellekens, D.: Flexible MicroTPMs through disembedding. In: Proceedings of ASIACCS (2009)
32. Lampson, B.: Usable security: How to get it. Communications of the ACM 52(11) (2009)
33. Lineberry, A., Strazzere, T., Wyatt, T.: Inside the Android security patch lifecycle. Presented at BlackHat (August 2011)
34. Mastin, M.: Square vs. intuit gopayment: Mobile credit card systems compared. PCWorld (September 2011), http://www.pcworld.com/businesscenter/article/239250/
35. McCammon, R.: How to build a more secure smartphone with mobile virtualization and other commercial off-the-shelf technology. Open Kernel Labs Technology White Paper (September 2010)

36. McCune, J.M., Li, Y., Qu, N., Zhou, Z., Datta, A., Gligor, V., Perrig, A.: TrustVisor: Efficient TCB reduction and attestation. In: Proceedings of the IEEE Symposium on Security and Privacy (May 2010)
37. Mills, E.: Researchers find avenues for fraud in square. CNET (August 2011), http://news.cnet.com/8301-27080_3-20088441-245/
38. Open Kernel Labs. OK Labs company datasheet (2010), http://www.ok-labs.com
39. Popek, G.J., Goldberg, R.P.: Formal requirements for virtualizable third generation architectures. Communications of the ACM, 17 (July 1974)
40. Sailer, R., Jaeger, T., Valdez, E., Cáceres, R., Perez, R., Berger, S., Griffin, J., van Doorn, L.: Building a MAC-based security architecture for the Xen opensource hypervisor. In: Proceedings of the Annual Computer Security Applications Conference (December 2005)
41. Schell, S.V., Narang, M., Caballero, R.: US Patent 2011/0269423 Al: Wireless Network Authentication Apparatus and Methods (November 2011)
42. Schwartz, M.J.: Apple iOS zero-day PDF vulnerability exposed. InformationWeek (July 2011), http://www.informationweek.com/news/231001147
43. Sun Microsystems, Inc. Java card specifications v3.0.1: Classic edition, Connected edition (May 2009)
44. TCG Mobile Phone Working Group. TCG mobile trusted module specification. Version 1.0, Revision 7.02 (April 2010)
45. Texas Instruments E2E Community. Setup of secure world environment using TrustZone. OMAP35X Processors Forum (August 2010), http://e2e.ti.com
46. US Department of Defense. Trusted computer system evaluation criteria (orange book). DoD 5200.28-STD (December 1985)
47. Wang, Z., Stavrou, A.: Exploiting smart-phone usb connectivity for fun and profit. In: Proceedings of the Annual Computer Security and Applications Conference, ACSAC (2010)
48. Winter, J.: Trusted computing building blocks for embedded linux-based ARM TrustZone platforms. In: Proceedings of the ACM Workshop on Scalable Trusted Computing (2008)
49. Xen.org. Xen ARM project, wiki.xen.org/wiki/XenARM. (accessed November 2011)
50. Yao, Y.: Security issue exposed by android accountmanager (January 2011), http://security-n-tech.blogspot.com/2011/01/security-issue-exposed-by-android.html
51. Zhang, X., Aciicmez, O., Seifert, J.P.: A trusted mobile phone reference architecture via secure kernel. In: Proceedings of the ACM Workshop on Scalable Trusted Computing (2007)
52. Zhou, Z., Gligor, V.D., Newsome, J., McCune, J.M.: Building verifiable trusted path on commodity x86 computers. In: Proceedings of the IEEE Symposium on Security and Privacy (May 2012)

Verifying System Integrity by Proxy*

Joshua Schiffman, Hayawardh Vijayakumar, and Trent Jaeger

Pennsylvania State University
{jschiffm,hvijay,tjaeger}@cse.psu.edu

Abstract. Users are increasingly turning to online services, but are concerned for the safety of their personal data and critical business tasks. While secure communication protocols like TLS authenticate and protect connections to these services, they cannot guarantee the correctness of the endpoint system. Users would like assurance that all the remote data they receive is from systems that satisfy the users' integrity requirements. Hardware-based integrity measurement (IM) protocols have long promised such guarantees, but have failed to deliver them in practice. Their reliance on non-performant devices to generate timely attestations and ad hoc measurement frameworks limits the efficiency and completeness of remote integrity verification. In this paper, we introduce the *integrity verification proxy* (IVP), a service that enforces integrity requirements over connections to remote systems. The IVP monitors changes to the unmodified system and immediately terminates connections to clients whose specific integrity requirements are not satisfied while *eliminating the attestation reporting bottleneck* imposed by current IM protocols. We implemented a proof-of-concept IVP that detects several classes of integrity violations on a Linux KVM system, while imposing less than 1.5% overhead on two application benchmarks and no more than 8% on I/O-bound micro-benchmarks.

1 Introduction

Traditionally in-house computing and storage tasks are becoming increasingly integrated with or replaced by online services. The proliferation of inexpensive cloud computing platforms has lowered the barrier for access to cheap scalable resources, but at the cost of increased risk. Instead of just defending locally administered systems, customers must now rely on services that may be unable or unwilling to adequately secure themselves. Recent attacks on cloud platforms [8] and multinational corporations [55] have eroded the public's willingness to blindly trust these companies' ability to protect their clients' interests. As a result, the need for effective and timely verification of these services is greater than ever.

Recent advances in trusted computing hardware [64,22,1] and integrity measurement (IM) protocols [39] aim to achieve this goal, but current approaches are insufficient for several reasons. First, existing protocols depend on *remote attestation* to convey information about a proving system's configuration to a relying party for verification. However, an attested configuration is only valid at the time the attention was generated,

---

* This material is based upon work supported by the National Science Foundation under Grant No. CNS-0931914 and CNS-1117692.

S. Katzenbeisser et al. (Eds.): TRUST 2012, LNCS 7344, pp. 179–200, 2012.

and any changes to that configuration may invalidate it. Since the proving system's components may undergo changes at anytime, a relying party must continually request fresh information to detect a potential violation of system integrity. This problem is made worse by the significant delay introduced by many IM protocols' reliance on the Trusted Platform Module [64] (TPM), a widely-deployed and inexpensive coprocessor, to generate attestations. Since the TPM was designed for cost and not speed, it is only capable of producing roughly one attestation per second [59,33,34]. This renders TPM-based protocols far too inefficient for interactive applications and high demand scenarios.

Another limitation of current IM approaches is how *integrity-relevant events* are monitored on the proving system. Systems undergo numerous changes to their configurations due to events ranging from new code execution to dynamic inputs from devices. While various measurement frameworks have been developed to enable these components to report arbitrary events and its associated content (e.g., memory pages and network packets), conveying everything is impractical due to the sheer volume of data and effort placed on relying parties to reason about it. Moreover, not every event may have a meaningful effect on the system and communicating such events is a further waste. Thus, proving systems often make implicit assumptions to remove the need to collect particular measurements (e.g., programs can safely handle all network input), which may not be consistent with the trust assumptions of the relying party. This problem stems from the onus placed on the proving system's administrator to choose and configure how the various IM components will collect information without knowledge of relying party's requirements.

To improve the utility of existing IM mechanisms, we propose shifting verification from the relying party to a *verification proxy* at the proving system. Doing so eliminates the bottleneck caused by remote attestation (and thus the TPM) from the critical path, by using traditional attestation protocols to verify the proxy and the proxy to verify the proving system's runtime integrity is maintained. Monitoring the system locally also permits the proxy to examine information relevant to the relying party's integrity requirements. Moreover, this approach supports the integration of fine-grain monitoring techniques like virtual machine introspection (VMI) into remote system verification that would otherwise be difficult to convey over traditional attestation protocols [16,17,30] or require modification to the monitored system.

In this paper, we present the *integrity verification proxy* (IVP), an integrity monitor framework that verifies system integrity at the proving system on behalf of the relying party clients. The IVP is a service resident in a virtual machine (VM) host that monitors the integrity of its hosted VMs for the duration of their execution through a combination of loadtime and VMI mechanisms. Client connections to the monitored VM are proxied through IVP and are maintained so long as the VM satisfies the client's supplied integrity criteria. The IVP framework is able to verify a variety of requirements through an extensible set of measurement modules that translate a client's requirements into VM-specific properties that are then tracked at runtime. When an event on the VM violates a connected client's criteria, immediate action is taken to protect that client by terminating the connection.

However, we faced several challenges in designing an IVP that can be trusted to verify the target system. First, the proxy itself must be simple to verify and able to maintain its integrity without the need for frequent attestation. We employed previous efforts in deploying static, verifiable VM hosts [46] to achieve this. Second, introspecting directly on the running VM can introduce significant performance overhead if done naively. Instead, we monitor the integrity of the VM's enforcement mechanisms by leveraging practical integrity models [28,60,49] to identify specific enforcement points that are critical for protecting the system's integrity. By monitoring these enforcement points, we reduce the frequency and impact of verification. Finally, managing multiple channels from the same and different clients introduces redundant criteria verification. We eliminate this redundancy by aggregating multiple connections for a single criteria.

We implement a proof-of-concept IVP for an Ubuntu VM running on a Linux Kernel-based Virtual Machine (KVM) host. We constructed both loadtime and custom CPU register-based VMI modules for monitoring VM enforcement mechanisms. We validated our proxy's ability to detect violations correctly by building and attacking a VM designed to satisfy integrity criteria based on a practical integrity models and several kernel integrity requirements. We further evaluated the performance impact the IVP imposed on monitored VMs, finding that it introduced less than 1.5% overhead on two application-level benchmarks.

The rest of this paper is organized as follows. Section 2 provides background on current IM approaches and elaborates on the limitation of current IM protocols. Section 3 enumerates our design goals, presents the IVP architecture broadly, and highlights the main design challenges. Section 4 describes of our implementation, which is followed by evaluation of functionality and performance in Section 5. Finally, we provide related work in Section 6 before concluding in Section 7.

2   Remote Integrity Verification

In this section, we present background on remote integrity verification and its building blocks: measurement and attestation. We then discuss the challenges current approaches face and show why they are insufficient for monitoring dynamic systems.

2.1   Integrity Verification Overview

Figure 1 provides a conceptual view of the remote integrity verification, where a *relying party* wants to determine whether a *proving system*'s current configuration (e.g., running code and data) satisfies the verifier's *integrity criteria* for a trustworthy system. The proving system has integrity measurement for its early boot layers that then measures the operating system code and data, which in turn may measure user code, data, and operations (e.g., VMs and processes). Each individual layer aims to measure the *integrity-relevant events* occurring at the layer above. The relying party *monitors* these events by requesting *attestations* of the measured events to evaluate satisfaction against the integrity criteria. If the proving system fails to satisfy the criteria, the monitor protects the relying party by denying access to the untrustworthy system. Thus, the monitor enforces an integrity policy (the criteria) over the communication to proving systems.

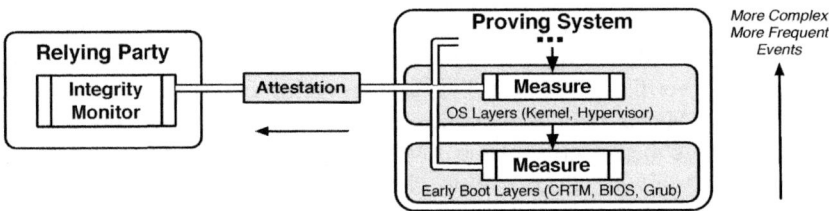

Fig. 1. A relying party's *integrity monitor* inspects a remote system's integrity by requesting *attestations* of *integrity-relevant events* collected by the proving system's layers of *integrity measurement*

Its role is similar to that of a reference monitor [2] that enforces access control policies over resources.

Traditionally, the monitor resides on the relying party and receives measurements provided by the proving system. *Remote attestation protocols* enable proving systems to attest to the integrity and authenticity of measurements collected on the system to relying parties. The Trusted Computing Group specifications use a request-response protocol to ensure freshness of attestations as well [43].

In order to assess system integrity accurately, the integrity monitor must observe events relevant to its integrity criteria. For example, criteria demanding enforcement of an information flow lattice might require that only trustworthy code are loaded into privileged processes and critical system files may only be written to by such processes. Thus, the monitor would require the combination of measurement mechanisms on the proving system (its *integrity measurement (IM) framework*) to record these events. We now provide a brief overview of existing measurement and attestation techniques to illustrate how an integrity monitor would use them, but provide a broader review in Section 6.

Measurement. A relying party's ability to judge system integrity is limited by which events are recorded and their detail. A framework with greater coverage of system events will be more capable of measuring the required integrity criteria for more complex configurations at higher layers. We divide these measurement techniques into two categories: (1) *loadtime* and (2) *runtime*. Loadtime measurements involve capturing changes to the system like code loading and data input *before* they occur. For example, the Integrity Measurement Architecture (IMA) measures binaries before they are mapped into a running process [43] and Terra hashes VM disk blocks before they are paged into memory [16]. Others like Flicker [33] and TrustVisor [32] leverage hardware isolation to reduce the TCB down to a single running process. To measure other events, such as the data read and written by processes, some IM approaches measure other loadtime events. For example, PRIMA [23] measures the mandatory access control policy governing processes at loadtime.

Loadtime only frameworks assume that system integrity is maintained if all loadtime measurements are trustworthy. However, unexpected runtime events like code injection attacks or difficult to assess inputs like arbitrary network packets can subvert system integrity. To address this, runtime measurement techniques have been designed to record this class of events. Furthermore, mechanisms like Trousers [65] for userspace processes and the vTPM [9] for virtual machines (VMs) enable these entities to report integrity-relevant events to an external IM framework.

However, mechanisms that report on a component's integrity from within run the risk of being subverted if the processes or VM is compromised. As an alternative, external approaches like VM introspection (VMI) enables a hypervisor to observe runtime events isolated from the watched VM [41,20,40]. Recent VMI techniques [30,50,25] use hardware memory protection and trampoline code to trap execution back to the host for further inspection. While runtime measurement can detect changes at a finer granularity than loadtime measurements, they also introduce greater complexity. In particular, external approaches introduce a semantic gap that require domain knowledge like memory layouts to detect malicious modifications [7].

Attestation. Early remote attestation efforts like Genuinity [26] and Pioneer [48] demonstrated the feasibility of software-based attestation, but were limited to specific, controlled environments. Specialized hardware approaches offered increased protection for the measurement framework by isolating it from the monitored system [4,42]. Hardware security modules (HSMs) like the IBM 4758 used an early attestation technique called Outbound Authentication [54] to certify the integrity of installed code entities via certificate chains. However, such specialized hardware imposed a significantly higher deployment cost and complexity.

The Trusted Platform Module (TPM) [64] was introduced to provide commodity HSMs across numerous consumer electronic devices. The TPM facilitates several cryptographic features like key generation, signing, and encryption. It also supports remote attestation through a set of platform configuration registers (PCRs) that store measurements (e.g., SHA-1 hashes) of integrity- relevant events. Measurements taken on the system are *extended* into the PCRs to form an append-only hash-chain. A relying party then requests an attestation of the recorded measurements by first providing a nonce for freshness. In response, the TPM generates a digital signature, called a *quote*, over its PCR values and the nonce. An asymmetric private key called an Attestation Identity Key (AIK) is used to sign this quote. The AIK is certified by a unique key burned into the TPM by the device's manufacturer, thereby binding the attestation to the physical platform. The proving system then provides the quote and list of measurements to the relying party. If the quote's signature is valid and the measurement list produces the same hash-chain as the quoted PCRs, then the measurements came from the proving system.

2.2 Integrity Monitoring Challenges

For the integrity monitor to verify system integrity accurately, its view of the proving system must be both fresh and complete. Stale or incomplete measurements limit the utility of the verification process. However, we find that current attestation-based verification model are insufficient for several reasons.

Stale Measurements. Attestation-based protocols introduce a window of uncertainty, which we illustrate in Figure 2. Here, the integrity monitor residing on the relying party requests an attestation at time t and finds it satisfies its integrity criteria. Since the prover

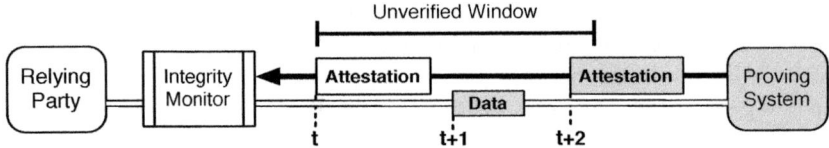

Fig. 2. A window between each attestation exists where the integrity of the proving system is unknown

is verified, the monitor permits it to send data to the relying party at $t + 1$. Later, the monitor requests a second attestation at $t + 2$ and finds the prover no longer satisfies the criteria. Because this violation could have happened at anytime between t and $t + 2$, it is not clear without additional information if the data at $t + 1$ was generated when the system was unacceptable. Classic attestation protocols like IMA [43] avoid this issue by buffering inputs until a later attestation is received, but this is not an option for high throughput or interactive applications.

Hardware Bottleneck. Many systems are dynamic and undergo numerous changes at any time. Thus, the monitor must continually poll for new attestations to detect changes. This problem is exacerbated by the TPM's design as a low performance device for attesting infrequent loadtime measurements like the boot process. In fact, current TPM implementations take approximately one second to generate a quote leading to major bottlenecks in any high demand scenario [59]. Designs that batch remote attestations to eliminate queueing delays have been proposed [34], but still incur a significant overhead.

Criteria Insensitive Measurements. A relying party's ability to assess system integrity is also limited by what events are measured. Since the proving system's administrator decides what the measurement framework will record, a remote verifier must often settle for the information provided by proving system. If that system provides only hashes of code loading operations, then a criteria requiring knowledge the possible runtime operations of those processes cannot be satisfied. However, it is difficult to know what information arbitrary clients require, which is especially challenging for public-facing services used across multiple administrative domains. On the other hand, designing an IM framework to record excessive measurements may be wasteful if they are inconsequential to the verifier's integrity criteria. Moreover, complex events occurring within an entity like may be difficult to assess. For example changes to kernel memory may indicate a rootkit, but it is hard to make that judgement without knowledge of where certain data structures are located. However, providing this context (i.e., entire memory layouts) via attestation can be impractical.

3   Integrity Verification Proxy

We now present the design of the *integrity verification proxy* (IVP), an integrity monitor framework that verifies system integrity at the proving system on behalf of the relying

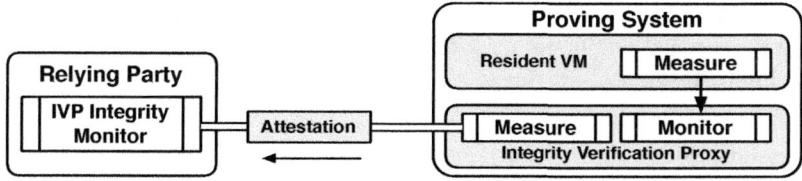

Fig. 3. The *integrity verification proxy* (IVP) acts as an integrity monitor on the proving system that monitors the resident VM to enforce the relying party's criteria over the communication channel. The long-term integrity of the IVP and its host (i.e., layers below the resident VM) is verified by traditional loadtime attestation.

party. By shifting a portion of the integrity monitor to the proving system, the IVP eliminates the need for continuous remote attestation and provides direct access to the system's IM framework to support a broad range of integrity criteria. We begin by describing our design goals and trust assumptions. We then give an overview of the IVP's architecture and detail how it achieves these goals.

3.1 Design Goals

Our aim is to extend the traditional notion of an integrity monitor into the proving system to overcome the limitations of current attestation-based verification protocols. Figure 3 shows the conceptual model of this approach. This model supports the following design goals.

Enforce Integrity Criteria at the Proving System. Monitoring system integrity remotely is insufficient because stale knowledge of the remote system's more complex events undermines the monitor's ability to correctly enforce its criteria. Instead, a relying party can establish trust in an integrity monitor on the proving system that enforces its integrity criteria. The IVP has direct access to resident VM's IM framework to eliminate the window of uncertainty caused by attestation protocols. Moreover, the IVP can terminate connections immediately when an integrity violation is detected to protect the relying party. If the relying party is also the administrator of the VM, the IVP can take further remedial measures such as rebooting the VM. However, the relying party must still monitor the IVP itself to justify such trust. Thus, the IVP must be deployed at a software layer whose integrity can be verified by the relying party without the need for continual attestation, or the purpose of moving monitoring to the proving system is defeated.

Criteria-Relevant Measurement. The problem with traditional IM frameworks is that they measure events irrespective of what the relying party requires. Moreover, entities on the resident VM may be implicitly trusted by the administrator and thus are not monitored. An effective IVP must support various integrity criteria that may even differ from administrator's criteria. To do this, the IVP leverages the available information about the resident VM to capture a broad set of integrity-relevant events to support differing criteria. In Figure 3, the IVP extracts information from both the IM framework on the proving system and additional information through external measurement techniques like VM introspection.

3.2 Assumptions

We make the following trust assumptions in the IVP design. First, we do not consider physical attacks on hardware, denial-of-service attacks, or weaknesses in cryptographic schemes. Next, we assume that the relying party and all the events allowed by the integrity criteria to be trustworthy. Moreover, we treat events that cannot be captured by the IM framework to be acceptable because we cannot say anything about their existence. It is important to note that such unobserved events may be harmful, but unless a mechanism can detect the degradation, it is hard to know the harm that has occurred. We consider the following threats in the IVP design. We assume a powerful external adversary who can produce external events upon the proving system that may exploit vulnerabilities. Such external events may affect both loadtime (e.g., modify files in a downloaded distribution) and runtime events (e.g., network communications). Finally, we consider attacks that modify remote storage and offline attacks on the proving system's local disk.

3.3 Architecture Overview

Figure 4 illustrates our architecture for enforcing the integrity criteria of a relying party (the client) over a network connection to an application VM. Here, the IVP is a service resident in the VM's host that verifies the integrity of the VM on behalf of the client. The client first (1) registers her integrity criteria with the IVP service. Next, (2) she establishes trust in the VM's host and IVP service by verifying their integrity through traditional attestation protocols. These components are designed to maintain their integrity at runtime, thereby enabling simple verification through loadtime measurements similar to existing protocols like IMA [43]. This verification is needed to trust the IVP to correctly enforce her criteria.

The client then requests a connection to a specific hosted VM the criteria to enforce over the channel. The IVP's *integrity monitor* is responsible for tracking the ongoing integrity of the hosted VMs relative to the client's criteria. It uses a set of *measurement modules* to interface directly with the host's IM framework and capture

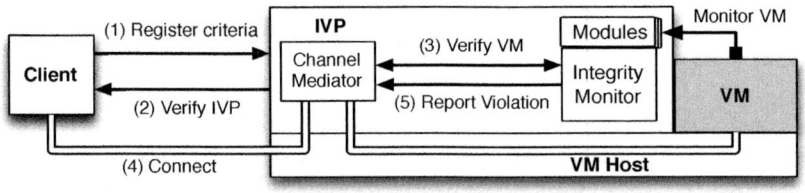

Fig. 4. Integrity verification proxy architecture

integrity-relevant events, which are reported back to the monitor. If the monitor (3) determines that the VM satisfies the client's criteria, it then (4) establishes a secured network tunnel between the client and VM through the IVP's *channel mediator*. The mediator associates each tunnel with the client's criteria. If the integrity monitor detects a that a VM has violated the criteria of any connect client, it notifies the mediator to (5) terminate each associated connection.

3.4   Verifying the IVP Platform

The IVP verifies VM integrity on behalf of the client, thereby requiring trust in the IVP. Since our aim is to reduce client verification effort and eliminate the need for repeated remote attestation, we want an IVP that can be verified by a single attestation at channel setup unless a reboot occurs. The challenge is then building IVPs and their hosting platform in such a way that they maintain their integrity to obviate the need for remote monitoring.

This endeavor is difficult in general because systems often have large TCBs consisting of numerous components that may not be trusted. Moreover, changes to these systems at runtime like upgrades may be overlooked without frequent monitoring. However, various research projects have explored techniques for building VM hosting platforms that may be small enough to verify formally [27,3,5,57,32,58]. While the design of a specific platform is outside the scope of this paper, we envision a host would incorporate such approaches. As for the IVP, it only relies on a small number of services, such as networking, the introspection interface, and VM management. Research projects like Proxos [61] and work by Murray et. al. [35], have demonstrated that it is possible to build minimal VMs that depend only on the VMM and use untrusted services in other VMs securely (e.g., by encrypting and integrity-protecting the data). This would enable the IVP to function as an independent service in the host without depending on a large host VM like in Xen Dom0. We intend to develop future IVP prototypes for various hypervisors that support this separation.

3.5   Channel Mediation

The IVP is responsible for mediating connections to ensure they are active only when their respective client's criteria are satisfied. The channel mediator creates an integrity association (IA) for each tunnel as the tuple (C, V, I), where C is the client, V is the VM, and I is the integrity criteria to check. Before a tunnel is brought up, the IA is registered with the integrity monitor to verify that V continues to satisfy I. If it does, the tunnel is brought up and shutdown either voluntarily or when the integrity monitor notifies the mediator that an I has been violated.

One challenge in designing the channel mediator is proving to clients that the channel is controlled and protected by the proxy. The connection is formed as an Ethernet tunnel between the client and the VM through a virtual network managed by the mediator. This effectively places the client and VM on the same local subnet. Other mediated connections to the VM connect over the same virtual network, but are isolated from each other by the mediator using VLAN tagging. During setup, the tunnel is protected via cryptographic protocols like TLS that mutually authenticate the client and mediator.

The VM is provided a certificate signed by the host's TPM at boot time to bind the platform's identity to the VM's credentials. This binding approach is similar to previous work on VM attestation [9,19]. The client can then setup further protections directly with the VM over the tunnel. Having direct control over the network tunnel also lets the mediator tear down the connections as soon as a violation is detected.

3.6   Integrity Monitoring

The IVP's integrity monitor is tasked with verifying each VM's integrity against integrity criteria registered by clients connected to it. To do this, the monitor collects events from its measurement modules (see Section 3.7) to update its view of each VM's configuration. When the mediator registers an IA, the monitor first checks if the IA's criteria is satisfied by the current VM configuration. If so, the monitor adds a reference to the IA to a list of IAs to verify. When the VM's configuration changes, (e.g., through code loading) the integrity monitor pauses the VM and checks whether any registered IA has been violated. If so, the channel mediator is notified of the invalid IA, so it may tear down the tunnel before the VM can send data on it. The monitor then resumes execution of the VM.

In order to verify a VM's integrity, the monitor must be able to capture all integrity-relevant changes from VM creation until shutdown. To monitor loadtime events, we give the integrity monitor direct control over VM creation through the platform independent virtualization API, libvirt. This lets the monitor collect information about the VM's virtual hardware, initial boot parameters, kernel version, and disk image. The monitor spawns individual watcher threads for each VM and registers with the IVP's measurement modules. When the modules capture an event at runtime, the watcher is alerted with the details of the change. Since multiple IAs to the same VM may have redundant requirements to verify, the monitor keeps a lookup table that maps IAs with the same criterion together. When a change to the VM is detected that violates one of these conditions, all IAs mapped to that criterion are invalidated by the monitor.

3.7   Measurement Modules

Integrity criteria consist of various loadtime and runtime requirements. The integrity monitor divides up these criteria into a set of discrete measurement modules tasked with tracking changes to specific aspects of the VM's configuration. The modules interface directly with the available IM framework to measure events in real time. For example, loadtime modules measure information like boot time parameters of the VM, while runtime modules attach a VMI to watch critical data structures. Since IM frameworks often consist of several components responsible for measuring various events, modularizing the interface allows for a more flexible design. Administrators can then write or obtain modules for the specific IM mechanism installed on the host without having to modify the monitor.

Capturing Runtime Events. Detecting violations at runtime requires modules to be able to capture events as they happen. The module must then notify the integrity monitor's watcher of the event before the VM continues to execute. We employ VMI to enable our modules to monitor runtime criterion. Many hypervisors now offer VMI mechanisms like xenaccess [40,15,21] in Xen and VMSafe [66] for VMware that enable direct access to VM resources. In addition, QEMU supports introspection through debugging tools like gdb and previous work has demonstrated the feasibility of VMI in KVM [50].

Each runtime module monitors a specific property on the VM. The modules actively monitor the VMs by setting *watchpoints* (e.g., locations in memory) that are triggered by integrity-relevant operations. Watchpoints can be set on sensitive data structures or regions of memory such as enforcement hooks [53], and policy vectors [37] stored in kernel memory. Other structures like function pointers and control flow variables are possible candidates [11]. Triggering a watchpoint pauses the executing VM so the module that set the watchpoint can examine the how the configuration has been altered. Pausing the VM prevents the VM from sending any data on the connection until the module can assess if the event violated an IA's criteria. After the module finishes invalidating any IAs, the VM is permitted to resume execution.

Improving Efficiency. VMI gives runtime modules direct memory access, but creates a semantic gap [12] when reading directly from the VM's memory. Since the module does not have the full context of the running system, changes to complex and userspace data structures are difficult to assess. Our modules leverage the VM's extant enforcement mechanisms to report events without having to pause the VM as often. For example, instead of pausing the VM to measure every executed program, we use Linux kernel's Integrity Module (LIM) [29] framework to record hashes of every previously unseen program and executable memory-mapped file before loading them. We set a watchpoint on the in-kernel measurement list to catch each addition to it. This way, the module can avoid pausing except when LIM detects new binaries. Other in-VM monitor techniques could be leveraged to report integrity measurements to the modules to reduce the overhead of pausing the VM. Virtual devices like the vTPM [9] and co-resident monitors like SIM [50] provide potential reporting frameworks.

4   Implementing an IVP

We implemented a proof-of-concept IVP for a Linux KVM system. Figure 5 illustrates the IVP's services residing in the host. Clients interact with the IVP through a *proxy manager* to (1) register their criteria, (2) request attestations of the host's configuration, and (3) manage connections to VMs. We used a TLS-protected VPN tunnel to the VM's virtualized private network to implement the IVP's channel mediator. Initially, VMs are firewalled from the client's tunnel and all clients are isolated from each other through the VPN as well. Once the tunnel is active, a client can establish an IA with a specific VM by first (3a) sending a request to the proxy manager and specifying which criteria previously registered should be used to mediate that connection. The proxy manager then creates the IA tuple and (3b) registers it with the integrity monitor, which in turn checks if the client's criteria are satisfied by the VM. If it is, the monitor (3c) informs the proxy manager to change the VPN firewall to allow the VM to send data to the client over the tunnel. The client can now receive data from the monitored VM as well as (4) authenticate the identity of the VM to establish an encrypted connection if desired.

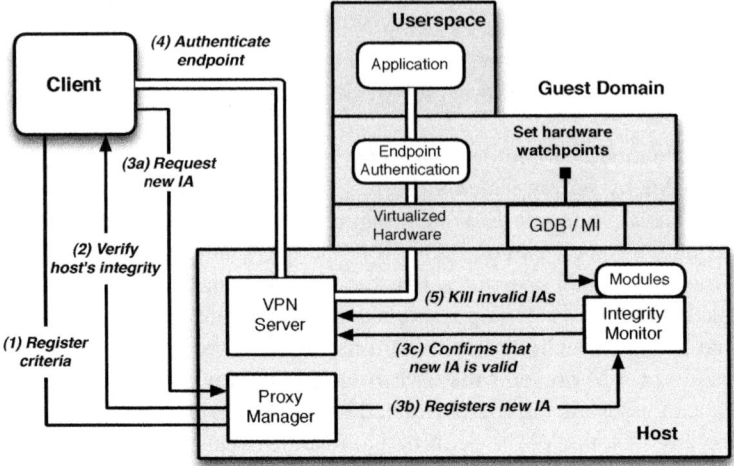

Fig. 5. IVP implementation and protocol

Finally, if at anytime the VM violates the IA's criteria, the integrity monitor (5) deletes the IA and informs the VPN server to firewall the client tunnel from the VM.

4.1   Verifying the Host

To verify the IVP platform's integrity, we use the Root of Trust for Installation (ROTI) approach to attest to the trusted distribution of the host [46]. At install time, a TPM signed proof is generated that binds the installed filesystem to the installer that produced it. We also employ the `tboot` bootloader to establish a measured launch environment (MLE) for the host using Intel's Trusted eXecution Technology (TXT) in recent CPUs [22]. The MLE establishes a dynamic root of trust for measurement (DRTM) through the processor that isolates, measures, and executes the kernel and initial ramdisk (initrd). This allows the boot process to be started from a trusted starting point. The initrd loads the system enforcement policies into the kernel and takes a measurement of the current filesystem before passing execution off to the root filesystem. When a client requests an attestation of the IVP platform, the ROTI proof is included with the normal attestation. The client then checks that the proof indicates no tampering with the installation has occurred and that the installer source is trusted to produce a system designed to maintain its integrity at runtime to meet the long-term integrity requirements of the IVP platform.

4.2   Channel Mediator

We implemented the channel mediator using OpenVPN server to manage Ethernet tunnels from remote clients to the internal virtualized network for the hosted VMs. All mediated connections from the client are aggregated through a single VPN tunnel with the individual VM endpoints permitted to transmit on that tunnel if a corresponding IA exists. VPN tunnels are established by first mutually authenticating the client's account certificate and a host certificate signed by the host's AIK. Each connection is TLS-protected and uses a Linux tap device to provide kernel supported Ethernet tunneling from the physical network interface to the virtual network bridge. Once connected, the OpenVPN server opens the firewall for traffic from the VM's virtual interface to the tunnel for each VM in the active IAs to the client. When the integrity monitor deletes an IA, it tells the OpenVPN server to firewall the VM from the client in the deleted IA.

4.3 Integrity Monitor

We created the integrity monitor as a 439 SLOC Python daemon that manages VM execution and monitors VM integrity. The daemon uses the hypervisor independent interface, libvirt, to start and stop VMs, collect information about virtual device settings, and control loadtime VM parameters. When the daemon receives a request to start a VM, it spawns a separate *watcher* thread to control the VM and monitor integrity information. When the proxy manager registers a new IA with the monitor, the monitor forwards the IA to the appropriate VM's watcher, which in turn checks that each criterion is satisfied by querying the registered measurement modules for current VM configuration. If all the modules indicate the requirements are satisfied, the watcher notifies the VPN server that the IA is valid.

The watcher registers with loadtime measurement modules to collect information about the VM before the VM is started. Next, the VM is created and the watcher attaches gdb to running VM process, which pauses the VM. We use gdb as a proof of concept VMI interface because VMs in Linux KVM run as userspace processes, making them it simple to monitor. Moreover, gdb can determine where kernel structures are in memory by reading debug information in the kernel or from a separate system map file that is easily obtained. The watcher then loads the runtime modules, which collect the necessary context from the paused VM and set any desired watchpoints through the gdb interface. After the runtime modules are registered, the VM resumes execution. When watchpoints are triggered at runtime, the VM is paused and control is passed from the watcher to the runtime module that set it. The module then introspects into the VM's memory and updates the accumulated VM configuration with any modified values detected during introspection. The module notifies the watcher if any values have changed, which checks if those changes have violated any of the registered IA's criteria. Finally, the module resumes the VM's execution.

We use hardware-assisted watchpoints in gdb to avoid modifying the VM code and introducing additional overhead. This raises an issue because the x86 architecture only contains 4 debug registers, which limits the number of hardware-assisted watchpoints that can be set for a process. Since software watchpoints require single stepping through the VM's execution, they are not a viable option. However, similar watchpoint functionally is feasible by using memory protection features of the KVM shadow page table for VMs as demonstrated in SIM [50]. While we did not implement this VMI approach, we plan to explore it and further implementation options in future work.

5 Evaluation

We evaluated our IVP implementation in terms of functionality and performance. First, we validated the IVP's ability enforce relying party criteria correctly by performing attacks that violated various integrity requirements. We then evaluated the performance overhead imposed on the monitored VM using both micro-benchmarks and application-level benchmarks performance.

Our experimental testbed consisted of a Dell OptiPlex 980 with a 3.46GHz Intel Core i5 Dual Core Processor, 8GB of RAM, and a 500GB SATA 3.0Gb/s hard disk. The Linux KVM host ran in an Ubuntu 10.10 distribution using a custom 2.6.35 Linux kernel. Our guest VMs were allocated a single 3.46GHz vCPU without SMP, 1GB of RAM, and an 8GB QCOW2 disk image connected via virtio drivers. Each VM ran an Ubuntu Linux 10.10 server distribution with default SELinux policy and a custom LIM module.

5.1 Functionality

To test the IVP's functionality, we designed a target application VM running the Apache webserver. We constructed a VM image that approximates the CW-Lite [49] integrity model and designed an integrity criteria for verifying that approximation. We then had a client connect to the VM through a mediated channel associated with the CW-Lite criteria. We performed several attacks on the VM's loadtime and runtime integrity both before and after the connection was established to see if the IVP would correctly detect the violations and terminate the connection.

Building a CW-Lite Enforcing VM. We constructed an application VM that satisfies the CW-Lite integrity model. This practical integrity model differs from strict integrity models like Biba [10] and Clark-Wilson [13] by allowing for an integrity policy that identifies trusted exceptions where illegal flows are required for the system to function properly. Other practical integrity models would also be viable [28,60]. To enforce CW-Lite, trusted processes with high integrity labels (e.g. privileged daemons) must only (1) load trustworthy code, (2) receive trustworthy inputs, and (3) handle untrusted inputs through designated filtering interfaces that can upgrade or discard low integrity data.

We configured our Apache VM with SELinux, which enforces a mandatory access control policy through Domain Type Enforcement [6]. This labels every process and system object with policy-defined types. We use the Gokyo [24] policy analysis tool to identify 79 labels from which data can flow to the Apache process and system TCB labels [49]. This included processes that access critical resources like kernel interfaces and privileged daemons. We then modified SELinux LSM to hook into the kernel's LIM [29] to receive hashes of code executed in trusted processes. The modified LSM module then denies execution of hashes that are not on a white list obtained from the Ubuntu 10.10 main repository. This secure execution monitor satisfies the first CW-Lite requirement because only trusted code from the hash list may run in trusted processes.

In addition to the identified trusted processes, several untrusted sources like the network provide necessary input to Apache. Per the third CW-Lite requirement, we must ensure untrusted inputs are only received by interfaces[1] designed to properly handle (e.g. sanitize) such input. To do this, we added additional checks to the LIM policy to whitelist only the Apache binary, designed to handle such inputs, to be loaded into the process with labels to access these interfaces. Before the interface is permitted to read data, our modified SELinux LSM checks if the interface is intended to receive untrusted data based on a CW-Lite policy and deny the read if it is not.

Specifying Integrity Criteria. We defined our client's integrity criteria with both load-time and runtime requirements. For loadtime criteria, we specified hashes of a trusted VM disk image, kernel, initrd, and CW-Lite enforcement policies to match those we created above. The runtime criteria, by contrast, checks for common signs of intrusion by rootkits and unexpected modification of the VM's enforcement mechanisms and policies at runtime.

For example, previous research [7] has shown that some rootkits modify the netfilter hook in the kernel to enable remote control of the system via specially crafted network packets [36]. Other attacks replace the binary format handlers to obtain privilege escalation triggered by program execution. We specified runtime criteria that require no changes to the kernel structures located by the kernel symbols `nf_hooks` for the netfilter and `formats` for binary format handlers attacks. We also identified function pointers used to hook execution by SELinux and LIM and in-kernel policy structures that should not be modified at runtime. Furthermore, we specified that only the Ubuntu repository code was to be executed in the TCB, which would catch the case where the secure execution protections were bypassed. To do this, we specified that all measurements of code loads taken by the LIM hooks should match the hash list we specified above.

Building Measurement Modules. We constructed several measurement modules to monitor various integrity requirements on the target VM. The modules were written in an inheritable base class that exposes a register function for setting watchpoints and a callback handler that is called when the watchpoint is triggered. Each module averaged 25 additional lines over the base class definition. The integrity monitor's watcher thread instantiates and registers loadtime modules before the VM is first created to measure the kernel, disk image, and enforcement policies.

Runtime modules are instantiated after VM initialization and set watchpoints through the `gdb` interface. When a watchpoint is triggered, the watcher is notified and invokes the appropriate module's callback to inspect the event. We placed watchpoints on various kernel structures including SELinux, LIM, and netfilter function pointers and the binary format handler list. We also monitored the in-kernel LIM policy by set a watchpoint on the kernel's `ima_measurements` list head. This traps to the runtime module whenever a new binary is executed. The module reads the hash from the list tail and adds it to the module's list of measured code. Doing this, we can monitor all code loaded in the TCB and check for inconsistencies between the expected LIM policy and executing programs. Leveraging the LIM framework to record new code hashes lets the integrity monitor pause the VM only when new binaries are loaded.

---

[1] Interface here refers to the read-like syscalls. While programs have many interfaces, only some are intended to handle untrusted inputs.

Detecting Violations. We tested if the IVP properly mediates the CW-Lite criteria before and after connecting a client to the VM over the mediated channel. We exercised each measurement module through a series of attacks on the VM's integrity. For load-time modules, we modified boot parameters, kernel versions, disk image contents, and policy files to values not permitted by the criteria. The modules then recorded these configuration values at VM creation. When the client initiated connection request to the IVP, the integrity monitor's watcher compared the measured values to the criteria and correctly rejected the connection. For our runtime modules, deployed attacks on the monitored data structures using attack code that exploits an x86 compatibility vulnerability in Linux kernels older than 2.6.36 [14]. This let us illegally change an unprivileged process' SELinux label to the full privileged `kernel_t` label, thereby enabling arbitrary code execution. We used this vector to easily modify kernel memory and modify the monitored structures to violate our runtime requirements. The IVP correctly detected these changes and disconnected the connection to the VM and prevented future connection requests.

5.2 Performance

Next, we examined the performance impact the IVP has on monitored application VMs. We first performed a series of CPU and I/O micro-benchmarks within the monitored VM to identify any overhead in system performance indicators. We then performed macro-benchmarks with a webserver and distributed compilation VM to see the impact at the application-level.

Passive Overhead. We first evaluated the impact of runtime monitoring on the VM when integrity-relevant events are not occurring. We used three types of benchmarks to test CPU, network, and disk performance of the VM with and without the IVP active. For CPU-bound benchmarking, we used the SPECINT 2006 test suite (see Table 1), which performs several training runs to identify the expected standard deviation (under 1.1%) before sampling. Most tests show negligible overhead with the IVP with the largest at 0.61%.

Table 3 shows our results for network and disk benchmarks after 30 runs of each. We used `netperf` to evaluate network overhead. It samples maximum throughput and transactions per second after saturating the network link. These tests also indicated negligible impact on networking. For disk I/O performance, we used the `dbench` benchmarking tool, which simulates a range of filesystem level operations using a configurable range of parallel processes. It presents results as the average throughput for the client processes. We found that the throughput was negatively affected as we increased the number of simultaneous clients. Our intuition for this trend was that more client processes led to more syscalls that, in turn, cause the VM process to raise signals to perform I/O through virtual devices. We profiled the VM with systrace while the benchmarks were executing and confirm this correlation. Since `gdb` uses the `ptrace` interface in the kernel to monitor processes for debug signals, every syscall incurred a small processing overhead by `gdb` to parse the signal and resume process execution. A possible solution for this would be to modify the ptrace interface to notify the `gdb` process only when debug signals are raised. Even with this overhead, our disk I/O benchmarks demonstrate overhead under 8% for 50 clients.

Table 1. Benchmarks with and without the IVP obtained by the median of three runs, as reported by the SPECINT 2006. The test suite does training and test runs in addition to the actual runs so the results are reproducible.

SPECINT '06 Benchmarks	Median (sec) Base	Test	Diff (%)
perlbench	403	404	0.25
bzip2	683	686	0.43
gcc	367	369	0.54
mcf	557	560	0.53
gobmk	467	467	0.00
hmmer	544	545	0.18
sjeng	575	576	0.17
libquantum	664	667	0.45
h264ref	762	763	0.13
omnetpp	494	497	0.61
astar	664	667	0.45

Table 2. Active Overhead Micro-benchmarks of overhead incurred when watchpoint is triggered. World switches and GDB contributes 82.2% of the trigger overhead excluding modules. Collected from 100 runs.

Operation	Mean ($\pm$ 95% CI) (ms)
Watchpoint Trigger	
VM Exit and Entry	.006 ($\pm$ 0.000)
QEMU overhead	.496 ($\pm$ 0.081)
GDB overhead	.327 ($\pm$ 0.054)
Monitor Overhead	0.172 ($\pm$ 0.028)
Runtime Modules	
Collect LIM Hash	66.76 ($\pm$ 0.215)
Read kernel variable	0.132 ($\pm$ 0.002)

We also tested the effect of our IVP on two real-world applications, an Apache web-server and a `distcc` compilation VM. We initiated all of our tests from a separate computer over the TLS-protected VPN tunnel setup by the IVP. We ran 30 runs of the `ab` tool to simulate 100 concurrent clients performing 100,000 requests on the Apache VM. For the `distcc` test, we compiled Apache-2.2.19 across 3 identical VMs on separate machines with 8 concurrent threads. Again, the average of 30 such runs are taken. Our results show that the IVP introduced a 1.44% and 0.38% overhead on Apache and distcc VMs, respectively. We suspect the primary cause for the Apache overhead is the frequent network requests and disk accesses made to service the requests.

Active Overhead. Finally, we explored the delays introduced by the IVP when handling changes to monitored data structures. We profiled our measurement modules using the ftrace framework in the Linux kernel by setting markers to synchronize timings between our userspace monitor and events happening in the kernel, such as VM exits and enters. Table 2 shows that interrupting the VM on a tripped watchpoint introduces a 1 ms pause regardless of the measurement module involved. For simple runtime modules that read single variables, approximately 100μs additional overhead is incurred. However, more complex measurement modules take more time. For example, the LIM measurement module reads a SHA1 hash from a nested kernel list, which causes a 67 ms delay. We found the majority of this is caused by `gdb` parsing the kernel symbol table to locate the memory addresses in the VM to read. Caching these addresses when the monitor is registered would greatly speed this measurement process. Regardless, measurement modules that perform more complex measurements like reading and parsing multiple structures will increase the time the VM is paused. Moreover, watchpoints on frequently modified memory locations will result in more pauses.

6   Related Work

Introduction of the TPM has led to numerous IM techniques (see the comprehensive survey by Parno et. al. [39]). Initial approaches focused on TCG-style verification of the boot process, the OS kernel, modules, userspace binaries [43,29] and system policies [23]. Application-level measurements through frameworks like Trousers [65] enable processes to pass measurements to the TPM for integrity protection and reporting. Other techniques measured VM integrity through hypervisor support [16,44,31] and even virtualized the TPM for VMs [9]. More recently, Sirer et. al. [52] proposed an authorization logic supported by a custom OS kernel that enables verification using high-level statements instead of binary hashes. This approach greatly simplifies the complexity of verifying attestations and provides a richer measurement framework for both local and remote entities. However, these approaches place the verification burden on the relying party to interpret potentially stale and incomplete information. The IVP can leverage these disparate measurement techniques to verify a relying party's criteria at the proving system and supplement them with more fine-grain monitoring.

Other approaches have focused on reducing the TCB that must be verified. Bind [51], Flicker [33], and TrustVisor [32] use CPU hardware support to measure and protect the execution environment of application code and associate it with the computation's result. These approaches provide guarantees to the relying party that the result was protected from external threats during execution, but still require verification of each result's attestation.

Instead of attesting system configurations, other research has focused on maintaining runtime integrity guarantees [47,30,17,50,45,5,56] that remote parties can verify are being enforced. For example, Terra's Optimistic Attestation ensure certain VM disk blocks are unaltered by shutting down the VM if a modification is detected at loadtime. These approaches offer a strong foundation for monitoring runtime integrity, but do not support verifying remote verifier specified requirements. Our IVP can leverage these runtime enforcement mechanisms to maintain the IVP host's integrity. Furthermore, remote parties can use the IVP to monitor the integrity of enforcement mechanisms in the VM and their policies. Also, our design does not explicitly provide remediation like shutting down the VM because we assume the remote clients are not administrators of the VM and may have differing criteria.

IM has also been incorporated into secure communication channels. Trusted Network Connect [63] requests periodic attestations of clients before and after they join a private network and evicts systems with invalid attestations. OpenTC PET [38] uses SSL proxies in a VM host to provide attestations of the VM to the remote client. However, the proxy simply provides attestations instead of verifying the VM's integrity on behalf of the connected client. Other work [19,62,9,18] has incorporated TPM attestations into public key certificates to bind integrity states to platform identities. However, the reported integrity of these approaches is only valid as long as the attested system's configuration does not change. This requires the client to continually request new certificates that function exactly like attestations. Our IVP eliminates the need for continual polling by enforcing the client's criteria at the VM's host.

Table 3. Network and disk benchmarks. `netperf` measures throughput (tcp_stream) and transactions per second (tcp_rr) after 30 second network saturation. `dbench` measures 20 seconds disk throughput intervals during a 10 minute read / write workload after 2 minute warmup. 30 runs per benchmark.

Benchmarks	Mean ± 95% CI		Diff
	Baseline	**With IVP**	**(%)**
Network: `netperf`			
TCP_STREAM (Mb/s)	268 ± 0.23	269 ± 0.22	0.2
TCP_RR (Trans/s)	1141 ± 5.65	1141 ± 1.96	0.05
Disk: `dbench`			
1 Client (Mb/s)	11.14 ± 0.02	11.12 ± 0.14	0.18
5 Clients (Mb/s)	32.64 ± 0.67	32.49 ± 0.76	0.46
10 Clients (Mb/s)	40.94 ± 1.01	40.21 ± 0.98	1.78
20 Clients (Mb/s)	47.46 ± 1.50	44.69 ± 1.12	5.83
50 Clients (Mb/s)	40.58 ± 3.09	37.41 ± 1.86	7.81

7   Conclusion

In this paper, we presented the integrity verification proxy (IVP), a service resident in a proving system that mediates connections on behalf of remote clients. By shifting the task of monitoring a client's integrity criteria to the proving system's host, we enable relying parties to connect to remote systems without the need for frequent attestations or further verification. We designed and implemented a proof of concept IVP for a Linux KVM host and evaluated its effectiveness and impact on performance. Our results show the IVP incurs only minor overhead for network and CPU-bound applications, but with additional delay that increases modestly as a function of I/O load. As future work, we plan to improve our VMI interface to minimize passive overhead and increase expressiveness of client's integrity criteria.

References

1. Processor-Based Virtualization, AMD64 Style,
   http://developer.amd.com/documentation/articles/pages/
   630200615.aspx
2. Anderson, J.P.: Computer Security Technology Planning Study. Tech. Rep. ESD-TR-73-51, The Mitre Corporation, Air Force Electronic Systems Division, Hanscom AFB, Badford, MA (1972)
3. Andronick, J., Greenaway, D., Elphinstone, K.: Towards Proving Security in the Presence of Large Untrusted Components. In: Proc. 5th Workshop on Systems Software Verification (2010)
4. Arbaugh, W.A., Farber, D.J., Smith, J.M.: A Secure and Reliable Bootstrap Architecture. In: Proc. IEEE SSP (1997)
5. Azab, A.M., Ning, P., Wang, Z., Jiang, X., Zhang, X., Skalsky, N.C.: HyperSentry: Enabling Stealthy In-Context Measurement of Hypervisor Integrity. In: Proc. 17th ACM Conference on Computer and Communications Security (2010),
   http://doi.acm.org/10.1145/1866307.1866313

6. Badger, L., Sterne, D.F., Sherman, D.L., Walker, K.M., Haghighat, S.A.: Practical domain and type enforcement for unix. In: IEEE Symposium on Security and Privacy (1995)
7. Baliga, A., Ganapathy, V., Iftode, L.: Automatic Inference and Enforcement of Kernel Data Structure Invariants. In: Proc. ACSAC (2008),
   http://dx.doi.org/10.1109/ACSAC.2008.29
8. BBC: Amazon apologises for cloud fault one week on,
   http://www.bbc.co.uk/news/business-13242782
9. Berger, S., et al.: vTPM: Virtualizing the Trusted Platform Module. In: USENIX Security Symposium (2006)
10. Biba, K.J.: Integrity Considerations for Secure Computer Systems. Tech. Rep. MTR-3153, MITRE (1975)
11. Carbone, M., Cui, W., Lu, L., Lee, W., Peinado, M., Jiang, X.: Mapping kernel objects to enable systematic integrity checking. In: Proceedings of the 16th ACM Conference on Computer and Communications Security
12. Chen, P.M., Noble, B.D.: When Virtual Is Better Than Real. In: Proc. HotOS (2001)
13. Clark, D.D., Wilson, D.R.: A Comparison of Commercial and Military Computer Security Policies. Security and Privacy (1987)
14. CVE-2010-3081,
    http://cve.mitre.org/cgi-bin/cvename.cgi?name=CVE-2010-3081
15. Fraser, T., Evenson, M.R., Arbaugh, W.A.: VICI Virtual Machine Introspection for Cognitive Immunity. In: Proceedings of the 2008 ACSAC (2008),
    http://dx.doi.org/10.1109/ACSAC.2008.33
16. Garfinkel, T., Pfaff, B., Chow, J., Rosenblum, M., Boneh, D.: Terra: A Virtual Machine-Based Platform for Trusted Computing. In: Proc. 19th ACM SOSP (2003)
17. Garfinkel, T., Rosenblum, M.: A Virtual Machine Introspection Based Architecture for Intrusion Detection. In: Proc. NDSS (2003)
18. Gasmi, Y., Sadeghi, A.R., Stewin, P., Unger, M., Asokan, N.: Beyond Secure Channels. In: Proc. ACM Workshop on Scalable Trusted Computing (2007)
19. Goldman, K., Perez, R., Sailer, R.: Linking Remote Attestation to Secure Tunnel Endpoints. In: Proc. First ACM Workshop on Scalable Trusted Computing (2006),
    http://doi.acm.org/10.1145/1179474.1179481
20. Haldar, V., Chandra, D., Franz, M.: Semantic remote attestation: a virtual machine directed approach to trusted computing. In: Proceedings of the 3rd Conference on Virtual Machine Research And Technology Symposium (2004)
21. Hay, B., Nance, K.: Forensics examination of volatile system data using virtual introspection. SIGOPS Oper. Syst. Rev. 42, 74–82 (2008)
22. Trusted Execution Technology, http://www.intel.com/technology/security/
23. Jaeger, T., Sailer, R., Shankar, U.: PRIMA: Policy-Reduced Integrity Measurement Architecture. In: Proc. 11th ACM SACMAT (2006)
24. Jaeger, T., Sailer, R., Zhang, X.: Analyzing Integrity Protection in the SELinux Example Policy. In: Proc. 12th USENIX-SS (2003)
25. Joshi, A., King, S.T., Dunlap, G.W., Chen, P.M.: Detecting past and present intrusions through vulnerability-specific predicates. In: SOSP. ACM (2005)
26. Kennell, R., Jamieson, L.H.: Establishing the genuinity of remote computer systems. In: USENIX Security Symposium (2003),
    http://portal.acm.org/citation.cfm?id=1251353.1251374
27. Klein, G., et al.: seL4: Formal Verification of an OS Kernel. In: SOSP (2009)
28. Li, N., Mao, Z., Chen, H.: Usable Mandatory Integrity Protection for Operating Systems. In: Proc. IEEE SSP (2007)
29. Integrity: Linux Integrity Module(LIM), http://lwn.net/Articles/287790/

30. Litty, L., Lagar-Cavilla, H.A., Lie, D.: Hypervisor Support for Identifying Covertly Executing Binaries. In: Proc. 17th Usenix Security Symposium (2008)
31. Maruyama, H., Seliger, F., Nagaratnam, N., Ebringer, T., Munetoh, S., Yoshihama, S., Nakamura, T.: Trusted Platform on Demand. Tech. Rep. RT0564. IBM (2004)
32. McCune, J.M., Li, Y., Qu, N., Zhou, Z., Datta, A., Gligor, V., Perrig, A.: TrustVisor: Efficient TCB Reduction and Attestation. In: Proc. IEEE SSP (2010),
    http://dx.doi.org/10.1109/SP.2010.17
33. McCune, J.M., Parno, B.J., Perrig, A., Reiter, M.K., Isozaki, H.: Flicker: An Execution Infrastructure for TCB Minimization. In: Proc. 3rd ACM SIGOPS/EuroSys (2008)
34. Moyer, T., Butler, K., Schiffman, J., McDaniel, P., Jaeger, T.: Scalable Asynchronous Web Content Attestation. In: ACSAC 2009 (2009)
35. Murray, D.G., Milos, G., Hand, S.: Improving xen security through disaggregation. In: VEE. VEE 2008. ACM (2008)
36. Linux Kernel Backdoors And Their Detection,
    http://invisiblethings.org/papers/ITUnderground2004_
    Linux_kernel_backdoors.ppt
37. Security-enhanced linux, http://www.nsa.gov/selinux
38. OpenTC: OpenTC PET,
    http://www.opentc.net/publications/OpenTC_PET_prototype_
    documentation_v1.0.pdf
39. Parno, B., McCune, J.M., Perrig, A.: Bootstrapping Trust in Commodity Computers. In: IEEE SP 2010 (2010)
40. Payne, B.D., Carbone, M., Lee, W.: Secure and Flexible Monitoring of Virtual Machines. In: ACSAC (2007)
41. Payne, B.D., Carbone, M., Sharif, M., Lee, W.: Lares: An architecture for secure active monitoring using virtualization. In: IEEE Symposium on Security and Privacy (May 2008)
42. Petroni, N.L., Timothy, J., Jesus, F., William, M., Arbaugh, A.: Copilot - A Coprocessor-based Kernel Runtime Integrity Monitor. In: Proc. 13th USENIX Security Symposium (2004)
43. Sailer, R., Zhang, X., Jaeger, T., van Doorn, L.: Design and Implementation of a TCG-based Integrity Measurement Architecture. In: USENIX Security Symposium (2004)
44. Santos, N., Gummadi, K.P., Rodrigues, R.: Towards Trusted Cloud Computing. In: HOT-CLOUD (2009)
45. Schiffman, J., Moyer, T., Shal, C., Jaeger, T., McDaniel, P.: Justifying integrity using a virtual machine verifier. In: Annual Computer Security Applications Conference, pp. 83–92(December 2009)
46. Schiffman, J., Moyer, T., Jaeger, T., McDaniel, P.: Network-based Root of Trust for Installation. IEEE Security & Privacy (2011)
47. Seshadri, A., Luk, M., Qu, N., Perrig, A.: Secvisor: A Tiny Hypervisor To Provide Lifetime Kernel Code Integrity For Commodity Oses. In: Proceedings of Twenty-First ACM SOSP (2007)
48. Seshadri, A., Luk, M., Shi, E., Perrig, A., van Doorn, L., Khosla, P.: Pioneer: Verifying Code Integrity And Enforcing Untampered Code Execution On Legacy Systems. In: Proceedings of the 20th ACM SOSP (2005)
49. Shankar, U., Jaeger, T., Sailer, R.: Toward Automated Information-Flow Integrity Verification for Security-Critical Applications. In: Proc. 2006 NDSS (2006)
50. Sharif, M.I., Lee, W., Cui, W., Lanzi, A.: Secure in-vm monitoring using hardware virtualization. In: Proceedings of the 16th ACM Conference on Computer and Communications Security (2009)
51. Shi, E., Perrig, A., van Doorn, L.: BIND: A Fine-Grained Attestation Service for Secure Distributed Systems. In: IEEE SP 2005 (2005)

52. Sirer, E.G., de Bruijn, W., Reynolds, P., Shieh, A., Walsh, K., Williams, D., Schneider, F.B.: Logical attestation: an authorization architecture for trustworthy computing. In: Proceedings of the Twenty-Third ACM Symposium on Operating Systems Principles, New York, NY, USA, pp. 249–264 (2011), http://doi.acm.org/10.1145/2043556.2043580

53. Smalley, S., Vance, C., Salamon, W.: Implementing SELinux as a Linux Security Module. Tech. Rep. 01-043, NAI Labs (2001)

54. Smith, S.W.: Outbound Authentication for Programmable Secure Coprocessors. In: Gollmann, D., Karjoth, G., Waidner, M. (eds.) ESORICS 2002. LNCS, vol. 2502, pp. 72–89. Springer, Heidelberg (2002)

55. Sony: Update on playstation network and qriocity (April 2011), http://blog.us.playstation.com/2011/04/26/update-on-playstation-network-and-qriocity

56. Srinivasan, D., Wang, Z., Jiang, X., Xu, D.: Process out-grafting: an efficient "out-of-vm" approach for fine-grained process execution monitoring. In: Proceedings of the 18th ACM Conference on Computer and Communications Security, New York, NY, USA, pp. 363–374 (2011), http://doi.acm.org/10.1145/2046707.2046751

57. St. Clair, L., Schiffman, J., Jaeger, T., McDaniel, P.: Establishing and Sustaining System Integrity via Root of Trust Installation. In: Annual Computer Security Applications Conference (2007)

58. Steinberg, U., Kauer, B.: Nova: a microhypervisor-based secure virtualization architecture. In: Proceedings of the 5th European Conference on Computer Systems, EuroSys 2010, pp. 209–222. ACM, New York (2010)

59. Stumpf, F., Fuchs, A., Katzenbeisser, S., Eckert, C.: Improving the scalability of platform attestation. In: ACM Workshop on Scalable Trusted Computing (2008)

60. Sun, W., Sekar, R., Poothia, G., Karandikar, T.: Practical Proactive Integrity Preservation: A Basis for Malware Defense. In: Proc. 2008 IEEE SSP (2008)

61. Ta-Min, R., Litty, L., Lie, D.: Splitting interfaces: making trust between applications and operating systems configurable. In: OSDI. USENIX Association, Berkeley (2007)

62. TCG: Infrastructure Subject Key Attestation Evidence Extension Version 1.0, Revision 5. Tech. report (2005)

63. TCG: Trusted Network Connect: Open Standards for Integrity-based Network Access Control. Technical report (2005), http://www.trustedcomputinggroup.org

64. TCG: Trusted Platform Module (2005), https://www.trustedcomputinggroup.org/specs/TPM/

65. Trousers, http://trousers.sourceforge.net/

66. VMWare VMsafe, http://www.vmware.com/go/vmsafe

Virtualization Based Password Protection against Malware in Untrusted Operating Systems

Yueqiang Cheng and Xuhua Ding

School of Information Systems,
Singapore Management University
{yqcheng.2008,xhding}@smu.edu.sg

Abstract. Password based authentication remains as the mainstream user authentication method for most web servers, despite its known vulnerability to keylogger attacks. Most existing countermeasures are costly because they require a strong isolation of the browser and the operating system. In this paper, we propose KGuard, a password input protection system. Its security is based on the hardware-based virtualization without safeguarding the browser or OS. A security-conscious user can conveniently and securely activate or deactivate the password protection by using key combinations. We have implemented KGuard and experimented our prototype on Windows with Firefox. The results show that no significant performance loss is induced by our protection mechanism when a user authenticates to commercial web servers.

1 Introduction

Password based authentication is the primary method for a remote server to check a user's identity. In a typical web authentication, a user password is transferred from the keyboard to the kernel, then to the browser before being sent out over the network to the web server through an SSL channel. One of the main threats to password authentication is kernel/application keyloggers which steal the password from its transferring path.

Any countermeasure to keyloggers must cope with both the attacks on the application which forwards the password to a remote server, and the attacks on the I/O path, namely from the keyboard to the application. Virtualization based isolation is the main approach as used in [6,9,8,3], where either the browser or the entire OS is isolated as a protected environment. This approach usually incurs significant cost due to the large code to isolate and the security assurance is not strong, though it addresses other related security problems, e.g., phishing attacks. Another approach, as suggested in Bumpy [16] and BitE [15], is to use an encryption-capable keyboard to protect the I/O path and rely on the latest processor features to isolate the application. However, most commodity platforms at present are not equipped with the needed keyboard.

In this paper, we propose a novel system to protect passwords against keyloggers in remote authentication without using a special keyboard or isolation like [6,9,8,3]. Note that in the remote authentication setting, it is unnecessary for the user's platform (including the OS and the application) to know the *actual* password as long as it can forward the authentication information to the server properly. Therefore, the high level idea of our work is that a hypervisor intercepts the user's password input; and whenever the

S. Katzenbeisser et al. (Eds.): TRUST 2012, LNCS 7344, pp. 201–218, 2012.

application needs to submit the password to the server through an SSL channel, it traps to the hypervisor which performs the desired encryption. In other words, the normal SSL connection between the application and the server is split into non-cryptographic operations and cryptographic operations, such that the latter are accomplished by the hypervisor holding the password.

In our system, the cleartext password is never exposed to the operating system or the application. As a result, a keylogger can only get a ciphertext version. The system is highly efficient because no extra computation or communication cost is incurred as compared to normal password authentication, except the keyboard interception and the trapping. It is entirely transparent to the operating system, though the application needs to have a plug-in in order to split the SSL operations. Furthermore, the system is user friendly as it results in little user experience change. (Note that anti-phishing is not in the scope of our work.)

In the rest of the paper, we present the design and implementation details of our password protection system named as *KGuard*. It is for password based web authentication using Firefox. We also report its performance in experiments with commercial websites such as Gmail. A novel building block of our system is a secure user-hypervisor interaction channel that allows a user to authenticate a hypervisor, which in itself is of research value as it addresses one of the challenges recently identified in [30]. KGuard can be extended for other password authentication systems (e.g., SSH) by replacing the browser plugin with the one for the application.

ORGANIZATION. In the next section, we discuss the related work. Then we present an overview in Section 3 with the emphasis on the methodology used in our design. In Section 4, we describe the details of our design. The implementation details and performance results are shown in Section 5 and Section 6, respectively. We discuss several important issues in Section 7 and conclude this paper in Section 8.

2   Related Work

BitE [15] and Bumpy [16] are two isolation based systems that defend user input against malware attacks. Both of them require an encryption-capable keyboard. BitE suffers from a large TCB since it contains the legacy OS and Window Manager. Bumpy reduces the TCB size by using Flicker [14]. However, it has a higher computation latency. The KGuard system does not leverage the encryption-capable keyboard, and the TCB size of the KGuard is larger than Bumpy, and smaller than BitE.

Password protection against malware is a sub problem of password management which deals with other issues like phishing attacks. A widely used approach in [19,8,3] is to set up a secure compartment which functions as a proxy to help the user's authentication. For instance, TruWallet [8] and TruWalletM [3] use different techniques to secure the authentication proxy which securely stores the user credentials and properly submits them to a remote server. The main disadvantages of these schemes are the architectural change (e.g., GUI parts are required to moved from the legacy OS) on the platform and the high cost (e.g., longer data flow path comparing with the legacy one). In addition, it is challenging to isolate the browser and the user interface due to the enormous code size. Oprea et. al. in [19] propose an approach to allow users possessing a trusted mobile device (e.g., PDA) to delegate their credentials (e.g., password) for performing a task (e.g., login). Other works in password management include PwdHash [22] which uses cryptographic techniques to cope with phishing attacks, and WebWallet [29] which checks user information submission and determines phishing attacks. Note that most secure password management systems are complementary to our work which focuses on password input.

Our work is also related to I/O protection in the kernel space. DriverGuard system [5] provides a generic solution to protect the confidentiality of I/O data from being attacked by a compromised kernel. However, it does not solve the password protection problem because it cannot protect the password residing in the application.

3   Overview

This section presents an overview of our work. We explain the design criteria and the rationale we follow, including the trust model and a high level explanation of our approach. We also show the architecture of the proposed system.

3.1   Design Criteria

Ideally, a password protection system should meet the following criteria. Firstly, the protection should offer the strongest security assurance. It should be able to defeat attacks from rootkits which subvert the operating system, as kernel rootkit keyloggers are not uncommon in the cyberspace. From the practicability perspective, the protection should induce little or no modification on the operating system and is fully compatible with existing browsers. This is due to the fact that proprietary operating systems such as Windows and Mac OS are more widely used than open-source operating systems. Furthermore, the password security should not be attained at the price of the easy-of-use of password authentication. On the user side, the protection scheme should be as simple as possible and does not require user possession of extra devices, such as a USB token and a mobile phone. On the server side, no changes should be needed. Last but not the least, the protection system should incur low cost. The cost is measured in terms of both the time delay during the password authentication session and the overall computation load on the platform. It is crucial that the user should not experience noticeable delay in an authentication session.

3.2   Design Rationale

In order to meet the criteria, we carefully assess a variety of design options. The foremost issue to consider is the trust model, i.e. which component in the platform can be considered as trustworthy.

Trust Model. We do not trust the operating system and applications running on top of it, in the sense that they can be compromised and attempt to steal user passwords.

Therefore, safeguarding user password necessitates a root of trust which should not be subverted by rootkits. One candidate for the root of trust is the TPM chip [28], which is expected to resist all software attacks. Nonetheless, despite of its high security assurance, the TPM chip offers rather primitive and inflexible functionalities and is slow in computation. These drawbacks make it ill-suited for password protection.

In this work, we choose the hypervisor (a.k.a. virtual machine monitor or VMM) as the root of trust, as in [24,25,4]. The main benefit is that it allows us to develop desirable protection functions within the hypervisor, and therefore facilitates the design and the implementation. The hypervisor is not as secure as the TPM chip since several attacks have been discovered to compromise some versions of hypervisors [27,7,11,21]. However, the security of the hypervisor can be ensured by three measures. Our design is based on hardware-assisted virtualization, such as Intel VT-x and AMD V, which significantly reduces the virtualization code of the hypervisor. In addition, TPM-based authenticated bootup can verify the integrity of the hypervisor when being launched. Thirdly, the hypervisor in our system is only for protection in a normal personal desktop setting, rather than a cloud server with a full-fledged virtualization for multiple VMs. Therefore, those unneeded services from the hypervisor are turned off so that only a minimal attack surface is exposed to the guest OS.

A secure hypervisor is capable to dynamically protect memory regions and I/O ports against direct malware accesses. In addition to that, the hypervisor also uses IOMMU to enforce the similar policies against malicious DMA operations launched by malware.

Protection Method. There exist several candidate methods to protect user passwords against rootkits. One is to follow the isolation approach as shown in [13]. The execution of routines processing the password is isolated from the rest of the platform to cordon off attacks. This method is not compatible with our design criteria because of its low performance. The frequent interrupt caused by user keystrokes for password inputting induces the expensive system thrashing between the protection mode and the regular mode. In addition, the isolation approach faces the difficulty of extracting appropriate Pieces of Application Logic (PAL) due to the complexity of the kernel's keyboard input processing and the browser's web page processing. Another possible method could be to escort the password data flow as shown in DriverGuard [5]. Nonetheless, this approach requires code modifications on the drivers, which does not satisfy our compatibility requirement. Moreover, DriverGuard by itself does not guarantee the security of password in the application level.

In this work, our method is based on the characteristics of the password authentication. Firstly, passwords are typically sent to a remote server through an SSL/TLS connection. It is *not* necessary for the local host to know the password in use. Secondly, passwords are fed to a system through keystrokes which can be intercepted by the hypervisor.

Based on these two observations, the basic idea of our protection method is to intercept the password keystrokes and then securely inject them back to the SSL/TLS connection established by the browser, however, with its cryptographic operations performed by the hypervisor. Therefore, the password is encapsulated using the web server's public key following the SSL/TLS specification without any exposure to the operating system or the browser.

Security Properties. The main challenge of realizing the proposed protection method is the gap between the hypervisor and the security-conscious user. In existing platforms, a user only interfaces with the operating system through the application, e.g., a browser.

This gap entails three problems to solve. The first is about the timing for protection. It is undesirable for the hypervisor to intervene in all keyboard inputs. Ideally, the protection is only activated by the user whenever needed. The *on-demand* protection brings up the second challenge: how the user is assured that the hypervisor is protecting the password input. Note that the operating system may cheat the user by simulating the hypervisor's behavior. Last but not the least, the hypervisor's SSL traffic assembling must use a proper public key certificate for encapsulation. Ideally, the hypervisor is capable of verifying whether the certificate belongs to the intended web server.

In this work, we design a dynamic secure channel for user-hypervisor interaction which bypasses the operating system. While the hypervisor's protection mechanism is dormant, the channel allows a security-conscious user to activate it through a key combination. In addition, the channel allows the user to verify whether it is indeed active. Note that it is not necessary for the hypervisor to authenticate the origin of the keystrokes, because a faked activation key combination, e.g., from the malware instead of the user, does not lead to password leakage[1].

For the aforementioned third problem, our design achieves the same level of security as the standard browser's dealing with SSL certificates, because a certificate misuse is essentially the traditional man-in-the-middle attack on SSL. Similar to the browser's certificate verification, the hypervisor ensures that the certificate is genuine and matches the SSL connection.

3.3   The Architecture

We consider a platform with an operating system running on top of a hypervisor. A user uses a web browser to login to a remote server by supplying the password. KGuard is designed to protect the user password from being stolen by kernel/application rootkits. The architecture of KGuard consists of three components:

1. A secure user-hypervisor interaction channel allows the user to activate or deactivate the password protection and authenticate the hypervisor. A user toggles the protection by pressing a prescribed key combination. In response, the hypervisor securely displays (on the screen) a secret message pre-shared with the user.
2. A routine in the hypervisor intercepts user keystrokes after the protection is activated. It also validates the authentication server's public key certificate supplied by the browser and encapsulates the password using encryption.
3. A browser plugin splits the SSL connection for password submission. Specifically, it requests the hypervisor to perform the needed cryptographic operations in a SSL connection and handles other non-cryptographic operations by itself.

Note that the hypervisor only performs cryptographic operations. It does *not* establish any SSL connection with the server. In a web authentication, the browser may establish

---

[1] The faked activation key combination can be considered as a denial of service attack. It will be quickly spotted by a user because as shown later, the hypervisor will respond to the user with a secret message pre-shared with the user.

multiple SSL connections. Only the one submitting the password is split by the plugin to get the needed cryptograms from the hypervisor. The benefit of this design is that it does not entail extra computation and communication cost and it can keep the hypervisor small without including the support for SSL.

4   The Design Details

4.1   User-Hypervisor Interaction

The user-hypervisor interaction channel is a duplex channel. In one direction, a user sends an activation command to the hypervisor by requesting the operating system to issue a hypercall. In the other direction, the hypervisor (on receiving the user's command) securely displays a secret message on the screen. Therefore, the user can verify whether the hypervisor receives the command or not.

Hypervisor Protection Activation. There exist several approaches for activation. One alternative design is for the hypervisor to listen to a prescribed hardware event, such as keystrokes, plugging a USB device etc. These methods can bypass the operating system. Nevertheless, it requires extra work from the hypervisor which has to keep listening to all events and filter them properly. In our system, we do not favor this approach because 1) we aim to minimize the load on the hypervisor, especially when the protection is not needed; and 2) bypassing the operating system is not necessary because no *data* is sent to the hypervisor for activation. In addition, the user can verify the activation by checking the returned secret message from the hypervisor.

In our design, the operation system is the medium transferring the user's activation command to the hypervisor. Specifically, we design an application routine, e.g. a browser extension, and install a new module to the OS, e.g. a virtual device in Windows. The application routine listens to a prescribed key combination (i.e., the activation command). When the event is captured, it issues a hypercall to inform the hypervisor. Specifically, in the system initialization phase, the hypervisor prepares a hypercall table and then the installed OS module maps the table into the kernel space. The module exports an interface (i.e., a system call) to applications. After getting input parameters from an application via the exported system call, the module is invoked and forwards these parameters to the hypervisor through a hypercall as the Xen Hypercall mechanism [1].

In response to the activation hypercall, the hypervisor clears the keyboard input buffer, starts to intercept the keyboard strokes as described in Section 4.2, and authenticates itself to the user as shown in the next subsection.

Visual Verification of Hypervisor Protection. The verification of hypervisor protection requires an output interface. To ensure its security, the output should not be captured or manipulated by malware in the guest OS. Otherwise, the guest can impersonate the hypervisor and give the user an illusion that the protection is activated.

The basic idea of our visual verification is that the hypervisor securely outputs to the monitor a secret text message priorly chosen by the user. Note that without involving the operating system, the monitor automatically and periodically fetches the display data *directly* from a memory region called the *display buffer*, whose location is determined by the hardware [10], and then it renders them on the screen. The hypervisor shows the secret message to the user by writing it into the display buffer. To prevent the operating system from attacking the secret, the hypervisor clears the _PAGE_PRESENT attribute bit of the corresponding page table entries. As a result, any guest access will be denied by the hardware.

The details of the visual verification are described below. Initially, the user chooses a random text message as his/her long term secret shared with the hypervisor. When the hypervisor boots up, the secret message is passed to the hypervisor as a booting parameter, which is the reason why the secret has to be text. Once taking control, the hypervisor stores the secret message into its own space. Since the hypervisor boots up before the operating system, the OS is not able to access this secret. To display it on a monitor in the graphics mode, the hypervisor derives the graphic version of the secret message by using the corresponding font bitmap for each character.

After receiving the activation hypercall, the hypervisor substitutes a part of the display buffer with the secret graphic data. As a result, the user secret message is displayed on the screen. The location of the message on the screen depends on its offset in the display buffer. Note that it is unnecessary to choose random locations. In addition, the hypervisor properly sets the attribute bits of the page table entries covering the graphic secret. Secret uploading and attribute bit setting up are an atomic operation. In other words, the hypervisor occupies the CPU without yielding it to the operating system until the attributes are set.

The hypervisor then sets up a timer whose duration is configured by the user during bootup. When the timer expires, the hypervisor restores the original display data, and finally returns the page access rights back to the guest OS.

Hypervisor Protection Deactivation. Protection deactivation requires a stronger authentication on the user than protection activation, since malware may attempt to impersonate the user to terminate the protection. Note that once the protection is activated, the hypervisor has cleared all previous data in the keyboard input buffer and intercepts all new keystrokes. As a result of the interception, no software can access the keyboard input buffer, either directly or through DMA operations, as explained in Section 4.2. Only the physical keyboard strokes can place inputs to the buffer.

Therefore, the hypervisor in KGuard is pre-configured with a deactivation command. Once it intercepts the command during its protection, it switches to the no-protection state by releasing the access control on the keyboard input buffer.

4.2   Keystroke Interception

After getting the activation key-combination command from the user, the hypervisor starts keystroke interception. Since the key stroke code is directly delivered to the guest's memory by the hardware using DMA, keystroke interception means that the hypervisor retrieves the keyboard scan code *before* the guest.

One potential approach is for the hypervisor to intercept all interrupts and intervenes if needed. The main drawbacks of this approach are twofold. This approach may fail because the guest OS can keep scanning the keyboard input buffer without waiting for the interrupt. Therefore, the guest OS may have the luck of getting the data prior to the interrupt. Secondly, the interrupt number can be shared by several devices. The hypervisor has to determine whether the interrupt is for the keyboard. Furthermore, the interrupt by itself does not provide sufficient information for the hypervisor to locate the data.

Since locating the keyboard input buffer is an indispensable step, we let the hypervisor intercept the guest access on the keyboard input buffer, rather than interrupt interception. This method reduces the burden of the hypervisor as the guest OS manages all interrupts and is forced by the hardware to alert the hypervisor for the scan code retrieval. For this purpose, the hypervisor sets up page-table based access control on both the keyboard I/O control region storing I/O commands and the keyboard input buffer storing the scan code. IOMMU is also configured such that no DMA command can be issued to access these protected regions. Consequently, both the guest OS's keyboard I/O command issuance and its data retrieval are intercepted by KGuard. For the I/O control, KGuard emulates the operations; for the data retrieval, it replaces the user keystroke with a dummy one and saves the original input into a buffer in the hypervisor space.

The actual access control mechanism for the keyboard input buffer depends on the keyboard interface. A PS/2 keyboard usually uses PIO to transfer data whereas a USB-keyboard uses DMA. It is easy to deal with port I/O keyboards. The technique for controlling I/O port has been demonstrated in [5]. The access control for USB-keyboard is more complex due to the USB architecture. The so-called *Universal Host Controller* hardware uses a 32-bit register called FLBASEADD to locate a list of *frame pointers*. A frame pointer points to a list of *Transfer Descriptors (TDs)*. A TD specifies the necessary I/O parameters for one DMA operation, including the input buffer address. After completing one keyboard I/O, the guest OS must either update the current TD or insert a new TD in order to read the next keyboard input. The keystroke interception for a USB keyboard follows the steps below.

Step 1. KGuard freezes the present frame list and all TDs by setting FLBASEADD and all memory regions occupied by the frame list data structure as *read-only* using I/O bitmap and page table respectively. Therefore, any attempts from the guest OS to relocate the input buffer will be monitored by KGuard.

Step 2. KGuard locates the keyboard input buffer following the path used by the host controller. The keyboard input buffer is then set as *inaccessible*.

Step 3. When the guest OS attempts to read the keyboard input buffer, a page-fault is generated and passes the control to KGuard which saves the scan code (which is one password character) in the input buffer and replaces it with a dummy one, and sets the buffer as *read-write*. The guest OS can have a full access to this buffer.

Step 4. When the guest OS prepares for the next keyboard I/O by updating the TD, a page-fault is generated. In response, KGuard emulates the update operation. To prevent malware from providing faked keystrokes, the hypervisor clears the content in the keyboard input buffer, which ensures that the data fetched in Step 3 is indeed from the keyboard.

Note that KGuard responds differently on the keyboard input buffer and the I/O region because one keyboard I/O only involves one TD update but may incur multiple accesses to the buffer depending on the driver's needs. Our approach avoids unnecessary hypervisor involvements.

We further remark that the keyboard interception is only activated based on the user's command. With the cooperation from the user, the incurred cost is therefore minimal to the platform's overall performance and it is reasonable for KGuard to treat all the intercepted keystrokes as the password. Even in case that the user and KGuard are out of synchronization, no user secret is compromised and the user can easily reset the protection.

4.3 Handling SSL Session

A normal web authentication may involve one SSL session comprising one or multiple SSL connections. Typically, when the user clicks a button for password submission, the browser sends out the encrypted password with other necessary information through an SSL connection.

In our system, the browser is deprived of the privilege of handling the password, because the encryption of the password and other authentication information must be performed in the hypervisor space, instead of in the untrusted guest domain. For this purpose, we design a dedicated browser extension for posting authentication information to the server through SSL. To achieve both security and compatibility, the extension is only responsible for non-critical operations in the SSL connection, while all cryptographic operations, such as master key generation and data encryption, are exported to KGuard.

The extension captures the login event and initiates a new SSL connection with the server. All keys used in this SSL connection are *newly* derived and only known by KGuard and the server. Note that this new connection will be immediately closed after the login event. Therefore, the browser does not need to maintain any extra connection. In the new SSL connection, the extension obtains the server's public key certificate. At the same time, it prepares a data blob containing all the data needed by the web server (except the password), e.g., the user name. It then submits to the hypervisor the data blob together with the server certificate. The hypervisor merges the blob with the intercepted user password, and encrypts them following the SSL specifications, on the condition that the provided public key certificate is valid. On receiving the resulting ciphertext from the hypervisor, the extension prepares the SSL data and sends them to the server. If the authentication succeeds, the server usually returns a URL with some cookies, which are decrypted by the hypervisor and forwarded to the extension. The extension then sets the cookies and redirects the browser to the URL. Now the extension terminates its SSL connection. Since neither the extension nor the browser possesses the keys for the SSL connection used for password submission, this SSL connection cannot be reused by the browser.

To avoid verbosity, we do not recite how the hypervisor generates the master key and performs the encryption, because it strictly follows the SSL/TLS specification. Out of the same reason, we do not explain how the extension prepares the data blob and the SSL traffic. However, it is worthwhile to elaborate how the server's public key certificate is validated by the hypervisor. Since we do not trust any software in the guest domain, the certificate forward by the extension to the hypervisor can be a malicious one.

If the adversary has the corresponding private key, the hypervisor's password encryption will be decrypted by the adversary. We leave the details of the browser extension in Section 5 because it is browser specific and more relevant to usability than security.

Server Certificate Verification. Certificate verification has long been considered as a thorny problem due to the trust on the public key infrastructure. The problem is even more complicated in our case because limited information is provided to the hypervisor for the sake of minimizing the hypervisor's size. Note that phishing detection is *not* within the scope of our study. Therefore, the criterion of a certificate's validity is not whether it matches the web server the user intends to login. Instead, a certificate is deemed as trusted as long as its root CA is trusted by the user.

In our system, the user may choose to trust all pre-loaded root CA certificates or import CA certificates she trusts. Once the user obtains a repository of trusted (root) certificates, the crux of our system is how the user securely passes them to the hypervisor. The difficulty is that the hypervisor does not have a file system and the whole guest is not trusted. The solution we propose relies on an additional trusted platform, or alternatively, the user may consider his/her platform in the initial state is trustworthy. On such a trusted platform, cryptographic tools such as OpenSSL, can be used to compute a HMAC key H_k and computes HMACs for each of the trusted certificate. Then, the user imports all trusted certificates as well as their corresponding HMAC tags into a file on the untrusted platform running with KGuard. During the platform's rebooting, the HMAC key H_k is passed to the hypervisor as a parameter. Therefore, the hypervisor knows whether a certificate is trusted by the user by checking its HMAC tag. Instead of using HMAC, the user may also apply digital signatures and pass the public key to the hypervisor, though this approach is not preferred because of its longer key and higher computation cost. Note that these above procedure is only executed *once*, i.e. for the first time using KGuard. All HMAC tags in the file are able to be reused after rebooting.

In runtime, the certificate verification proceeds as follows.

Step 1. The browser extension receives the public key certificate from the server and composes a certificate chain such that the last certificate in the chain is a trusted certificate imported by the user. For ease of description, we denote the certificate chain as $(Cert_0, \cdots, Cert_k)$ where $Cert_0$ is the server's certificate and $Cert_i$ is the issuer of $Cert_{i-1}$ for $1 \leq i \leq k$. In most cases in practice, $k = 1$ or 2. Note that only $Cert_k$ is the trusted certificate while all others are not. It is not necessary to obtain the issuer for $Cert_k$ even if it is not a root, because it is already trusted.

Step 2. The extension transfers $(Cert_0, \cdots, Cert_k, \sigma)$ to KGuard, where σ is the HMAC tag for $Cert_k$. In addition, the extension transfers the server's host name to KGuard. The transferring is accomplished by a hypercall.

Step 3. In response, KGuard first checks whether σ is a valid HMAC for $Cert_k$ using the HMAC key provided by the user during bootup. If the checking fails, KGuard rejects the certificate chain and aborts.

Step 4. KGuard then verifies the certificate chain in the same ways as the browser's verification, by treating $Cert_k$ as a trusted CA. Namely, it checks $Cert_i$'s signatures with the public key in $Cert_{i+1}$ for $0 \leq i \leq k - 1$, and make sure that they are not expired, and checks whether $Cert_0$'s subject name matches the given server hostname (domain name). If all certificates pass the checking, KGuard accepts $Cert_0$ as the server's public key and uses it to encrypt the pre-master secret key in the current SSL connection.

The hypervisor calculates an HMAC value of each certificate in the verified certification chain, and returns them back to the guest if the certificate chain passes all checks. The browser inserts the certificate with its HMAC tag into the trusted certificate repository. This is to save the hypervisor's verification time when this certificate is reused in the user's future logins. Note that the new website certificates are accepted once the root certificate is trusted by the user.

4.4   Security Analysis

The security of the proposed password protection mechanism relies on the security of the hypervisor and the user cooperation. With the assumption on both conditions, the user-hypervisor channel ensures that the password is typed in only when KGuard is in position for keystroke interception, which saves the real password in the hypervisor space. The hypervisor and the guest space isolation enabled by the virtualization techniques prevents the guest from accessing the password. When the browser runs an SSL connection to submit the password, all cryptographic operations are performed by the hypervisor. The browser and the guest OS only get the ciphertext of the password. The hypervisor security is discussed in the Section 7.

5   Implementation

5.1   KGuard in the Hypervisor

We have built a prototype of KGuard on Xen 4.1.0 on a desktop with an Intel(R) Core(TM) i7 CPU-860 @2.80GHz processor and 4GB main memory. We choose a USB-keyboard as the experiment device. The implementation of KGuard does not depend on the design of Xen and can be easily migrated to other hypervisors.

KGuard consists of around 1500 SLOC for its main functions except cryptographic functions. We import the needed crypto functions (about 5000 SLOC) from [23]. The main cost is due to AES and RSA algorithms which need about 3500 SLOC. Nonetheless, comparing with the Xen code base (around 225,000 SLOC), we only increase the code size 2.885%. In fact, most of the code in Xen are not used by our system. Therefore, it is one of our future work to customize Xen for KGuard.

Visual Verification. One of the implementation issues about the user's visual verification of the hypervisor verification is to choose a proper secret message. It is similar to a password in the sense that it should not be random enough to resist dictionary attacks, and it should be easy to remember. Since the user does not type in the message at runtime, the message can be much longer than a password. For instance, we choose the string $"ApBlE@8s\_BaeuTifu10O"$ as the user secret in our experiment.

Another issue is the position of the text message on the screen. We do not change the position for two reasons. Firstly, it does not enhance the security. If malware can breach the access control, it may grab the entire display buffer data. Secondly, from the usability perspective, it is inconvenient for users to find the message over the whole screen. We choose the top-left corner of the screen as the location because it is less likely to be overlapped with the web page in use.

The third concerns in visual verification is the performance overhead due to the slow speed of the display memory. It requires twice display memory access for the hypervisor to save the present content and to write the secret message. In our implementation, we use the following trick to save one display memory access. We do not save the original data. Instead, we impose the font bitmap of characters in the message upon the existing content. By performing the XOR operation, all the bits corresponding to the characters are flipped. As a result, the shape of the character is displayed on the screen. Although the content is not saved, it can be recovered by running the XOR operations again.

Note that our current implementation requires to work with the VGA compatible graphics cards.

5.2 Browser Extension and Plugin

Benefiting from the virtualization features of the Intel processor, we launch a hardware virtual machine (HVM) running Windows. The HVM guest domain runs a installation of Windows 7 Professional version with default configuration. We choose the popular firefox (version 3.6) as the test browser, and extend it with a plug-in and an extension.

The main part of the browser plug-in is based on CyaSSL v2[2]. It interacts with the hypervisor using hypercalls to build a separated SSL channel with a web server. Specifically, The plug-in interacts the hypervisor in the SSL handshake phase for four times: to transfer the server certificate chain; to provide the key materials for pre-master key generation; to provide the authentication data for encryption; and to provide a finish-message to terminate the SSL handshake phase. The plugin finishes the SSL protocol and forwards the server response data to the browser extension.

The browser extension is implemented using Firefox XML User interface Language (XUL) and JavaScript. One of the tasks of the extension is to listening to the user activation key combination and then sends a hypercall to KGuard. The other two tasks are to integrate the password protection with the browser. The first task is to intercept the authentication data submitted to the server. Since KGuard is transparent to the browser, it proceeds as usual in password submission though with a dummy password.

The events generated by Firefox after the login button is clicked are shown in Figure 1. We choose to intercept the *HTTP Request Event*, the last event right before Firefox is about to pass the data to the SSL layer. The benefit of this choice is that this event implies that the browser has prepared all the data (including the HTTP header) expected by the web server. Therefore, the extension does not need to handle the nuisance of gathering all kinds of POST data required by the web server.

---

[2] CyaSSL is a C-Langue SSL library for embedded and realtime operating systems, and in regular desktop and enterprise environments [12].

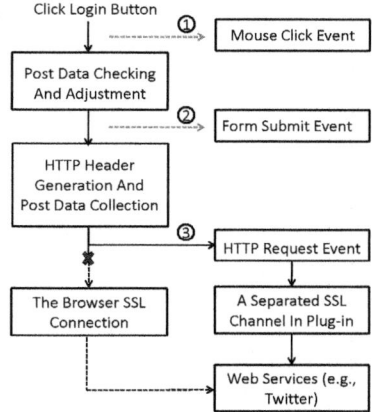

Fig. 1. Firefox events in the login session where the third one is intercepted by the extension

The second task is to navigate the browser to the destination URL that is in the server response packages. After receiving the response packages returned by the plug-in from its own SSL channel, the extension extracts the cookies and the redirection URL by parsing the header and body. It updates the cookies in the browser, and requests it to refresh the current page to the redirection URL. For the following connections, no matter whether they are HTTPS or HTTP connections, the browser will send the request with corresponding cookies, and continue the web session as normal. Note that the browser is not aware of the existence of the separated SSL connection, thanks to the statelessness of HTTP and HTTPS protocols.

5.3   Hypercall Support in the HVM

In the Windows kernel space, we build a virtual device module using the Windows Driver Kit (WDK) [17]. The module first uses the instruction *CPUID* to find registers that contain the size and the location of the hypercall table. Then it maps the hypercall table into its own memory space. Using the mapped hypercall table, the module is able to issue hypercalls to communicate with the hypervisor.

The module also exports a *DeviceIOControl* interface for application usage. According-ing to the *dwIoControlCode* parameter in the *DeviceIOControl* interface, the module can request different services by issuing different types of hypercalls to the hypervisor.

6   Performance Evaluation

We have run experiments and evaluated the performance and usability with legitimate web servers, including Google, Groupon, Twitter and Amazon, and Microsoft Hotmail. We divide the total authentication session into two phases to facilitate the evaluation. The first phase is user password input and the second is password submission. We have measured the time overhead in each of them. Note that our protection is the "on-demand" mode, therefore, there are no extra cost for the system when the protection is inactive.

6.1   Overhead for Password Input

Table 1 lists the time costs for the procedures taking place during a user's password inputting. The password input phase begins with protection activation and ends with protection deactivation. The main overhead is due to the hypervisor's responses to the activation/deactivation command and its interception of keyboard strokes. The activation cost mainly includes a guest system call, a hypercall, a series of access control setup, and two accesses on the display memory. The deactivation cost only includes the removal of access control on the relevant regions. The keystroke-interception cost is the CPU time spent for intercepting one keystroke. It includes two exceptions, emulation of the refreshing of TD and processing the keystroke.

Note that the user secret message is written to the display memory, instead of the main memory. Its speed is only 27 MHZ, much slower than the main memory chip. Therefore, the secret message displaying dominates the overhead of protection activation. Nonetheless, it is still negligible to the user as compared to the human keystroke speed. The removal of the secret message is not considered as the overhead, because with a high likelihood, it is completed between the user's two keystrokes.

Table 1. The performance overhead for password input protection in KGuard

Components	Protection Activation	Protection Deactivation	Keystroke Interception	Displaying Message
Time	$1.71ms$	$3.5\mu s$	$0.12\mu s$	$1.67ms$

6.2   Overhead for Password Submission

In the password submission procedure, we evaluate the extra operations introduced by our scheme, i.e. those not appearing in normal web authentication. The extra operations include the extension's HTTP Request event interception and extracting data from the login (POST) request, which cost about $4ms$ in total. Note that the extension is written in JavaScript, whose best timing granularity is in milliseconds. The extra operations also include transferring data between the guest and the hypervisor; HMAC verification for the certificate's trustworthiness. The measurement results are listed in Table 2.

We have also measured the turnaround time to evaluate the overall delay a user may experience with KGuard. The turnaround time refers to the period from the moment when the login button is clicked, to the moment when the browser begins refreshing the page. We have tested KGuard with Twitter and a local web server which resides in the same platform with the browser so that no network delay variation disturbs the results. The results are shown in Table 3. Note that the results from the tests with Twitter are not sufficiently accurate due to the large variance of network round trip time.

Table 2. The performance overhead of each component for password submission

	Event interception and data extraction	Data transferring cost during in hypercalls	HMAC computation
Time	$4ms$	$1.38ms$	$0.02ms$

Table 3. The overall performance measurement in the login procedure

	Login without KGuard	Login with KGuard	Extra Cost
Twitter	$1.10s$	$1.11s$	$10ms$
Local Web Site	$201ms$	$207ms$	$6ms$

7 Discussions

7.1 Hypervisor Security

The hypervisor security is the bedrock of the proposed password protection system. It is known that both the code size and the interfaces affect the hypervisor security. According to [2,20], the size of the source code is proportional to the number of vulnerabilities (bugs). We choose Xen for our prototype building instead of the other mainstream hypervisor VMware ESXi, because the former has a smaller code size according to [26] and is open source. In principle, KGuard can also be built on those tiny hypervisors developed by researchers, such as SecVisor [24], BitVisor [25] and Nova [26]. Unfortunately, they are not supported by the Intel processor used in our platform. As mentioned in [18], interfaces are the main source of critical errors. In the current Xen hypervisor, all default hypercalls for a HVM domain are only used during HVM loading. Therefore, we turn off all of them to enhance security to minimize the attack surface.

In the future work, we aim to reduce the hypervisor code size by removing unnecessary code. Besides the basic hardware virtualization functions, our initial study shows that the functionalities required by KGuard include: 1) memory management, including data transferring and address translation between the guest and the hypervisor; 2) access control on all I/O ports and memory regions; 3) interceptions on interrupts and exceptions; 4) basic crypto algorithms, such as RSA, AES and SHA1; 5) certain instruction emulations; and 6) asynchronization support (e.g., timer).

7.2 Trusted Certificate Updates

The user may need to insert or delete entries in the trusted certificate repository. It is relatively straightforward to add a new trusted certificate. The user simply calculates the HMAC value on a clean system and adds the certificate and its HMAC into the repository.

However, it is costly to revoke a trusted certificate from the repository. One solution is that the user chooses a new HMAC key and re-computes the HMAC tags for all trusted certificates excluding those revoked ones. Once the new key is updated to the hypervisor, the revoked certificates will not pass the verification. Alternatively, the user can prepare a Certificate Revocation List (CRL) whose integrity is protected by the HMAC tag. Whenever the plugin sends the server certificate to the hypervisor, the CRL is attached. The hypervisor then checks whether the certificate in use is on the CRL. Both methods have pros and cons. The former requires more user involvement while the latter increases the hypervisor's code size and causes more runtime overhead.

7.3   Sensitive Keyboard Input Protection

The KGuard system proposed in this paper focuses on password protection. We can easily extend it to protect other sensitive inputs from the keyboard, such as CAPTCHA, credit card numbers or driver license numbers. KGuard is able to intercept and replace the sensitive inputs whenever the user activates the protection. By inserting them back into an SSL/TLS connection or forwarding them to a trusted domain, all sensitive inputs are free from malware attacks.

The challenge is to maintain the user's experience. For a normal password input, the browser only displays a string of '*'. The user feels the same even if KGuard replaces the original password with dummy ones. However, for other types of inputs, the user may feel discomfort when seeing dummy characters instead of the expected ones. Another issue on the user interface is how a user determines the correctness of the input, since a wrong key may have been pressed accidentally. One possible solution is that KGuard echoes each input on the screen in the same ways as in the visual verification. Alternatively, KGuard can display the entire input string and ask for user confirmation. This method does not work well for protecting a large amount of sensitive inputs (e.g., private document editing) due to the heavy load on the hypervisor and the slow responses. In addition, it would add too much code into the hypervisor and possibly weakens the security strength.

8   Conclusion

To conclude, this paper has presented a virtualization based password input protection system, which is composed of a novel user-hypervisor interaction channel, a keyboard stroke interception mechanism, and a hypervisor-based SSL client. Our method does not require specialized hardware and is fully transparent to the operating system and the browser. The prototype implementation and testing have demonstrated that the protection system incurs insignificant overhead on the platform and maintains the user-friendliness of password authentication in web services.

Acknowledgements.   The authors are grateful to anonymous reviewers for their valuable feedback. This work is partially supported by Centre for Strategic Infocomm Technology (CSIT) Technology Innovation Fund (TIF) Project #PO2011240001 and by Singapore Management University (SMU) Office of Research under the project #12-C220-SMU-003.

References

1. Barham, P., Dragovic, B., Fraser, K., Hand, S., Harris, T., Ho, A., Neugebauer, R., Pratt, I., Warfield, A.: Xen and the art of virtualization. In: SOSP 2003: Proceedings of the Nineteenth ACM Symposium on Operating Systems Principles, pp. 164–177. ACM, New York (2003)
2. Basili, V.R., Perricone, B.T.: Software errors and complexity: an empirical investigation. Commun. ACM 27, 42–52 (1984)

3. Bugiel, S., Dmitrienko, A., Kostiainen, K., Sadeghi, A.-R., Winandy, M.: TruWalletM: Secure Web Authentication on Mobile Platforms. In: Chen, L., Yung, M. (eds.) INTRUST 2010. LNCS, vol. 6802, pp. 219–236. Springer, Heidelberg (2011)

4. Chen, X., Garfinkel, T., Christopher Lewis, E., Subrahmanyam, P., Waldspurger, C.A., Boneh, D., Dwoskin, J., Ports, D.R.K.: Overshadow: A virtualization-based approach to retrofitting protection in commodity operating systems. In: Proceedings of the 13th International Conference on Architectural Support for Programming Languages and Operating Systems (ASPLOS 2008), Seattle, WA, USA (March 2008)

5. Cheng, Y., Ding, X., Deng, R.H.: DriverGuard: A Fine-Grained Protection on I/O Flows. In: Atluri, V., Diaz, C. (eds.) ESORICS 2011. LNCS, vol. 6879, pp. 227–244. Springer, Heidelberg (2011)

6. Cox, R.S., Hansen, J.G., Gribble, S.D., Levy, H.M.: A safety-oriented platform for web applications. In: Proceedings of IEEE Symposium on Security and Privacy (2006)

7. CVE-2008-0923 (2008),
   http://cve.mitre.org/cgi-bin/cvename.cgi-?name=cve-2008-0923

8. Gajek, S., Löhr, H., Sadeghi, A.-R., Winandy, M.: Truwallet: trustworthy and migratable wallet-based web authentication. In: Proceedings of the 2009 ACM workshop on Scalable trusted computing, STC 2009, pp. 19–28. ACM, New York (2009)

9. Grier, C., Tang, S., King, S.: Secure web browsing with the OP web browser. In: Proceedings of IEEE Symposium on Security and Privacy (2008)

10. IBM. IBM VGA Technical Reference Manual,
    http://www.mca-mafia.de/pdf/ibm_vgaxga_trm2.pdf

11. King, S.T., Chen, P.M., Wang, Y.-M., Verbowski, C., Wang, H.J., Lorch, J.R.: Subvirt: Implementing malware with virtual machines. In: Proceedings of the 2006 IEEE Symposium on Security and Privacy, pp. 314–327. IEEE Computer Society, Washington, DC (2006)

12. Sawtooth Consulting Limited. CyaSSL Embedded SSL Library,
    http://www.yassl.com/yaSSL/Products-cyassl.html

13. McCune, J.M., Li, Y., Qu, N., Zhou, Z., Datta, A., Gligor, V., Perrig, A.: Trustvisor: Efficient tcb reduction and attestation. In: Proceedings of the 2010 IEEE Symposium on Security and Privacy, SP 2010, pp. 143–158. IEEE Computer Society, Washington, DC (2010)

14. McCune, J.M., Parno, B., Perrig, A., Reiter, M.K., Isozaki, H.: Flicker: An execution infrastructure for TCB minimization. In: EuroSys 2008 (2008)

15. McCune, J.M., Perrig, A., Reiter, M.K.: Bump in the ether: a framework for securing sensitive user input. In: Proceedings of the Annual Conference on USENIX 2006 Annual Technical Conference, p. 17. USENIX Association, Berkeley (2006)

16. McCune, J.M., Perrig, A., Reiter, M.K.: Safe passage for passwords and other sensitive data. In: Proceedings of the Symposium on Network and Distributed Systems Security (NDSS) (February 2009)

17. Microsoft. About the Windows Driver Kit (WDK), http://goo.gl/DfSRi

18. Murray, D.G., Milos, G., Hand, S.: Improving xen security through disaggregation. In: Proceedings of the Fourth ACM SIGPLAN/SIGOPS International Conference on Virtual Execution Environments, VEE 2008, pp. 151–160. ACM, New York (2008)

19. Oprea, A., Balfanz, D., Durfee, G., Smetters, D.K.: Securing a remote terminal application with a mobile trusted device. In: 20th Annual Computer Security Applications Conference, pp. 438–447. IEEE (2004)

20. Ostrand, T.J., Weyuker, E.J.: The distribution of faults in a large industrial software system. In: Proceedings of the 2002 ACM SIGSOFT International Symposium on Software Testing and Analysis, ISSTA 2002, pp. 55–64. ACM, New York (2002)

21. Rafal, W., Joanna, R., Alexander, T.: Xen 0wning trilogy (2008),
    http://invisible-thingslab.com/itl/Resources.html

22. Ross, B., Jackson, C., Miyake, N., Boneh, D., Mitchell, J.: Stronger password authentication using browser extensions. In: Proceedings of the 14th USENIX Security Symposium (2005)

23. Limited Sawtooth, Consulting. Ctaocrypt embedded cryptography library, http://www.yassh.com/yaSSL/Docs_CTaoCrypt_Usage_Reference.html

24. Seshadri, A., Luk, M., Qu, N., Perrig, A.: Secvisor: a tiny hypervisor to provide lifetime kernel code integrity for commodity oses. In: Proceedings of Twenty-First ACM SIGOPS Symposium on Operating Systems Principles, SOSP 2007, pp. 335–350. ACM, New York (2007)

25. Shinagawa, T., Eiraku, H., Tanimoto, K., Omote, K., Hasegawa, S., Horie, T., Hirano, M., Kourai, K., Oyama, Y., Kawai, E., Kono, K., Chiba, S., Shinjo, Y., Kato, K.: Bitvisor: a thin hypervisor for enforcing i/o device security. In: Proceedings of the 2009 ACM SIG-PLAN/SIGOPS International Conference on Virtual Execution Environments, VEE 2009, pp. 121–130. ACM, New York (2009)

26. Steinberg, U., Kauer, B.: Nova: a microhypervisor-based secure virtualization architecture. In: Proceedings of the 5th European Conference on Computer Systems, EuroSys 2010, pp. 209–222. ACM, New York (2010)

27. The Blue Pill, http://blackhat.com/presentations/bh-usa-06/BH-US-06-Rutkowska.pdf

28. Trusted Computing Group. TPM main specification. Main Specification Version 1.2 rev. 85 (February 2005)

29. Wu, M., Miller, R.C., Little, G.: Web wallet: Preventing phishing attacks by revealing user intentions. In: Proceedings of the Symposium on Usable Privacy and Security (SOUPS), pp. 102–113. ACM Press (2006)

30. Zaharia, M., Katti, S., Grier, C., Paxson, V., Shenker, S., Stoica, I., Song, D.: Hypervisors as a foothold for personal computer security: An agenda for the research community. Technical report (January 2012)

SmartTokens: Delegable Access Control with NFC-Enabled Smartphones

Alexandra Dmitrienko[1], Ahmad-Reza Sadeghi[2],
Sandeep Tamrakar[3], and Christian Wachsmann[4]

[1] Fraunhofer SIT Darmstadt, Germany
[2] Technische Universität Darmstadt & Fraunhofer SIT Darmstadt, Germany
[3] Aalto University School of Science, Finland
`sandeep.tamrakar@aalto.fi`
[4] Technische Universität Darmstadt (CASED), Germany
`{alexandra.dmitrienko,christian.wachsmann,`
`ahmad.sadeghi}@trust.cased.de`

Abstract. Today's smartphones and tablets offer compelling computing and storage capabilities enabling a variety of mobile applications with rich functionality. The integration of new interfaces, in particular near field communication (NFC) opens new opportunities for new applications and business models, as the most recent trend in industry for payment and ticketing shows. These applications require storing and processing security-critical data on smartphones, making them attractive targets for a variety of attacks. The state of the art to enhance platform security concerns outsourcing security-critical computations to hardware-isolated Trusted Execution Environments (TrEE). However, since these TrEEs are used by software running in commodity operating systems, malware could impersonate the software and use the TrEE in an unintended way. Further, existing NFC-based access control solutions for smartphones are either not public or based on strong assumptions that are hard to achieve in practice. We present the design and implementation of a generic access control system for NFC-enabled smartphones based on a multi-level security architecture for smartphones. Our solution allows users to delegate their access rights and addresses the bandwidth constraints of NFC. Our prototype captures electronic access to facilities, such as entrances and offices, and binds NFC operations to a software-isolated TrEE established on the widely used Android smartphone operating system. We provide a formal security analysis of our protocols and evaluate the performance of our solution.

1 Introduction

Modern smartphones are equipped with a variety of communication interfaces and enable mobile access to many different services, including Internet, web services, e-mail, multi-media entertainment, navigation and location-based services. The integration of additional communication interfaces, in particular near field

S. Katzenbeisser et al. (Eds.): TRUST 2012, LNCS 7344, pp. 219–238, 2012.

communication (NFC) [36], greatly enlarges the application area of smart devices. NFC-based access control systems on smartphones and commercial NFC-based applications for ticketing and payment are particularly promoted by industry.

Electronic access control tokens for smartphones offer a variety of appealing features: they can be distributed and revoked remotely, delegated by users, and may support context-aware and time-limited access control policies. There are already some commercial systems on the market, including electronic hotel room keys [1,7,15] that are sent to the customer via SMS or email, and electronic car keys [14,41]. These applications require storing and processing security-critical data on smartphones, raising risks of being targeted by attacks. However, the security properties of current solutions are unclear, in particular because their design and implementation details are not publicly available and most operating systems for smartphones are vulnerable to malware [32,33].

A vast amount of research (such as in [16,26,11]) has been performed on hardening platform security based on secure hardware that is already available in many smartphones, such as M-Shield [3] and ARM TrustZone [2] on Nokia devices. Existing security hardware typically provides a trusted execution environment (TrEE) that enforces secure and isolated execution of small programs. However, currently available TrEEs are typically resource-constrained and prevent the implementation of important security functionalities, such as secure user interfaces [11]. Further, even the verification of X.509 certificates within a TrEE is challenging and requires a number of subsequent invocations of the TrEE [11], which introduces additional performance overhead. Hence, practical security architectures built on top of existing TrEEs must rely on additional trusted components in the operating system.

The secure implementation of security critical NFC-based applications on smartphones, such as electronic payment, ticketing and access control systems, requires the underlying security architecture to isolate trusted and untrusted components to prevent leakage and unintended manipulation of security-critical data, such as authentication secrets. Furthermore, the underlying protocol design must consider the bandwidth constraints of NFC.

Contribution and Outline. We present the design and implementation of an access control system for NFC-enabled smartphones. The unique feature of our scheme is that users can delegate (part of) their access rights to other users without contacting a central token issuer. Our contributions are as follows:

Multi-level Platform Security Architecture. Our SmartToken application runs on top of a security architecture that protects the underlying authentication secrets. The architecture combines a hardware-supported trusted execution environment (TrEE) to handle cryptographic keys with software-based isolation of trusted code controlling access to the TrEE (Section 2). The architecture provides a two-line defense against software attacks and a trade-off between security and resource constraints of common security hardware.

Delegatable SmartToken System. We present a generic token-based access control system for NFC-enabled smartphones that, in contrast to previous solutions, supports delegation of access rights without contacting a central token issuer and that addresses the bandwidth constraints of NFC (Section 3). Our solution is suitable for various applications, ranging from access control solutions for digital objects, such as electronic documents, to physical resources like rooms or cars. Further, we prove the security properties of our system (Section 4).

Reference Implementation. We instantiate the SmartToken system for electronic access control tokens (Section 5). The implementation is based on TrustDroid [10], which extends the widely used Android smartphone operating system with software-based isolation of trusted and untrusted compartments. Further, we conceptually consider binding NFC operations to a hardware-based trusted execution environment (TrEE).

2   Multi-level Security Architecture

In this section we describe our multi-level security platform architecture, which we deploy to protect user credentials on the device.

2.1   Model and Requirement Analysis

In the following, we describe our system model, formulate security objectives and requirements, and define our trust and adversary model.

System Model. We consider mobile platforms that (1) run untrusted code, such as user applications downloaded from untrusted sources, (2) store user credentials, such as user passwords and cryptographic secrets that are used in cryptographic protocols to authenticate the user to some service provider, and that (3) run security-critical code that, e.g., operates on security sensitive data, such as cryptographic keys.

Security Objectives and Requirements. The objective of our overall solution is to prevent the adversary from being able to authenticate to a service provider. While attacks against the authentication protocols must be prevented by protocol design (Section 3), the platform security architecture must ensure (1) that the adversary cannot access user credentials stored on the platform and (2) that he cannot exploit or modify code using them. More specifically, the objective of the platform security architecture is to ensure *confidentiality* of and to enforce *access control* to credentials, i.e., that any application on the platform can use only those credentials that have been created or enrolled by this application before. This results in the following security requirements:

- *Confidentiality of user credentials:* User credentials created or enrolled by security-critical code must not be accessible by untrusted and other security-critical code while stored or used on the platform.
- *Code isolation:* Security-critical code that processes user credentials must be isolated from untrusted and other security-critical code on the platform.
- *Code access control:* Only authorized code instances must be able to invoke execution of security-critical code that has access to user credentials.

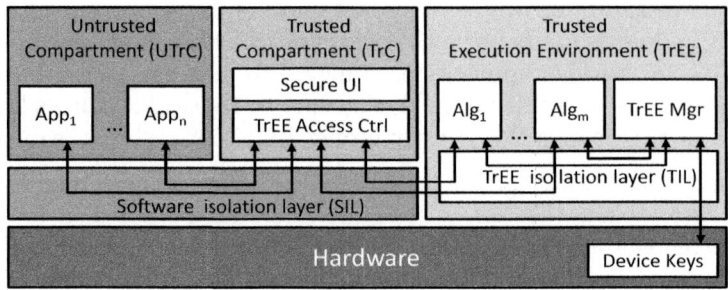

Fig. 1. Generic multi-level platform security architecture

- *Code integrity:* The integrity of security-critical code that has access to user
  credentials and the integrity of untrusted code that can invoke security-
  critical code must be preserved.

Trust and Adversary Model. The adversary can perform software attacks
and install, modify or compromise arbitrary code on the device. However, he
cannot access or modify the hardware of the platform and its trusted computing
base, i.e., the code that enforces access control or isolation on the device.

2.2   Generic Security Architecture

Figure 1 illustrates our multi-level security platform architecture. At a high level,
the execution environment of the device is split into three isolated compartments
(Figure 1): an untrusted compartment UTrC, a trusted compartment TrC and a
trusted execution environment TrEE. TrEE is isolated from the rest of the system by the underlying security hardware and protected against software-based
attacks. However, TrEE is a resource-constrained component. UTrC is free of strict
resource constraints and isolated from the untrusted compartment by means of
software, which is less reliable compared to hardware-based isolation since isolation can be broken upon successful compromise of the software isolation layer.
TrEE is used to run secure code that operates on user credentials, while TrC
handles system components that exceed the capabilities of TrEE. Particularly,
TrC provides a secure user interface SecureUI, which is used to collect security-
sensitive user input (such as passwords) or to display output. Further, TrC includes the TrAC component, which enforces access control to the code running
within TrEE.[1]

Security-sensitive applications are split into an untrusted host application
App_i running in UTrC and one or more security-sensitive algorithms Alg_j that
are executed by TrEE and that can be invoked by App_i when necessary (Figure 1).
Communication between App_i and the algorithms Alg_j within TrEE is mediated

---

[1] Note, that both SecureUI and TrAC have been shown to exceed resource-constraints
of commodity TrEEs [28,11].

by TrAC, which ensures that App_i can communicate only to those Alg_j App_i is supposed to communicate to. The software isolation layer verifies the integrity of host applications (e.g., by comparing the hash digest of the application binary to a reference value or by verifying the application's signature upon application loading) and reports it to TrAC, which then grants or denies access to the TrEE based on the integrity of the host application.

Algorithms executed within TrEE may belong to different host applications and thus are mutually untrusted. Thus, they are isolated from each other, which is enforced by the TrEE isolation layer. Furthermore, TrEE includes the TrEEMgr component, which has direct access to platform keys stored in secure memory and that provides a sealing/unsealing functionality to the algorithms. More specifically, TrEEMgr encrypts/decrypts user credentials with a key that is cryptographically bound to the platform key and the identity of the algorithm (such as the hash digest of its binary).

The trusted computing base of our architecture includes the software isolation layer, trusted compartment, TrEE isolation layer and the TrEE manager.

Fulfillment of the Security Requirements. Our security architecture achieves the security requirements described in Section 2.1: confidentiality of user credentials is ensured by a trusted TrEEMgr component, which stores user credentials only in an encrypted form and such that they can be decrypted only by authorized algorithms (sealing). Isolation of security-critical code from untrusted code is enforced by a hardware-isolated TrEE, while isolation from other security-critical code is provided by the trusted isolation layer within the TrEE. Access control to security-critical code is enforced by the TrAC component. The integrity of security-critical code is ensured by the sealing functionality of TrEEMgr, which ensures that user credentials can be decrypted only if the integrity of the algorithm is preserved. Integrity of untrusted code is enforced by the software isolation layer, which measures and verifies the application integrity upon loading the application and denies access to TrC if the application has been modified.

Our security architecture provides higher security guarantees than approaches using pure software-based isolation and solutions that rely only on hardware-based TrEEs (such as [29,20,26,11]), where the secure user interface and access control to the TrEE is typically outsourced to the untrusted commodity operating system that is vulnerable to various attacks.

2.3 Architecture Instantiation

Our security architecture can be instantiated based on different types of security hardware and different approaches to software-based isolation. For instance, the TrEE can be instantiated using ARM TrustZone [2], M-Shield [3], embedded or removable secure elements, such as SIM cards, universal integrated circuit cards (UICC), or secure memory cards (SMC). A detailed discussion of different types of hardware security modules can be found in [35].

Software-enforced isolation can be implemented based on virtualization technology or hardened operating systems that enforce domain isolation by mandatory access control. Examples include the OKL4 microvisor [24], domain isolation based on security kernels [43], and the TrustDroid [10] security enhancement of the Android operating system.

Instantiation for Android Devices. We aim to instantiate our multi-level security architecture on Android-powered devices, since Android is the most popular smartphone operating system worldwide [19] and first NFC-enabled Android devices appear on the market. On the other hand, most secure NFC-based applications target Nokia smartphones, most probably since NFC-enabled Nokia smartphones are already available for some time and equipped with secure hardware. At the time of writing, we are not aware of any instantiation of a secure access control application for Android devices and aim to fill this gap.

To enforce the software isolation required by our architecture, we could follow the virtualization approach, e.g., based on the OKL4 microvisor that can run multiple instances of L4Android, as well as native applications. However, as supported by OKL4-based developments [17], a number of challenges has to be solved with regard to performance, power consumption and drivers portability before virtualization approaches become a practical solution for mobile devices. Thus, we opted for a more practical solution and adopted the TrustDroid security extensions [10] to enforce isolation.

TrustDroid applies a coloring approach to isolation that has its origins in information-flow theory [37]. Particularly, it uses the concept of application identifiers on Android and colors (tags) applications and application data upon application installation. Based on the assigned colors, TrustDroid organizes applications along with their data in logical domains. At runtime, communication across domains is prevented by means of mandatory access control applied on all communication channels between applications, including inter-process communication (IPC) calls, Linux sockets, file system access and local network connections. We extended TrustDroid to form isolated domains and enabled inter-domain communication through well-defined interfaces, as required by our architecture. The details of our implementation can be found in Section 5.

3   Smart Token System

We present a generic access control system that allows users to maintain their access credentials for different resources on their smartphone. One of the key features of our scheme is that users can delegate their credentials to other users without contacting a central token issuer. The system is applicable to various applications, ranging from access control solutions for digital objects, such as electronic documents, to physical resources like rooms and cars.

3.1   Overview

The entities in our system are at least a token issuer $\mathcal{I}$, a set of resources $\mathcal{R}$ (such as electronic documents or doors) and a set of users $\mathcal{U}$ (Figure 2). We denote the adversary with $\mathcal{A}$. Each $\mathcal{U}$ possesses a mobile platform $\mathcal{P}_\mathcal{U}$, such as a smartphone or tablet. $\mathcal{I}$ is a central authority that defines which $\mathcal{U}$ is allowed to access which

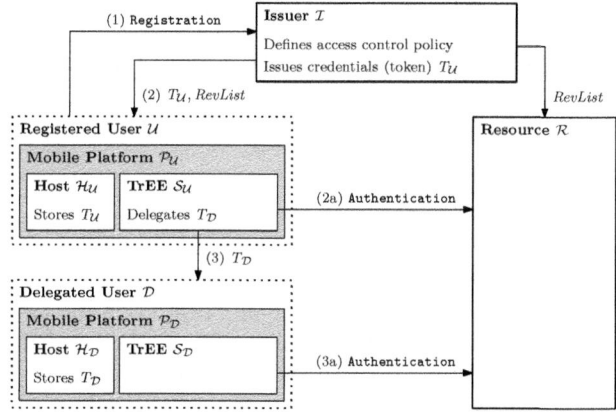

Fig. 2. SmartToken system overview

$\mathcal{R}$. Further, $\mathcal{I}$ issues credentials (SmartTokens) $T_\mathcal{U}$ to each $\mathcal{U}$, which are used later by $\mathcal{U}$ to authenticate to $\mathcal{R}$. We distinguish between registered users and delegated users. A registered user $\mathcal{U}$ can delegate his token $T_\mathcal{U}$ to a delegated user $\mathcal{D}$, while a delegated user $\mathcal{D}$ cannot delegate his token $T_\mathcal{D}$.

Objectives. The objectives of our solution are as follows:

- *Access control.* Access to a resource $\mathcal{R}$ is granted only (1) to a registered user $\mathcal{U}$, who got a token $T_\mathcal{U}$ for $\mathcal{R}$ from issuer $\mathcal{I}$, and (2) to a delegated user $\mathcal{D}$, who got a token $T_\mathcal{D}$ for $\mathcal{R}$ from a registered user $\mathcal{U}$ with $T_\mathcal{U}$ for $\mathcal{R}$.
- *Delegation.* Issuer $\mathcal{I}$ can allow registered users to delegate (share) their tokens with other users.
- *Revocation.* Issuer $\mathcal{I}$ can revoke tokens of regular and/or delegated users. Revoking token $T_\mathcal{U}$ of a registered user $\mathcal{U}$ automatically revokes all delegated tokens $T_\mathcal{D}$ based on $T_\mathcal{U}$.

Note that our scheme provides basic protection against denial-of-service attacks that permanently prevent a user from using the SmartToken scheme. However, since the focus of this paper is delegatable authentication for NFC-enabled smartphones, we did not consider countermeasures against denial of-service attacks.

Protocols. Our scheme is composed of the following protocols:

- *System initialization:* Issuer $\mathcal{I}$ generates its authentication secrets and encryption keys. Moreover, $\mathcal{I}$ generates and initializes each resource $\mathcal{R}$ with an authentication secret and encryption key.
- *User registration:* User $\mathcal{U}$ registers its mobile platform $\mathcal{P}_\mathcal{U}$ with $\mathcal{I}$ and becomes a registered user.
- *Token issuing:* $\mathcal{I}$ generates and sends the authentication key, the delegation key and token $T_\mathcal{U}$ to the mobile platform $\mathcal{P}_\mathcal{U}$ of a registered user $\mathcal{U}$.

- *Token delegation:* A registered user $\mathcal{U}$ delegates its smart token (its access rights) to a user $\mathcal{D}$, who then becomes a delegated user.
- *User authentication:* $\mathcal{U}$ or $\mathcal{D}$ authenticate to $\mathcal{R}$. Access to $\mathcal{R}$ is granted or denied based on the result of the authentication protocol.
- *Token and user revocation:* $\mathcal{I}$ revokes one or all tokens of $\mathcal{U}$ by updating the revocation list *RevList* on each $\mathcal{R}$.

Our scheme is inspired by Kerberos [31], which is a widely deployed and extensively analyzed authentication protocol. Kerberos provides strong authentication for client/server applications based on symmetric cryptography. Our protocols follow a similar approach to distribute authentication secrets with tokens issued by a key distribution center (KDC), which corresponds to the issuer in our scheme. However, in contrast to Kerberos our scheme enables delegation of tokens by clients (mobile devices) without contacting the KDC. Further, tokens are bound to the identity and the platform of their user by means of a one-time password and a device-specific platform key, respectively.

Trust Model and Assumptions. We assume that each registered user $\mathcal{U}$ and each delegated user $\mathcal{D}$ possesses a mobile platform $\mathcal{P}$, which consists of an untrusted operating environment (host) $\mathcal{H}$ and a trusted execution environment (TrEE) $\mathcal{S}$ (Figure 2). In Section 5, we show how the TrEE can be implemented based on an isolated trusted software compartment. Further, we assume issuer $\mathcal{I}$, resource $\mathcal{R}$ and $\mathcal{S}$ to be trusted. Moreover, we assume that an authentic and confidential out-of-band channel between $\mathcal{I}$ and $\mathcal{U}$ is available once before the user registration protocol, and between $\mathcal{U}$ and $\mathcal{D}$ once before the token delegation protocol. Note that this is very natural since in many access control scenarios users typically have to prove their identity (e.g., by showing their identity card) to $\mathcal{I}$ during registration and/or will get a personal welcome letter with their access credentials from $\mathcal{I}$. Furthermore, $\mathcal{S}$ provides countermeasures against dictionary attacks.

Adversary Model. We consider adversaries $\mathcal{A}$ that have full control over the communication between $\mathcal{I}$, $\mathcal{R}$, $\mathcal{U}$ and $\mathcal{D}$, which means that $\mathcal{A}$ can eavesdrop, modify, insert, delete and re-route protocol messages.[2] Further, $\mathcal{A}$ can compromise the untrusted part $\mathcal{H}$ of the user's mobile platform $\mathcal{P}$ and gain access to all information stored in $\mathcal{H}$. However, as mentioned in assumptions, $\mathcal{A}$ cannot compromise issuer $\mathcal{I}$, resource $\mathcal{R}$ or TrEE $\mathcal{S}$ of $\mathcal{P}$. In particular, $\mathcal{A}$ cannot change the functionality of $\mathcal{S}$ and $\mathcal{A}$ cannot obtain any secret information stored in $\mathcal{S}$.

3.2   Notation and Preliminaries

We denote with $a \in_R A$ the uniform sampling of an element a from a set A. Let A be a probabilistic algorithm. Then $y \leftarrow \mathsf{A}(x)$ means that on input x, algorithm

---

[2] Note that we exclude relay attacks since the focus of this paper is delegatable authentication for NFC-enabled smartphones. Relay attacks can be mitigated by distance bounding techniques, which can be integrated into our scheme.

$\mathcal{A}$ assigns its output to variable y. Probability $\epsilon(l)$ is called *negligible* if for all polynomials $f(\ )$ it holds that $\epsilon(l) \leq 1/f(l)$ for all sufficiently large l. Further, ID_X is the unique identifier, sk_X the secret key, and pk_X the public key of entity X, respectively.

Encryption Schemes. An encryption scheme ES is a tuple of algorithms (Genkey, Enc, Dec) where Genkey is the key generation, Enc is the encryption and Dec is the decryption algorithm. A public-key encryption scheme is said to be CPA-secure [22,4] if every probabilistic polynomial time (p.p.t.) adversary $\mathcal{A}$ has at most negligible advantage of winning the following security experiment: an algorithm $\mathcal{C}_{sk}^{\mathrm{CPA}}$ (CPA-challenger), generates an encryption key pk and decryption key sk using Genkey(1^l), chooses $b \in_R \{0,1\}$, encrypts $c_b \leftarrow$ Enc($pk; m_b$) and returns c_b to $\mathcal{A}$. Eventually, $\mathcal{A}$ must return a bit b' that indicates whether c_b encrypts m_0 or m_1. $\mathcal{A}$ wins if $b' = b$. Note that for symmetric encryption schemes $sk = pk$.

Random Oracles. A random oracle RO [6] is an oracle that responds with a random output to each given input. More precisely, RO starts with an empty look-up table Γ. When queried with input m, RO first checks if it already knows a value $\Gamma[m]$. If this is not the case, RO chooses $r \in_R \{0,1\}^\alpha$ and updates Γ such that $\Gamma[m] = r$. Finally, RO returns $\Gamma[m]$. Random oracles model the ideal security properties of cryptographic hash functions.

Note that our protocols use the MAC-then-encrypt paradigm [5], where for a given plaintext m, first the message digest $\sigma = $ RO(m) is computed and then (m, σ) is encrypted with a CPA-secure encryption scheme.

3.3 Protocol Specification

System Initialization. Each mobile platform $\mathcal{P}$ has a unique platform key pair $(sk_\mathcal{P}, pk_\mathcal{P})$, where $sk_\mathcal{P}$ is only known to trusted execution environment (TrEE) $\mathcal{S}$ of platform $\mathcal{P}$. Further, host $\mathcal{H}$ of $\mathcal{P}$ stores a certificate $cert_\mathcal{P}$ issued by, e.g., the platform manufacturer, which contains $pk_\mathcal{P}$ and attests that $pk_\mathcal{P}$ is the public key of a genuine TrEE $\mathcal{S}$ and that $sk_\mathcal{P}$ is securely stored in and never leaves $\mathcal{S}$. Issuer $\mathcal{I}$ initializes the revocation list $RevList \leftarrow \emptyset$ and each resource $\mathcal{R}$ with $RevList$, a resource-specific authentication key $K_{\mathrm{Auth}}^\mathcal{R}$ and a resource-specific encryption/decryption key $K_{\mathrm{Enc}}^\mathcal{R}$.

User Registration. When a user $\mathcal{U}$ wants to register, $\mathcal{I}$ sends a new one-time password $pwd_\mathcal{U}$ to $\mathcal{U}$ over an authentic and confidential out-of-band channel. After that, $\mathcal{U}$ can register as follows (Figure 3): $\mathcal{U}$ sends its identifier $ID_\mathcal{U}$ and $pwd_\mathcal{U}$ to TrEE $\mathcal{S}_\mathcal{U}$ of its mobile platform $\mathcal{P}_\mathcal{U} = (\mathcal{H}_\mathcal{U}, \mathcal{S}_\mathcal{U})$. Then $\mathcal{S}_\mathcal{U}$ sends $ID_\mathcal{U}$ and a random $N_{\mathrm{reg}}^\mathcal{U}$ to host $\mathcal{H}_\mathcal{U}$, which sends both values and the platform certificate $cert_\mathcal{P}^\mathcal{U}$ to $\mathcal{I}$. Next, $\mathcal{I}$ verifies $cert_\mathcal{P}^\mathcal{U}$ and generates a new authentication secret $K_{\mathrm{Auth}}^{\mathcal{U},\mathcal{I}}$ and an encryption/decryption key $K_{\mathrm{Enc}}^\mathcal{U}$ for $\mathcal{U}$, which are used later in the token issuing protocol. Further, $\mathcal{I}$ derives a temporary authentication secret K

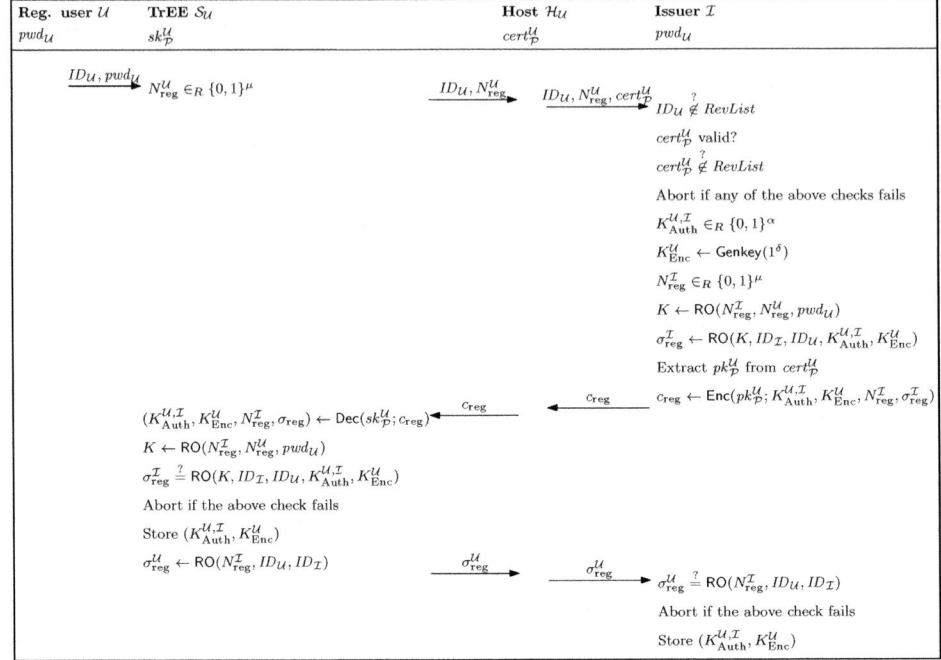

Fig. 3. User registration protocol

from $pwd_\mathcal{U}$, computes authenticator $\sigma_{\mathrm{reg}}^\mathcal{I}$ for $K_{\mathrm{Auth}}^{\mathcal{U},\mathcal{I}}$ and $K_{\mathrm{Enc}}^\mathcal{U}$, encrypts both keys and $\sigma_{\mathrm{reg}}^\mathcal{I}$ with the platform key $pk_\mathcal{P}^\mathcal{U}$ of $\mathcal{S}_\mathcal{U}$, and sends the resulting ciphertext c_{reg} to $\mathcal{S}_\mathcal{U}$. On receipt of c_{reg} $\mathcal{S}_\mathcal{U}$ decrypts c_{reg} and, in case the verification of σ_{reg} is successful, stores $(K_{\mathrm{Auth}}^{\mathcal{U},\mathcal{I}}, K_{\mathrm{Enc}}^\mathcal{U})$. Then, $\mathcal{S}_\mathcal{U}$ sends authenticatior $\sigma_{\mathrm{reg}}^\mathcal{U}$ to $\mathcal{I}$, which verifies $\sigma_{\mathrm{reg}}^\mathcal{U}$ and, in case the verification was successful, stores $(K_{\mathrm{Auth}}^{\mathcal{U},\mathcal{I}}, K_{\mathrm{Enc}}^\mathcal{U})$. In case $\mathcal{I}$ already stores an authentication secret and encryption/decryption key for $\mathcal{U}$, $\mathcal{I}$ deletes the old keys and stores the newly generated ones.

Token Issuing. The token issuing protocol is depicted in Figure 4: user $\mathcal{U}$ initiates the protocol at TrEE $\mathcal{S}_\mathcal{U}$ of its mobile platform $\mathcal{P}_\mathcal{U}$, which then sends $ID_\mathcal{U}$ and a random N_{iss} to $\mathcal{I}$. Next, $\mathcal{I}$ generates authentication secret $K_{\mathrm{Auth}}^{\mathcal{U},\mathcal{R}}$, delegation secret $K_{\mathrm{Del}}^\mathcal{U}$ and token $T_\mathcal{U}$ for $\mathcal{U}$, which are used later by $\mathcal{U}$ in the authentication and delegation protocols. Further, $\mathcal{I}$ computes σ_{iss} that authenticates $K_{\mathrm{Auth}}^{\mathcal{U},\mathcal{R}}$, $K_{\mathrm{Del}}^\mathcal{U}$ and $T_\mathcal{U}$, encrypts these keys, $T_\mathcal{U}$ and σ_{iss} with $K_{\mathrm{Enc}}^\mathcal{U}$, and sends the resulting ciphertext c_{iss} to host $\mathcal{H}_\mathcal{U}$ of $\mathcal{P}_\mathcal{U}$, which passes c_{iss} to $\mathcal{S}_\mathcal{U}$. Next, $\mathcal{S}_\mathcal{U}$ decrypts c_{iss} and, in case the verification of σ_{iss} is successful, stores $(K_{\mathrm{Auth}}^{\mathcal{U},\mathcal{R}}, K_{\mathrm{Del}}^\mathcal{U})$. Eventually, $\mathcal{S}_\mathcal{U}$ sends $T_\mathcal{U}$ to $\mathcal{H}_\mathcal{U}$.

Authentication of Registered Users. The authentication protocol for registered users is depicted in Figure 5: user $\mathcal{U}$ initiates the protocol at TrEE $\mathcal{S}_\mathcal{U}$ of its mobile platform $\mathcal{P}_\mathcal{U}$, which sends an authentication request to resource $\mathcal{R}$.

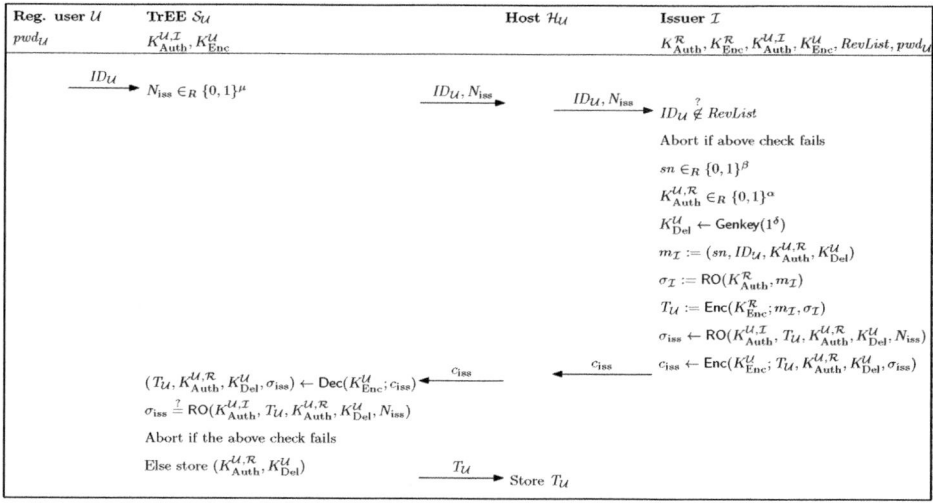

Fig. 4. Token issuing protocol

Then $\mathcal{R}$ sends its identifier $ID_{\mathcal{R}}$ and a random N to $\mathcal{S}_{\mathcal{U}}$, which replies with $\sigma_{\mathcal{U}}$ to $\mathcal{H}_{\mathcal{U}}$ that sends $(\sigma_{\mathcal{U}}, T_{\mathcal{U}})$ to $\mathcal{R}$. Next, $\mathcal{R}$ decrypts $T_{\mathcal{U}}$ with $K_{\text{Enc}}^{\mathcal{R}}$ to obtain $K_{\text{Auth}}^{\mathcal{U},\mathcal{R}}$, verifies $\sigma_{\mathcal{I}}$ and $\sigma_{\mathcal{U}}$ using $K_{\text{Auth}}^{\mathcal{R}}$ and $K_{\text{Auth}}^{\mathcal{U},\mathcal{R}}$, respectively, and accepts only if both verifications are successful. Otherwise, $\mathcal{R}$ rejects.

Token Delegation. Registered user $\mathcal{U}$ and delegated user $\mathcal{D}$ establish a new one-time secret $pwd_{\mathcal{D}}$ over an authentic and confidential out-of-band-channel. Then, the token delegation protocol (Figure 6) starts: $\mathcal{D}$ sends its identifier $ID_{\mathcal{D}}$ and $pwd_{\mathcal{D}}$ to TrEE $\mathcal{S}_{\mathcal{D}}$ of its mobile platform $\mathcal{P}_{\mathcal{D}} = (\mathcal{S}_{\mathcal{D}}, \mathcal{H}_{\mathcal{D}})$, which then sends a random $N_{\text{del}}^{\mathcal{D}}$ to host $\mathcal{H}_{\mathcal{D}}$ that passes $(ID_{\mathcal{D}}, N_{\text{del}}^{\mathcal{D}})$ together with the platform certificate $cert_{\mathcal{P}}^{\mathcal{D}}$ of $\mathcal{P}_{\mathcal{D}}$ to host $\mathcal{H}_{\mathcal{U}}$ of the registered user's mobile platform $\mathcal{P}_{\mathcal{U}} = (\mathcal{S}_{\mathcal{U}}, \mathcal{H}_{\mathcal{U}})$. $\mathcal{H}_{\mathcal{U}}$ then sends $(ID_{\mathcal{D}}, N_{\text{del}}^{\mathcal{D}}, cert_{\mathcal{P}}^{\mathcal{D}})$ and token $T_{\mathcal{U}}$ of $\mathcal{U}$ to $\mathcal{S}_{\mathcal{U}}$. Next, $\mathcal{S}_{\mathcal{U}}$ verifies $cert_{\mathcal{P}}^{\mathcal{D}}$, generates authentication secret $K_{\text{Auth}}^{\mathcal{P}}$ for $\mathcal{D}$, computes authenticator $\sigma_{\mathcal{U}}$ and delegated token $T_{\mathcal{D}}$. Further, $\mathcal{S}_{\mathcal{U}}$ derives a temporary authentication secret K from $pwd_{\mathcal{D}}$ and uses K to compute authenticator σ_{del}. Moreover, $\mathcal{S}_{\mathcal{U}}$ encrypts $(K_{\text{Auth}}^{\mathcal{D}}, T_{\mathcal{D}}, T_{\mathcal{U}})$ with the platform key $pk_{\mathcal{P}}^{\mathcal{D}}$ of $\mathcal{S}_{\mathcal{D}}$ and sends the resulting ciphertext c_{del} to $\mathcal{S}_{\mathcal{D}}$. Next, $\mathcal{S}_{\mathcal{D}}$ decrypts and, in case the verification of σ is successful, stores $K_{\text{Auth}}^{\mathcal{D}}$ and sends $(T_{\mathcal{D}}, T_{\mathcal{U}})$ to $\mathcal{H}_{\mathcal{D}}$, which are used later in the authentication protocol.

Authentication of Delegated Users. Authentication of delegated users is similar to authentication of registered users (Figure 5). The only difference is that a delegated user $\mathcal{D}$ sends in addition to its delegated token $T_{\mathcal{D}}$ also the token $T_{\mathcal{U}}$ of user $\mathcal{U}$ that created $T_{\mathcal{D}}$. Further, $\mathcal{R}$ first decrypts $T_{\mathcal{U}}$ to obtain $K_{\text{Del}}^{\mathcal{U}}$, which is then used to decrypt $K_{\text{Auth}}^{\mathcal{D}}$ from $T_{\mathcal{D}}$. The rest of the authentication protocol is the same as in Figure 5.

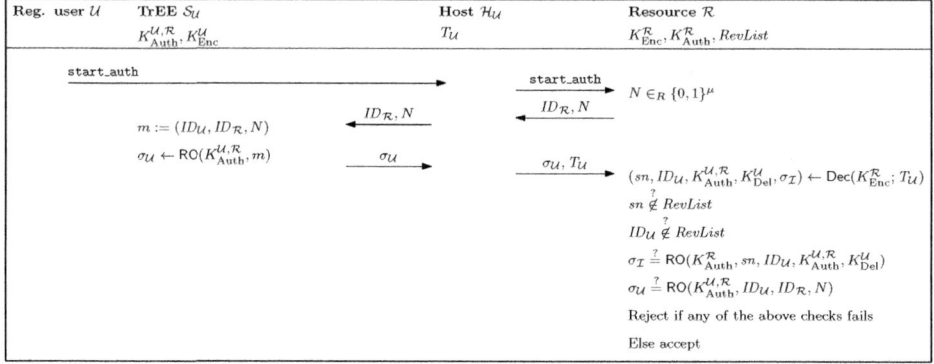

Fig. 5. Authentication protocol for registered users

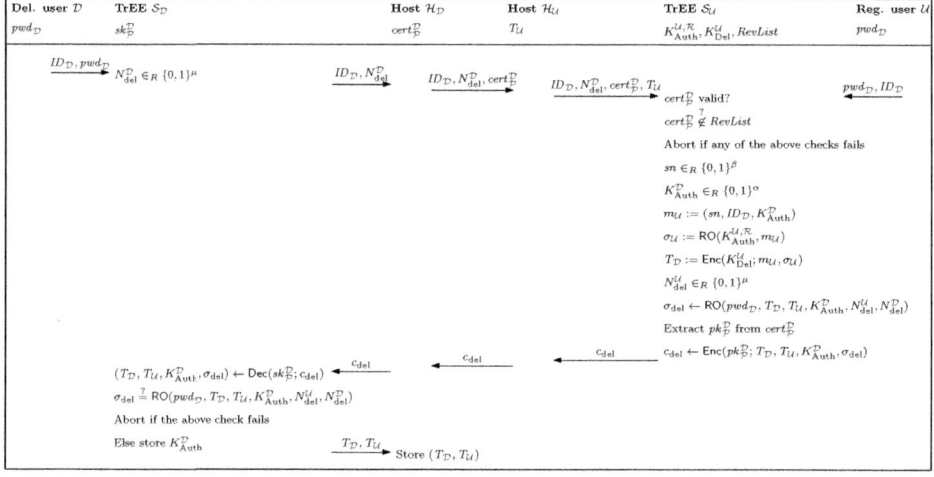

Fig. 6. Token delegation protocol

Token and User Revocation. To revoke a token $T_{\mathcal{U}}$ (or all tokens of user $\mathcal{U}$), sn (or $ID_{\mathcal{U}}$) is added to *RevList*.

4 Security Analysis

The security goal of the authentication scheme in Section 3.3 is *token authentication*, which means that only registered and delegated users, whose smartphone has a valid token T and knows the corresponding authentication secret K_{Auth}, can make an honest resource $\mathcal{R}$ accept. This can be formalized by a security experiment $\mathbf{Exp}_{\mathcal{A}}^{\text{Auth}}(q) = out_{\mathcal{R}}^{\pi}$, where a probabilistic polynomial time (p.p.t.) adversary $\mathcal{A}$ must make an honest resource $\mathcal{R}$ to authenticate $\mathcal{A}$ either as a registered user $\mathcal{U}$ or delegated user $\mathcal{D}$ by returning $out_{\mathcal{R}}^{\pi} = 1$ in some instance π of one of the authentication protocols (Section 3.3). Following the approach by Canetti et al. [12], $\mathcal{A}$ can arbitrarily interact a limited number of times q with $\mathcal{I}$, $\mathcal{U}$, $\mathcal{D}$ and their mobile platforms $\mathcal{P} = (\mathcal{H}, \mathcal{S})$ and knows all information stored on $\mathcal{H}$. However, since we do not consider relay attacks, $\mathcal{A}$ is not allowed to just forward all messages from $\mathcal{S}$ to $\mathcal{R}$ in instance π. Hence, at least some of the protocol messages that made $\mathcal{R}$ accept must have been (partly) computed by $\mathcal{A}$ without knowing the secrets of $\mathcal{S}$. Note that, as discussed in Section 3.1, by assumption $\mathcal{A}$ does not know any value, including intermediate computation results, stored in $\mathcal{S}$ at any time and can only obtain the messages sent to $\mathcal{S}$ and its responses.

Definition 1. *A token-based authentication scheme achieves token authentication if for every p.p.t. adversary $\mathcal{A}$* $\Pr\left[\mathbf{Exp}_{\mathcal{A}}^{\mathrm{Auth}}(q) = 1\right]$ *is negligible in q.*

Theorem 1. *The authentication scheme in Section 3.3 achieves token authentication (Definition 1) in the random oracle model under the assumption that the underlying encryption schemes are CPA-secure (Section 3.2).*

We give only a proof sketch here, while the full proof can be found in the full version of the paper [18].

Proof (Sketch). Assume by contradiction that $\mathcal{A}$ is an adversary with non-negligible success probability. We show that $\mathcal{A}$ can be used to construct an adversary $\mathcal{B}$ that violates the definition of the underlying random oracle RO or the CPA-security of the underlying encryption schemes (Section 3.2). More detailed, $\mathcal{B}$ simulates the protocols in Section 3.3 according to their specification except that $\mathcal{B}$ simulates all ciphertexts and tokens by encrypting random plaintexts. Following the approach by Shoup [38], we show that the CPA-security of the underlying encryption schemes ensures that the simulation by $\mathcal{B}$ has a negligible effect on $\mathcal{A}$'s success probability. $\mathcal{A}$ is allowed to arbitrarily interact with RO and the simulation by $\mathcal{B}$. Eventually, in protocol session π, $\mathcal{A}$ responds to message $(ID_{\mathcal{R}}, N)$ generated by $\mathcal{B}$ with $out_{\pi}^{\mathcal{A}}$, which is used by $\mathcal{B}$ to compute either a collision for RO or to predict the output of RO with non-negligible probability, which violates the definition of RO (Section 3.2). Hence, RO and the CPA-security of the underlying encryption schemes ensure that there is no p.p.t. $\mathcal{A}$ that violates token authentication (Definition 1) with non-negligible probability.   □

5   SmartTokens Reference Implementation

In this section, we describe the implementation of the SmartToken design presented in Section 3.3 based on the security architecture described in Section 2. We exemplarily consider the scenario, where a company plays the role of issuer $\mathcal{I}$, while users $\mathcal{U}$ correspond to employees and delegated users $\mathcal{D}$ to temporary visitors or other employees. The resources $\mathcal{R}$ are the company premises, including buildings and rooms.

5.1   Instantiation of the Multi-level Platform Security Architecture

In our current implementation, we instantiated a modified multi-level security architecture that slightly differs from the one described in Section 2. The reason

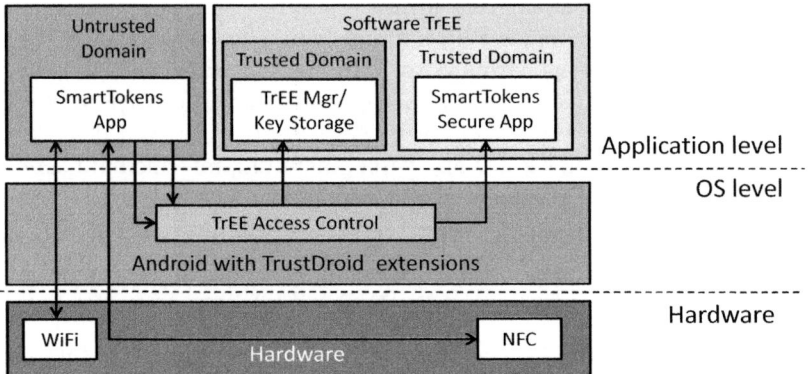

Fig. 7. Implemented Platform Security Architecture

is that we could not identify any Android device featuring both NFC and security hardware that can be used by third party developers. In particular, we could not find Android devices with M-Shield or ARM TrustZone, while Android platforms with SIM cards or universal integrated circuit cards (UICC) do not allow accessing the secure hardware. Moreover, there seems to be no Android device on the market that provides both an NFC interface and a microSD slot, which would have allowed using a removable secure memory card (SMC) as TrEE. However, we envision the availability of such devices in the near future and designed our implementation such that it can be easily ported to these security modules upon availability.

Due to this temporal limitation, our current prototype uses software-based isolation to establish a trusted execution environment (TrEE) on the device. The refined security platform architecture is depicted in Figure 7. It builds on the top of TrustDroid [10], a security framework that enhances the standard Android operating system with mandatory access control at all operating system levels, wich allows to establish isolated compartments (or domains) on the device. Further, TrustDroid allows to define inter-domain communication rules by specifying system-centric security policies.[3] We realized acces control to the TrEE as a security service of TrustDroid (thus, it resides at the level of the operating system), while TrEE is realized as a number of application-level isolated compartments. One TrEE-based compartment contains the TrEE Manager, while other compartments are intended to run secure code associated with host applications running in an untrusted compartment.

Implementation Details. We implemented the SmartToken scheme in Section 3.3 on Nexus S smartphones running Android 2.3.3 patched with Trust-Droid security extensions. The prototype implementation of resources uses a

---

[3] TrustDroid applies very simple rules that restrict inter-domain communication. However, the TrustDroid framework itself allows defining more sophisticated security policies, e.g., to prevent application-level privilege escalation attacks [9,8].

commodity NFC reader (ACS ACR 122 U) connected to a Linux PC running Ubuntu Oneiric.

NFC Communication Mode. We implemented our protocols using Android NFC card reader and writer APIs, which provide direct access to different NFC tag technologies using tag-specific application protocol data unit (APDU) command and response structures. Specifically, we use the ISO Dep Android API that allows direct access to smartcard properties and read/write operations according to the widely used ISO 14443-4 standard for contactless smartcards. The NFC reader emulates NFC Forum type 4 contactless smartcards that communicate according to ISO 14443-4. We used libnfc open source libraries[4] for accessing the NFC reader from the Linux PC. The implementation of the token authentication and user delegation protocol (Figure 5 and 6) uses ISO/IEC 7816-4 and ISO/IEC 7816-8 specific APDUs. ISO/IEC 7816-4 defines a standard interface for identifying applications and accessing files and data on smartcards, while ISO/IEC 7816-8 defines commands for security operations on smartcards. Further, we implemented an application on the Linux PC emulating the resource in the token authentication protocols.

Primitives and Parameter Sizes. Random oracle RO is implemented as HMAC based on SHA-1, where $\alpha = 160$. For the symmetric encryption scheme ES we used AES, i.e., $\delta = 128$. To achieve CPA-security (Section 3.2), which is required by the MAC-then-encrypt paradigm [5] used in our protocols and our security proof, AES is used in CBC mode with random padding. The public-key encryption scheme is implemented based on RSA with random padding, which means that platform keys are $2,048$ bit RSA keys. Further, we use $\beta = 64$ for token serial numbers sn and $\mu = 128$ for nonces. All identifiers ID are random 64 bit strings. For the one-time passwords pwd used in the user registration (Figure 3) and token delegation protocol (Figure 6), we use $\rho = 128$. Note that long passwords can be encoded in a barcode or data-matrix that can be printed on the user's welcome letter and scanned with the smartphone's camera. For delegated users, the barcode can be shown on the display of the registered user's smartphone and scanned by the camera of the delegated user's phone.

Performance Analysis. We measured the time required to complete an authentication protocol session between the NFC reader and the phone for a registered user and a delegated user. Table 1 shows the time for exchanging different protocol messages and the overall authentication session completion time. The average data transmission rate between NFC reader and phone is around 10 kbps. Our measurements show that it requires about 540 ms to complete an authentication session for a registered user and about 565 ms for a delegated user.

6   Related Work

There are several NFC-based applications for smartphones, including key storage and management, payment and ticketing systems, and remote attestation.

---

[4] www.libnfc.org

Table 1. Transmission times for authentication protocol messages (units are in milliseconds with 95% confidence interval)

User Type	Connection Estb.	Start Msg.	Reading $(ID_\mathcal{R}, N)$	Sending (σ_D, T_D, T_U)	Session Time
Registered	245.17(± .18)	42.19(±.52)	59.6 (± .51)	98.4 (± .53)	441.8(± .54)
Delegated	245.17(± .18)	42.19(±.52)	59.6 (± .51)	121.6 (± .54)	473.55 (± .54)

Key Storage and Management. Mantoro et al. [30] propose a scheme to protect the cryptographic keys of a PC by securely storing them in the SIM card of an NFC-enabled phone. However, the scheme protects only against offline attacks aiming to recover keys from the PC memory and is vulnerable to runtime attacks since keys are uploaded to the PC when used and thus can be accessed by malware. Noll et al. [34,27] propose a key management architecture that uses a SIM card to securely manage the authentication secrets of a smartphone. They describe several use cases, including an NFC-based access control system that allows distributing electronic keys via SMS. However, the security of their scheme is unclear since the use case is only sketched and neither protocols nor a security analysis is provided.

NFC-Based Payment Systems. Chen et al. [13] propose an NFC-based mobile payment system leveraging SIM-based authentication capabilities of GSM networks. However, their scheme requires all involved parties to be subscribed to the same mobile operator, which is not always guaranteed in practice and not required in our scheme. Another NFC-based mobile payment system by Kadambi et al. [26] is based on payment authorization tokens that are used to authorize transactions. Their scheme protects privacy-sensitive user data, such as credit card numbers, even against merchants. Although their solution uses secure hardware, access to the secure environment is controlled by a commodity operating system that may be vulnerable to various attacks [32,33]. In contrast, in our scheme access control to the TrEE is enforced by trusted software components. Gauthier et al. [20] propose an offline payment system based on digital vouchers that can be transferred from one to another device over NFC. However, their scheme heavily relies on public-key operations resulting in low performance, while our scheme uses only efficient symmetric techniques and tackles the bandwidth limitations of the NFC interface (for the protocol running over NFC). The Merx system [39] provides a solution for delegated electronic payments. Its system model involves four parties: (1) a customer, (2) a concierge, (3) a merchant and (4) a bank, which can be mapped to the entities of our model as follows: (1) a user, (2) a delegated user, (3) a resource and (4) an issuer, respectively. The system requires online interactions between merchant and bank on each purchase, which is common for payment systems. However, when mapped into our use case, this scheme would require an online connection between the issuer and the resource upon each access of the user to the resource, which is highly undesirable in our use case and not required by our scheme.

NFC-Based Ticketing Systems. Tamrakar et al. [40] present an NFC-based authentication scheme for electronic transport tickets. However, their scheme is vulnerable to replay attacks and assumes the mobile device to be equipped with a trusted time source, which is hard to achieve in practice and not required in our scheme. Ghìron et al. [21] present a prototype implementation of an NFC-enabled ticketing system. However, their work focuses on usability rather than security aspects.

NFC-Enabled Remote Attestation. Toegl et al. [25,42] propose verifying the integrity of public terminals, such as ticket vending machines, using NFC-enabled smartphones. Their scheme requires terminals to be equipped with NFC-enabled TPMs, which are not conform to the latest TPM specification [23] and not available on the market.

7   Conclusion and Future Work

We present the design of a token-based access control system for NFC-enabled smartphones that can be used in many applications. The scheme allows users to delegate (part of) their access rights to other smartphone users without involvement of a central authority (a token issuer). Our scheme considers the bandwidth constraints of NFC by using only symmetric cryptographic primitives for the protocols running over NFC. We provide a formal security analysis of our scheme and instantiate it in the application scenario, where access control tokens are used as electronic door keys. We propose an implementation of our system for Android-powered Nexus S smartphones. Our performance analysis shows that authentication can be performed within 474 ms. Furthermore, we present a multi-level security architecture to protect the underlying authentication secrets of our protocols. The architecture combines a hardware-assisted trusted execution environment (TrEE) with software-based isolation and overcomes the drawbacks of existing solutions.

Future work includes extending the implementation of our multi-level security architecture for Android-based smartphones with security hardware, when these devices are available on the market. Moreover, we are implementing the token-based access control system and the multi-level security architecture on Nokia C7 phones, which feature an NFC interface and ARM TrustZone security hardware.

Acknowledgements. We thank our anonymous reviewers for their helpful comments and Raphael Friedrich, Stephan Heuser and Daniel Steinmetzer for supporting the implementation. This work has been supported in part by the European Commission through the FP7 programme under contract 238811 UNIQUE.

References

1. VingCard Elsafe's NFC locking solution wins prestigious gaming industry technology award,
   http://www.hotel-online.com/News/PR2011_3rd/Aug11_VingCardHOT.html

2. Alves, T., Felton, D.: TrustZone: Integrated hardware and software security. Information Quaterly 3(4) (2004)
3. Azema, J., Fayad, G.: M-Shield mobile security technology: making wireless secure. Texas Instruments White Paper (2008), http://focus.ti.com/pdfs/wtbu/ti_mshield_whitepaper.pdf
4. Bellare, M., Desai, A., Pointcheval, D., Rogaway, P.: Relations among Notions of Security for Public-Key Encryption Schemes. In: Krawczyk, H. (ed.) CRYPTO 1998. LNCS, vol. 1462, pp. 26–45. Springer, Heidelberg (1998)
5. Bellare, M., Namprempre, C.: Authenticated Encryption: Relations among Notions and Analysis of the Generic Composition Paradigm. In: Okamoto, T. (ed.) ASIACRYPT 2000. LNCS, vol. 1976, pp. 531–545. Springer, Heidelberg (2000)
6. Bellare, M., Rogaway, P.: Random oracles are practical: A paradigm for designing efficient protocols. In: ACM Conference on Computer and Communications Security (ACM CCS), pp. 62–73. ACM, New York (1993)
7. Brown, C.: NFC room keys find favour with hotel guests, http://www.nfcworld.com/2011/06/08/37869/nfc-room-keys-find-favour-with-hotel-guests/
8. Bugiel, S., Davi, L., Dmitrienko, A., Fischer, T., Sadeghi, A.R.: Xmandroid: A new Android evolution to mitigate privilege escalation attacks. Technical Report TR-2011-04, Technische Universität Darmstadt (2011)
9. Bugiel, S., Davi, L., Dmitrienko, A., Fischer, T., Sadeghi, A.R., Shastry, B.: Towards taming privilege-escalation attacks on Android. In: 19th Annual Network & Distributed System Security Symposium, NDSS (2012)
10. Bugiel, S., Davi, L., Dmitrienko, A., Heuser, S., Sadeghi, A.R., Shastry, B.: Practical and lightweight domain isolation on Android. In: ACM CCS Workshop on Security and Privacy in Mobile Devices (SPSM). ACM Press (2011)
11. Bugiel, S., Dmitrienko, A., Kostiainen, K., Sadeghi, A.-R., Winandy, M.: TruWalletM: Secure Web Authentication on Mobile Platforms. In: Chen, L., Yung, M. (eds.) INTRUST 2010. LNCS, vol. 6802, pp. 219–236. Springer, Heidelberg (2011)
12. Canetti, R., Krawczyk, H.: Analysis of Key-Exchange Protocols and Their Use for Building Secure Channels. In: Pfitzmann, B. (ed.) EUROCRYPT 2001. LNCS, vol. 2045, pp. 453–474. Springer, Heidelberg (2001)
13. Chen, W., Hancke, G.P., Mayes, K.E., Lien, Y., Chiu, J.H.: NFC mobile transactions and authentication based on GSM network. In: International Workshop on Near Field Communication (NFC), pp. 83–89. IEEE Computer Society, Washington, DC (2010)
14. Clark, S.: NXP launches NFC car key, http://www.nfcworld.com/2011/06/22/38196/nxp-launches-nfc-car-key/
15. Clark, S.: VingCard launches NFC room key system for hotels, http://www.nfcworld.com/2011/06/28/38366/vingcard-launches-nfc-room-key-system-for-hotels/
16. Costan, V., Sarmenta, L.F.G., van Dijk, M., Devadas, S.: The Trusted Execution Module: Commodity General-Purpose Trusted Computing. In: Grimaud, G., Standaert, F.-X. (eds.) CARDIS 2008. LNCS, vol. 5189, pp. 133–148. Springer, Heidelberg (2008)
17. Davi, L., Dmitrienko, A., Kowalski, C., Winandy, M.: Trusted virtual domains on OKL4: Secure information sharing on smartphones. In: ACM Workshop on Scalable Trusted Computing (ACM STC). ACM Press (2011)
18. Dmitrienko, A., Sadeghi, A.R., Tamrakar, S., Wachsmann, C.: Smarttokens: Delegable access control with NFC-enabled smartphones (extended version). Cryptology ePrint Archive, Report 2012/187 (2012)

19. Gartner Inc.: (2011), http://www.gartner.com/it/page.jsp?id=1689814
20. Gauthier, V.D., Wouters, K.M., Karahan, H., Preneel, B.: Offline NFC payments with electronic vouchers. In: ACM Workshop on Networking, Systems, and Applications for Mobile Handhelds (MobiHeld), pp. 25–30. ACM, New York (2009)
21. Ghiron, S.L., Sposato, S., Medaglia, C.M., Moroni, A.: NFC ticketing: A prototype and usability test of an NFC-based virtual ticketing application. In: International Workshop on Near Field Communication (NFC), pp. 45–50. IEEE Computer Society, Washington, DC (2009)
22. Goldwasser, S., Micali, S.: Probabilistic encryption. Journal of Computer and System Sciences 28, 270–299 (1984)
23. Trusted Computing Group: TPM Main Specification, Version 1.2 rev. 103 (2007), https://www.trustedcomputinggroup.org
24. Heiser, G., Leslie, B.: The OKL4 microvisor: Convergence point of microkernels and hypervisors. In: ACM Asia-pacific Workshop on Systems (APSys), pp. 19–24. ACM, New York (2010)
25. Hutter, M., Toegl, R.: A trusted platform module for near field communication. In: International Conference on Systems and Networks Communications (ICSNC), pp. 136–141. IEEE Computer Society, Washington, DC (2010)
26. Kadambi, K.S., Li, J., Karp, A.H.: Near-field communication-based secure mobile payment service. In: International Conference on Electronic Commerce (ICEC), pp. 142–151. ACM, New York (2009)
27. Kalman, G., Noll, J., UniK, K.: SIM as secure key storage in communication networks. In: International Conference on Wireless and Mobile Communications, ICWMC (2007)
28. Kostiainen, K., Asokan, N., Afanasyeva, A.: Towards User-Friendly Credential Transfer on Open Credential Platforms. In: Lopez, J., Tsudik, G. (eds.) ACNS 2011. LNCS, vol. 6715, pp. 395–412. Springer, Heidelberg (2011)
29. Kostiainen, K., Ekberg, J.E., Asokan, N., Rantala, A.: On-board credentials with open provisioning. In: ACM Symposium on Information, Computer, and Communications Security (ASIACCS), pp. 104–115. ACM (2009)
30. Mantoro, T., Milisic, A.: Smart card authentication for Internet applications using NFC enabled phone. In: International Conference on Information and Communication Technology for the Muslim World, ICT4M (2010)
31. Massachusetts Institute of Technology: Kerberos: The network authentication protocol, http://web.mit.edu/kerberos/
32. McAfee Labs: McAfee threats report: Second quarter (2011), http://www.mcafee.com/us/resources/reports/rp-quarterly-threat-q2-2011.pdf
33. McAfee Labs: McAfee threats report: Third quarter (2011), http://www.mcafee.com/us/resources/reports/rp-quarterly-threat-q3-2011.pdf
34. Noll, J., Lopez Calvet, J.C., Myksvoll, K.: Admittance services through mobile phone short messages. In: International Multi-Conference on Computing in the Global Information Technology, pp. 77–82. IEEE Computer Society, Washington, DC (2006)
35. Reveilhac, M., Pasquet, M.: Promising secure element alternatives for NFC technology. In: International Workshop on Near Field Communication (NFC), pp. 75–80. IEEE Computer Society, Washington, DC (2009)
36. Robertson, T.: Eight industries that will benefit from NFC technology, https://www.x.com/devzone/articles/eight-industries-will-benefit-nfc-technology

37. Rushby, J.M.: Design and verification of secure systems. In: ACM Symposium on Operating Systems Principles, SOPS (1981)
38. Shoup, V.: Sequences of games: A tool for taming complexity in security proofs. Cryptology ePrint Archive, Report 2004/332 (2004)
39. Soghoian, C., Aad, I.: Merx: Secure and Privacy Preserving Delegated Payments. In: Chen, L., Mitchell, C.J., Martin, A. (eds.) Trust 2009. LNCS, vol. 5471, pp. 217–239. Springer, Heidelberg (2009)
40. Tamrakar, S., Ekberg, J.E., Asokan, N.: Identity verification schemes for public transport ticketing with NFC phones. In: ACM workshop on Scalable Trusted Computing (STC), pp. 37–48. ACM, New York (2011)
41. Telecom Innovation Laboratories: Mobile Wallet turns cell phones into digital car keys (2011),
    http://www.laboratories.telekom.com/public/English/Newsroom/news/Pages/
    digitaler_Autoschluessel_Mobile_Wallet.aspx
42. Toegl, R., Hutter, M.: An approach to introducing locality in remote attestation using near field communications. J. Supercomput. 55(2), 207–227 (2011)
43. Zhang, X., Acıçmez, O., Seifert, J.P.: A trusted mobile phone reference architecture via secure kernel. In: ACM workshop on Scalable Trusted Computing (ACM STC), pp. 7–14. ACM, New York (2007)

A Belief Logic for Analyzing Security of Web Protocols

Apurva Kumar

IBM Research, India
kapurva@in.ibm.com

Abstract. Many useful transactions on the web are implemented as a sequence of interactions that a user performs with multiple collaborating providers. Safety of such transactions requires the user to not only trust individual providers and communication channels, but also the web protocols that manage security of these transactions. A protocol can be trusted for a particular usage, if the guarantees that it provides its participants are considered acceptable in the context. An important set of approaches for cryptographic protocol analysis are based on the so-called BAN logic which is used to reason about beliefs established at protocol participants. In this paper, we attempt at providing a similar approach for web protocols. The new logic extends BAN and supports key concepts that simplify security analysis of web protocols. It also takes into account additional challenges introduced due to browser-based interaction. Through examples of two leading cross-domain identity and access management protocols, we demonstrate efficacy of our analysis in establishing precisely what a protocol achieves, in deciding whether it can be trusted for a particular need and in proposing fixes that improve trust levels.

Keywords: security protocol analysis, belief logic, identity federation, delegated authorization.

1 Introduction

While most security protocols are relatively simple to describe, the problem of ensuring that they can achieve certain guarantees in the presence of intruders that are allowed to intercept, alter, delete messages and collude with dishonest principals has proven to be a hard one. Analysis of cryptographic protocols (i.e. protocols that use cryptographic techniques for distributing keys and authenticating principals over a network) has been an active research area over the past three decades.

Approaches for security protocol analysis can be broadly classified under two categories. Inference construction approaches, first popularized by the publication of Burrows, Abadi, Needham (BAN) [1] logic, attempt to use inference in specialized logics to establish required beliefs at protocol participants. Attack construction approaches attempt to construct attacks by modeling an intruder and using algebraic properties of the messages being transmitted.

In the last decade or so, a new set of protocols has emerged that manage specific transactions on the web. The protocols are characterized by a user interacting with

S. Katzenbeisser et al. (Eds.): TRUST 2012, LNCS 7344, pp. 239–254, 2012.

multiple collaborating providers using standard web security mechanisms over a web-browser. Examples of such transactions are cross-domain single sign-on, electronic payments, sharing content with third parties etc. Some popular protocols that have been used to implement such transactions are Security Assertion Markup Language (SAML) [2], OpenID [3] and OAuth [4].

Security analysis of such web 'transaction protocols' poses several new challenges. Firstly, there is a need to model users without identifying keys and identities that are not global. Secondly, there is need for a framework for reasoning about user actions. Users contribute in these protocols through actions like submitting a request, signing in, accepting terms, clicking a link etc. When identities are not global, establishing that a user has recently performed an action is often more important than knowing its identity. Thirdly, browser-based communication allows new types of attacks based on using the browser as a confused deputy which have to be accounted for. Finally, there is a need to support common security mechanisms such as SSL/TLS based transport layer as a primitive construct to simplify modeling of web protocols. Due to the above challenges, there is lack of an established framework for modeling and analyzing security of web protocols.

We feel that inference construction based approaches (also termed as belief logics) are ideally suited for analyzing security of web protocols. The higher abstraction level and their ability to establish what a protocol achieves without explicitly modeling the intruder make them attractive for analyzing complex web environments. However, little work has been done in extending belief logics to the web domain. In this paper, our aim is to provide a robust logic for analyzing security of web protocols.

While there have been several extensions to BAN logic, our work generalizes some basic concepts of the logic, e.g. the type of beliefs that it can represent and the types of principals it can support. We define a set of intuitive inference rules that greatly simplify analysis of web based protocols. We also address implications of common browser based attacks such as request forgery. The vocabulary of the logic is extensible through constructs like actions and parameters that allow problem domain specific elements to be introduced.

To illustrate effectiveness of the extended logic in analyzing security of web protocols, we analyze two relatively complex browser-based protocols. SAML Identity Linking protocol is an extension of the more popular SAML single sign-on (SSO) protocol. Our analysis shows that the protocol is unable to establish required belief to securely link identities. We describe an attack that can be used to exploit this weakness. Next, we consider the OAuth protocol which is fast becoming the ad-hoc standard for authorizing third parties on the web. We determine the guarantees that the protocol provides and show that they can be inadequate in some situations. In both cases, the attacks identified have not been reported earlier. We also use insight from the analyses to propose fixes for the broken protocols.

We discuss related work in Section 2 and overview of BAN logic in Section 3. In Section 4, we introduce syntax and axioms of the proposed logic. In Sections 5 and 6, we take up the example analyses and discuss our contribution in Section 7.

2   Related Work

In the previous section, we mentioned two types of approaches for security protocol analysis. In this section, we review existing work in each type of approach.

Inference construction approaches attempt to use inference in specialized logics to establish required beliefs at the protocol participants. The logic of authentication described in [1], commonly known as BAN, was one of the first successful attempts at representing and reasoning about security properties of protocols. In [6], minor improvements to the logic's syntax and inference rules suggested to remove some ambiguity. Authors of [7] introduced the concept of 'recognizability'. Logic in [5] introduces the concept of possession along with belief and uses it to support constructs like 'not originated here'. In [8] authors attempt to consolidate good features from earlier belief logic approaches. These logics have the advantage of being usually decidable and efficiently computable. There have been efforts to automate verification for these logics. In [9], a transformation of BAN logic and inference rules to first order formula is performed and theorem prover SETHEO is used for finding proofs. In [10], the authors attempt to embed BAN logic in EVES theorem prover.

Attack construction approaches on the other hand do not try to establish beliefs at the participants but use model-checking techniques to construct attacks. The states and transitions used for modeling the protocol include modeling the structure of the message passing over the channel and a model of the intruder. The intruder is usually based on a Dolev-Yao model [11], and is allowed to perform any sequence of operations such as data interception, concatenation, deconcatenation, encryption, decryption etc. These complexities result in such approaches suffering from state-space explosion problem. We note that protocol modeling is usually quite complex in these approaches and even automated analysis often depends on user inputs at various stages of the state exploration process.

Few works that are representative of this class of approaches are mentioned below. The first such approach was introduced in [11], but the class of protocols studied in this work was very limited. In [12] the author modeled an extension of Dolev-Yao model in a specialized Prolog based model-checker, the NRL protocol analyzer. Other approaches in this area include the use of FDR model checker for CSP [13], use of SAT based model-checking techniques to solve a simplified version of the protocol insecurity problem [14] and on-the-fly model-checker (OFMC) [18], a semi-decision procedure which explores the search space system in a demand-driven way. [14] and [18] have been employed as backend model-checkers in the AVISPA tool [19] for automated validation of security protocols. An alternative to state-based analysis is the strand-space based approach [20] which uses a graph-theoretic interpretation of Dolev-Yao model. The protocol analyzer, Athena [21] is based on this approach. Also noteworthy is [22], in which authors propose some new threat models for the web platform. They use an attack construction approach to analyze effectiveness of some proposed web mechanisms against attacks targeting the browser.

Another relevant work which analyzes an important browser based protocol is the analysis of SAML in [15]. However, the author does not propose a framework for analyzing similar protocols. Finally, in our earlier work [23] a logic for analysis of web protocols is proposed. However, the logic introduced in this preliminary work is not robust enough to address challenges specific to browser based communication e.g. requests forgery by third parties. We build upon the approach of [23] and address its shortcomings. The protocols analyzed in [23] (SAML SSO and OAuth Core 1.0) are different from those analyzed in this paper (SAML Identity Linking and OAuth 1.0 revision A). In this paper, we are driven by the goal of providing a robust logic for analyzing security in web protocols. We refer to [9], [10], [23] for automating analysis for such logics.

3   Overview of Logic of Authentication

BAN Statements. A formula in BAN logic [1] is constructed using operators from Table 1. P and Q range over principals. The three statements about keys and secrets represent atomic statements. X represents a BAN formula constructed using one or more BAN operators. The expression $\sharp X$ means that the message X is fresh and has not been used before the current run of the protocol. This is especially true for a nonce, a sequence number or timestamp generated with this specific purpose. Nonces are used in protocols to defeat replay attacks from previous executions of the protocol.

Table 1. Operators in BAN Logic. X is a statement of the logic

Notation	Meaning	Notation	Meaning
$P \models X$	P believes X	$P \xleftrightarrow{K} Q$	Shared key K
$P \triangleleft X$	P sees X	$\mapsto_K Q$	Q has public key K
$P \mid\sim X$	P said X	$P \overset{Y}{\rightleftharpoons} Q$	Shared secret Y
$P \mid\Rightarrow X$	P controls X	$\sharp X$	X is fresh.
$\{X\}_K$	X encrypted by K	$\langle X \rangle_Y$	X combined with Y

Inference Rules. There is a set of inference rules for deriving new beliefs from old ones. E.g. the *message-origin* inference rule below states that if P knows that K is a secret key between itself and Q and it sees a message X encrypted by K, then P is entitled to believe that Q said X. Similar inference rules about public keys and shared secrets are also provided, as shown below. K^{-1} represents the private key corresponding to public key K.

$$\frac{P \models Q \xleftrightarrow{K} P, P \triangleleft \{X\}_K}{P \models Q \mid\sim X} \qquad \frac{P \models \mapsto_K Q, P \triangleleft \{X\}_{K^{-1}}}{P \models Q \mid\sim X}$$

$$\frac{P \models Q \overset{Y}{\rightleftharpoons} P, P \triangleleft \langle X \rangle_Y}{P \models Q \mid\sim X}$$

$$(R1)$$

A *nonce-verification* rule (R2) states that, in addition if the message is known to be fresh, then P believes that Q must still believe X. Further, the *jurisdiction rule* (R3) states that, if in addition, P also believes that Q is an authority on the subject of X (i.e. Q controls X), then P is entitled to believe X itself.

$$\frac{P \mid\equiv Q \mid\sim X, P \mid\equiv \sharp X}{P \mid\equiv Q \mid\equiv X} \tag{R2}$$

$$\frac{P \mid\equiv Q \mid\equiv X, P \mid\equiv Q \mid\Rightarrow X}{P \mid\equiv X} \tag{R3}$$

Idealization. Each message exchanged in the protocol is idealized into a BAN formula representing meaning of the message including any facts that the sending of the message implies. Consider for example, the second message in the Needham-Schroeder Symmetric Key protocol [17] in which a server S sends a response to an initiator A containing a session key K_{ab}, along with a message for another principal B encrypted using B's key containing the same session key and A's identity. In typical Alice-Bob notation used in literature this can be expressed as:

$$S \rightarrow A : \{N_a, B, K_{ab}, \{K_{ab}, A\}_{K_{bs}}\}_{K_{as}}$$

where N_a is a nonce value. K_{as} and K_{bs} represent keys shared between A and S, B and S respectively. The message is idealized in [1] as follows:

$$S \rightarrow A : \{N_a, (A \xleftrightarrow{K_{ab}} B), \sharp(A \xleftrightarrow{K_{ab}} B), \{A \xleftrightarrow{K_{ab}} B\}_{K_{bs}}\}_{K_{as}}$$

The idealization makes explicit that the server says that K_{ab} is a shared key for communication between A and B and also that it is fresh (due to the presence of the nonce).

Analysis. Protocol analysis in inference construction approaches involves two main tasks: (*i*) identification of an initial set of beliefs i.e. assumptions at each principal. (*ii*) message-by-message manual reasoning based on combining formula (idealized messages) that a principal sees with what it knows using inference rules of the logic.

4   Extending Belief Logic

4.1   Introducing New Concepts and Syntax

Our goal is to extend BAN for analysis of generic browser based web transactions. This involves extending logic of authentication in the following ways.

Support for Principals without Identifying Keys. Existing techniques for security protocol analysis require principals to possess identifying keys. However, it is common for users to authenticate to websites using passwords over secure connections. A *secure channel* in this paper refers to a transport layer security mechanism e.g. SSL, TLS that provides server authentication, confidentiality and integrity in message exchanges. We introduce a new sort (type) in the many sorted BAN logic called *user* which represents the client side of a secure connection.

Support for Passing Domain Specific Information. We also allow for *parameters* to be used in idealized expressions representing a protocol. These are named variables belonging to a particular sort of the logic and assigned to a constant symbol of that sort in a particular execution of the protocol.

Support for User Actions and Secrets. While principals make statements signed using identifying keys, users interact with principals (usually servers) over secure channels. We define the concept of an action and allow it to be associated with a user. We allow secrets to be associated with actions in order to identify a user that performed the action (possibly at a different place or time). An action has a *type* and can be parameterized by a set of arguments belonging to the sorts of the logic. E.g. the act of signing in as principal Q is represented as *SignIn(Q)*.

The new concepts are represented using the notation described in Table 2. *Aname* ranges over action types while *Pname* ranges over parameter names.

Table 2. Additional operators used in our extended belief logic

Notation	Meaning	Notation	Meaning
$P \overset{\Delta}{\leftrightarrow} U_c$	C is a secure channel between U_c and P.	$X \rightsquigarrow action$	Secret X is associated with *action*.
$[\![X]\!]_C$	Formula X exchanged over secure channel C.	$U_c \ni X$	U_c possesses secret X.
$U_C \triangleright action$	U_C performs *action*	$Pname = val$	*Pname* has value '*val*'.

4.2   Implications of Forged Requests

An additional challenge, that belief logics for the web must contend with, is request forgery. In cryptographic protocols a principal is always aware of the content of messages it sends (unless it is relaying an encrypted message). In browser-based protocols a user can be induced into clicking a link or submitting a form at a malicious website. Both the content of the message and the receiving end-point can thus be controlled by an attacker. Moreover, an HTTP cookie identifying any context information (e.g. login context) is automatically included by the browser if the request is directed to a URL within the scope (defined as a combination of domain and path) of the cookie. Such attacks are termed as cross-site request forgery (CSRF). Since secrets and actions are also message content, this has an obvious implication on the reasoning in our logic. There are two cases to handle:

(*i*) *Faked actions*: Since user performs actions on web pages created by a server, we assume that the server always knows whether an action was forged or not by checking for a secret that it has included in the web page. An action *act* seen by a principal *P* who knows it was not forged is represented as act^P in our notation.

(*ii*) *Faked secrets*: In our analysis we make the assumption that the attacker cannot tamper with cookies stored in a user's browser. We assume that any other secrets carried in a user request might be faked. We allow a user to assert actions corresponding to faked secrets. However, if a request contains two secrets *s1* and *s2* corresponding to actions *act1* and *act2*, we do not conclude that principal who performed *act1* performed also performed *act2*. To be able to make such conclusions, we require one of the actions to be additionally associated with a valid cookie which the server believes to be associated with the action. In a common scenario one of the actions is a sign-in action and the logic is used to associate the other action with the signed in principal.

4.3   Reasoning about Users, Actions and Secrets

The following new inference rules have been defined to reason about users, their actions and associated secrets. Rule R4 says that if a principal (usually server) believes that a user U_C communicates over a secure channel C, then any actions it sees over the secure channel C can be attributed to user U_C. The superscript P over the action name represents that P believes the action is not forged (through verification of a secret as described in Section 4.2).

$$\frac{P \models (P \overset{\Delta}{\longleftrightarrow} U_C), P \lhd [\![action^P]\!]_C}{P \models (U_C \rhd action)} \tag{R4}$$

The above rule requires the believer to be a direct observer of the action. Rule R5, on the other hand, allows belief about an action based on a secret associated with the action. It says if P believes that secret S is associated with an action, and it sees that user U_C connected over a secret channel possesses the secret, then it believes that the action was performed by U_C.

$$\frac{P \models (S \rightsquigarrow action), P \models (P \overset{\Delta}{\longleftrightarrow} U_C), P \lhd [\![S]\!]_C}{P \models (U_C \rhd action)} \tag{R5}$$

Rules R4 and R5 do not require a user to be authenticated. Rule R6 and R7 are corresponding rules for authenticated users. Rule R6 says that if P is connected to U_C over a secure channel and believes that U_C is currently signed in as Q, then P can attribute any actions performed on the channel to the principal Q. We use the predicate $SignedIn(U_C, Q)$ to denote that U_C is signed in as Q.

$$\frac{P \models (P \overset{\Delta}{\longleftrightarrow} U_C), P \models SignedIn(U_C, Q), P \lhd [\![action^P]\!]_C}{P \models (Q \rhd action)} \tag{R6}$$

For browser based protocols, there is a simple check for *SignedIn*. If the request contains a valid cookie (*ck*) which is associated with the *SignIn(Q)* action, then *P* assumes U_C to be signed in as *Q*. In addition, if the principal is the direct observer of the action over a secure channel and the action is not forged, then *P* is entitled to believe that action was performed by *Q*.

$$\frac{P \mid\equiv (P \overset{\Delta}{\longleftrightarrow} U_c), P \mid\equiv ck \rightsquigarrow SignIn(Q), P \lhd [\![\{ck, action^P\}]\!]_C}{P \mid\equiv (Q \rhd action)} \quad \text{(R6.1)}$$

R7 is the rule for attributing actions not directly observed by *P* to an authenticated user. Like R7 it postulates that *P* is connected to U_C over a secure channel and believes that U_C is currently signed in as *Q*. If *P* then sees a secret *T* which it believes to be associated with a particular action, then *P* believes that *Q* performed *action*.

$$\frac{P \mid\equiv (P \overset{\Delta}{\longleftrightarrow} U_c), P \mid\equiv SignedIn(U_c, Q), P \mid\equiv (T \rightsquigarrow action), P \lhd [\![T]\!]_C}{P \mid\equiv (Q \rhd action)} \quad \text{(R7)}$$

We now translate this rule for browser based protocols. The above rule can be seen as associating another action with a principal who is believed to perform sign-in action. As per handling described in Section 4.2, we use another secret (*S*) shared with the signed in principal (*Q*) and contained in the message body along with the secret *T* to ensure that *T* is not faked. This results in the following rule:

$$\frac{P \mid\equiv (P \overset{\Delta}{\longleftrightarrow} U_c), P \mid\equiv ck \rightsquigarrow SignIn(Q), P \mid\equiv P \overset{S}{\rightleftharpoons} Q, P \mid\equiv T \rightsquigarrow action, P \lhd [\![\{ck, \langle T \rangle_S\}]\!]_C}{P \mid\equiv (Q \rhd action)} \quad \text{(R7.1)}$$

A more generic form of the rule does not require one of the actions to be sign-in action. The notation R_{action} is used to identify an unauthenticated principal who is aware of performing *action*.

$$\frac{P \mid\equiv (P \overset{\Delta}{\longleftrightarrow} U_c), P \mid\equiv ck \rightsquigarrow act1, P \mid\equiv P \overset{S}{\rightleftharpoons} R_{act1}, P \mid\equiv T \rightsquigarrow act2, P \lhd [\![\{ck, \langle T \rangle_S\}]\!]_C}{P \mid\equiv (R_{act1} \rhd act2)} \quad \text{(R7.2)}$$

5   Analysis of SAML Identity Linking Protocol

5.1   Protocol Description

In addition to the well-known web single sign-on (SSO) protocol, the SAML specification also features an identity linking protocol. The objective of this protocol is to allow linking of user identity across security domains. Despite being a widely deployed identity federation protocol, it does not appear to be the subject of scrutiny in a prior security analysis work.

A user authenticated at an identity provider (IdP) as principal Q_p, chooses to be transferred to the service provider (SP) site. The redirect includes a signed SAML token asserting the identity of the user at IdP (i.e. Q_p). Once at the service provider (SP) site, user is requested to sign-in. The user signs in as principal R_c. SP links local principal name R_c with remote principal name Q_p. In future, when SP sees a user carrying a SAML token from IdP asserting identity Q_p, it automatically signs in the user as R_c. The message exchange is illustrated in Fig. 1.

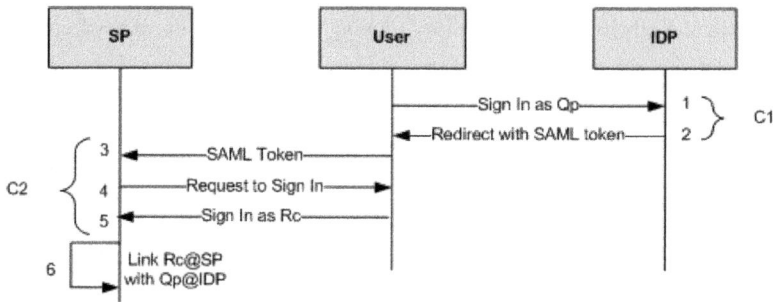

Fig. 1. SAML identity linking protocol

5.2   Modeling and Analysis

The idealized protocol shown below retains only messages received by either SP or IdP. SP is denoted as principal C, while IdP is denoted as P. All communication is assumed to take place on secure (SSL/TLS) channel. Message 1 represents the sign-in action user performs at the IdP. Message 3 is the redirect from IdP being received at SP. The message contains SAML token (T) signed by IdP which is associated with the action $SignIn(Q_p)$. We combine a request identifier and timestamp sent in the message in a single nonce value N_{cp}. Two domain specific parameters *prov* and *cons* are introduced representing protocol roles of assertion provider (IdP) and assertion consumer (SP) respectively. Message 5 represents user sign-in action at SP:

Message 1 $\quad U_{C1} \rightarrow P: \quad [\![SignIn(Q_p)]\!]_{C1}$

Message 3 $\quad U_{C2} \rightarrow C: \quad [\![\{ N_{cp}, T, T \rightsquigarrow SignIn(Q_p), prov = P, cons = C \}_{K_r^{-1}}]\!]_{C2}$

Message 5 $\quad U_{C2} \rightarrow C: \quad [\![SignIn(R_c)]\!]_{C2}$

Assumptions for the protocol can be expressed by the following statements.

$$C \models C \overset{\triangle}{\leftrightarrow} U_{C2} \qquad\qquad P \models P \overset{\triangle}{\leftrightarrow} U_{C1}$$
$$C \models \sharp(N_{cp}) \qquad\qquad P \models \sharp(N_{cp})$$
$$C \models \mapsto_{K_p} P \qquad\qquad P \models \mapsto_{K_c} C$$
$$C \models (P \mapsto SignIn(x))$$

The first two assumptions are about secure channels *C1* and *C2*. The next four are beliefs about nonces and keys while the last one is the belief that IdP (P) controls the sign-in action.

The goal of the protocol is to establish $C \models R_c \rhd SignIn(Q_p)$. Details of analysis of the protocol are provided in Table 3. We observe that using inference rules of the logic, C can only associate actions with U_{C2} and not with principal R_c. R7.1 cannot be applied on receipt of message 3 because it requires user to be signed in locally at C. Hence, we conclude that the protocol does not establish sufficient beliefs for the identity linking operation to be considered safe. Using this knowledge, we were also able to construct the following attack on SAML identity linking.

Table 3. Analysis of SAML Identity Linking. Recipient is shown in parentheses

Msg.	Rule Used	Inference	Reasoning
3(C)	R1,R2	$P \models (prov = P, cons = C)$	Combine message with assumptions about K_c and N_{cp}
3(C)	R5	$U_{C2} \rhd SiginIn(Q_p)$	Using assumption about jurisdiction of P over sign-in.
5(C)	R4	$U_{C2} \rhd SiginIn(R_c)$	Combine message with assumption about channel C2.

Attack Description. An attacker having a valid account A at IdP authenticates itself and chooses to be redirected to SP. However, instead of following the redirect request from IdP, it extracts the request parameters and induces the victim into clicking a link or submitting a form (depending on whether HTTP redirect binding or POST binding is used for the exchange). Following the link takes the victim to the SP site, unwittingly carrying the SAML token issued to the attacker. The victim has an account (say V) at the SP site and is requested to sign-in. On signing in, SP links local identity V with attacker's identity A at IdP. In future, attacker can sign-in at IdP, get redirected to SP and automatically get access to the victim's account at SP.

5.3   Fixing Identity Linking

The analysis above provides a hint to the possible fix of the protocol. R7.1 can only be applied at C if user is already signed in locally. Thus the token from IdP must be received after step 5 of the protocol. One simple way to achieve this is for SP to simply initiate an SSO flow after step 5. This is exactly what is shown in the modified protocol of Fig. 2. However, since the user already has a valid login context at IdP (it signed in at P in step 1), it does not need to sign-in again.

The additional steps of the protocol (with recipient as C or P) can be idealized as follows:

Message 7 $U_{C3} \to P$: $[\![\{N'_{cp}, prov = P, cons = C\}_{K_C^{-1}}, ck_q]\!]_{C3}$
Message 9 $U_{C4} \to C$: $[\![\{\langle T' \rangle_{N'_{cp}}, T' \rightsquigarrow SignIn(Q_p), prov = P, cons = C\}_{K_P^{-1}}, ck_r]\!]_{C4}$

Additional assumptions are noted below. Cookies ck_q and ck_r are assumed to be associated with sign-in actions $SignIn(Q_p)$ and $SignIn(R_c)$ respectively. In addition, N'_{cp} the unique identifier of the SAML request is assumed to be a secret shared with R_c.

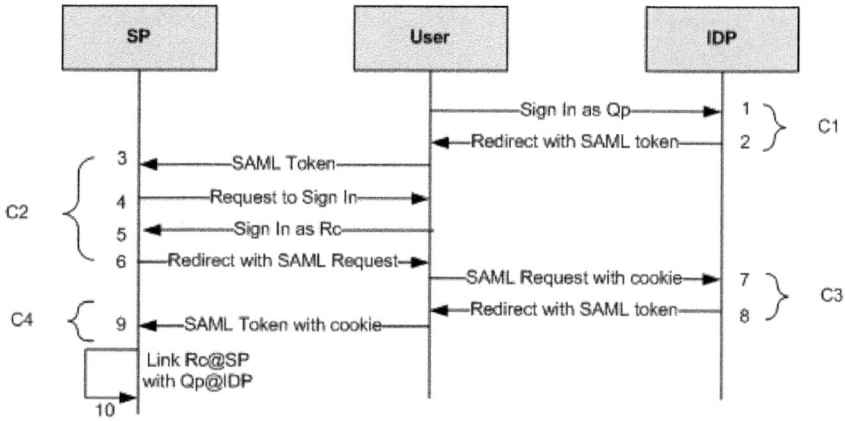

Fig. 2. Modified Identity Linking Flow

$$C \models ck_r \leadsto SiginIn(R_c), \quad C \models C \xrightarrow{N_{cp}'} R_c \qquad\qquad P \models ck_q \leadsto SiginIn(Q_p)$$

Combining the assumptions with message 9 using R7.1, we have all the premises satisfied, leading to the conclusion $C \models R_c \rhd SignIn(Q_p)$ which satisfies the goal.

6   Analysis of OAuth Protocol

6.1   Protocol Description

The OAuth protocol [4] provides a web based workflow that allows a user to temporarily delegate privileges of his account at a provider to a third party without sharing his login credentials. Privileges could for example mean access to pictures, friend list, blogs etc. OAuth is the primary protocol used by Google, Facebook and Twitter to allow third party access to their users' content.

In [23], the original version of the protocol, OAuth Core 1.0 [24], was analyzed using a belief logic. Model driven analysis was used to demonstrate insecurity of the protocol which explained a known session-fixation attack [16]. The issue was identified and fixed which resulted in OAuth Core 1.0 Revision A. This version was later approved and published as an IETF RFC [4] *OAuth 1.0 Protocol*[1]. This improved version [4], is the subject of analysis in this paper. The protocol flow is shown in Fig. 3 and described below.

Steps 1-4, user requests service S from consumer (C).   The service requires a set of privileges (permissions) *Priv* to the user account at provider (P). Consumer registers delegation request with P and gets returned a request token N_b. C redirects user to P

---

[1] We note that some providers like Google and Facebook have moved to OAuth 2.0 [25] which bears little resemblance with the original protocol. Other providers e.g. Twitter have chosen to stay with the IETF approved version [4].

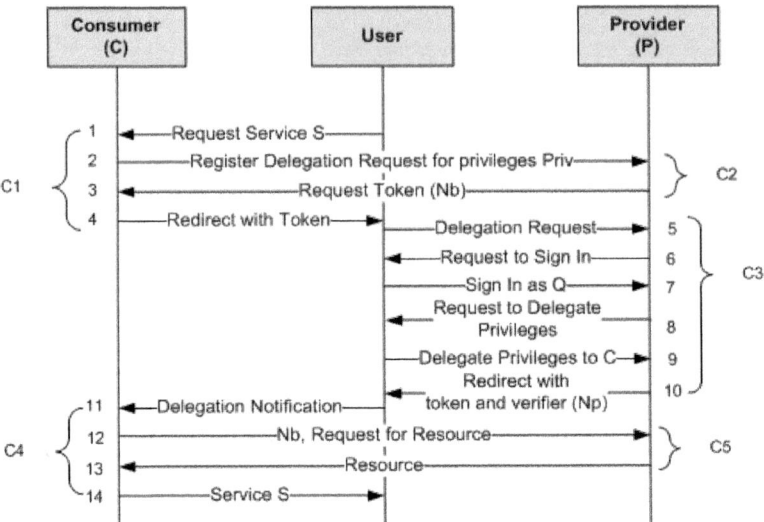

Fig. 3. The OAuth 1.0 protocol (as described in RFC 5849)

with this token. *Steps* 5-10, user is requested to sign in and delegate set of privileges *Priv* to C. User signs in as principal Q and performs requested delegation. User is redirected back to C with the request token and another *verifier* token N_p. *Steps 11-14*, C uses the two tokens N_b and N_p to access a protected resource at P. All communication happens over secure SSL/TLS channels and requests from consumer are signed and verifiable at the provider. The secure channels used are identified as C1-C5 in Fig. 3.

6.2   Modeling and Analysis

The protocol is idealized as shown below. As usual only messages received by either C or P are idealized because we are interested in beliefs at only these principals.

$$
\begin{aligned}
&Message\,1 \quad U_{C1} \to C: \quad [\![Request(S)]\!]_{C1} \\
&Message\,2 \quad C_{C2} \to P: \quad [\![\{C, N_1, scope = \text{Priv}\}\kappa_c^{-1}]\!]_{C2} \\
&Message\,3 \quad P \to C_{C2}: \quad [\![N_b]\!]_{C2} \\
&Message\,5 \quad U_{C3} \to P: \quad [\![N_b]\!]_{C3} \\
&Message\,7 \quad U_{C3} \to P: \quad [\![SignIn(Q)]\!]_{C3} \\
&Message\,9 \quad U_{C3} \to P: \quad [\![Delegate(scope, C), Ck_Q]\!]_{C3} \\
&Message\,11 \quad U_{C4} \to C: \quad [\![N_b, N_p]\!]_{C4} \\
&Message\,12 \quad C_{C5} \to P: \quad [\![C, N_2, N_b, N_p, \{p1\}]\!]_{C5} \\
&Message\,13 \quad P \to C_{C5}: \quad [\![(N_b, N_p) \rightsquigarrow Delegate(\text{Priv}, C)]\!]_{C5}
\end{aligned}
$$

Apart from the sign-in action, we have two other actions. Requesting service S is represented as *Request(S)* while delegating a set of permissions *Priv* to C is represented as *Delegate(Priv, C)*. The parameter *scope* is assigned to a set of privileges to be delegated in an execution of the protocol.

Idealization of messages 1, 7 and 9 represent the user actions performed in the protocol. Cookie Ck_Q represents login context for user signed in as principal Q at P. Messages 2 and 12 are direct requests from C to P for request token and protected resource respectively. In message 2, the set of privileges $Priv$, for which delegation is required, is included. In message 12, a protected resource requiring a privilege $p1$ $\in Priv$ is requested. If the provider allows access to protected resource in message 13, it is interpreted as verifying association of secrets N_b and N_p with the delegation action. This is made explicit in the idealization. N_1 and N_2 are nonces (combination of a timestamp and nonce in actual protocol). Assumptions at C and P are given below:

$$C \models C \overset{\leftrightarrow}{} U_{C1}, C \models C \overset{\leftrightarrow}{} U_{C4} \qquad P \models P \overset{\leftrightarrow}{} U_{C3}$$
$$C \models P \overset{\leftrightarrow}{} C_{C2}, C \models P \overset{\leftrightarrow}{} C_{C5} \qquad P \models P \overset{\leftrightarrow}{} C_{C2}, P \models P \overset{\leftrightarrow}{} C_{C5}$$
$$C \models \sharp N_1 \qquad\qquad\qquad P \models \sharp N_1$$
$$C \models \sharp N_2 \qquad\qquad\qquad P \models \sharp N_2$$
$$C \models N_b \rightsquigarrow Request(S) \qquad P \models Ck_Q \rightsquigarrow SignIn(Q)$$
$$\qquad\qquad\qquad\qquad\qquad P \models (N_b, N_p) \rightsquigarrow Delegate(\text{Priv}, C)$$
$$C \models (P \mapsto Delegate(r, y))$$

The first seven assumptions are about secure channels C1-C5. The next four assumptions are about freshness of nonces N_1 and N_2. The next three are beliefs about secrets N_p, N_b and cookie Ck_q being associated with the three user actions. The last belief says that C trusts P for the delegation action. A reasonable goal for the protocol seems to be to establish the following belief:

$$P \models Q \triangleright Delegate(\text{Priv}, C) \quad\text{and}\quad C \models U_{C4} \triangleright Delegate(\text{Priv}, C) \qquad (G1)$$

G1 requires P to establish that delegation was performed by the resource owner and that C should provide service (in step 14) to a user (U_{C4}) that it believes has performed the delegation action. We consider a stricter goal of additionally satisfying:

$$C \models R_{Request(S)} \triangleright Delegate(\text{Priv}, C) \qquad (G2)$$

G2 requires C to believe that the principal performing request action in step 1 has also performed the delegation action.

Analysis of the protocol is described in Table 4. We can easily see that goal statement G1 is satisfied by inferences made in step 9 at P and step 13 at C. We also observe that the belief required by G2 has not been established.

While satisfying G1 may be sufficient in most applications using the protocol, there are cases where the additional goal G2 is important. This is demonstrated by the following attack, not reported previously.

An attacker performs steps 1-10 of the protocol and delegates access to its account X at P for a limited period of time to C. However, instead of getting redirected to C, it induces a victim - having a valid account V at C – to click a link that contains both request token and verifier. On clicking the link, V is transferred to C, where it either starts a new session or continues with an existing session. C thinks that the valid

Table 4. Analyzing the OAuth 1.0 protocol

Msg.	Rule Used	Inference	Reasoning
7(P)	R4	$U_{C3} \triangleright SiginIn(Q)$	Combining received message with assumption about C3.
9(P)	R6	$Q \triangleright Delegate(R,C)$	Combining received message with assumption about C3 and Ck.
11(C)	R6	$U_{C4} \triangleright Request(S)$	Combining received message with assumption about C4 and Nb.
13(C)	R3	$(N_b, N_p) \rightsquigarrow$ $Delegate(\text{Priv}, C)$	Combining message 13 with C's trust in P for delegation action.
13(C)	R5	$U_{C4} \triangleright Delegate(\text{Priv}, C)$	Using previous conclusion with message 11, assumption about C4.

request token and verifier are for V's account at P, while they are actually associated with the attacker's account X. If V accesses a service at C that requires information to be shared with a remote account at P (e.g. backing up an address book), C releases the sensitive information to the attacker.

6.3   Fixing OAuth Protocol

Clearly the attack could be averted if we had been able to establish G2 since it ensures that the same principal performs steps 1 and 11 of the protocol. From the discussion in Section 4.2, we recall that making statements linking more than one action with the same user requires that at least one of them is associated with a valid cookie. The fix we propose introduces a cookie, ck, which is returned by C to the user (in step 2) who executed the request action. Rewriting idealization for messages 11-13 below:

$$Message\ 11\ \ U_{C4} \rightarrow C: \ \ [\![\langle N_b, N_p \rangle_{N_b}, ck]\!]_{C4}$$
$$Message\ 12\ \ C_{C5} \rightarrow P: \ \ [\![C, N_2, N_b, N_p, \{p1\}]\!]_{C5}$$
$$Message\ 13\ \ P \rightarrow C_{C5}: \ \ [\![(N_b, N_p) \rightsquigarrow Delegate(\text{Priv}, C)]\!]_{C5}$$

We write the additional assumptions about cookie ck. $R_{Request(S)}$ is used to identify the unnamed principal who performed the request action.

$$C \models ck \rightsquigarrow Request(S), C \stackrel{ck}{\rightleftharpoons} R_{Request(S)}$$

Combining messages 11, 13 with the new assumptions about ck using R7.2 results in the following belief being established which achieves the additional goal G2 (while still satisfying G1).

$$C \models R_{Request(S)} \triangleright Delegate(\text{Priv}, C)$$

7   Conclusions

We have proposed a new logic for analyzing security in web protocols. It extends the BAN logic which has been successfully used to analyze many cryptographic authentication and key exchange protocols. Our logic supports several concepts like principals without identifying keys, secure channels and user actions that greatly simplify modeling of web protocols. It provides a framework for reasoning about user actions based on cookies, tokens, secrets thus allowing belief logics to move beyond analyzing authentication protocols to addressing security of a wide range of business transactions. The framework is designed to be resilient in a realistic web environment where requests can be forged.

We use the extended logic to analyze two important web protocols. SAML Identity Linking protocol is seen to be deficient in its goal of securely linking identities across domains and a previously unreported attack against the protocol is discovered. We also analyze OAuth, a mainstream web protocol used for third party authorization. We analyze a version of the protocol which addresses a known session-fixation bug and is believed to be secure. Our analysis reveals that the protocol suffers from another insecurity not reported earlier and the corresponding attack. For both protocols we use insights from our analysis to propose fixes that resolve security issues.

Belief logic based security protocol analysis results in decidable and efficiently computable formulations and analysis can be easily automated. We believe that our work will allow benefits of these approaches to become available to web protocols.

References

1. Burrows, M., Abadi, M., Needham, R.: A Logic of Authentication. ACM Transactions on Computer Systems (TOCS) 8(1), 18–36 (1990)
2. OASIS SAML Specifications. SAML v2.0, Core, http://saml.xml.org/saml-specifications
3. OpenID 2.0 Specifications, http://openid.net/specs/openid-authentication-2_0.html
4. Hammer, E.: The OAuth 1.0 Protocol, Internet Engineering Task Force, Request for Comments (RFC): 5849, http://www.rfc-editor.org/rfc/rfc5849.txt
5. Gong, L., Needham, R., Yahalom, R.: Reasoning about Belief in Cryptographic Protocols. In: Proceedings 1990 IEEE Symposium on Research in Security and Privacy (1990)
6. Abadi, M., Tuttle, M.R.: A semantics for a logic of authentication. In: Proceedings of the ACM Symposium of Principles of Distributed Computing (1991)
7. Kessler, V., Wedel, G.: AUTLOG: An advanced logic of authentication. In: Proceedings of Computer Security Foundation Workshop VII, pp. 90–99 (1994)
8. Syverson, P., van Oorschot, P.: On unifying some cryptographic protocol logics. In: Proceedings of the Symposium on Security and Privacy, Oakland, CA, pp. 14–28 (1994)
9. Schumann, J.: Automatic Verification of Cryptographic Protocols with SETHEO. In: McCune, W. (ed.) CADE 1997. LNCS, vol. 1249, pp. 831–836. Springer, Heidelberg (1997)
10. Craigen, D., Saaltink, M.: Using EVES to analyze authentication protocols. Technical Report TR-96-5508-05, ORA Canada (1996)

11. Dolev, D., Yao, A.: On the security of public key protocols. IEEE Trans. Inform. Theory IT-29, 198–208 (1983)
12. Meadows, C.: Applying formal methods to the analysis of a key management protocol. Journal of Computer Security 1, 5–53 (1992)
13. Lowe, G.: Breaking and Fixing the Needham-Schroeder Public-Key Protocol Using FDR. In: Margaria, T., Steffen, B. (eds.) TACAS 1996. LNCS, vol. 1055, pp. 147–166. Springer, Heidelberg (1996)
14. Armando, A., et al.: An Optimized Intruder Model for SAT-based Model-Checking of Security Protocols. Elec. Notes in Theoret. Comp. Sci. 125(1) (March 2005)
15. Groß, T.: Security analysis of the SAML single sign-on browser/artifact profile. In: Proceedings of 19th ACSAC 2003, pp. 298–307. IEEE Computer Society Press (2003)
16. Hammer-Lahav, E.: Explaining the OAuth Session Fixation Attack, http://hueniverse.com/2009/04/explaining-the-oauth-sessionfixation-attack/
17. Needham, R., Schroeder, M.: Using encryption for authentication in large networks of computers. Communications of the ACM 21(12), 993–999 (1978)
18. Basin, D., Mödersheim, S., Viganò, L.: An On-the-Fly Model-Checker for Security Protocol Analysis. In: Snekkenes, E., Gollmann, D. (eds.) ESORICS 2003. LNCS, vol. 2808, pp. 253–270. Springer, Heidelberg (2003)
19. Armando, A., Basin, D., Boichut, Y., Chevalier, Y., Compagna, L., Cuellar, J., Drielsma, P.H., Heám, P.C., Kouchnarenko, O., Mantovani, J., Mödersheim, S., von Oheimb, D., Rusinowitch, M., Santiago, J., Turuani, M., Viganò, L., Vigneron, L.: The AVISPA Tool for the Automated Validation of Internet Security Protocols and Applications. In: Etessami, K., Rajamani, S.K. (eds.) CAV 2005. LNCS, vol. 3576, pp. 281–285. Springer, Heidelberg (2005)
20. Javier, F., Fabrega, T., Herzog, J.C., Guttman, J.D.: Strand spaces: Why a security protocol is correct? In: Proceedings of IEEE Symposium on Security and Privacy, pp. 160–171 (1998)
21. Dawn, S., Berezin, S., Perrig, A.: Athena: a novel approach to efficient automatic security protocol analysis. Journal of Computer Security 9, 47–74 (2001)
22. Akhawe, D., Barth, A., Lam, P.E., Mitchell, J., Song, D.: Towards a Formal Foundation of Web Security. In: Proceedings of 23rd IEEE Computer Security Foundations Symposiym (CSF), pp. 290–304 (2010)
23. Kumar, A.: Model Driven Security Analysis of IDaaS Protocols. In: Kappel, G., Maamar, Z., Motahari-Nezhad, H.R. (eds.) ICSOC 2011. LNCS, vol. 7084, pp. 312–327. Springer, Heidelberg (2011)
24. The OAuth Core 1.0 Specification, http://oauth.net/core/1.0
25. Hammer, E., Reardon, D., Hardt, D.: The OAuth 2.0 Authorization Protocol, Network Working Group, Internet Draft (work in progress), http://tools.ietf.org/html/draft-ietf-oauth-v2-xx

Provenance-Based Model for Verifying Trust-Properties

Cornelius Namiluko and Andrew Martin

Oxford University Department of Computer Science,
Wolfson Building, Parks Road, Oxford OX1 3QD, UK
firstname.lastname@cs.ox.ac.uk

Abstract. Trust establishment requires evidence about the system's ability to operate as expected. However, the nature of this evidence and its representation and usage in trust evaluation still remains an open problem. Current mechanisms for collecting this evidence, such as the TCG integrity schema, do not support the linkage of this evidence and therefore limit the kinds of properties that can be verified. We argue that provenance provides more comprehensive evidence that can be represented in a manner that eases trust evaluation. Towards this end, we propose a *provenance-based* model for reasoning about a system's ability to satisfy trust properties of interest. This approach enables interoperability, supports multiple abstractions and enables evaluation of varying trust properties. Its application on verifying properties of platforms for use in a trust domain demonstrate its feasibility and flexibility.

1   Introduction

Distributed systems have the potential to deliver cheaper, flexible and scalable computation and data storage solutions. However, security and trust still pose a significant challenge towards their wider adoption [3]. This subject has received considerable attention and several systems that use trusted computing [1,10] have been proposed to address this challenge. These systems provide information about their configurations, which can be used to determine whether or not the system's behaviour conforms to expectations. However, the question of what information is necessary, how it can be represented and how it can be used in trust evaluation is still an open problem.

We argue that provenance provides more comprehensive evidence (including integrity of the components and activities that occur on the system such as events, processes, interactions e.t.c.) which can be captured in a manner that eases trust evaluation. Towards this end, and motivated by the realisation that trusted computing and provenance seek to address similar issues [7], we propose a *provenance-based model* which captures activities on a system as a *provenance graph*. The model extends the Open Provenance Model (OPM) [9] to enable provenance to be captured in a manner that supports verification of trust properties.

S. Katzenbeisser et al. (Eds.): TRUST 2012, LNCS 7344, pp. 255–272, 2012.

This approach has a number of advantages including: i) ability to provide a more comprehensive view of a system; ii) support for multiple abstractions; iii) support for interoperability; and iv) support for varying complexity in the types of properties that can be expressed. We apply this approach to the verification of platforms for use in a *trust domain*.

1.1 Virtual Platforms for Trust Domains

Information sharing is crucial for any successful collaboration. However, the sensitive nature of certain information may prevent or discourage entities from sharing it. To overcome this challenge, the Trust Domains Project[1] proposes the concept of a *trust domain* as a means of capturing the state and processes that allow information to be shared among entities that exhibit shared and predictable behaviour to protect the information.

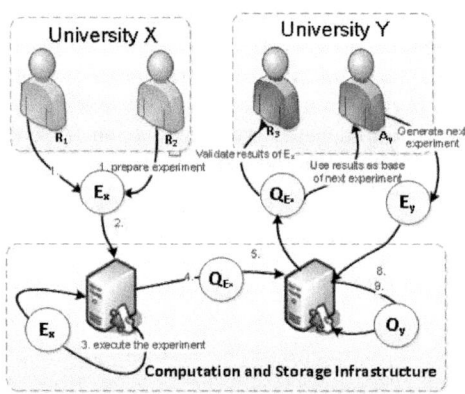

Fig. 1. A shared infrastructure used to execute experiments. E_x is an experiment set-up and Q_{E_x} is the completed experiment containing results.

Figure 1 illustrates an application of such a concept. In this scenario, researchers collaborate on a number of projects, each of which is comprised of a number of experiments. Researchers from university X may create an experiment which might be validated or used in the next series of experiments by other researchers from Y. To facilitate this, experiments are created as virtual appliances (VA) — ready-to-use virtual machine images configured with an operating system and a software stack necessary for a particular experiment. However, since the virtual appliances are created outside of their control, researchers need to establish whether or not virtual appliances will enforce appropriate data flow control before entrusting them with data for the experiment. This can be achieved by collecting evidence that could support a VA's behavioural characteristics and representing such evidence in a manner suitable for trust evaluation.

---

[1] The Trust Domains project is a TSB and EPSRC funded project that aims to build a framework for controlled information sharing. Further details are available on http://www.hpl.hp.com/research/cloud_security/TrustDomains.pdf

2   Related Work

Our work is motivated by Lyle and Martin [7] who note that provenance and trusted computing could complement each other. We build on our previous work [4] on a trace-based model for verifying properties of virtual appliances and on an open provenance model (OPM) [9]. This work proposes the semantics of a model that can be used to capture trust-relevant evidence. It differs from our previous work in that it is more general, i.e. the trace of events considered is in fact a subset of provenance, and has a simplified means of specifying trust properties, as opposed to the CSP specifications mechanism proposed in [4].

The idea of collecting provenance from virtual appliances has also been investigated by Wei [8]. Our work differs in that we are interested in the evaluation of trustworthiness of a system using the generated provenance rather than the trustworthiness of provenance records. The idea of developing a more comprehensive view of the system configurations has also been discussed in [14,2]. Presti [14] proposes the notion of a tree of trust as a mechanism for representing verification data. Schmidt et. al. [2] builds on this structure and proposes modifications to the TPM command set and data structures to support the derivation of tree-formed verification data. In our case, the TPM does not require any modifications. Instead it is simply used to validate the authenticity of the nodes in the graph. Whereas in a tree structure there is only one way of getting to a particular node, our graph-based approach provides a richer semantics — enabling verifiers to consider multiple paths to a node. Furthermore, our model is extensible and supports interoperability.

The TCG Infrastructure Working Group recognises that trust establishment must consider the origin, condition and history of components used to construct the platform. However, the proposed architecture[2] is limited to capturing components that exist on a system rather than how those components interact or how they are related. Our approach is more comprehensive in that it includes the activities that occur on the system in question and relations among components involved in those activities.

3   Trust Properties and Evidence

The TCG defines trust in terms of the expectations of a relying party on the behaviour of the system they wish to rely on. These expectations can be considered constraints on the behaviour of the system being relied on. We call these constraints *trust properties* and define them as *constraints that capture a trustor's expectations on the behaviour of the system*. But what kinds of constraints are necessary to arrive at a particular trustworthiness decision? What kind of information is necessary to support such decisions?

The answers to these questions will depend on a number of factors such as the level of trust desired, the amount of information available and the ability

---

[2] http://www.trustedcomputinggroup.org/files/resource_files/
87651761-1D09-3519-AD6C5B3E41547285/IWG_ArchitecturePartII_v1.0.pdf

of the trustor to use this information. In this section, we describe the kind of information, which we refer to as *evidence* that can be collected in the scenario described in Section 1.1 and the trust properties applicable to it.

3.1 Trust Properties

We identify four categories of trust properties as follows:

1. *Possible future behaviour*: seek to determine whether or not a VA will exhibit certain behavioural patterns when executed. Examples include: i) an executable will use known configurations; ii) a given executable will run before another executable; or iii) cryptographic keys will be reset at start-up.
2. *Processes performed and parameters used*: identify the processes carried out during the creation of a VA, the order in which they were performed and the parameters that were used as input to the processes. Examples include: i) a certain package was installed; ii) a package was configured as expected; or iii) certain privileges were assigned to a given object.
3. *Data sources and integrity*: seek to establish the authenticity of data such as packages included on a VA. Some examples include: i) packages installed were downloaded from trusted sources; ii) all critical packages installed were of a known integrity; or iii) a given file was obtained from a known package.
4. *Integrity of processes*: seek to determine whether or not the software components that executed as part of the build process, described below, behaved as expected. These may include: i) the executed programs have known integrity values; or ii) a particular process used the expected executable files.

3.2 Evidence Classification

The properties discussed above can be determined by collecting evidence from three main sources: *build platform*; *build process*; and *verification meta-data*.

1. *Build platform* — provides services for creating VAs and thus determines the behaviour of the resulting VA. Evidence from the build platform may include: i) components executed e.g. VA build tools, package managers; ii) configurations of the components e.g. ports open, digital signature checks or enabled services; or iii) dependency resolution among components e.g. versions of libraries used by the components.
2. *Build process* — involves a number of steps including package download and installation, configuration changes and execution of specified scripts. Evidence from this process might include: i) integrity values of the input and output e.g. command line parameters, environment variables; ii) configuration settings for virtual appliance, e.g. user accounts and privileges, network configurations and start-up scripts; and iii) virtual appliance contents e.g. software packages installed or files copied to the disk image.
3. *Verification metadata* — provides information about the format or validity of other pieces of evidence. Examples include: i) integrity schemas and reference manifests; ii) digital signatures; and iii) meta-data about the repositories from where packages are downloaded.

4   Graph-Based Representation

To enable meaningful trust evaluation, the evidence, discussed above, must be captured in an interoperable manner (since the producer may be different from the consumer of the evidence) and must include relationships among the parts of the evidence. Towards this end, we propose a provenance-based model that extends the open provenance model (OPM) [9] to capture the evidence.

The model is based on the idea that information about the data used, processes performed, entities that perform these processes and any new data generated is captured as a set of RDF triples, where each triple (X, Y, Z) specifies that a component X was related to another component Z through the property Y. In the rest of this section, we describe the extensions to OPM necessary to support reasoning about trust properties.

4.1   A Summary of OPM Semantics

Since our model builds on OPM, we begin with a summary of the main semantics of OPM, a detailed discussion of which can be found in Groth and Moreua [9].

OPM defines three main entities in a provenance record. These include: *Agent*, *Artifact* and *Process*, where an agent is an entity capable of performing a process, an artifact is an immutable piece of state and a process is a series of actions that use artifacts and generate new artifacts. These entities are related through a number of properties as depicted in Figure 2. The *wasTriggeredBy* (WTB) defines a relationship in which one process is made operational by another process. A process can be specified to have been controlled by multiple agents through the *wasControlledBy* (WCB) property. Artifacts used in a process are indicated through the *used* property while those that are created by a process are related to the process that created them through the *wasGeneratedBy* (WGB) property. The *used* and *WGB* properties must occur after the process has been created. To maintain the link between those artifacts that are used and those created, the *wasDerivedFrom* (WDF) property is used to specify that one artifact was derived from another. However, these semantics introduce some limitations (as discussed in the following sections) towards capturing the evidence for the purpose of trust evaluation.

4.2   Program Execution

A program can be captured as an agent in OPM. However, the semantics of the properties defined in OPM limit the ability to express execution relationships

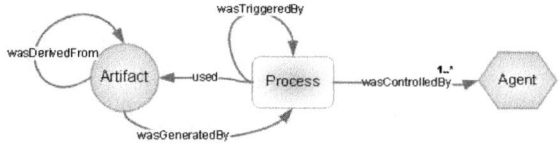

Fig. 2. An illustration of the main components of OPM. Artifacts are illustrated with a circle, agents by a hexagon and processes by rectangles.

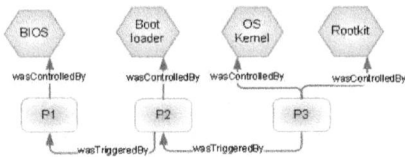

Fig. 3. Capturing the boot phase using OPM. Shows that a process can be controlled by multiple programs.

among programs. Consider the boot phase of a system in which the BIOS executes the boot loader, which in turn executes the operating system kernel. Using OPM, this scenario can be captured as illustrated in Figure 3. The BIOS controls a process, $P1$, which triggers another process, $P2$, controlled by the boot loader. $P2$ triggers $P3$, which is controlled by the operating system kernel. The semantics of the *WCB* property, however, imply that a single process can in fact be controlled by multiple programs (e.g. $P3$ *wasControlledBy* OS Kernel and Rootkit in Figure 3). Alternatively, the concept of *role* defined in OPM could be used to specify the role played by each program linked through the *WCB* property. However, roles are defined as labels and would still require a similar effort in defining semantics to make them useful in trust evaluation.

An alternative approach would be to use the TCG integrity architecture to create a chain of trust which captures the notion that a program in the chain executed and transferred control to the next program in the chain. However, such an approach is not sufficient to capture the idea that other activities could have been happening at the same time as the execution of programs in the chain. To overcome these limitations, we propose an extension to OPM that captures aspects about program execution. The extension, illustrated in Figure 5.A, enables programs to be related to the processes through which they are executed and the component executing them. This has an advantage that when establishing trust not only is the resulting chain of execution checkable, but also the processes in which the chain was created. We formally define the extension to include *ExecutionProcess* and *BootstrapProcess* processes and a number of properties that relate programs to the processes through which they were executed

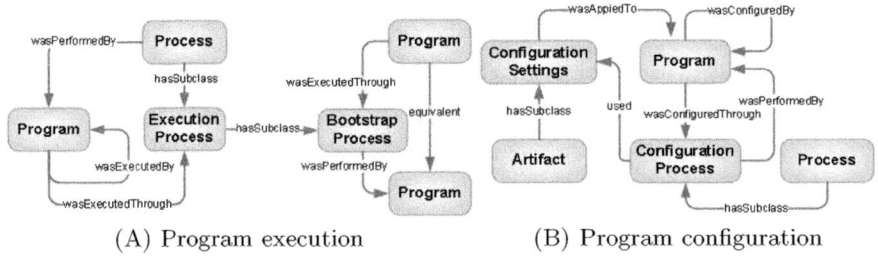

(A) Program execution   (B) Program configuration

Fig. 4. Conceptual representation of extensions to support program execution and configuration

as well as to the program that initiated the execution (note: *ran* is a *Z* function which returns the range of a given relation).

$wasPerformedBy : Process \rightarrow Program$
$ExecutionProcess : \mathbb{P}\ Process$
$wasExecutedThrough : Program \rightarrow Process$
$wasExecutedBy : Program \rightarrow Program$
$wasExecutedAt : Program \rightarrow Time$
$BootstrapProcess : \mathbb{P}\ ExecutionProcess$

$ExecutionProcess = \mathrm{ran}\ wasExecutedThrough$
$\forall\, p1, p2 : Program\ \bullet$
    $wasExecutedBy\ p2 = p1 \Leftrightarrow (\exists\, e : ExecutionProcess\ \bullet$
        $wasPerformedBy\ e = p1 \land wasExecutedThrough\ p2 = e)$
$\forall\, e : ExecutionProcess\ \bullet$
    $e \in BootstrapProcess \Leftrightarrow (\exists\, p1 : Program\ \bullet$
        $wasPerformedBy\ e = p1 \land wasExecutedThrough\ p1 = e)$

Intuitively, an *ExecutionProcess* is performed by a specific program and yields another program (i.e. the new program goes into the running state). A special type of execution process in which the program that performs the execution is the same as the program that is yielded is referred to as a *BootstrapProcess*.

4.3 Program Configuration

Configuration settings play an important role in determining the behaviour of a program. Grawrock [5] notes that in any non-trivial system, there will be a number of configuration options that may affect how a system behaves. For this reason, configuration settings used in a system must be considered when evaluating the system's trustworthiness.

In OPM, configuration settings can be captured as a type of *Artifact*. This artifact can then be linked to the process that uses it through the *used* property to capture the idea that a process is configured with the configuration settings specified. However, as discussed in the previous section, the semantics of *WCB* imply that configuration settings used by a process cannot be linked to the specific program being configured because multiple programs are linked to the same process that uses the artifact. Furthermore, the semantics of *used* imply that a process has to start its operation *before* it can be configured. However, for trust evaluation it is important to capture the idea that a program was configured in a certain way before it engaged in some other activities. To achieve this, we define an extension to OPM, illustrated in Figure 5.B, in which *ConfigurationSettings* is defined as a type of artifact that can be used to configure a program in a process called *ConfigurationProcess*. We capture this extension formally as follows.

$ConfigurationSettings : \mathbb{P}\, Artifact$
$ConfigurationProcess : \mathbb{P}\, Process$
$wasAppliedTo : ConfigurationSettings \mapsto Program$
$wasConfiguredBy : Program \mapsto Program$
$wasConfiguredThrough : Program \mapsto ConfigurationProcess$

$\forall p : Process \bullet p \in ConfigurationProcess \Leftrightarrow$
$\quad (\exists c : ConfigurationSettings \bullet c \in used(\!|\, p \,|\!))$
$\forall c : ConfigurationSettings;\ p : Program \bullet p \in wasAppliedTo (\!|\, c \,|\!) \Leftrightarrow$
$\quad (\exists e : ConfigurationProcess \bullet c \in used(\!|\, e \,|\!) \wedge e \in wasConfiguredThrough(\!|\, p \,|\!))$
$\forall p1, p2 : Program \bullet p1 \in wasConfiguredBy(\!|\, p2 \,|\!)) \Leftrightarrow$
$\quad (\exists e : ConfigurationProcess, c : ConfigurationSettings \bullet$
$\qquad wasPerformedBy\ e = p2 \wedge p1 \in wasAppliedTo (\!|\, c \,|\!))$

This extension allows us to capture properties such as "a program X configured another program Y with settings Z".

4.4 Integrity Measurement

Integrity measurement can be captured as a process using OPM, so that the entity being measured is linked to the integrity measurement process through the *used* property while the resulting integrity value is linked to the process that performs the measurement through the *WGB* property. However, the semantics of *used* imply that only artifacts can be integrity measured because the used relationship can only be applied to artifacts. To overcome this limitation, we introduce an extension to OPM, illustrated in Figure 5.A and formally defined below, which includes a type of process referred to as *IntegrityMeasurementProcess*, an artifact called *IntegrityValue*, a *Measurable* type and a number of properties that relate these concepts (and those already defined in OPM).

$IntegrityMeasurementProcess : \mathbb{P}\, Process$
$performedOn : IntegrityMeasurementProcess \rightarrow Measurable$
$IntegrityValue : \mathbb{P}\, Artifact$
$integrityOf : IntegrityValue \nrightarrow Measurable$
$measured : Program \mapsto Measurable$

$Measurable = (Artifact \cup Agent)$
$\forall p : Program;\ m : Measurable \bullet measured\ p = m \Leftrightarrow$
$\quad (\exists e : IntegrityMeasurementProcess \bullet performedOn\ e = m$
$\qquad \wedge performedBy\ e = p)$

The extension specifies that *IntegrityMeasurementProcess* is a process that can take agents, in addition to artifacts, as input and produce another artifact of type *IntegrityValue*. The entity whose integrity is being taken can be linked to the resulting integrity value through the *integrityOf* property and to the *IntegrityMeasurementProcess* through the *performedon* property.

4.5   Communication

Components on a system communicate through various means to provide services to one another (e.g. remote procedure calls), inform each other about their activities or observations (e.g. events, message broadcasts) and exchange information for use in computations. For example, in the scenario described in Section 1.1 a package manager communicates with the repository to download packages for installation on a virtual appliance. This communication creates interactions which determine the flow of information within and across systems. Of particular interest to the scenario is the ability to track the source of packages that are installed on a VA.

To cater for communication aspects of the system, we make use of a combination of the D-profile proposed by Groth and Moreau [13] and the common module defined for the open provenance model vocabulary (OPMV)[3]. The D-profile defines the relationship between a sender process and the message it sends as well as the receiver process and the message it receives. This is useful for capturing communication. However, if we need to capture interactions resulting from this communication, the D-Profile falls short. To solve this, we complement it with concepts defined in the common module. More specifically, we use *Download, downloadUri, connection* defined in the namespace, *http://purl.org/net/opmv/types/common#* and *Connection* defined in the namespace, *http://www.w3.org/2006/http#*.

4.6   Assertion Model

We have so far defined a way of capturing the various kinds of evidence as provenance statements. However, these statements are only sound if they can be traced to a *root of trust*. Groth and Moreau [13] note that in distributed systems, where there may be multiple monitoring and reporting components, each provenance entry must be linked to the entity that reports it. They introduce the *attributedTo* property to link an account of provenance to an entity responsible for it. However, the soundness of these attributions can only be determined if a link can be created between the attributing (*assertor*) entity and a root of trust, i.e. a root of trust for assertion.

To achieve this, we propose an extension to OPM, called *Assertion Model*, which makes use of the earlier defined extensions to create links between the assertor to other components which could potentially serve as roots of trust. In other words, this can be used to create multiple chain of trust (based on different aspects of the system, not just the measure-before-load [5] as is the case for TCG based chain of trust) with the assertor at one end of the chain and a root of trust for assertion at the other end.

In this model, each triple (s, p, o) is linked to an assertor to create a pair $(A, (s, p, o))$, which we refer to as an *assertion*. This specifies that an agent A

---

[3] Common Module is a specialisation of OPMV that defines commonly used terms not defined in the OPM specifications, see
http://code.google.com/p/opmv/wiki/GuideOfCommonModule for details.

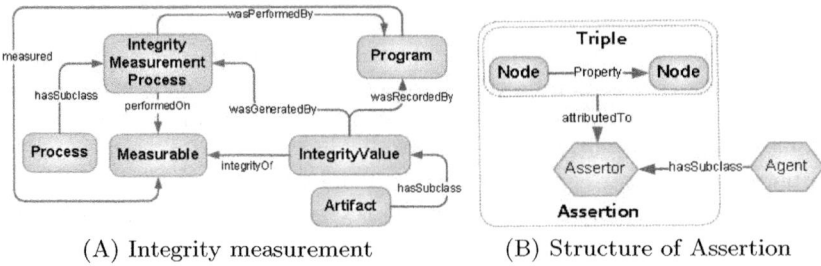

(A) Integrity measurement   (B) Structure of Assertion

Fig. 5. (A) depicts the integrity measurement extension while (B) shows the structure of an assertion for use in the assertion model

asserts that a subject s is related to an object o through a property p. Figure 5.B depicts how each assertion is captured.

$$Property == \{wasConfiguredBy, wasPerformedBy, wasExecutedThrough,$$
$$wasExecutedBy, ...\}$$

$$Assertor : \mathbb{P} \, Agent$$
$$Assertion : (Assertor \times (Node \times Property \times Node))$$
$$attributedTo : (Node \times Property \times Node) \to Assertor$$
$$occuredAt : (Node \times Property \times Node) \to Time$$

$$Node = (Process \cup Agent \cup Artifact)$$
$$\forall \, x, y : Node; \; p : Property; \; a : Assertor \bullet$$
$$(a, (x, p, y)) \in Assertion \Leftrightarrow y \in p(\!|\, x \,|\!) \land attributedTo \, (x, p, y) = a$$

5   Reasoning about Trust-Properties

The graph representation discussed above provides a means of representing the evidence about the activities on a system. But how useful is this evidence and how does the graph representation help in trust evaluation? This section addresses these questions by proposing an approach in which the evidence is validated against a set of criteria which aim to determine its soundness before verifying it to determine if certain properties can be satisfied by the graph.

5.1   Evidence Validation

The evidence presented in a provenance graph can come from multiple sources. As discussed in Section 4.6, for the purpose of trust evaluation, this evidence must be linked to the entities that generate it. Therefore, we consider evidence to be valid if it can be liked to an entity that can be securely identified. The use of the assertion model simplifies this by providing a link between the assertions and the assertors so that validation is based on the ability to securely identify assertors for either the entire set of evidence or a subset of it. To achieve this, we develop three validation rules, which when taken together specify that evidence presented in a particular subset of the graph is sound.

$$G = \{(A, (s, p, o)) \mid s, o \in Node;\ p \in Property;\ A \in Assertor\}$$

1. *RULE 1*: each assertion (s, p, o) must have been asserted by some agent that exists within the system (SystemComponents is a set of components in a system's architecture).

$$\forall\, a : G \mid valid(a) \Leftrightarrow a.1 \in SystemComponents$$

2. *RULE 2*: if the assertor is a program, then it must have been executed before performing the assertion.

$$\forall\, g : G \mid g.1 \in Program \bullet$$
$$valid(a) \Leftrightarrow wasExecutedAt\ a.1 < occuredAt\ a.2$$

3. *RULE 3*: the assertor must be securely identifiable (this does not necessary mean that the identity is the expected one, this is checked during verification).

$$\forall\, g : G \mid valid(g) \Rightarrow (\exists\, iv : IntegrtiyValue \bullet integrityOf\ iv = g.1)$$

5.2   Property Specification and Verification

Our verification model is based on RDF graph pattern matching provided in SPARQL [6]. First, each property specification, discussed in the previous section, is captured as a basic graph pattern (BGP) — a set of triples which may have some of the elements represented by variables. Then the obtained BGP is mapped to the graph (or a sub-graph) to determine if there is an entailment relationship between the BGP and the graph. In the remainder of this section, we discuss how properties are specified and verified on a given graph.

Presence/Absence of Triple Patterns: properties can be specified in terms of the presence or absence of certain triples. For example, to specify that a firewall was installed, one can check the graph to determine whether or not the triples $(installProcess, wasPerformedBy, rpm)$ and $(installProcess, used, firewall.rpm)$ exist. This is achieved by specifying the triples to be checked as a BGP (when the values of the triple elements are important) or graph templates (when certain values can be ignored). Verification is achieved by performing a query in the form of *ASK*, which returns true or false, depending on whether the specified triples can be found in the graph. Listing 1.1 shows how the example of firewall installation can be verified.

Listing 1.1. Example query for determining presence/absence of triples

```
ASK
    { :installProcess :wasPerformedBy :rpm . }
    { :installProcess :used :firewall.rpm . }
```

Values of Triple Elements: elements of a triple have values which can be used to infer certain information about the behaviour of a system. In the TCG-based integrity mechanism, for instance, trust is based on the presence of components with known integrity values. We support specification of triple element values using the FILTER feature of SPARQL. For example, to determine that in a given execution, the installed firewall had a certain integrity value, a query such as that shown in Listing 1.2 can be specified.

Listing 1.2. Example query for determining triple element values

```
ASK
    { :installProcess    :used         :firewall.rpm .
      ?iv               :integrityOf   :firewall.rpm .
      FILTER ( ?iv = "cdf84324"^^xsd:string )}
```

Supporting Multiple Abstractions: the property that any set of triples can be defined as a graph enables us to provide multiple abstractions. So that a subgraph that concentrates on certain types of assertions can be obtained from a provenance graph. This is achieved by specifying a graph template that includes properties useful for a certain abstraction. For example, to capture a graph that can be used to determine an execution chain of trust on a system, a graph template such as *?x :wasExecutedBy ?y* can be used to return all triples that have a *wasExecutedBy* property between any two entities (represented by the variables x and y). Such a graph can be obtained by using the *CONSTRUCT* query form on a provenance graph, which returns a graph matching the triples specified. For example, the query in Listing 1.3 returns a graph which only includes assertions related to programs executed on a system. The resulting graph can be subjected to further analysis as discussed above.

Listing 1.3. Example query to create abstraction for executions

```
CONSTRUCT    { ?x ?p      ?y .}
WHERE        { ?x :wasExecutedBy ?y .}
```

Sequencing of Triples: in most cases, a triple taken in isolation does not provide much information. To develop a more meaningful judgement of the behaviour of the system requires a way of relating the triples. One such relationship is the sequencing of triples. For example, to specify that a given program was configured in a certain way before it participated in a process, would involve checking that the program configuration occurred before a particular process was performed. Triple sequencing can be specified using the assertion model, where each assertion is linked to the time instance at which a particular triple occurred, using the *occuredAt* property. Given a sequence of triples $T =< t1, t2, ...tn >$, the FILTER construct can be used to relate the times at which each triple occurs. Listing 1.4 shows an example (s = subject, p = property and o = object).

Listing 1.4. Example query to determine sequence of triples

```
ASK
    {t1.s            t1.p            t1.o  .
    t1.(s,p,o)      :occuredAt      ?x1  .
    t2.s            t2.p            t2.o  .
    t2.(s,p,o)      :occuredAt      ?x2  .
    ...
    tn.s            tn.p            tn.o  .
    tn.(s,p,o)      :occuredAt      ?xn  .
    FILTER ( ?x1 < ?xn <...<?xn )}
```

6 Verifying Virtual Appliances

In this section, we describe an experiment that demonstrates how our proposed model can be used to verify trust properties of platforms before they can be admitted into a trust domain.

6.1 Set-Up and Provenance Collection

The experiment was set-up as illustrated in Figure 6. A build platform was setup using openSUSE 11.3 running on a kernel compiled with IMA support. Kiwi imaging system[4] and *strace*[5] packages were installed and a simple shell script was set-up to execute Kiwi using *strace* as a tracing tool. Execution traces were collected including log files from Kiwi, integrity measurement log (an extract of which appears in Listing 1.5) and a trace generated by *strace* (an extract appears in Listing 1.6), which were processed and verified on a separate platform.

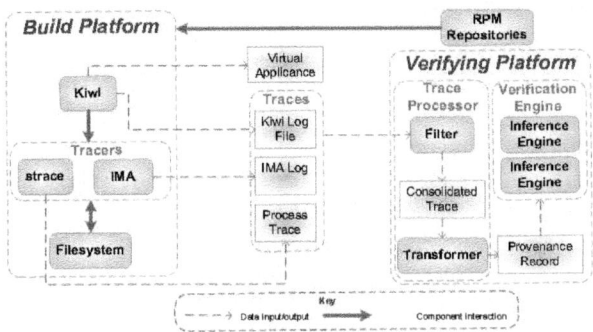

Fig. 6. An experimental setup for generating provenance for virtual appliances that will be used in a trust domain

---

[4] Kiwi is a tool, from openSUSE Build Services, used for creating VM images.
[5] Strace is a UNIX tool for tracing system calls.

Listing 1.5. Example IMA log showing a selected list of log entries with hash values truncated to six digits

```
10  000000  ima  000000  boot_aggregate
10  7ba06b  ima  095baf  /init
...
10  ba0922  ima  bb4476  ./build.sh
10  f80069  ima  e54a84  /usr/bin/strace
10  f97bd8  ima  e10ec0  /usr/sbin/kiwi
....
10  1125be  ima  908990  config.xml
10  b97636  ima  185cb1  KIWIConfig.sh
....
10  6b81fa  ima  cc622c  /usr/bin/zypper
....
10  988080  ima  bddd59  zypper.conf
10  229eb6  ima  6bf998  opensuse.org_distr_xx_.repo
...
10  2d6856  ima  3b2310  openSUSE−xx−.i586.rpm
10  e828ee  ima  b0d515  filesystem−xx−.i586.rpm
10  827556  ima  bc4d2a  vim−base−7.xx.i586.rpm
....
10  d9545c  ima  f56808  config.sh
```

Listing 1.6. Example entries in strace output

```
3056  18:19:08  clone(child_stack=0,....) = 3057
3057  18:19:08  execve("/usr/bin/zypper", ....) = 0
...
3057  18:19:42  clone(child_stack=0,....) = 3069
3069  18:19:42  execve("/bin/rpm",..,http:download.
      opensuse.org..openSUSE−xx−.i586.rpm
...
4354   18:21:51  open("/tmp/prov−va/tmp/config.sh",..
```

6.2   Graph Representation

A provenance graph that conforms to the model described in Section 4 was generated from the collected traces. The integrity measurement log provides integrity values of the components on the platform and therefore enables us to create instances of *IntegrityValue* and specify the *integrityOf* property. The trace generated by *strace* provides information about relationships among the programs executed and the data they use.

A slice of the resulting graph is shown in Figure 7. The graph shows how programs and data used in various processes that occurred on a VA are related and how IMA provides assertions about integrity values.

6.3   Verification

We demonstrate some of the trust properties that can be verified for VAs.

Verifying Package Authenticity: can be determined in two ways: check the integrity values recorded for each of the ".*rpm*" packages or determine whether they were obtained from a trusted repository. Listing 1.7 and 1.9 shows two queries and the results obtained are shown in Listing 1.8 and 1.10, respectively.

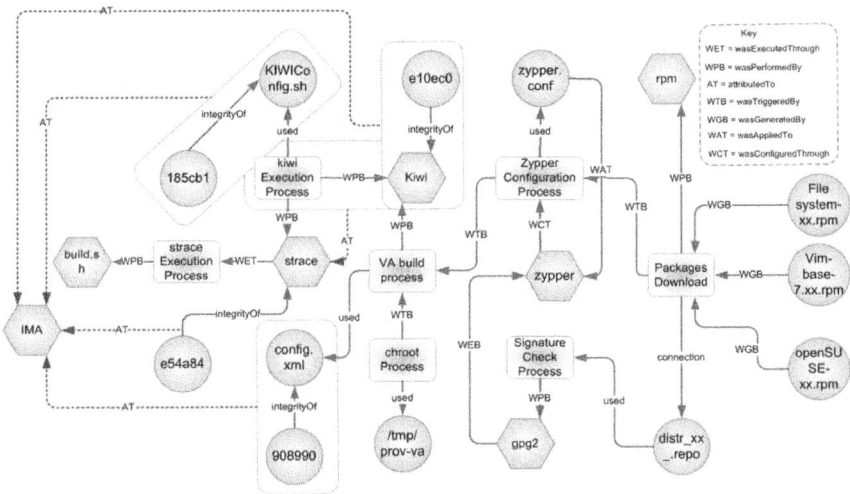

Fig. 7. A simplified provenance graph — showing only a small number of integrity values. The full graph includes a link between an integrity value for each of the artifacts and programs to the IMA.

Listing 1.7. Query that returns the integrity of all the packages installed

```
SELECT      {?pkg ?iv }
WHERE       {?pkg   :wasGeneratedBy ?x .
     ?iv       :integrityOf      ?pkg .
     FILTER  regex(?x,"rpm")}
```

Listing 1.8. Results of package source query

```
Artifact                    IntegrityValue
"filesystem −xx−.i586.rpm"    "b0d515"
"vim−base−7.xx.i586.rpm"      "bc4d2a"
"openSUSE−xx−.i586.rpm"       "3b2310"
```

Listing 1.9. Query to return the mapping of the packages to the source

```
SELECT      {?pkg    ?y }
WHERE       {?x    :connection       ?y .
     ?x rdf:type   :Download .
     ?pkg       :wasGeneratedBy ?x .}
```

Listing 1.10. Results of package source query

```
Artifact                    Connection
"filesystem −xx−.i586.rpm"    opensuse.org_distr_xx_.repo
"vim−base−7.xx.i586.rpm"      opensuse.org_distr_xx_.repo
"openSUSE−xx−.i586.rpm"       opensuse.org_distr_xx_.repo
```

Verifying Configurations Applied: can be verified by checking the integrity values of the configuration settings that have a *wasAppliedTo* relationship with programs. Listing 1.11 shows the query performed.

Listing 1.11. Example query to check configurations

```
SELECT    { ?y ?x ?z}
WHERE           { ?x :integrityOf    ?y .
    ?p  rdf:type  :ConfigurationProcess  .
    ?p  :used       ?y .
    ?z  :wasConfiguredThrough  ?p  .
    ?y  :wasAppliedTo  ?z}
```

Listing 1.12. Results of the checking program configurations

```
ConfigurationSettings    IntegrityValue  Program
"zypper.conf"            "bddd59"        "zypper"
"KIWIConfig.sh"          "185cb1"        "Kiwi"
```

Verifying Startup Scripts : is accomplished by checking the integrity of the programs or artifacts that have been placed in a certain location. Listing 1.13

Listing 1.13. Example query to determine the scripts that will be executed

```
SELECT    {?x ?y }
WHERE     {?x rdf:type :artifact  .
          ?y :integrityOf ?x
          FILTER regex(?x, "^init")  }
```

Listing 1.14. Results of checking scripts copied

```
Artifact IntegrityValue
"config.sh" "3de324"
"image.sh" "359aa3"
```

7   Discussion

7.1   Interoperability and Extensibility

Our model can be extended with semantics useful for a given application domain by defining new concepts or extending existing concepts. The new concepts can then be linked to concepts that exist in the model or to other new ones by defining or using existing properties. For example, entities in the TCG schemas can be mapped to either programs or artifacts to take advantage of the interrelations among components and thus enable a more comprehensive verification of platform configurations.

7.2   Collecting and Securing the Evidence

One key issue with the use of provenance in verifying trustworthiness is establishing the trustworthiness of the provenance itself. Considerable effort [12,11] has been directed towards this end and it is not our intention to provide a solution for this problem. Instead, we have assumed that this information is secured and concentrated on developing a model that enables one to use this information in trustworthiness verification. The evidence can further be tagged with trust values to indicate the belief that the assertor has in the assertions [11], allowing quantitative measurement of trust.

7.3   Assumption on Infrastructure

In this paper, we consider trust properties that can be established through evidence obtained from the build platform. There are other aspects that could affect the behaviour of a virtual appliance when launched. For example, two identically configured VAs could behave differently if the runtime parameters passed from the hypervisor are different. We assume that the hypervisor would launch all VAs with identical parameters. We intend to investigate how such parameters could affect the behaviour as part of our future work.

8   Conclusions and Future Work

The nature of evidence for use in trust evaluation and how it can be represented and used is still an open problem. Existing mechanisms such as the TCG integrity schema are limited to a specific aspect of a system's operation (e.g. chain of program execution). We have proposed a provenance-based model in which evidence is represented as a provenance graph which captures activities that occur on a system. This model specifies relationships among system components and data to enable evaluation against certain trust properties. Our application to virtual platforms for use in a trust domain demonstrate that the approach enables verification of more comprehensive properties. The model will be incorporated as part of the trust domain framework.

Acknowledgements. The work described here was supported by the Trust Domains project funded by UK TSB and EPSRC, reference TS/I002634/1. We thank David Power and the anonymous reviewers for their insightful comments.

References

1. Cooper, A.: Towards a Trusted Grid Architecture. PhD thesis, Oxford University (2008)
2. Schmidt, A.U., Leicher, A., Shah, Y., Cha, I.: Tree-formed verification data for trusted platforms. CoRR, abs/1007.0642 (2010)

3. Kandukuri, B.R., Paturi, V.R., Rakshit, A.: Cloud security issues. In: IEEE International Conference on Services Computing, SCC 2009, pp. 517–520 (September 2009)
4. Namiluko, C., Huh, J.H., Martin, A.: Verifying Trustworthiness of Virtual Appliances in Collaborative Environments. In: McCune, J.M., Balacheff, B., Perrig, A., Sadeghi, A.-R., Sasse, A., Beres, Y. (eds.) Trust 2011. LNCS, vol. 6740, pp. 1–15. Springer, Heidelberg (2011)
5. Grawrock, D.: Dynamics of a Trusted Platform: A Building Block Approach. Intel Press (2009)
6. Prud'hommeaux, E., Seaborne, A.: SPARQL query language for RDF. Technical report, World Wide Web Consortium (January 2008)
7. Lyle, J., Martin, A.: Trusted computing and provenance: better together. In: Proceedings of the 2nd Conference on Theory and Practice of Provenance, TAPP 2010, p. 1. USENIX Association, Berkeley (2010)
8. Wei, J., Zhang, X., Ammons, G., Bala, V., Ning, P.: Managing security of virtual machine images in a cloud environment. In: Proceedings of the 2009 ACM Workshop on Cloud Computing Security, CCSW 2009, pp. 91–96. ACM, New York (2009)
9. Moreau, L., Freire, J., Futrelle, J., McGrath, R., Myers, J., Paulson, P.: The open provenance model (December 2007)
10. Santos, N., Gummadi, K.P., Rodrigues, R.: Towards trusted cloud computing. In: Proceedings of the 2009 Conference on Hot Topics in Cloud Computing, HotCloud 2009. USENIX Association, Berkeley (2009)
11. Hartig, O.: Querying Trust in RDF Data with tSPARQL. In: Aroyo, L., Traverso, P., Ciravegna, F., Cimiano, P., Heath, T., Hyvönen, E., Mizoguchi, R., Oren, E., Sabou, M., Simperl, E. (eds.) ESWC 2009. LNCS, vol. 5554, pp. 5–20. Springer, Heidelberg (2009), doi:10.1007/978-3-642-02121-3_5
12. Groth, P., Moreau, L.: Recording process documentation for provenance. IEEE Transactions on Parallel and Distributed Systems 20(9), 1246–1259 (2009)
13. Groth, P., Moreau, L.: Representing distributed systems using the open provenance model. Future Generation Computer Systems 27(6), 757–765 (2011)
14. Presti, S.L.: A tree of trust rooted in extended trusted computing. In: Proceedings of the Second Conference on Advances in Computer Security and Forensics Programme (ACSF), pp. 13–20 (2007)

On the Practicality of Motion Based Keystroke Inference Attack

Liang Cai and Hao Chen

University of California, Davis
lngcai@ucdavis.edu, hchen@cs.ucdavis.edu

Abstract. Recent researches have shown that motion sensors may be used as a side channel to infer keystrokes on the touchscreen of smartphones. However, the practicality of this attack is unclear. For example, does this attack work on different devices, screen dimensions, keyboard layouts, or keyboard types? Does this attack depend on specific users or is it user independent? To answer these questions, we conducted a user study where 21 participants typed a total of 47,814 keystrokes on four different mobile devices in six settings. Our results show that this attack remains effective even though the accuracy is affected by user habits, device dimension, screen orientation, and keyboard layout. On a number-only keyboard, after the attacker tries 81 4-digit PINs, the probability that she has guessed the correct PIN is 65%, which improves the accuracy rate of random guessing by 81 times. Our study also indicates that inference based on the gyroscope is more accurate than that based on the accelerometer. We evaluated two classification techniques in our prototype and found that they are similarly effective.

1 Introduction

Modern mobile devices, such as smartphones and tablets, are equipped with multiple sensors. While these sensors enable exciting new applications, they also pose new security and privacy risks. The risks of some of these sensors are easily understood. For example, when an attacker can access the microphone, camera, or GPS, she can eavesdrop on the sound, image, and location of the user [5,24,23]. Therefore, most mobile platforms protect these sensors by requiring access permissions to these sensors. By contrast, the security risks of motion sensors, such as the accelerometer and gyroscope, are not as well understood. For example, applications need no permission to access motion sensors on Android. As another example, W3C's *DeviceOrientation* Event Specification [19] allows any web application to access the accelerometer and gyroscope, which was adopted by both Android since version 3.0 and iOS since version 4.2.

However, recent researches have shown that motion sensors can leak sensitive information [4,17]. The attacker may use motion sensors as a side channel to infer keystrokes typed on on-screen keyboards, which may help the attacker recover important information about the user, such as his passwords or credit card numbers. This *motion-based keystroke inference attack* is based on the observation that device vibration during a keystroke is correlated to the key typed.

S. Katzenbeisser et al. (Eds.): TRUST 2012, LNCS 7344, pp. 273–290, 2012.

Although previous studies showed that motion sensors leak information about keystrokes, they have yet to demonstrate the practicality of this attack. Those studies were based on a single smartphone and a few users. However, for this attack to be practical, we must evaluate whether it is robust against:

- **Hardware variation:** Different devices may use different sensor chips, which may have different sampling rates and precisions. Also the motion sensors may be embedded at different locations on the mobile devices. Does this attack work on different devices?
- **Dimension variation:** Previous work studied only smartphones. Lately, larger devices, such as tablets, are becoming popular. Does this attack work better or worse on these larger devices?
- **Keyboard layout variation:** Device vibration during a keystroke is correlated to the location of the key, which is determined by both the key and the keyboard layout. Furthermore, keyboard layout often affects how the user holds the device and types. During our experiment, we observed that on regular keyboards in portrait mode, users usually held the device in one hand and typed with fingers in the other hand; however, on split keyboards in landscape mode, users usually held the device using both hands and typed with both thumbs. Does this attack work on different keyboard layouts?
- **User variation:** Device vibration during keystrokes may depend on the user's typing style, such as the force of her finger, the tilt angle of the device, and anchor of her holding hand on the device. Does this attack work on different users?

Besides the above questions regarding the robustness of this attack, a successful attack must address the following questions in its design and implementation:

- **Extracting keystroke-relevant signal from motion sensor data.** Although the attacker, through his malware installed on the victim device, can read from the motion sensors, he does not know when a keystroke starts and ends in the continuous data stream. To recognize keystrokes, he must divide the continuous sensor data stream into segments for each keystroke.
- **Selecting the motion sensor.** A device may have multiple motion sensors, such as an accelerometer and a gyroscope. Previous work studied only the accelerometer, but a shrewd attacker would choose the sensor that provides the best results.
- **Selecting the inference techniques.** Multiple techniques exist for inferring keystrokes based on device motion. No previous study compared the alternative techniques, but a shrewd attacker would choose the best technique.

To answer the above questions and to evaluate the practicality of the motion-based keystroke inference attack, we conducted a user study where 21 participants typed on four different mobile devices consisting of two smartphones and two tablets. We asked each participant to type in each of six settings to evaluate various factors affecting the attack and collected a total of 47,814 keystrokes.

We developed a prototype attack and applied the attack on the collected keystrokes. We evaluated how variations in hardware, device dimension, keyboard layout, and user habit affect the attack. To make the attack more effective, we investigated how to extract data segments representing keystrokes from a continuous stream of motion sensor data, the difference between different motion sensors, and the difference between two classifiers. Our evaluation shows that on a number-only keyboard, after the attacker tries 81 4-digit PINs, the probability that she has guessed the correct PIN is 65%, which improves the accuracy rate of the random guessing attack by 81 times.

2   Background

2.1   Motion Based Keystroke Inference Attack

Keyboards are the most common input device. We use keyboards to input a variety of information, some of which is highly valuable, such as passwords, PINs, social security numbers, and credit card numbers. It came as no surprise that keystroke logging [1] is a favorite tool of the trade by attackers. The attacker can install a Trojan program on the victim computer to log keystrokes, or use out-of-band channels to infer keystrokes. An acoustic key logger, for example, can infer keystrokes from acoustic frequency signatures [2], timings between two keystrokes [8], or language models [25]. Electromagnetic emanations of keyboards have also been studied for keylogging [21].

Touch screen mobile devices have changed the paradigm of user interaction. Most touch screen mobile devices have no physical keyboard. Instead, the user types on the software keyboard on the screen. Since there is neither sound nor electromagnetic emanation from a virtual keyboard, the attacker can no longer infer keystrokes based on these signals. Moreover, mobile operating systems, such as Android and iOS, have security design that thwarts Trojan based keyloggers. For instance, on the Android platform, each app runs in its own Linux process and is assigned a unique user ID. An application cannot read keystrokes unless it is active and receives the focus on the screen. In most cases, it seems that key loggers, at least the traditional ones described above, face severe obstacles on touch screen mobile devices.

However, a new approach for keystroke logging on touch screen smart phones has been recently proposed in [4,17]. The new attack exploits the output of motion sensors, such as accelerometers, to infer keystrokes. When the user types on the soft keyboard on her smartphone (especially when she holds her phone by hand rather than placing it on a fixed surface) it causes slight phone vibrations, which can be detected by motion sensors. The keystroke induced vibration on touch screens is correlated with the location of keys being typed. This can be observed from the shifting reflection of distant objects on the device screen when we type. It is possible to estimate the approximate location where a user's finger hit the screen by analyzing the output of motion sensors. Given the keyboard layout is known, it is then straightforward to infer the keystroke value from the location.

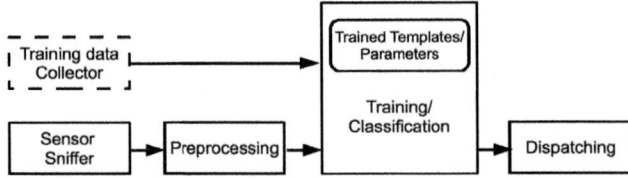

Fig. 1. Architecture of a motion based keystroke inference app

A keystroke inference malware should have at least four components– sensor sniffer, preprocessor, classifier and dispatcher, as shown in Figure 1. The sniffer reads the motion sensor output from a background process. After preprocessing, the sensor data is sent to the classifier, which extracts features and maps the data to a keystroke value. The dispatcher eventually sends the inference result to a remote server controlled by the attacker. If the attack is user dependent, the attacking program should also contain a component to collect a certain amount of training data (sensor data labeled with key values). The training data set is sent to generate templates or parameters used in classification.

2.2   Motion Sensor Data

There are two possible hardware motion sensors available on mobile devices: accelerometer and gyroscope. Accelerometers are already widely adopted by mobile devices. Recently, a gyroscope has been integrated in a number of smartphones and tablets to allow for more accurate recognition of rotating movement within a 3D space. The device movement caused by keystroke is the combination of both shift and rotation. However, since we have observed that the rotation is more related to the key locations, precisely capturing the device rotation is of more interests in keystroke inference. In general it is believed that the accelerometer is designed for recognizing the linear shift component of device movement and the gyroscope is better at recognizing device rotation. But the reality is both of them can detect rotation. With a fixed reference from gravity, accelerometers provide a better measurement tracking pitch and roll when the device is not moving. Gyros provide a higher accuracy when the device is in motion [15]. In this paper, we compared the keystroke inference results based both on accelerometer and gyroscope.

Another important specification of motion sensor data is the sampling rate. Unlike audio input, the motion data is not sampled in a fixed rate. Instead, all of the motion sensors return multi-dimensional arrays of sensor values in terms of sensor events, i.e. new sensor values are reported only when they are different from those reported in the previous event. We list the average and standard deviation of intervals in motion sensor data from different devices we used for evaluation in Table 1.

Mobile platforms allow applications to specify different data delays when reading motion sensor output to trade off between efficiency and accuracy. In this

Table 1. Interval of motion sensor output for difference devices

Device	Accelerometer		Gyroscope	
	average (ms)	stdev	average (ms)	stdev
Google Nexus S	20.07	0.77	1.18	0.11
HTC Evo 4G	22.04	1.93	n/a	n/a
Galaxy Tab 10.1	10.10	0.23	10.10	0.23
Motorola Xoom	10.05	0.36	1.15	0.18

paper we focus mainly on the inference rate rather than the efficiency so that the sensor data delay has been always set to zero.

3   Related Works

Previous research [5] has raised the awareness of privacy attacks on smartphone sensors. Besides the obvious privacy concern over the GPS sensor, researchers have shown attacks using the camera [23] and microphone [24]. These attacks are less insidious because these sensors are protected with access permission by mobile operating systems.

Researchers have studied keystroke inference based on side channels, such as sound [2,25], electromaganetic wave [21], and timing [20]. Since these attacks exploit characteristics of physical keyboards, they become ineffective on smartphones with soft keyboards.

Applications exploiting motion sensors have been extensively researched. Most of these works focus on human activity or gesture recognition. Activity recognition is an important topic in the area of pervasive computing. Researchers have proposed schemes to detect user's activity in choreography [3], food preparation [18], and in medical research [14]. In [11], Lester, etc. tried to determine whether two devices are worn by the same person based on motion signals. The main application for gesture recognition is user interaction [12,6,10,22]. Some also use it for authentication[16,7]. In [13], users can authenticate two devices by attaching them together and shaking. It is also based on accelerometer data. These works use a wide variety of approaches for classification, ranging from frequency domain analysis[11,3,13], Time series analysis [14], Template matching[12,18] to statistical learning[22]. Although their experience on processing motion sensor signal can be borrowed, several major differences between these researches and motion based keystroke inference must be noticed. First, the duration of keystroke induced device movement is much shorter than that caused by a gesture or human activity such as walking or dancing. Second, many of the previous research collect sensor data from a customized devices or Wii remote. The motion sensor signals from these devices usually have constant sampling rate. On a smartphone, the motion data is reported via motion events asynchronously. Finally, the movement caused by keystrokes are not perceptible as user activity or gesture. For example, it is hard for users to control the magnitude of movement.

This paper is directly related to [4] and [17], as they all focus specifically on motion based keystroke inference attack. However, our paper provides a more thorough investigation on the practicality of such attack. We conducted a user study of many more users, devices and settings, and compared the performance of different classification schemes. To the best of our knowledge, this paper is also the first one to investigate output of gyroscopes on mobile devices.

4 Methodology

4.1 Data Acquisition

The attacker can read the motion sensor data through either a web application or an application installed on the victim mobile device. For example, the attacker can embed the code for sniffing the motion sensors in an otherwise legitimate application. Since Android requires no permission for reading motion sensors, these applications are unlikely to raise suspicion.

We record the stream of motion sensor events in a sequence of tuples $(t^i, V^i = \{v_x^i, v_y^i, v_z^i\}), i = 1 \ldots N$, where t_i is the time when the i_{th} sensor event occurs, V^i contains sensor reading on three dimensions, and N is the total number of sensor events. For the accelerometer, V_i contains the acceleration force in m/s^2 along the x, y and z axis, respectively. For the gyroscope, V^i contains the rate of rotation in rad/s around the x, y and z axis.

4.2 Preprocessing

De-jittering: Many signal analysis methods require constant-interval sampling. However, motion sensors usually do not generate new events until the reading has changed (Table 1). Therefore, we dejitterize the motion events as follows:

1. Calculate the average interval Δ of sensor events in each stream.
2. For any event $e^i = \{t^i, V^i\}$, if $t^i - t^{i-1} > \frac{4}{3}\Delta$, we insert M events evenly between e^{i-1} and e^i such that $\frac{2}{3}\Delta \leq \frac{t^i - t^{i-1}}{M+1} < \frac{4}{3}\Delta$. We set the sensor values in all these new events to be equal to that in V^{i-1}, because a long interval with no event indicates that the sensor reading has not changed.
3. For any event $e^i = \{t^i, V^i\}$, if $t^{i+1} - t^{i-1} < \frac{2}{3}\Delta$, then we delete e^i.

Low-pass Filtering: The interpolation in the previous step converts the stream of sensor events into a time series. To remove spurious high frequency spikes, we apply an IIR Low-pass filter whose cutoff frequency is 30Hz.

Calibration: When the motion data is received from the accelerometer, we must calibrate it to remove the projection of gravity on each axis. Although typing may cause slight device movement, the total rotation and shift of the device are negligible during the short time of each keystroke. Therefore, we calibrate the accelerometer data by subtracting the average value from each data point on each axis, resulting in $(t^i, V^i = \{v_x^i - \bar{v_x}, v_y^i - \bar{v_y}, v_z^i - \bar{v_z}\})$. In theory, the average gyroscope value on each axis is zero. In our experiments, however, we observed that the average values were small but non-zero, possibly due to hardware or driver imprecision. Thus we must calibrate the gyroscope data similarly.

Segmentation: After calibration, we obtain a series of motion sensor data, from which we must extract segments of motion data where each segment corresponds to one keystroke. In other words, we must recognize the start and end of each keystroke from the motion data series. We build a library of waveform patterns of keystroke motion and use them to determine the segment of each keystroke in the motion data.

4.3   Classification

We use and compare two classification techniques: Dynamic Time Warping(DTW) and Support Vector Machine(SVM). They have been extensively used in user activity and gesture recognition. DTW is a template matching technique that uses a time function as the feature, while SVM is a statistical learning technique that uses a vector of parameters as the feature.

Feature Selection. Feature selection extracts relevant information from input data to feed to classifiers. The input to our keystroke inference tool is motion data, which may look similar to the input to user activity or gesture recognition superficially. However, a key difference is in the magnitude and stability of the data. In user activity and gesture recognition, the user perceives and controls the device motion consciously; therefore, the magnitude of motion data can often be used as a good feature in recognizing activities or gestures. By contrast, magnitude is a poor feature in keystroke inference, as motion is a byproduct of typing and is never controlled by the user consciously. Therefore, we need to explore features other than magnitude.

The motion data on the z-axis from the accelerometer mainly reflect the shift component of the device movement, and the motion data on the z-axis from the gyroscope reflect the rotation around the z-axis. Since neither of them is closely related to the keys being typed, we drop them from further consideration.

Dynamic Time Warping. Dynamic Time Warp is a common template matching approach for motion sensor analysis [12,18,6,10]. Likely because of the relatively high variance in the sampling rate of our data, we find that DTW works better than other template matching algorithms, such as Euclidean Distance. Another factor in favor of DTW is the varying number of motion data points for different key presses. For example, when the user types continuously and quickly, a new keystroke can interrupt the device vibration caused by the previous keystroke. We observed in our data that the duration of a keystroke can be as short as 100ms, less than half of the duration of a typical keystroke. DTW substring matching handles varying length of input nicely.

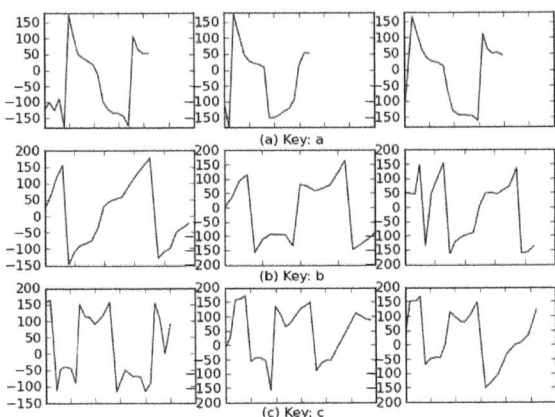

Fig. 2. Sample DTW features extracted from the data by same user

Existing works on activity or gesture recognition based on DTW use the magnitude of motion data on the three dimensions as input to DTW. However, as we discussed earlier, magnitude of motion data is not a good feature in inferring keystrokes, and neither is motion data on the z-axis. Therefore, from the motion data, we compute $h_i = arctan(v_y^i/v_x^i) \times 180/\pi$ as the DTW feature. Figure 2 plots the values of this feature on sample keystrokes. Our experiments show that this feature gives better results than the magnitudes on three axes.

During training, among all the data segments of the same key, we choose as a template the segment that minimizes its total distance to all the other segments.

Support Vector Machine. Support Vector Machine(SVM) is a statistical learning technique used in related research [22]. Unlike template matching, Support Vector Machine uses parameter features extracted from the motion data. Common features used in SVM can be either from time domain or frequency domain. We choose to use time domain features only because the relatively small number of data points in the motion data segment of each keystroke makes frequency domain features unreliable. We also avoid features that are determined solely by the magnitude of motion, as discussed earlier. Our features include:

- **Segment duration:** the duration of the motion data segment.
- **Peak time difference:** $p_x - p_y$, where $v_x^{p_x}$ and $v_y^{p_y}$ are the first peaks on the x-axis and y-axis respectively.
- **Spike number on X (and Y):** the number of spikes on X(and Y) axis.
- **Peak interval on X (and Y) axis:** $p_{x'} - p_x$ (and $p_y' - p_y$), where $v_x^{p_x}$ and $v_x^{p_{x'}}$ (and $v_y^{p_y}$ and $v_y^{p_{y'}}$) are the first and second peaks on X (and Y) axis.
- **Attenuation rate on X (and Y) axis:** $v_x^{p_x}/v_x^{p_{x'}}$ (and $v_y^{p_y}/v_y^{p_{y'}}$).
- **Vertex angles:** $arctan(v_y^p/v_x^p)$ and $arctan(v_y^{p'}/v_x^{p'})$, where p and p' is the time of the first and second peaks on $(v_x)^2 + (v_y)^2$.

The basic form of SVM makes binary classification decisions. To apply SVM as a multi-classifer to infer keystrokes, we build a binary decision tree [9] based on the geometric distribution of keys on each keyboard.

5 Evaluation

To answer the questions raised in Section 1, we conducted a user study in which we collected typing-induced motion data from 21 users on 4 mobile devices in 6 settings. We designed and implemented a prototype system for keystroke inference as described in Section 4. We ran the system on the data collected in our user study.

5.1 User Study

Participants. With the approval of our university IRB, we recruited 21 participants for our user study. They were all undergraduate students. Before the user study, we told them that the purpose was to study the usability of onscreen keyboards. We purposely did not disclose the true purpose of this study so as not to prime the participants to our security evaluation. All the participants have used smartphones and 1/3 of them have also used tablets.

Procedure. We developed an application for recording keystrokes and their corresponding motion data and installed it on two smartphones and two tablets all running Android. We gave each participant a set of random strings and ask him to type each string in six different settings with regard to device type, key set, device orientation, and keyboard layout (Table 2). In each setting, we collected around 30 keystrokes per key from each participant.

It took each participant around one hour to finish the study. To prevent fatigue, our application reminded the participant to take a break after every few strings. Before the application started to record keystrokes, we allowed all the participants enough time to play with the devices to find the most comfortable way to type. The only restriction is that they could not place the devices on any fixed surfaces. We found that all the participants held the devices with one hand and typed with the other in every setting except the one that used a split software keyboard. However, the typing styles, such as the tilt of the devices and the anchor points of their hands on the devices, varied greatly between different participants and even between different strings typed by the same participant.

Settings. Participants type each string in each of six settings, which differ in device type, key set, device orientation, and keyboard layout.

- *Device types*: We used four Android devices in the user study: two smartphones (Nexus S and HTC Evo) and two tablets (Motorola Xoom and Samsung Galaxy Tab 10.1). All the devices except the HTC Evo have both an accelerometer and a gyroscope. Table 1 shows that the motion sensors in

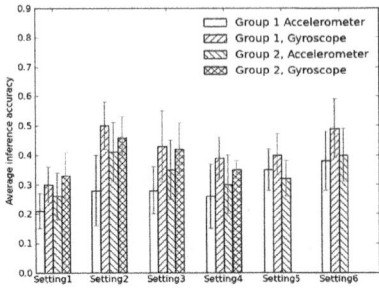
(a) Using dynamic time warping

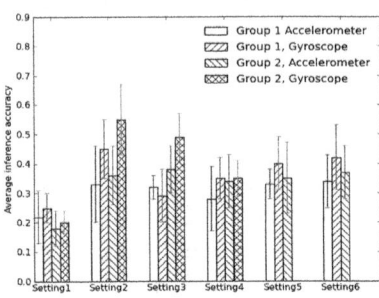
(b) Using supporting vector machine

Fig. 3. Keystroke inference accuracy in different settings. There are only three bars in Setting 5 and 6 of Group 2 because HTC Evo has no gyroscope.

different devices have different sampling rates. The OS on both smartphones is Android 2.3.1 (Gingerbread) and on both tablets is Android 3.0 (Honeycomb). We randomly divided all the users into two groups: 10 Users were in group 1 while the remaining were in group 2. Users in group 1 typed on Nexus S and Motorola Xoom while users in group 2 typed on HTC Evo and Samsung Galaxy Tab.

- *Key sets*: The keystroke inference attacker may know the set of keys in certain scenarios. For example, during phone calls the user can type only numbers because phone dialing pads have only numbers. Intuitively, one expects lower inference rate on an alphabet-only keyboard than on a number-only keyboard because the former has more keys to distinguish between. To evaluate this conjecture, we chose only alphabet characters in all the strings in setting 1 of our study, and chose only numbers in all the rest 5 settings of our study.
- *Screen orientation*: All software keyboards have different layouts for different orientations of the screen. Typically the keyboard is larger in landscape mode than in portrait mode. The screen was in portrait mode in one setting and in landscape mode for the other five.
- *Keyboard layout*: On an Android smartphone, the layout of the default software keyboard can be configured. For instance, an app can display the keyboard with the QWERTY layout by choosing *text* class, or with phone dialing pad layout by choosing *phone* class. Users can enter numbers in either layout. In the *text* class, number keys are located only in the first row of the keyboard while in the *phone* class, number keys occupy most area of the keyboard. In our user study, uses entered numbers in both keyboard layouts on smartphones.

We compared two keyboard layouts on tablets. One is the QWERTY layout of default Android keyboard. The other is a split layout provided by a third party input method called *Tablet Keyboard Free*. In the split layout, the QWERTY keyboard is divided into a left pane and a right pane, located

Table 2. Users type each key in all six settings, varied by device, orientation, keyboard layout, and key set

	Devices		Key set	Orientation	Keyboard Layout
	Group 1	Group 2			
1	Motorola Xoom	Galaxy tab 10.1	alphabet only	landscape	default keyboard
2	Motorola Xoom	Galaxy tab 10.1	number only	landscape	default keyboard
3	Motorola Xoom	Galaxy tab 10.1	number only	portrait	default keyboard
4	Motorola Xoom	Galaxy tab 10.1	number only	landscape	split keyboard
5	Nexus S	HTC Evo	number only	landscape	default keyboard, text class
6	Nexus S	HTC Evo	number only	landscape	default keyboard, phone class

in the lower left and right corners of the screen, respectively. A split keyboard allows users to hold the device with two hands and to type with both thumbs.

Table 2 lists the six settings for both participant groups. The order of settings in which each participant types is randomized.

5.2 Finding

Overview. We collected valid data for 47,814 keystrokes in total. Figure 3 shows the inference accuracy rate for each setting. It shows that we correctly inferred 30% - 33% of the keystrokes within 26 letters (from the gyroscope reading), which is more than 8 times as good as a random guess. The average inference accuracy on number only keystrokes is as high as 55%, which is 5.5 times as good as a random guess. Even on a smartphone with a smaller screen, the inference accuracy on number-only keystrokes is 49%. These results confirmed that motion sensors are a significant side channel for leaking sensitive information.

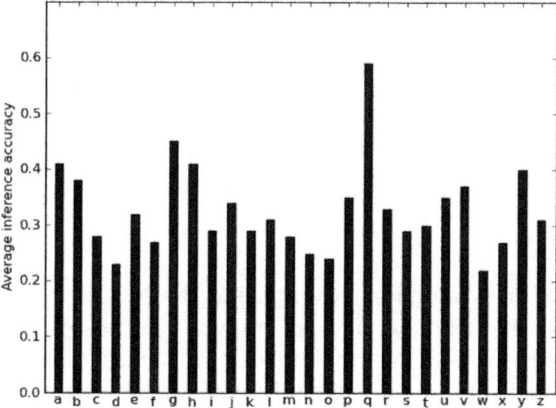

Fig. 4. Average inference accuracy of each key on the default QWERTY keyboard in setting 1 on Motorola Xoom using dynamic time warping

Figure 4 shows that the average inference accuracies of different keys on the default keyboard are close to each other except for one key. We have found no evidence to suggest that inference accuracy differs on different areas on the keyboard.

User Dependency. The above results are based on user-dependent inference, where the training and testing data sets are from the same user. Figure 5 compares the accuracy of user dependent inference with that of user independent inference. In user independent inference, we picked a random user and used his data to train all the classifiers, and then tested the classifiers on all the other users' data. Figure 5 shows that user independent inference has much lower accuracy. It indicates that keystroke inference depends heavily on the user's typing style. However, even though user independent inference is less accurate, it still leaks useful information about keystrokes. For example, the average accuracy rate in Setting 1 is 12%, which is 3 times as good as random guessing.

Minimum Training Set Size. To evaluate the effect of training set size on the accuracy in user dependent inference, we repeated the classification with training sets of different sizes. For each size, the test was done in repeated random sub-sampling cross validation. Figure 6 shows the results using dynamic time warping. Initially, the inference accuracy increases when the training set becomes larger. However, the curves become flat when the training set reaches a certain size (12 for the alphabet-only keyboard and 8 for the number-only keyboard). We found a similar correlation between training set size and inference accuracy when using support vector machine as the classifier.

Device Variation. The participants in our user study were divided into two groups. Each group was assigned a different set of devices, which use different motion sensor chips. Although the precision and sampling rate of sensor data that we obtained from the two groups are different, the results on keystroke inference were very close.

Layout Variation. In Figure 3 we can see the accuracies in setting 2 is slightly higher than those in setting 3. It suggests that keystroke inference is more accurate on a keyboard in landscape mode than in portrait mode. This is not surprising because the keyboard in landscape mode is larger and the keys are separated farther.

Device Dimension Variation. Comparing the results in setting 2 and those in setting 5 shows that the inference accuracy is affected by device dimension. In both settings the users were typing number-only strings on the default keyboard (text class) in landscape mode. Using dynamic time warping, the inference accuracy based on the output of tablet gyroscope is 50%, while that of inference based on the smartphone gyroscope is 41%. Using support vector machine, the accuracies are 45% and 36% respectively. In both cases, the inference accuracy

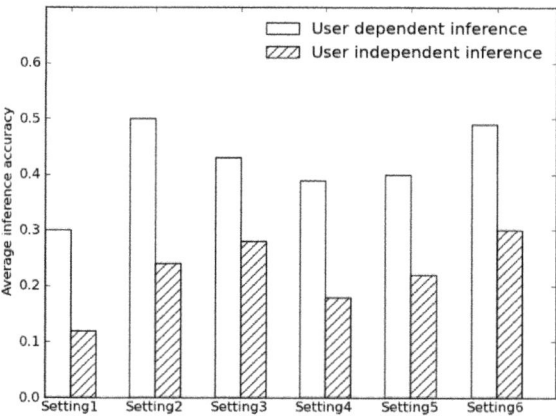

Fig. 5. Average inference accuracy is much higher when the attack is user dependent

on a tablet is higher. Because all other factors — keyboard layout, key set, device orientation, data sampling rate, and users — are identical, we believe the difference in accuracy is caused by device dimension.

The variables in setting 5 and 6 are all the same except the keyboard layout. In setting 5, the number keys use only one row of the QWERTY keyboard. By contrast, the number keys almost occupy the whole keyboard in setting 6. Intuitively, the inference accuracies in setting 6 are higher than those in setting 5, which is confirmed in Figure 3. Comparing the results in setting 2 and 4 further supports our conclusion.

Finally, keystroke inference is affected by the size of the key set, as we expected. The users typed alphabet-only strings in setting 1 and number-only strings in setting 2, with all other variables identical. The inference accuracies in setting 1 are always lower than those in setting 2.

5.3 Motion Sensor Selection

Figure 3 suggests that the gyroscope is a better side channel than the accelerometer for keystroke inference. In almost every setting, gyroscope data result in higher inference accuracy. In the beginning, we suspected that it is due to the higher sampling rate of the gyroscope sensors in both Motorola Xoom and Nexus S, but comparing the results between Setting 1 and Setting 4 of Group 2 disapproved our suspicion because both motion sensors on Samsung Galaxy Tab 1.0 have exactly the same sampling rate. One possible explanation for the superiority of gyroscope data is the effect of gravity on the accelerometer data. We can see from the recorded data that the projection of gravity on each axis of the accelerometer data is changing over time, which makes it hard to eliminate the gravity during data calibration. It suggests that the angle between the device and the desk surface is changing when users type. Such movement introduces

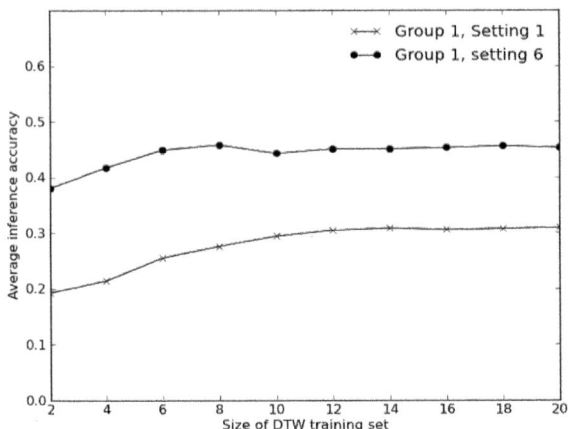

Fig. 6. Average inference accuracy by the size of training set used in dynamic time warping when the inference is user dependent

noise to the accelerometer output and reduces keystroke inference accuracy. On the other hand, type induced device movement includes both rotation and shifting. Ideally we want to extract the rotation to differentiate keystrokes because it is better related to the location of the key on the screen. Both the accelerometer and the gyroscope can be used to measure device rotation, but the gyroscope is better at capturing high frequency rotation (> 0.5Hz) while the accelerometer is more accurate when the rotation has a lower frequency (< 0.1Hz) [15]. The data we collected indicate that typing-induced movement lasts only about 200ms, which supports the observed superiority of gyroscope data. In the rest of the paper, we focus on keystroke inference based on gyroscope data.

5.4   Classification Techniques

We chose both dynamic time warping and support vector machine as the classifer in our prototype. Our results show no strong evidence that one is superior to the other. Other than these two classifiers, we also tried time series analysis techniques, such as Linear predictive coding. All of them have inferior performance.

6   Discussions

6.1   Inference Precision

Our evaluation shows that the accuracy for inferring a single keystroke is about 33% for the alphabet only keyboard and about 50% for the number only keyboard. Moreover, when the inference is incorrect, the probability that the falsely inferred key belongs to a small set of keys surrounding the correct key is high.

Figure 7a shows that on a number-only keyboard, the probability that the inferred key belongs to a set of three keys (including the correct key) is about 90%. Therefore, after the attacker records the motion data of a four-key PIN on this keyboard, he can try $3^4 = 81$ different PINs and the probability that one of these PINs is correct is $0.9^4 = 0.65$. By comparison, when the attacker has no motion data and therefore has to guess each key randomly, after 81 tries the probably that he has guessed a correct PIN is $0.3^4 = 0.0081$. Our motion-based keystroke inference has improved the success probability by 81 times.

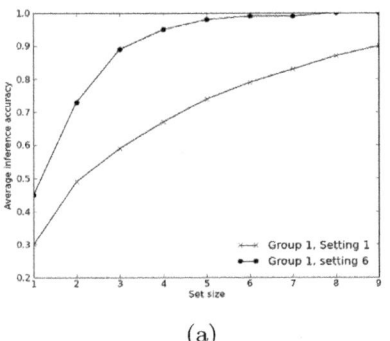
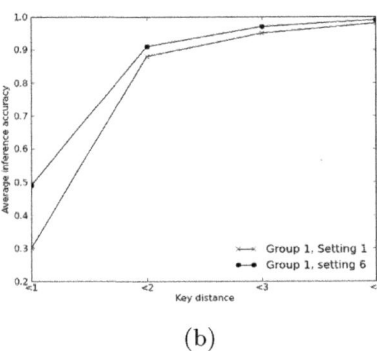

(a)   (b)

Fig. 7. Inference precision: (a)Probability that the inferred key belongs to a set of keys (the correct key and its neighboring keys) using dynamic time warping; (b)Accuracy rate described by the distance of the inferred key from the correct key using dynamic time warping

The incorrectly inferred keys are usually nearby the actual key. Figure 7b shows the distribution of *key distance* [17]. It indicates that almost 90% of inferred keys are either the actual key pressed or only one key distance away.

6.2   Multiple Templates in DTW

We observed in the user study that many participants switched among a set of fixed typing style rather than changing randomly. This reminds us that a user may feel comfortable typing in several styles. To account for this, we tried matching multiple templates in dynamic time warping classification and found that it works better than matching a single template. Figure 8a shows the DTW classifier has a higher accuracy when the data is matched against multiple templates. However, the classification takes longer as the template number increases. We chose to use three templates in setting 1 and two templates in setting 6 even though the accuracy is higher if 7 templates are used as in setting 6.

6.3   Multi-class SVM

SVM is a binary classifier. To apply it to keystroke inference, a variety of techniques are available for decomposition of the multi-class problem. We compared

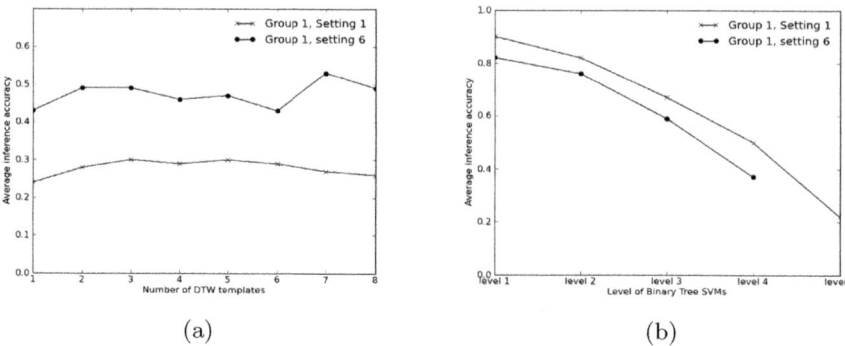

(a)   (b)

Fig. 8. Classifier parameters slection: (a)Average inference accuracy by different template number using dynamic time warping; (b)Average inference accuracy by the level binary tree SVMs(BTS). The more levels of the BTS the lower the accuray.

two approaches: One-against-all(OvA) and Binary tree of SVM (BTS) and the latter shows a much better performance. Moreover, BTS has a useful feature in keystroke inference. The SVM on the first level only determines whether the key is on the left side or the right side of the keyboard. But the SVM on the last level need to make a decision between two adjacent keys. Thus it is reasonable that SVM on the lower level node has lower inference accuracy. As shown in Figure 8b, the inference accuracy decreases when the input goes through more classifiers. The results suggest that the medium output of BTS can be used for determining approximation of the key. For example, the accuracy inferring a key on the alphabet only keyboard with a BTS classification of 5 levels is only 22%, but the accuracy after the 4th SVM is 50%, i.e, the chance that the actual key is one of two keys is 50%. This is consistent to what we observed from Figure 7a.

7   Conclusion

To evaluate the practicality of motion-based keystroke inference attack, we conducted a user study where 21 participants typed a total of 47,814 keystrokes on four different mobile devices in six settings. We developed a prototype attack and applied the attack on the users' keystrokes. Our results show that this attack remains effective even though the accuracy is affected by user habits, device dimension, screen orientation, and keyboard layout. On a number-only keyboard, after the attacker tries 81 4-digit PINs, the probability that she has guessed the correct PIN is 65%, which improves the accuracy rate of random guessing by 81 times. Our study also indicates that inference based on the gyroscope is more accurate than that based on the accelerometer. We evaluated two classification techniques in our prototype and found that they are similarly effective.

Acknowledgments. This material is based in part upon work supported by the National Science Foundation under Grant Numbers 0644450 and 1018964. Any opinions, findings, and conclusions or recommendations expressed in this material are those of the author(s) and do not necessarily reflect the views of the National Science Foundation.

References

1. Keystroke logging wiki page, http://en.wikipedia.org/wiki/Keystroke_logging
2. Asonov, D., Agrawal, R.: Keyboard acoustic emanations. In: Proceedings of IEEE Symposium on Security and Privacy, pp. 3–11 (May 2004)
3. Aylward, R., Lovell, S.D., Paradiso, J.A.: A compact, wireless, wearable sensor network for interactive dance ensembles. In: International Workshop on Wearable and Implantable Body Sensor Networks, BSN 2006, pages 4, p. 70 (April 2006)
4. Cai, L., Chen, H.: Touchlogger: inferring keystrokes on touch screen from smartphone motion. In: Proceedings of the 6th USENIX Conference on Hot Topics in Security, HotSec 2011, p. 9 (2011)
5. Cai, L., Machiraju, S., Chen, H.: Defending against sensor-sniffing attacks on mobile phones. In: Proceedings of the 1st ACM Workshop on Networking, Systems, and Applications for Mobile Handhelds, MobiHeld 2009, pp. 31–36 (2009)
6. Choe, B., Min, J.-K., Cho, S.-B.: Online Gesture Recognition for User Interface on Accelerometer Built-in Mobile Phones. In: Wong, K.W., Mendis, B.S.U., Bouzerdoum, A. (eds.) ICONIP 2010, Part II. LNCS, vol. 6444, pp. 650–657. Springer, Heidelberg (2010)
7. Chong, M.K., Marsden, G., Gellersen, H.: Gesturepin: using discrete gestures for associating mobile devices. In: Proceedings of the 12th International Conference on Human Computer Interaction with Mobile Devices and Services, MobileHCI 2010, pp. 261–264 (2010)
8. Kune, D.F., Kim, Y.: Timing attacks on pin input devices. In: Proceedings of the 17th ACM Conference on Computer and Communications Security, CCS 2010, pp. 678–680 (2010)
9. Madzarov, D.G.G., Chorbev, I.: A multiclass svm classifier utilizing binary decision tree. In: Informatica33, pp. 233–241 (2009)
10. Hancke, G.P.: Gesture recognition as ubiquitous input for mobile phones (2008)
11. Lester, J., Hannaford, B., Borriello, G.: "Are You with Me?" - Using Accelerometers to Determine If Two Devices Are Carried by the Same Person. In: Ferscha, A., Mattern, F. (eds.) PERVASIVE 2004. LNCS, vol. 3001, pp. 33–50. Springer, Heidelberg (2004)
12. Liu, J., Wang, Z., Zhong, L., Wickramasuriya, J., Vasudevan, V.: uwave: Accelerometer-based personalized gesture recognition and its applications. Pervasive and Mobile Computing 5, 1–9 (2009)
13. Mayrhofer, R., Gellersen, H.-W.: Shake Well Before Use: Authentication Based on Accelerometer Data. In: LaMarca, A., Langheinrich, M., Truong, K.N. (eds.) Pervasive 2007. LNCS, vol. 4480, pp. 144–161. Springer, Heidelberg (2007)
14. Min, C.-H., Tewfik, A.H.: Automatic characterization and detection of behavioral patterns using linear predictive coding of accelerometer sensor data. In: Proceedings of the International Conference of IEEE Engineering in Medicine and Biology Society, vol. 2010, pp. 220–223 (2010)

15. Nasiri, S., Sachs, D., Maia, M.: Selection and integration of mems-based motion processing in consumer apps (July 2009),
    http://invensense.com/mems/gyro/documents/whitepapers/
    Selection-and-integration-of-MEMS-based-motion-processing-in-
    consumer-apps-070809-EE-Times.pdf
16. Niu, Y., Chen, H.: Gesture authentication with touch input for mobile devices. In: 3rd International Conference on Security and Privacy in Mobile Information and Communication Systems, MobiSec 2011 (May 2011)
17. Owusu, E., Han, J., Das, S., Perrig, A., Zhang, J.: Accessory: password inference using accelerometers on smartphones. In: Proceedings of the Twelfth Workshop on Mobile Computing Systems and Applications, HotMobile 2012, pp. 9:1–9:6. ACM, New York (2012)
18. Pham, C., Plötz, T., Olivier, P.: A Dynamic Time Warping Approach to Real-Time Activity Recognition for Food Preparation. In: de Ruyter, B., Wichert, R., Keyson, D.V., Markopoulos, P., Streitz, N., Divitini, M., Georgantas, N., Mana Gomez, A. (eds.) AmI 2010. LNCS, vol. 6439, pp. 21–30. Springer, Heidelberg (2010)
19. Popescu, A., Block, S.: DeviceOrientation event specification, editor's draft 9 (February 2011), http://dev.w3.org/geo/api/spec-source-orientation.html
20. Song, D.X., Wagner, D., Tian, X.: Timing analysis of keystrokes and timing attacks on ssh. In: Proceedings of the 10th conference on USENIX Security Symposium, vol. 10, p. 25 (2001)
21. Vuagnoux, M., Pasini, S.: Compromising electromagnetic emanations of wired and wireless keyboards. In: Proceedings of the 18th Conference on USENIX Security Symposium, SSYM 2009, pp. 1–16 (2009)
22. Wu, J., Pan, G., Zhang, D., Qi, G., Li, S.: Gesture Recognition with a 3-D Accelerometer. In: Zhang, D., Portmann, M., Tan, A.-H., Indulska, J. (eds.) UIC 2009. LNCS, vol. 5585, pp. 25–38. Springer, Heidelberg (2009)
23. Xu, N., Zhang, F., Luo, Y., Jia, W., Xuan, D., Teng, J.: Stealthy video capturer: a new video-based spyware in 3G smartphones. In: Proceedings of the Second ACM Conference on Wireless Network Security, WiSec 2009, pp. 69–78 (2009)
24. Zhang, K., Zhou, X., Intwala, M., Kapadia, A., Wang, X.: Soundcomber: A stealthy and context-aware sound trojan for smartphones. In: Proceedings of the 18th Annual Networkand Distributed System Security Symposium, NDSS 2011 (2011)
25. Zhuang, L., Zhou, F., Tygar, J.D.: Keyboard acoustic emanations revisited. ACM Transactions on Information and System Security 13, 3:1–3:26 (2009)

AndroidLeaks: Automatically Detecting Potential Privacy Leaks in Android Applications on a Large Scale

Clint Gibler[1], Jonathan Crussell[1,2], Jeremy Erickson[1,2], and Hao Chen[1]

[1] University of California, Davis
{cdgibler,jcrussell,jericks}@ucdavis.edu, hchen@cs.ucdavis.edu
[2] Sandia National Labs*, Livermore, CA
{jcrusse,jericks}@sandia.gov

Abstract. As mobile devices become more widespread and powerful, they store more sensitive data, which includes not only users' personal information but also the data collected via sensors throughout the day. When mobile applications have access to this growing amount of sensitive information, they may leak it carelessly or maliciously.

Google's Android operating system provides a permissions-based security model that restricts an application's access to the user's private data. Each application statically declares the sensitive data and functionality that it requires in a manifest, which is presented to the user upon installation. However, it is not clear to the user how sensitive data is used once the application is installed. To combat this problem, we present AndroidLeaks, a static analysis framework for automatically finding potential leaks of sensitive information in Android applications on a massive scale. AndroidLeaks drastically reduces the number of applications and the number of traces that a security auditor has to verify manually.

We evaluate the efficacy of AndroidLeaks on 24,350 Android applications from several Android markets. AndroidLeaks found 57,299 potential privacy leaks in 7,414 Android applications, out of which we have manually verified that 2,342 applications leak private data including phone information, GPS location, WiFi data, and audio recorded with the microphone. AndroidLeaks examined these applications in 30 hours, which indicates that it is capable of scaling to the increasingly large set of available applications.

1 Introduction

As smartphones have become more popular, the focus of mobile computing has shifted from laptops to phones and tablets. There are several competing mobile platforms. As of this writing, Android has the highest market share of any

---

* Sandia National Laboratories is a multi-program laboratory managed and operated by Sandia Corporation, a wholly owned subsidiary of Lockheed Martin Corporation, for the U.S. Department of Energys National Nuclear Security Administration under contract DE-AC04-94AL85000.

S. Katzenbeisser et al. (Eds.): TRUST 2012, LNCS 7344, pp. 291–307, 2012.

smartphone operating system in the U.S. [8]. Android provides the core smartphone experience, but much of a user's productivity depends on third-party applications. To this end, Android has numerous marketplaces where users can download third-party applications. In contrast to the market policy for iOS, in which every application is reviewed before it can be published [15], most Android markets allow developers to post their applications with no review process. This policy has been criticized for its potential vulnerability to malicious applications. Google instead allows the Android Market to self-regulate, with higher-rated applications more likely to show up in search results and reported malicious applications removed.

Android sandboxes each application from the rest of the system's resources in an effort to protect the user [2]. This attempts to ensure that one application cannot tamper with another application or the system as a whole. If an application needs to access a restricted resource, the developer must statically request permission to use that resource by declaring it in the application's manifest file. When a user attempts to install the application, Android will warn the user that the application requires certain restricted resources (for instance, location data), and that by installing the application, she is granting permission for the application to use the specified resources. If the user declines to authorize these permissions, the application will not be installed.

However, statically requiring permissions does not inform the user how the resource will be used once granted. A maps application, for example, will require access to the Internet in order to download updated map tiles, route information and traffic reports. It will also require access to the phone's location in order to adjust the displayed map and give real-time directions. The application's functionality requires sending location data to the maps server, which is expected and acceptable given the purpose of the application. However, if the application is ad-supported it may also leak location data to advertisers for targeted ads, which may compromise a user's privacy. Given the only information currently presented to users is a list of required permissions, a user will not be able to tell how the maps application is handling her location information.

To address this issue, we present AndroidLeaks, a static analysis framework designed to identify potential leaks of personal information in Android applications on a large scale. Leveraging WALA [7], a program analysis framework for Java source and byte code, we create a call graph of an application's code and then perform a reachability analysis to determine if sensitive information may be sent over the network. If there is a potential path, we use dataflow analysis to determine if private data reaches a network sink.

Our contributions in this paper are as follows:

- We have created a set of mappings between Android API methods and the permissions they require to execute using static techniques. We use a subset of this mapping as the sources and sinks of private data for our dataflow analysis.
- We present AndroidLeaks, a static analysis framework for finding potential leaks of private information in Android applications. We evaluated

AndroidLeaks on 24,350 Android applications, finding potential privacy leaks involving uniquely identifying phone information, location data, WiFi data, and audio recorded with the microphone. AndroidLeaks identifies APKs and provides a set of leaks most likely to be of interest to a security researcher.
- We designed and implemented taint-aware slicing and an approach for identifying taint sources in callbacks, which is used extensively in Android applications.
- We compare the prevalence of several popular ad libraries and the private data they leak.

2   Background

Android applications are primarily written in Java. Unlike standard Java applications, after being compiled into Java bytecode Android applications are converted into the Dalvik Executable (DEX) format. This conversion occurs because Android applications run in the Dalvik [6] virtual machine, rather than the Java virtual machine. We use *ded* [11] and *dex2jar* [17] to convert applications back into Java source code or byte code, respectively.

Android applications are distributed in compressed packages called Android Packages (APKs). APKs contain everything that the application needs to run, including the code, icons, XML files specifying the UI, and application data. Android applications are available both through the official Android Market and other third-party markets. These alternative markets allow users freedom to select the source of their applications.

The official Android Market is primarily user regulated. The ratings of applications in the market are determined by the positive and negative votes of users. Higher ranked applications are shown first in the market and therefore are more likely to be discovered. Users can also share their experiences with an application by submitting a review. This can alert other users to avoid poorly behaving applications. Google is able to remove any application not only from the market, but also from users' phones directly, and has done so when users reported malicious applications [16,20]. However, recent research [10] shows that many popular applications still leak their users' private data.

Android applications are composed of several standard components which are responsible for different parts of the application functionality. These components include: Activities, which control UI screens; Services, which are background processes for functionality not directly tied to the UI; BroadcastReceivers, which passively receive messages from the Android application framework; and ContentProviders, which provide CRUD operations[1] to application-managed data. In order to communicate and coordinate between components, Android provides a message routing system based on URIs. The sent messages are called Intents. Intents can tell the Android framework to start a new Service, switch to a different Activity, or to pass data to another component.

---

[1] Create, Read, Update, and Delete operations.

294   C. Gibler et al.

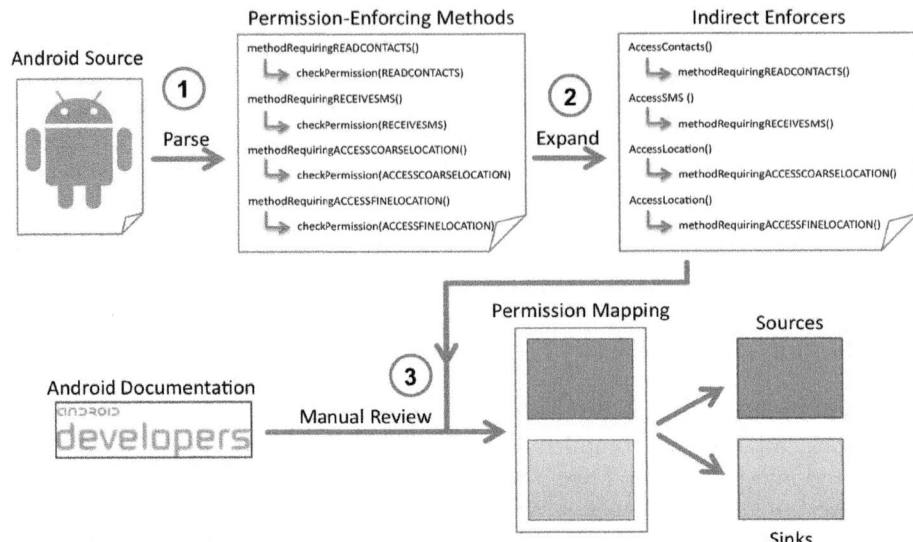

Fig. 1. Creating a Mapping between API Methods and Permissions

Each Android application contains an important XML file called a manifest [1]. The manifest file informs the Android framework of the application components and how to route Intents between components. It also declares the specific screen sizes handled, available hardware and most importantly for this work, the application's required permissions.

Android uses a permission scheme to restrict the actions of applications [2]. Each permission corresponds to protecting a type of sensitive data or specific OS functionality. For example, the INTERNET permission is required to initiate network communications and READ_PHONE_STATE gives access to phone-specific information. Upon application installation, the user is presented with a list of required permissions. The user will be able to install the application only if she grants the application all the permissions. Without modifying the Android OS, there is currently no way to install applications with only a subset of the permissions they require. Additionally, Android does not allow any further restriction of the capabilities of a given application beyond the permission scheme. For example, one cannot limit the INTERNET permission to only certain URLs. This permission scheme provides a general idea of an application's capabilities; however, it does not show how an application uses the resources to which it has been allowed access.

3   Threat Model

In this work we consider a *privacy leak* to be any transfer of personal or phone-identifying information off of the phone. We do not attempt to distinguish personal data used by an application for user-expected application functionality from unintended or malicious use; nor do we attempt to differentiate between benevolent and malicious leaks. Identifying if personal data is used for expected functionality requires understanding the purpose of the application as well as the intention of the developer during its creation, neither of which we attempt to do. Thus we classify transfer of personal information off of the phone as a privacy leak regardless of its use, e.g., malware authors may maliciously leak private data, ad libraries may leak it for more targeted ads, and applications may use it for their functionality. We focus on tracking private information flow in real applications at a large scale, but leave determining the intent of private information leaks to future work.

Our work focuses on Android applications leaking private data within the scope of the Android security model [2]. We are not concerned with vulnerabilities or bugs in Android OS code, the SDK, or the Dalvik VM which runs applications. For example, a Webkit[2] bug that causes a buffer overflow in the browser leading to arbitrary code execution is outside the scope of our work. Our trusted computing base is the Linux kernel and libraries, the Android framework, and the Dalvik VM.

We do not attempt to track private data specific to an application, such as saved preferences or files, since determining which application-specific data is private requires knowledge of the application's purpose and therefore is difficult to automate. We also do not attempt to find leaks enabled by the collaboration of applications. To find such leaks, we would need to extend AndroidLeaks to analyze potential interactions between applications, which we leave for future work.

Currently AndroidLeaks does not analyze native code. We do not believe this significantly affects our results as only 7% of our Android applications include native code. Even if an application is written in native code to defeat Java-based analyses such as AndroidLeaks, it cannot hide its access of private data because it may read private data only through Android's Java APIs. AndroidLeaks could be extended so that, when an application reads private data and then passes it to native code, AndroidLeaks would pass the analysis on to existing binary analysis tools, such as BitBlaze [3].

4   Methodology

In this section we discuss the architecture and implementation of AndroidLeaks. First, we create a *permission mapping* — a mapping between Android API calls and permissions they require to execute — to be used in all application analyses. We use a subset of this mapping for our dataflow *sources* and *sinks*. A *source* is a method that accesses personal data; for example, a phone number, unique device ID, or the phone's GPS location. A *sink* is a method that can transmit local data to an external entity; for instance, submitting a HTTP request. Next, for each application, AndroidLeaks generates a call graph to determine the call sites which invoke source or sink methods. Applications without at least one source and sink are not analyzed, as they cannot leak private data. For applications

---

[2] Webkit is a rendering engine used by Android's browser.

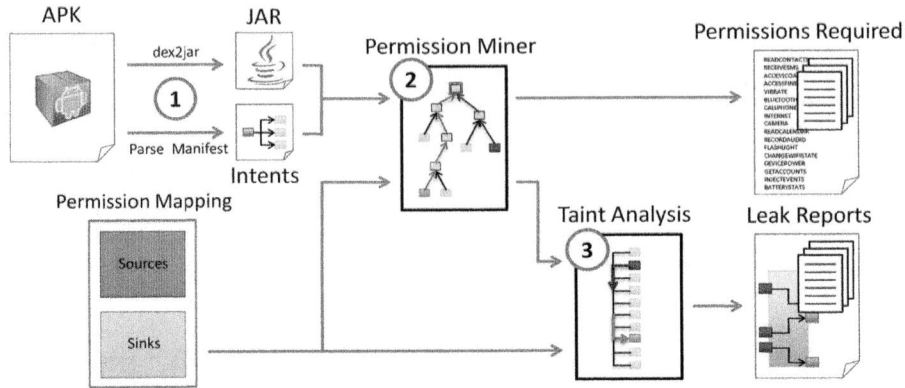

Fig. 2. AndroidLeaks Analysis Process. 1. Preprocessing. 2. Recursive call stack generation to determine where permissions are required. 3. Dataflow analysis between sources and sinks.

that have the potential to leak, we perform static taint analysis to determine if data from a source method reaches a sink.

4.1   Permission Mapping

To determine if an application is leaking sensitive data, first one must define what should be considered sensitive. Intuition and common sense may give a good starting point; however, in Android we can do much better since access to restricted resources is protected by permissions. Of these restricted resources, some control access to sensitive data, such as precise geographic location. It is likely that API calls that require sensitive permissions are *sources* of private data.

Ideally this mapping between API methods and the permissions they require would be stated directly in the documentation for Android. It would be useful for developers because it would help them better understand the permissions required by their desired functionality. Unfortunately, the Android documentation is incomplete, and only a partial mapping is provided. To address this issue, we attempt to automatically build this mapping by directly analyzing the Android framework source code. Figure 1 visualizes our process.

Intuitively, for a permission to protect restricted functionality, there must be points in the code where the permission is checked. In manual analysis of the Android source, we found a number of helper functions that enforce a permission, such as *Context.enforcePermission(String, int, int)*, where the first parameter is the name of the permission. For every method in every class of the Android framework, we recursively determined the methods called by each method in the framework, building a call stack, a process we call *mining*. Our miner will use all possible targets of virtual methods, erring on the side of completeness, rather than precision. If our mining encounters one of these enforcement methods, we inspect the value of the first parameter in order to determine the name of the permission being enforced. We then propagate the permission requirement to all the methods in the current call stack. After the permission mining is complete, we have a mapping between methods and the permissions they require. A subset of the methods in this mapping are API methods which are directly available to developers through the SDK.

Though this process gave us many mappings, it does not find permission checks that are implemented outside the Android framework and can not propagate permission requirements along edges connected by Intents or by IPC to a system process. To supplement our programmatic analysis, we manually reviewed the Android documentation to add mappings we may have missed. While this may seem significant, we note that we only found two permissions enforced outside of Java. The first of these two permissions is INTERNET, for which we manually added a very complete mapping. The second is WRITE_EXTERNAL _STORAGE, which is unimportant for our current work. Additionally, at some points in the Android framework, it may check, but not enforce a permission using a method such as *Context.checkPermission(String, int, int)*. For each of these points in the code, we determined how the check was used and what method actually requires that permission and add it to our permission mapping before the mining process. Currently we have mappings between over 2000 methods and the permissions they require. To check the completeness of our mapping, we plan to collaborate with the group that worked on [12], which has also created a permission mapping but with dynamic testing.

4.2   Android Leaks

In this section we describe AndroidLeaks' analysis process. See Fig. 2 for a visual representation. Before we attempt to find privacy leaks, we perform several preprocessing steps. First, we convert the Android application code (APK) from the DEX format to a JAR using *ded* [11] or *dex2jar* [17]. AndroidLeaks can also use any other tool that converts DEX to a JAR or to Java source.

Using WALA, AndroidLeaks then builds a call graph of the application code and its included libraries. It iterates through the application classes and determines the application methods that call *source* and *sink* API methods. It also keeps track of which other application methods can call these application methods that require permissions, as reviewing the call stacks can give insight into the flow of the application's use of permissions. If the application contains a combination of permissions that could leak private data, such as READ_PHONE_STATE and INTERNET, it then performs dataflow analysis to determine if information from a source of private data may reach a network sink.

Taint Problem Setup. The two main components of taint problems are determining the sources and sinks.

Sources. We have selected all the API methods requiring permissions for location, network state, phone state, and audio recording as sources, as discussed in Sect. 4.1. Android has two categories of location data: coarse and fine. Coarse location data uses triangulation from the cellular network towers and nearby wireless networks to approximate a device's location, whereas fine location data uses the GPS module on the device itself. We do not differentiate between coarse and fine location data as we believe any leakage of location information to be important.

Sinks. We have selected methods that require access to the Internet as sinks. We discovered that the Internet permission is enforced by the Android sandbox, which will cause any open socket command to fail if the INTERNET permission has not been granted. As discussed in Sect. 4.1, we manually reviewed the standard APIs available to Android applications to ensure our mapping contained every method that allows an application to send network data.

Taint Analysis. First, we use WALA to construct a context-sensitive System Dependence Graph (SDG). Since context-sensitive pointer analysis is resource intensive, we chose to use a context-insensitive overlay to show heap dependencies in the SDG. The SDG is a graph that describes the inter- and intraprocedural control and data dependencies of an application. Using the SDG, for each source method, we compute forward slices from our set of tainted data, initially populated by the return value of the source method. We use the return value because all the sources that we have identified return sensitive data through the return values only (and not through other means, such as side-effects on the parameters). On each iteration, we obtain a new slice of tainted data to which we apply supplemental taint-forwarding procedures. We then analyze the slice to determine if any parameters to sink methods are tainted, i.e., if they are data dependent on the source method. If so, we report a potential leak of private data.

WALA's built-in SDG and forward slicing algorithms are insufficient for analyzing Android applications, because they fail to handle callbacks, which are used extensively in Android applications, or do taint-aware slicing.

Handling Callbacks. Private data may enter Android applications via API methods identified as sources in Sect. 4.2. However, they may also enter applications via callback parameters, which are used extensively in Android. For example, an application may access location information either by asking the LocationManager for the last known location or by registering with the LocationManager as a listener. For the latter, the LocationManager provides regular updates of the current location to the registered listener. For API methods labeled as sources, we can taint the return values of these methods; however, this approach does not work for callbacks since neither the return value of the callback nor the return value of the registration is tainted. Therefore, we automatically identified calls to the register listener method while mining the application code and then inspected the parameters to determine the type of the listener. We then tainted the parameters of the callback method for the listener's class. This approach allows us to compute forward slices for both types of access in the same way.

Taint-Aware Slicing. Rather than modify WALA internally as done in [19] to achieve taint-aware slicing, we decided to analyze the computed slices and compute new statements from which to slice. We implemented the following logic to compute these new statements:

1. Taint all objects whose constructor parameters are tainted data.
2. Taint entire collections if any tainted object is added to them.
3. Taint whole objects which have tainted data stored inside them.

By applying these propagation rules to the slice computed for the source method, we create a set of statements that are tainted but would not be included in the original slice. This is because the original slice only shows statements that are data dependent, which is only part of how taint propagates. We then compute forward slices for each of these new statements and all others derived in the same manner from subsequent slices until we encounter a sink method or run out of statements from which to slice.

Preventing over-tainting without missing taint propagation is a difficult problem in static analysis, especially when complex objects handle both tainted and untainted data. Since we do not wish to miss any taint propagation, we conservatively track all potential taint propagation, which may result in false positives. We note that [19] also has high false positives in certain cases.

5   Evaluation

We evaluated AndroidLeaks on 25,976 unique free Android applications obtained from thirteen Android markets, including the official Android Market [14] and third-party American and Chinese markets.[3] We exclude multiple versions of the same application and duplicate copies of the same application on multiple markets.

1,626 applications require no permissions. Since these applications cannot access private data nor leak it, we exclude them from the analysis. We found potential privacy leaks in 7,414 of the remaining 24,350 applications.

Running AndroidLeaks on one server-grade computer we were able to analyze all 24,350 applications in 30 hours- over 800 APKs per hour. Collectively we processed over 531,249 unique Java classes.

We chose to focus on 4 types of privacy leaks: uniquely identifying phone information, location data, WiFi state and recorded audio. Examples of uniquely identifying phone information include the unique device ID (IMEI for GSM phones, MEID or ESN for CDMA phones) and the subscriber ID (IMSI for GSM phones). For location data, AndroidLeaks tracks accesses to both "coarse" and "fine" GPS data. WiFi state information includes the SSID and BSSID of the current access point as well as the MAC address of the phone's WiFi adapter. Though information about the WiFi networks seen by a phone may not seem sensitive, correlating this with a broad knowledge of the location of wireless networks can yield a device's specific location. In fact, Android phones already offer the option in the phone's "Location and Security" settings to use

---

[3] Including SlideMe [18] and GoApk [4].

Table 1. Breakdown of Leaks by Type

Leak Type	# Leaks	% of all Leaks	# apps with leak	% apps with leak
Phone	53,281	92.99%	6912	28.39%
Location	3,405	5.94%	969	3.98%
WiFi	266	0.46%	79	0.32%
Record Audio	347	0.61%	115	0.47%

nearby wireless networks to determine the phone's location. Finally, we include audio recorded with the phone's microphone.

The importance of a given privacy leak varies depending on the sensitivity of the data being leaked and the privacy concerns of the user. We designed AndroidLeaks to find leaks ranging in sensitivity to allow users of AndroidLeaks to focus on findings at their desired level of privacy.

5.1   Potential Privacy Leaks Found

We found a total of 57,299 leaks in 7,414 Android applications. 7,870 of these are unique leaks, varying by source, sink or code location (Table 1). 36,388 were leaks found in ad code, which comprises 63.51% of the total leaks found. In Fig. 3 we show the source of leaks of phone and location data, divided into leaks found in application code and ad libraries. We do not include pie charts for WiFi and record audio leaks because all of these leaks were found in application code. Ad libraries were responsible for 65% of the total phone data-related leaks with the top four ad libraries accounting for 43%. Application code contained 46% of the location-related privacy leaks and the top four ad libraries were responsible for 51%. Figure 4a shows a breakdown of the leaks found by the type of leak and its source. Figure 4b displays the number of applications we found containing each type of leak, organized by the source of the leak. We found that in most cases where phone identifying information is leaked, the advertising library is solely responsible.

Verification. Due to the large number of APKs analyzed and leaks found, it is difficult to manually verify all the leaks. Therefore, we prioritize the task by initially focusing on verifying leaks in ad code. By verifying one leak in a given ad library we can extend that result to identical leaks in other applications containing the same version of the same ad library. We determine leaks to be identical if they share the same source and sink method as well as the class and method where each is called.

We manually verified 60 leaks, most of which occurred in the ad libraries shown in Fig. 3. Of these, we found 39 to be true positives, yielding a false positive rate of 35%. The false positives tended to occur most commonly in applications that contained ad libraries in addition to the one containing the leak being verified. As multiple ad libraries may populate UI components on the same screen, our analysis may conservatively say that it is possible for sensitive data accessed by one ad library to propagate to its containing Activity or other ad libraries that

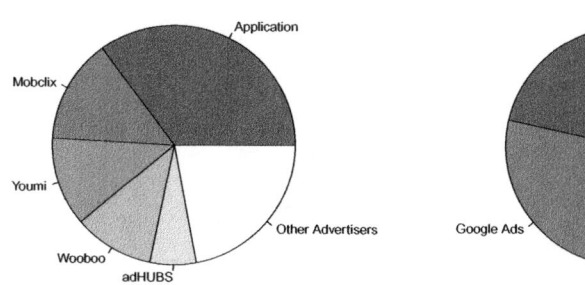
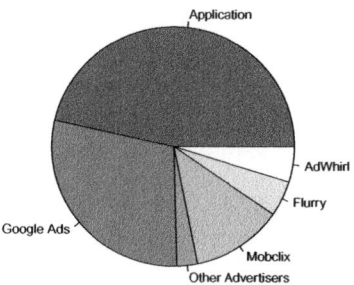

(a) Sources of leaks of phone id   (b) Sources of leaks of location information

Fig. 3. Source of leaks

share the same Activity. The 39 leaks we verified are repeated 5,007 times and occur in 2,342 unique applications. Therefore, at least 32% of the leaky APKs AndroidLeaks found have confirmed leaks.

Additionally, we verified a random set of 15 applications collectively containing several leaks of each type in application code. Several of the microphone leaks we verified turned out to be in IP camera applications, such as "SuperCam" or "IP Cam Viewer Lite." Figure 5 and Table 3 show the total number of verified leaks and leaky applications.

After AndroidLeaks reports potential privacy leaks, a security auditor can manually verify these leaks. To help with the manual verification, AndroidLeaks specifies the containing class and method as well as each leak's source and sink.

Ad Libraries. Nearly every ad library we looked at leaked phone data and, if available, location information as well. We hypothesize that nearly any access of sensitive data inside ad code will end up being leaked, as ad libraries provide no separate application functionality which requires accessing such information.

As an application developer, knowledge of the types of private information an ad library may leak is valuable. One may use this knowledge to select the ad library that best respects the privacy of users and possibly warn users of potential uses of private information by the advertising library.

One solution is to watch an application that uses a given ad library using dynamic analysis, such as TaintDroid. However, one runs into limitations of dynamic analysis, such as difficulty in achieving high code coverage. Manually driving applications through all code paths is infeasible at the rate new Android applications are being published, between 7,500 and 22,500 per month according to [5]. But even with maximum possible code coverage using dynamic taint analysis, there are further challenges on Android. Many ad libraries we

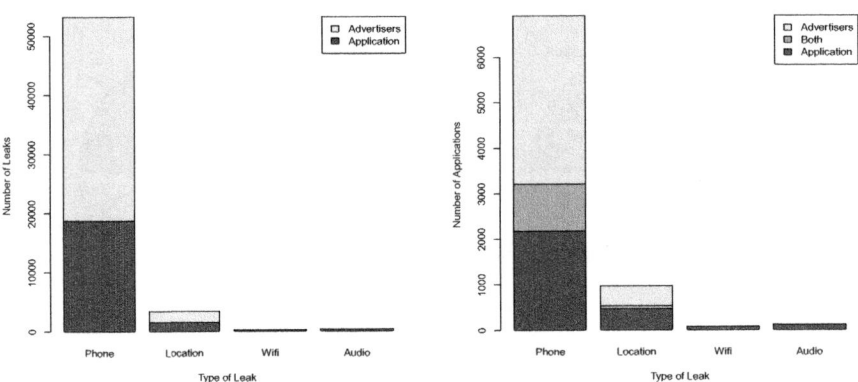

(a) Number of unique leaks broken down by their sources

(b) Number of applications that leak in ad code, app code, or both

Fig. 4. Number of unique leaks and leaky applications

examined check if the application they were bundled with has a given permission, oftentimes the ability to access location data. Using this information, they could localize ads, potentially increasing ad revenue by improving click through rates. However, there is nothing preventing ad libraries from checking if they have access to any number of types of sensitive information and attempting to leak them only if they are able. A dynamic analysis approach could watch many applications with a malicious advertising library and never see this functionality if none of the applications declared the relevant permissions. Using our static analysis approach we do not have this limitation and would be able to find these leaks regardless of the permissions required by the application being analyzed.

Ad libraries tend to be distributed to developers in a precompiled format, so it is not easy for an application developer to determine the information the ad library uses for user analytics. This is important for developers that include ad libraries in highly sensitive applications because the developer is ultimately responsible for any information leaked by libraries they choose to include. Additionally, a developer wanting to use an ad library is forced to use the ad library as it comes, with no option to remove features or modify the code. Since there is no mechanism in Android that allows one to restrict the capabilities of a specific portion of code within an application — all ad libraries have privilege equal to the application with which they are packaged. We note that a need for sandboxing a subset of an application's code is not an issue specific to Android; it is an open issue for many languages and platforms. However, the issue is especially relevant on mobile platforms because applications commonly include unverified third-party code to add additional features, such as ads.

Table 2 and Fig. 5 shows the total verified number of unique leaks and number of leaky applications.

Table 2. Verified number of unique leaks and leaky applications

Leak Type	# verified leaks	# apps with verified leak
Phone	3731 (84.91%)	2083 (8.55%)
Location	646 (14.70%)	323 (1.33%)
WiFi	0 (0%)	0 (0%)
Record Audio	17 (0.39%)	9 (0.04%)

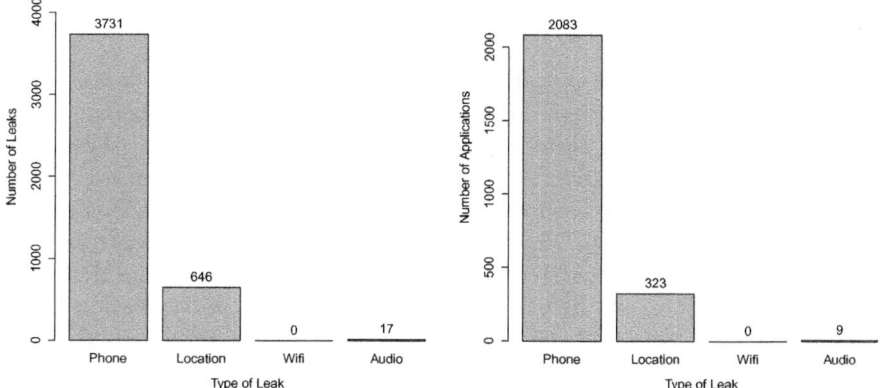

(a) Verified number of unique leaks   (b) Verified number of leaky applications

Fig. 5. Verified number of unique leaks and leaky applications

Table 3 shows the number of unique leaks of each data type in the 15 applications that we manually verified. Of these data types, device ID, subscriber ID, line one number, and SIM serial number all uniquely identify a phone.

After AndroidLeaks reports potential privacy leaks, a security auditor can manually verify these leaks. To help with the manual verification, AndroidLeaks specifies the containing class and method as well as each leak's source and sink. AndroidLeaks drastically reduces the number of applications and the number of traces that a security auditor needs to verify manually.

5.2   Miscellaneous Findings

Unique Android Static Analysis Issues. During the course of our analysis, we found several issues unique to Android that impacted our false positive and false negative rate. A common programming construct in ad libraries is to check if the currently running application has a certain permission before executing functionality that requires this permission. Many ad libraries do this to serve localized ads to users if the application has access to location data. An analysis that does not take this into account would find all such libraries as requiring access to location data and would possibly find leaks involving location data when in reality neither are valid because the application does not have access to location data.

Table 3. Number of leaks by data type in 15 manually verified applications

Leak Type	# Verified leaks
Device ID	9
Line 1 Number	3
Subscriber ID	2
SIM Serial Number	2
Other Phone Data	10
Location Data	9
Recorded Audio	4

Native Code. Native code is outside the scope of our analysis, however, it is interesting to see how many applications use native code. The use of native code is discouraged by Android as it increases complexity and may not always result in performance improvements. Additionally, all Android APIs are accessible to developers at the Java layer, so the native layer provides no extra functionality. We found that 1,988 out of 25,976 applications (7%) have at least one native code file included in their APK. Of the total 3,902 shared objects in APKs, a majority (2,014, 52%) of them were not stripped. This is interesting because stripping has long been used to reduce the size of shared libraries and to make them more difficult to reverse engineer, however, a majority of the applications we downloaded contained unstripped shared objects. This may be a result of developers using C/C++ who aren't familiar with creating libraries.

6   Limitations

Approach Limitations. There are several inherent limitations to static analysis. Tradeoffs are often made between speed, precision, and false positives. AndroidLeaks errs on the side of false positives rather than false negatives, as we intend AndroidLeaks to provide potential leaks to security auditors.

While a dynamic approach would have high precision due to the fact that privacy leaks are directly observed at run-time, achieving high path coverage is challenging. Moreover, dynamic analysis tools [10] tend to be manually driven, which does not scale to the massive number of Android applications. Combining AndroidLeaks with a dynamic approach would have great potential, as AndroidLeaks can quickly analyze a larger number of applications and then feed potential leaky applications to further dynamic analysis. We leave combining AndroidLeaks with a dynamic analysis approach for future work.

Implementation Limitations. AndroidLeaks does not yet analyze Android-specific control and data flows. This includes Intents, which are used for communication between Android and application components, and Content Providers, which provide access to database-like structures managed by other components.

7   Related Work

Chaudhuri et al. present a methodology for static analysis of Android applications to help identify privacy violations in Android with SCanDroid [13]. They used WALA to analyze the source code of applications, rather than Java byte code as we do. While their paper described mechanisms to handle Android specific control flow paths such as Intents which our work does not yet handle, their analysis was not tested on real Android applications.

Egele et al. perform similar analyses with their tool PiOS [9], a static analysis tool for detecting privacy leaks in iOS applications. AndroidLeaks and PiOS both found privacy leaks related to device ID, location and phone number. PiOS additionally considered the address book, browser history and photos while we consider several other types of phone data, WiFi data and audio recorded with the microphone. PiOS ignored leaks in ad libraries, claiming that they always leak, while one of the focuses of our work is giving developers insights into the behavior of ad libraries.

In comparison to AndroidLeaks's static analysis approach, TaintDroid [10] detects privacy leaks using dynamic taint tracking. Enck et al. built a modified Android operating system to add taint tracking information to data from privacy-sensitive sources. They track private data as it propagates through applications during execution. If private data is leaked from the phone, the taint tracker records the event in a log which can be audited by the user. Many of the differences between AndroidLeaks and TaintDroid are fundamental differences between static and dynamic analysis. Static analysis has better code coverage and is faster at the cost of having a higher false positive rate. One benefit of AndroidLeaks over the implementation of TaintDroid is that AndroidLeaks is entirely automated, while TaintDroid requires manual user interaction to trigger data leaks. We believe that AndroidLeaks and TaintDroid are in fact complementary approaches, AndroidLeaks can be used to quickly eliminate applications from consideration for dynamic testing while flagging areas to test on applications that are not eliminated.

Zho et al. presented a patch to the Android operating system that would allow users to selectively grant permissions to applications [21]. Their patch gives users the ability to revoke access to, falsify, or anonymize private data. While this is an effective way to limit permissions granted to applications, it requires flashing the phone's ROM, which voids most phone warranties and is too technical for many users.

Enck et al. [11] created *ded*, a tool that decompiles DEX to Java source code. They used *ded* to convert 1,100 free Android applications to Java source code that they then analyzed with a commercial static analysis tool. Because they used a commercial tool but never described its analysis algorithms, it is difficult to compare the merit of our analyses directly. From their preliminary results, we can note that Androidleaks is faster and therefore can run on a much larger scale. While just *ded*'s decompilation took approximately 20 days on 1,100 applications, our conversion and analysis time for 24,000 applications was approximately 30 hours. Their analysis time was not specified.

Felt et al. investigated permission usage in 940 Android applications using their tool STOWAWAY [12]. In order to determine the API method to permissions mapping, they generated unit tests for each method in the Android API and observed if the execution caused a permission check. This dynamic approach is very precise, however, it may be incomplete if the automated test construction failed to call API methods with arguments that cause the method to perform a permission check. Selectively combining their mapping with our statically generated one could produce a very complete and precise mapping.

8   Conclusion

Android users need a way to determine if applications are leaking their personal information. To this end we present AndroidLeaks, a static analysis tool for finding potential privacy leaks in Android applications. In order to make AndroidLeaks, we created a mapping between API calls and the permissions they require. AndroidLeaks is scalable to the current rate of new applications being submitted to markets, capable of analyzing 24,350 in 30 hours. During analysis, AndroidLeaks found 57,299 potential privacy leaks in over 7,400 applications, out of which we have manually verified that 2,342 applications leak private data. AndroidLeaks drastically reduces the number of applications and the number of traces that a security auditor has to verify manually.

Acknowledgments. The authors would like to thank Ben Sanders and Justin Horton for helping us obtain Android applications and our anonymous reviewers for their input. This material is based in part upon work supported by the National Science Foundation under Grant Numbers 0644450 and 1018964. Any opinions, findings, and conclusions or recommendations expressed in this material are those of the author(s) and do not necessarily reflect the views of the National Science Foundation.

References

1. Android developer reference, http://d.android.com/ (accessed March 30, 2012)
2. Android security and permissions,
   http://d.android.com/guide/topics/security/security.html
   (accessed March 30, 2012)
3. Bitblaze, http://bitblaze.cs.berkeley.edu/
4. Go Apk. Go apk market, http://market.goapk.com (accessed March 2011)
5. AppBrain. Number of available android applications,
   http://www.appbrain.com/stats/number-of-android-apps
   (accessed August 15, 2011)
6. Bornstein, D.: Dalvik vm internals (2008), http://goo.gl/knN9n
   (accessed March 18, 2011)
7. IBM T.J. Watson Research Center. T.j. watson libraries for analysis (wala)
   (March 2011) (accessed March 30, 2012)

8. The Nielsen Company. Who is winning the u.s. smartphone battle?,
   http://blog.nielsen.com/nielsenwire/online_mobile/
   who-is-winning-the-u-s-smartphone-battle (accessed March 17, 2011)

9. Egele, M., Kruegel, C., Kirda, E., Vigna, G.: Pios: Detecting privacy leaks in
   ios applications. In: Proceedings of the Network and Distributed System Security
   Symposium (2011)

10. Enck, W., Gilbert, P., Chun, B.G., Cox, L.P., Jung, J., McDaniel, P., Sheth, A.N.:
    Taintdroid: an information-flow tracking system for realtime privacy monitoring
    on smartphones. In: Proceedings of the 9th USENIX Conference on Operating
    Systems Design and Implementation, pp. 1–6. USENIX Association (2010)

11. Enck, W., Octeau, D., McDaniel, P., Chaudhuri, S.: A study of android application
    security. In: Proc. of the 20th USENIX Security Symposium (2011)

12. Felt, A.P., Chin, E., Hanna, S., Song, D., Wagner, D.: Android permissions demys-
    tified. In: Proceedings of the 18th ACM Conference on Computer and Communi-
    cations Security, pp. 627–638. ACM (2011)

13. Fuchs, A.P., Chaudhuri, A., Foster, J.S.: Scandroid: Automated security certifica-
    tion of android applications. Univ. of Maryland (2009) (manuscript),
    http://www.cs.umd.edu/~avik/projects/scandroidascaa

14. Google. Google play , http://market.android.com (accessed March, 2011)

15. Apple Inc. App store review guidelines,
    http://developer.apple.com/appstore/guidelines.html (accessed March 30,
    2012)

16. Pachal, P.: Google removes 21 malware apps from android market (March 2011),
    http://www.pcmag.com/article2/0,2817,2381252,00.asp (accessed March 18,
    2011)

17. pxb1988. dex2jar: A tool for converting android's .dex format to java's .class for-
    mat, https://code.google.com/p/dex2jar/ (accessed March 30, 2012)

18. SlideMe. Slideme: Android community and application marketplace,
    http://slideme.org/ (accessed March 30, 2012)

19. Tripp, O., Pistoia, M., Fink, S.J., Sridharan, M., Weisman, O.: Taj: effective taint
    analysis of web applications. In: ACM Sigplan Notices, vol. 44, pp. 87–97. ACM
    (2009)

20. Yin, S.: 'most sophisticated' android trojan surfaces in china (December 2010),
    http://www.pcmag.com/article2/0,2817,2374926,00.asp (accessed March 18,
    2011)

21. Zhou, Y., Zhang, X., Jiang, X., Freeh, V.W.: Taming Information-Stealing Smart-
    phone Applications (on Android). In: McCune, J.M., Balacheff, B., Perrig, A.,
    Sadeghi, A.-R., Sasse, A., Beres, Y. (eds.) Trust 2011. LNCS, vol. 6740, pp. 93–107.
    Springer, Heidelberg (2011)

Why Trust Seals Don't Work:
A Study of User Perceptions and Behavior

Iacovos Kirlappos[1], M. Angela Sasse[1], and Nigel Harvey[2]

[1] University College London, Department of Computer Science,
London, United Kingdom
{i.kirlappos,a.sasse}@cs.ucl.ac.uk
[2] University College London, Department of Psychology,
London, United Kingdom
n.harvey@ucl.ac.uk

Abstract. Trust seals, such as the *VeriSign* and *TRUSTe* logos, are widely used to indicate a website is reputable. But how much protection do they offer to on-line shoppers? We conducted a study in which 60 experienced online shoppers rated 6 websites – with and without trust seals - based on how trustworthy they perceived them to be. Eye tracking data reveals that 38% of participants failed to notice any of the trust seals present. When seals were noticed, the ratings assigned to each website were significantly higher than for the same website without a seal, but qualitative analysis of the interview data revealed significant misconceptions of their meaning (e.g. *"presence of seals automatically legitimizes any website"*). Participants tended to rely on self-developed – but inaccurate – heuristics for assessing trustworthiness (e.g. perceived investment in website development, or references to other recognizable entities). We conclude that trust seals currently do not offer effective protection against scam websites; and suggest that other mechanisms – such as automatic verification of authenticity are required to support consumers' trust decisions.

Keywords: trust signaling, e-commerce, trust seals.

1   Introduction

Trust plays a vital role in the commercial world: people and organizations cooperate to achieve mutual benefits, and the success of business transactions depends on both parties behaving in a collaborative way. The wide success of e-commerce since the early 2000's [1] posed a major challenge for consumers and merchants: how to reach a transaction-enabling level of trust between them, without the traditional trust development medium - face-to-face interaction [2]. Attackers soon exploited the opportunities this new setting created: they started setting up fake online stores, pretending to sell popular products at tempting prices, but actually stealing consumers' money and credit card details [3],[1]. At best, consumers receive counterfeit goods. At worst, they receive no goods, lose money and suffer identity theft. Some financial institutions, like credit card issuers, have introduced buyer protection mechanisms that cover

S. Katzenbeisser et al. (Eds.): TRUST 2012, LNCS 7344, pp. 308–324, 2012.
© Springer-Verlag Berlin Heidelberg 2012

their customers for any monetary losses [4], but consumers still have to go through time-consuming processes to obtain new credit cards, and monitor their accounts and credit reports to prevent identity theft using their stolen credentials.

A number of different measures have been introduced to address this problem: anti-phishing tools, trust seals and user education. But the number of scam websites and the reported losses are still alarmingly high [5-8] – UK card fraud crime amounted to £365.4 million in 2011 [9], and in the US online merchants lost $2.7 billion to fraud in 2010 only [10]. The persistence of criminals operating online suggests that it is worth their effort.

Trust seals were created to make it easier for consumers to identify trustworthy websites. Their effectiveness has been discussed by a number of research reports [11-18], but all used experimental designs that explicitly drew respondents' attention to presence of the trust seals (e.g. surveys). This paper presents an experiment in which we observed participants' reaction to the same websites with and without trust seals, without directing their attention to them. We also conducted a detailed debrief to elicit their *"folk perceptions"* [19] of trustworthiness indicators in a website, including trust seals. We identified a number of trust-development heuristics consumers use to verify a website's authenticity, and identify those as targets for future security awareness approaches.

2   Background

2.1   E-Commerce and Trust

Trust plays a significant role in online environments, as it enables transactions between parties that are separated in both space and time. Riegelsberger et al. [2] outline the basic trustor-trustee interaction in technology-mediated interactions (Figure 1): a consumer (trustor) uses the signals (1) emitted by the merchant (trustee) to assess their trustworthiness before proceeding to the trusting action (2a) [2], which increases their exposure to a trustee's potential misbehavior, but provides the potential for positive gains if the merchant fulfills (3a). In e-commerce, increased exposure comes as a result of sharing financial and personal details with a website, as consumers now rely on the merchant's behavior to reduce the likelihood of a negative outcome (e.g. goods not arriving, selling of counterfeit products, credit card details compromised, identity theft) [20]. As a result, the higher the perceived trustworthiness of the website, the more likely a consumer is to proceed to initiating a transaction.

Other researchers have also stressed the importance of trust to enable successful commercial transactions over the Internet. Nielsen [21] defines e-commerce related trust as *"A user's willingness to risk time, money and personal data on a website"*, and others have underlined its importance for the success of e-commerce [11-13],[22]: the lower the transaction-related uncertainty appears to be to a consumer, the more likely they are to act in a way that renders them vulnerable to the behavior of an online merchant.

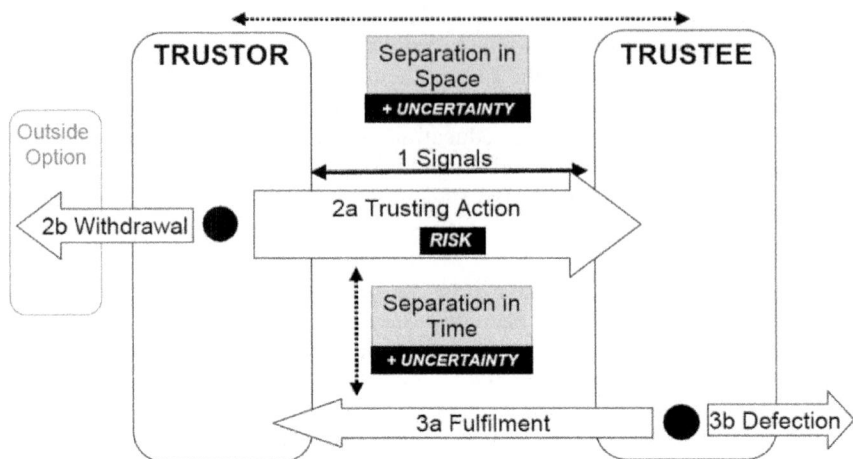

Fig. 1. The basic trustor-trustee interaction (Source: Riegelsberger et al. [2])

Another challenge to designing for trust in e-commerce environments is that, after a small number of successful transactions, consumers expect all further transactions to be successful, too – they now are in a state of *reliance,* rather than trust [2]. They extrapolate their past positive or negative experiences with some websites to new ones, resulting to a *"trust spillover"* effect: After a number of successful transactions, consumers are less likely to check for the *trust-warranting* [2] properties they searched for on the very first time they bought something online, or they may spend less time doing so. As a result trustworthy behavior of some merchants can lead to trust in the entire online market [23-25].

2.2   How Attackers Exploit Trust

Consumers shopping online are looking for 'good deals': trying to save money on regular purchases, or acquire something they would otherwise not be able to afford. In this situation, the classic economics problem of *information asymmetry* [26] applies: the lack of personal interaction results to consumers having less knowledge on the intentions of the merchant to fulfill in the transaction or the quality of the products offered [14],[27],[28]. The merchant, on the other hand possesses the advantage to wait until they have received full payment before shipping out any products [20]. This asymmetric nature of the interaction makes the exploitation of human needs easier for attackers, who are extremely skillful in exploiting human vulnerabilities [29]: Once they know what consumers want, they tempt them with *"too good to miss"* deals, but ship either counterfeit products or nothing at all.

2.3   Trust Signaling

The trustor's perceived uncertainty in the outcome of a transaction can be reduced by communicating information about the trustee's ability and motivation to fulfill. In online markets, technology is not only the medium over which an interaction happens, but also the medium over which both parties signal the trust-warranting properties required to allow the formation of positive expectations on the behavior of each other, which then provide the level of trust required by the trustor to initiate the interaction. Riegelsberger et al. [30] identify two main types of signals of trustworthiness trustees can emit:

- *Symbols*: They have arbitrarily assigned meaning, and were designed specifically to signal the presence of trust-warranting properties, so the trustor needs certain knowledge be able decode them. In e-commerce, trust symbols are all the mechanisms that aim to directly signal a merchant's trustworthiness to potential customers (e.g. trust seals issued by certification authorities - CAs).
- *Symptoms*: These are trust signals that were not specifically designed to signal trust-warranting properties; they are given off as by-products when honest actors go about their business, at little or no cost to honest actors. But if an attacker were to try and mimic these, it would be at great cost. In an e-commerce setting, symptoms are all the website properties and information consumers draw on to assess the trustworthiness of a merchant (e.g. well-known brand name and reputation amongst friends and relatives).

The opportunistic attempt of non-trustworthy actors to appear trustworthy by emitting manipulated signals (symptoms or symbols) is defined as *mimicry* [31]. Mimicry will occur only if emitting the signal required to appear trustworthy comes to a lower cost to untrustworthy actors than the potential benefit of doing so [2]. Symbols are much easier to mimic than symptoms, as attackers can simply place those in their websites at minimal costs, while symptoms require more effort, which can outweigh any potential benefits for an attacker.

2.4   Trust Symptoms - User Trust Assessment Heuristics

Consumers use a wide range of symptoms to assess the trustworthiness of a merchant. Those are mostly based on self-developed heuristics[1], a number of which have been reported by past research:

- Perceived professionalism and reputation of a company, e.g. well-known branding [13],[22],[28]
- Ability of the merchant to fulfill – usually revealed by positive user reviews [22],[32]
- Relationship with other known entities e.g. other well-known merchants [33]
- Willingness to customize products and services [13]
- Usefulness and ease of use of the website [21],[28],[32]
- Perceived security control e.g. providing reassurances in case of fraud [32]

The major drawback of all the aforementioned reports is that the proposed heuristics are either not supported by experimental verification ([21],[28],[32]), or were based on experimental designs that did not accurately capture the complete picture of the actual trust development process:

---

[1] Merriam Webster heuristic definition: "involving or serving as an aid to learning, discovery, or problem-solving by experimental and especially trial-and-error methods".

1) Experiments in [22] and [13] were based on pre-defined hypotheses by researchers (i.e. *"Would you trust this website if it had this property?"*), which results to reporting only the effect the properties they targeted have on a website's perceived legitimacy (e.g. [22] tested for the effect of size and reputation on trust development, but explicitly presented size and reputation information for each website to the participants). This setup also hinders the ecological validity of the results as it explicitly draws the participants' attention to website properties they may have failed to notice by themselves.

2) In [33] the focus of the experiment conducted was to test for the effectiveness of an anti-phishing indicator; trust development factors were identified afterwards, based on analysis of self-reports by participants in post-experiment interviews.

2.5   Trust Seals

Trust seals are extra-legal, symbol-based trust-signaling mechanisms, introduced to provide trustworthiness information on a merchant to potential customers from Trusted Third Parties (TTPs) – Certification Authorities (CA). They are logos added in websites to signal that a certified organization (TTP) has granted the right to use those, based on some rules of conduct (e.g. reliability as a merchant, correct private data handling or website security). They are used to facilitate trust-building in online commerce environments [14], decreasing the perceived transaction-related risk by consumers, thus increasing their willingness to engage in it [12].

The purpose of trust signaling mechanisms is similar to the way risk communication is used to advise the general public on issues of public concern: they act as advisors to consumers on the risk they accept by engaging in a transaction. Twyman et al. [34] classify trust in advisors in two major categories:

- *Trust in Motives*: Consumers identify the similarity of values between them and the TTP: they both benefit from successful interactions and it is of interest to the TTP to provide them with reliable information.
- *Trust in Competence*: Consumers have received reliable information from a specific TTP in the past so they are more likely to trust the information they receive from it. This explains past research reports that consumers are more likely to buy from an unknown website that bears a trust seal than one which does not [11].

Both forms of trust can be destroyed, if they are manipulated by untrustworthy actors. Attackers can easily add trust seals to their websites (*mimicry* – [31]) and negative experiences with trust seals will result to the corresponding signals losing significance [2]. This can undermine trust in the competence of the seals, and the trust certification approach in general.

Research opinion on the effectiveness of trust seals is divided: some researchers report that trust seals help to improve consumer purchasing decisions [11],[15-17], but others report that they fail to do so [13][18]. The problem with all the previous research is that they drew participants' attention to the presence of trust seals and explicitly asked if they influenced their decision to trust a website. Testing if consumers take trust seals into account if they notice their presence, is a valid question, but accounts only for a sub-set of the decision-making process. Previous experiments also did not test whether trust seals lead to *correct trust decisions*; if a trust seal is present, consumers are more likely to buy from it - but that might include buying from fraudulent sites that carry mimicked seals. We need trust signals that help consumers to make better decisions, not just manipulate their trust perceptions.

2.6   Public Awareness Campaigns

A number of awareness campaigns have been set up by governments and commercial organizations to inform consumers on the potential dangers they may face while shopping online [35-38]. They provide a range of advice on what consumers can use to protect themselves:

- Make sure they have antivirus, firewall and anti-spyware software installed and keep operating system and browser up to date.
- Check merchants out before first time purchases. Locate contact details and whether refunds are provided in case things go wrong.
- Verify the website's legitimacy using *https://* indicators and closed padlocks; also never make purchases through unsecured wireless networks.
- Only provide a website with the information required to complete the transaction.
- Check who the website is registered to and how long has it been registered.
- Check for website reviews on the Internet.

Whilst we would not argue that this advice is wrong, it ignores some key factors that drive consumers' behavior in these situations:

- When presented with a 'good deal', consumers may be tempted to accept a higher risk in order to reap the potential benefits. This risk propensity can be leveraged by attackers emphasizing the "limited offer duration" (*time principle* – [29]), putting time pressure on consumers to quickly seize the deal, otherwise lose it.
- Providing consumers with widely varying advice ([36] mentions 9 different website properties that require 3-4 verification checks each) causes confusion. Faced with too much information, consumers try to reduce it to a manageable level, but the process of selecting factors is haphazard [39]. Finally, consumers can follow the advice, and still fall for a scam, as many scam websites are well-designed and resemble legitimate ones, in their attempt to appear trustworthy. When this happens, consumers' trust in the competence of the advisors is undermined, making it less likely that they will pay attention to advice from that source next time [34].

2.7   Summary

The continuing high level of online scams suggests that existing security measures and advice are not working. Even though trust seals are widely used, there are conflicting reports on their effectiveness. Past research lacked ecological validity: to accurately capture the trust development process, consumers need to be presented with trust seals in the same way as they would in a home setting, without the experimenters drawing their attention to any specific trust development factors.

3   Experiment

3.1   Aim

The aim of our experiment was to evaluate the effectiveness of trust seals in a realistic setting (see 3.2) that would improve on the validity and applicability of our findings. We designed a study to test the following hypothesis:

> *H1: Website ratings will increase when participants notice the presence of trust seals*

We used eye-tracking and screen recordings to guide a set of post-experiment interviews, where we questioned our participants on their eye-gaze fixations during the experiment. We analyzed interview data using qualitative methods, aiming to:

- Capture the participants' *perception of the meaning* of trust seals.
- Identify other elements they used to assess the trustworthiness of a website.

3.2   Method

We asked participants to browse through six websites that sell tickets for a music festival in London (*Wireless Festival in Hyde Park*) and asked them to rate each website based on how likely they were to buy from it. We chose online ticket sales for our study because they represent a large and constantly growing number of online scams: the UK National Fraud Authority reported a number of half a million ticket scam victims in the UK in 2010, each losing an average of £80 [40].

Apparatus and Materials. A pre-experiment questionnaire was designed to identify participant demographics, computer experience, online shopping habits and past experience with internet scams. During the experiment, screen and eye-gaze recordings were taken using a Tobii X50 eye tracker and Tobii Studio 2.0.4 software. The experiment took place in a usability laboratory on a computer running Windows XP and websites were displayed using Mozilla Firefox 3.5 web browser. Post-experiment interviews with participants were audio recorded.

Websites. Using a search engine, 6 websites selling tickets for the event were identified, and downloaded locally using the HTTRack free website copier tool (*http://www.httrack.com*). Three of the websites had a trust seal positioned on the main page and other parts of the ticket selection process. To test for the effectiveness of trust seals two different conditions were created (Table 1):

- *Original*: All websites were used unmodified in the experiment.
- *Modified*: Trust seals were removed from the websites that originally carried those and a fake trust symbol was placed in the other three websites (that originally did not have them) as a plain image, without any links to verify its authenticity. The fake symbol was positioned in easy to spot positions in the websites.

Table 1. The conditions assigned to the websites used in the experiment

Website name	Original	Modified
www.eventim.co.uk	No trust seal	Trust seal
www.getmein.com	Trust seal	No trust seal
www.gigantic.com	No trust seal	Trust seal
www.hmvtickets.com	Trust seal	No trust seal
www.seetickets.com	No trust seal	Trust seal
www.skiddle.com	Trust seal	No trust seal

The local copies of the websites were setup on a university server and the DNS mapping was modified so that the participants could see the real website URL (e.g. *www.eventim.co.uk*) in the address bar.

Participants. Participants were recruited through the university's psychology department subject pool. They had to be over 18, use online shopping regularly, and be available to visit the lab for a 1-hour session. They all received payment of £12 for their time. The university's ethics procedures on experiments involving human participants were followed. (No application to the Research Ethics Committee was required since our participants were not identifiable, no personal information was kept after the experiment, and there was no deception involved).

62 participants took part in the study, but data from two had to be discarded due to lack of accurate eye-tracking recordings. Of the remaining 60:

- 36 (60%) were female and 24 (40%) male.
- Their average age was 24 years (Standard Deviation = 4.9).
- They had an average computer experience of 12 years (SD = 3.3).
- They browse the Internet daily for 4.9 hours (SD = 2.88).
- They receive 18 (SD = 14.7) emails per day.
- 51 (85%) of them have checked their account balance online.
- 50 (83%) had transferred money to other people's accounts using online banking services.
- 11 (18%) had configured a firewall in the past.
- 21 (35%) had designed a website.
- 15 (25%) had registered a domain name.
- 17 (28%) had been victims of an online scam, or knew someone that has been.

Procedure. A between-subjects design was chosen to prevent habituation effects. Participants were equally divided between the two conditions. The websites were pre-opened in six browser tabs in randomized order, and participants had 5 minutes to browse through those. After signing the consent form and completing a screening questionnaire, they were presented with the experiment scenario: "*You want to attend the Wireless Festival 2011 in Hyde Park. You have used a search engine to find six websites that claim to sell tickets. Friends have warned you that festival tickets sell out very quickly so you only have five minutes to look at the websites. You can browse through the websites with no limitations. Warnings will be given to you when* *two and one minutes are left. After the end of the 5-minute period you will be asked to indicate how much you trust each of the websites presented to you. To do so you need to assign a grade between -2 and +2 (-2,-1,0,1,2) to each website with -2 being the lowest and 2 the highest"*. After reading the scenario, they were asked to confirm they understood how the rating grades reflect their level of trust for each website.

During the 5-minute browsing period the experimenter was present, but participants were told they could not ask questions during this part of the session. They were allowed to distribute their browsing period in any way they wanted across websites, so they carry out all the checks as if they were shopping on their own computers (e.g. check delivery policy, FAQs etc.) and when they had enough information to make a decision proceed to the next website. Participants were not prohibited from using external sources (i.e. other websites) to check for a website's reputation, but none attempted to do so during the experiment.

After participants rated the websites, there was a de-briefing session: the eye-tracking recording of their browsing period was replayed to them, and questions about their behavior asked, based on their eye-gaze fixations. When the recordings showed a fixation on any visual element of a website (e.g. reading through the text on a page), participants were asked to explain how each of those elements affected the trust rating they assigned to each website. Participants were then pointed to the trust seals in the sites and were asked to explain what they signal to them, and whether they knew how to verify their authenticity. This aimed to provide data that could be used to identify whether consumers perceive the meaning of trust seals correctly, which is important if trust seals affect their decisions, as incorrect understanding can result to misplaced trust. The questions on trust seals were asked at the final part of the interview, to avoid drawing the participants' attention to their presence. The interviews were audio recorded and analyzed after the experiment, using a Grounded Theory analysis combining open, axial and selective coding procedures [41].

4   Results

4.1   Effectiveness of Trust Seals

The analysis of eye-tracking data revealed that only 12 (20%) participants noticed all three trust seals they encountered during their browsing session (Table 2), and more than a third did not notice any of them (23 – 38%). We tested our *H1* hypothesis by comparing the ratings participants assigned to a website when they noticed the presence of the trust seal in it against the ratings when the trust seal was not noticed or was not present. This revealed a significant tendency ($t(5) = 3.3786$, $p = 0.0099$) to rate websites higher when participants noticed a trust seal on a website (Table 3).

Table 2. Number of trust seals noticed by participants

No of seals noticed	No of participants
0	23
1	12
2	13
3	12

Table 3. The assigned ratings on websites when trust seals were present

Website name	Number of partici-pants who noticed	Rating when noticed seals	Rating when not noticed seals or seals not present
www.eventim.co.uk	18	0.94	0.00
www.getmein.com	15	0.73	-0.04
www.gigantic.com	14	0.64	-0.11
www.hmvtickets.com	8	1.25	1.04
www.seetickets.com	11	0.27	0.37
www.skiddle.com	5	0.40	-0.40

After participants' attention was drawn to the presence of trust seals, we asked what they signified, and received a variety of responses - all incorrect (see Table 4).

Table 4. The responses participants gave on the meaning of trust symbols

Comment	No of participants
Seals mean a website is safe for Credit Card details	18 (30%)
Completely ignore what trust seals are and what they mean	15 (25%)
They know that trust seals can be spoofed	11 (18%)
Payment method symbols mean the website is verified by the payment method company (e.g. VISA, PayPal, MasterCard)	11 (18%)
Seals provide confirmation that website is genuine (could not explain why)	10 (17%)
Authority exists that grants rights to use the seal to trustworthy merchants, punishing the misuse of those	9 (15%)
Seen some trust symbols in websites they use often, assumed that their presence in a website automatically signifies its legitimacy	7 (12%)
Seals are meaningless as they could be copied by anyone	6 (10%)
Seals mean a website has no viruses	1 (2%)

4.2   Factors Affecting Trust in Websites

The Grounded Theory analysis of the interview data revealed a number of factors other than trust seals that affected the participants' trust development decisions. These factors can be classified in two major categories: Those that affected the *perceived professionalism* of the company and those that affected the *perceived competence* of it as an online merchant.

1. **Trustee's Professionalism.** Participants attempted to assess the professionalism of the company running a website, which they reported as a combination of many different factors (Table 5):

Table 5. The factors affecting the perceived professionalism of a website

Comment	No of participants
Perceived amount of effort invested in a website - indicated by factors like aesthetically pleasing design, well-formed layout.	45 (75%)
Presence of company information e.g. physical location, contact details etc	43 (72%)
Variety of products available	23 (38%)
Inclusion of Terms and Conditions/Privacy Policy	16 (27%)
Large amount of information on event of interest (opening times, venue information etc), good presentation of it with rich media (e.g. maps and pictures)	14 (23%)
Ease of use, self-explanatory labeling - to aid navigation around the website	8 (13%)
Well-formed URL - participants argued that scam websites have long, non-meaningful URLs	6 (10%)

2. **Trustee's Competence.** Participants attempted to assess a website's competence by looking for a number of different website properties (Table 6):

Table 6. The factors affecting the perceived competence of a website

Comment	No of participants
Indicators of past trustworthy behavior - Name and reputation of a company were the major factors participants used to assess this: positive expectation about a merchant's behavior was formed if participants recognized a company's name or had previous experience with it (online or in the real-world).	45 (75%)
Trust transfer - Inclusion of other recognizable entities affected the decisions of participants e.g. claims by a website that they are subsidiary of *Ticketmaster* (UK's biggest ticket merchant), advertisements of known companies or presence of a charity logo together with claims that part of the profits is donated to them.	30 (50%)
Social Networking links - Believed that they could find information on the merchant's past behavior by following those links	28 (47%)
Assurances provided – The ticket purchases and financial details are safe and that tickets will be sent via secure postage	19 (32%)
User reviews – Present inside the website (did not check for off-site reviews)	16 (27%)

5   Discussion

5.1   Trust Seals Are Not Effective

Our findings suggest that trust seals do not improve on consumers' ability to make accurate trust assessment of websites: despite a significantly increased rating amongst participants who noticed trust seals, only 20% noticed those on all 3 websites they encountered, and over a third of participants (38%) did not notice any of the 3. It is reasonable to suspect that the same is true for consumers - unless their attention is specifically drawn to the presence of a seal on a site. Our participants also had significant misconceptions about what the seals stood for (see Table 4). Those participants who noticed trust seals during the experiment interpreted the mere presence of those as proof of a website's competence (hence the statistical significance in Table 3), and felt no need to check that they were genuine.

We also observed a trust "*spillover effect*". Early research on trust seal effectiveness [42] pointed out that their presence does not legitimize a website, but consumers are still not aware of this: seven participants (12%) had previously seen some trust seals in websites they use, and incorrectly assumed that these mean the website is legitimate. This misconception makes consumers highly vulnerable to mimicry attempts.

Another problem with trust seals can be attributed to bad practice by merchants. In one of the websites we presented to participants, the trust seal present was a plain image, instead of linking to the verification pages provided by the seal issuers (e.g. whenever a VeriSign trust seal is present, it should be a clickable link, bringing up a verification page with the details of the company to which the website was registered [43]). If legitimate merchants implement trust seals incorrectly, the task of identifying mimicry attacks becomes almost impossible for consumers (even though our participants did not attempt to verify the seals).

The large number of different trust seals used is a further source of confusion for consumers, and thus undermines the effectiveness of trust seals. The *www.truste.com* [44] website lists 9 different certifications covering Privacy, Security (2 for SSL encryption, 2 for malware and vulnerability scans), Reputation and Reliability (which can be either review-based or granted by another authority). Such a complex system does not help consumers trying to detect online fraud - and how many consumers know what SSL encryption is, or what risks malware presents to them?

The creators of trust seals and website owners who use them expect consumers to search for trust seals, check their authenticity, and understand what protection their offer. Based on our results, we argue that these expectations are unrealistic. Usable security researchers have long argued that security is not the primary concern of people using computer systems [45],[46]: the need to be careful about scams is a minor consideration in the context of the consumer's main activity – to find and buy something they want. Expecting consumers to interrupt this activity to find and check trust seals before every purchase is expecting too much. Like most security mechanisms, the effort involved is just too high for ordinary consumers [47] – so they either ignore them altogether, or associate those with a simple, but incorrect meaning. In both cases, consumers are left vulnerable.

5.2   Trust Assessment Heuristics and Consumer Awareness

The trust assessment heuristics we present in Section 4 partly confirm past research findings [13],[21],[22],[28],[32],[33], but the most worrying observation is that none of our participants attempted to verify the authenticity of the signals they used. This means that even simple mimicry attacks can succeed: attackers copy genuine websites, register well-formed web addresses and use search engine advertisements or phishing emails to direct consumers to them [7],[48]. None of the websites used in our experiment included a way to verify claimed affiliations (social network links, charity organizations or advertisements), which means that even if consumers were prepared to check for their authenticity, there would be little they could do. An example of how the identified heuristics can be manipulated by attackers are account takeovers, reported by eBay as a major source of threat for their customers [49], as consumers blindly trusting reputable retailers are left vulnerable against those attacks.

Our observations demonstrate that the advice given by awareness campaigns is not effective, either: No participant checked for *https://* indicators, padlocks in the address bar or who the website owner is. The advice *"Only provide a website with the information required to complete the transaction"* also seems ill-posed: what is more sensitive than the credit card information required to complete a transaction? Consumers transfer trust perceptions from physical world settings (e.g. the reputability of a brand name or claimed affiliations with other well-known organizations), unaware that these are easily and cheaply mimicked in the online world. This leaves them vulnerable to the techniques attackers use, like including well-known names in their website without any proof for their affiliations, and which awareness campaigns fail to address effectively: despite telling consumers to look for specific trust signals, they fail to equip them with the skills required to verify their authenticity, doing nothing to protect them from any potential mimicry attempts.

6   Conclusions

Our results demonstrate that trust seals do not effectively support consumers making decisions about websites. A significant part of consumers does not notice them, and most of those who do, do not understand what protection they offer and how to verify their authenticity. We thus argue that trust seals may currently do more harm than good, because they leave consumers vulnerable against even the simplest attacks (e.g. inclusion of fake trust seals in websites). To overcome these problems, a significant shift is required from the way trust signaling mechanisms are used today. Technology needs be used to aid correct trust placement by automatically performing any verification required, alerting consumers when potential risks are identified, aiding their accurate assessment of the dangers they may face when they need to make trust-related decisions and reducing the potential of being victimized by online scams.

6.1   What Needs to Be Done

Use Automatic Verification Mechanisms. More radical measures are required to reduce the potential of successful mimicry attempts. Mechanisms that automatically verify a seal's authenticity need to be developed, which will alert consumers when seal misuse is detected. The backbone of this technology already exists: The SOLID authentication tool (developed by the UK firm First Cyber Security) *"gives the owner of a logo, trademark or certificate the ability to authenticate its use on other websites"*, using a *Secure On Line ID 3rd Party Validation* mechanism, which identifies unauthorized use of symbols registered by their original owners [50]. This, or other similar systems, can be used as the basis of a larger implementation, developed in collaboration with web browser creators, which will automatically alert crime prevention authorities and Internet Service Providers (ISPs) when scam websites are detected, who can then act to block traffic to those and take them offline. A widely-adopted automatic verification approach can also be used to provide shoppers with merchant information, like registration details of the company owning the domain name, contact details, where the product will be shipped from etc. – eliminating the need to find that information by looking around various websites on the Internet. The technology to implement this also exists - organizations like VeriSign already provide information on the owner of a website when consumers click on the VeriSign trust logo, but currently require consumers to notice the presence of that logo to do so.

The alerts an automatic verification mechanism presents to consumers should use meaningful messages, explaining what the identified problem is and how to protect themselves. Those messages should appear as active warnings, which are proven to be more effective than asking the consumers to stop and search for security indicators [51]. To avoid habituation issues, consumers' should only be interrupted when seal misuse is detected and presented with a short and clear warning that the website they are browsing is using unauthorized symbols. When no problem exists a passive window can be present in the consumer's browser providing information on the merchant. This will minimize the cognitive load imposed on them when they attempt to assess a merchant's trustworthiness and can result to more accurate trust-placement decisions. The success of any attempt to implement a mechanism like this requires the involvement of all interested stakeholders (merchants, certification authorities, ISPs, crime prevention authorities) and a good implementation can significantly improve on the public perception of e-commerce as a safe and trustworthy service.

Re-focus Awareness Campaigns. Research has already reported that current security awareness campaigns are not well-aligned with actual consumer behavior in online environments [33]; future campaigns should focus on widely-held misconceptions. Automatic website verification can significantly reduce the amount of information that needs to be communicated to consumers, and the effort they have to make to check the authenticity of a site. They only need to be made aware of the fact that they may be targeted by scams (e.g. a website you access may be fraudulent and you may receive nothing for the money you pay) and what they need to do to protect themselves (e.g. make sure your browser is up to date). This can result to a significant decrease in the confusion amongst them and aid safer decisions when shopping online.

6.2   Research Limitations

The study aimed to create a scenario that would closely resemble the conditions under which consumers shop online: The need for them to accurately assess the trustworthiness of a merchant to avoid being victimized. A potential limitation that may have affected the ecological validity of our quantitative results is the fact that participants did not risk losing any money or having any personal details compromised, which would be the consequences of incorrect trust decisions while shopping online. This could have an effect on the ratings participants assigned to websites, but testing for this was not possible due to time and resource limitations. Despite that, the main issues we raise on the ineffectiveness of trust seals (failure to notice those and misunderstanding of their purpose) and the failure of awareness campaigns are well supported by the qualitative analysis of the interview data, where the identified misconceptions on trust seal meaning and trust development heuristics are unlikely to have been affected by this limitation.

References

1. The UK Cards Association,
   http://www.financialfraudaction.org.uk/cms/assets/1/be%20car
   d%20smart%20release%20final%20-%2024%20nov%2011%20(nfa).pdf
2. Riegelsberger, J., Sasse, M.A., McCarthy, J.D.: The mechanics of trust: a framework for research and design. International Journal of Human-Computer Studies 62(3), 381–422 (2005)
3. Financial Fraud Action UK,
   http://www.financialfraudaction.org.uk/cms/assets/1/fraud%20
   figures%20release%202010%20mar%2010.pdf
4. DirectGov, UK,
   http://www.direct.gov.uk/en/Governmentcitizensandrights/Cons
   umerrights/Howtocomplainaboutgoodsandservices/DG_196229
5. Publicservice.co.uk,
   http://www.publicservice.co.uk/news_story.asp?id=18293
6. Mail Online,
   http://www.dailymail.co.uk/femail/article-2073344/
   Will-fall-Santa-frauds-Britain-flooded-designer-Christmas-
   gifts-actually-dangerous-fakes.html?ito=feeds-newsxml
7. Retail Digital,
   http://www.retail-digital.com/consumer_trends/
   top-retail-scams
8. BBC News, http://news.bbc.co.uk/2/hi/8392600.stm
9. UK Cards Association,
   http://www.theukcardsassociation.org.uk/
   media_centre/press_releases_new/-/page/1323/
10. http://www.internetretailer.com/2011/01/18/fraud-losses-fall
11. Hu, X.R., Lin, Z.X., Zhang, H.: Myth or reality: effect of trust promoting seals in electronic markets. In: Proceeding of the Eleventh Annual Workshop on Information Technologies and Systems (WITS), New Orleans, Louisiana, pp. 65–70 (2001)
12. Resnick, P., Zeckhauser, R., Friedman, E., Kuwabara, K.: Reputation systems: facilitating trust in internet interactions. Communications of the ACM 43(12), 45–48 (2000)
13. Kim, D., Ferrin, D., Rao, H.: A trust-based consumer decision-making model in electronic commerce: The role of trust, perceived risk, and their antecedents. Decision Support Systems 44(2), 544–564 (2008)
14. Ba, S., Whinston, A.B., Zhang, H.: Building trust in online auction markets through an economic incentive mechanism. Decis. Support Syst. 35(3), 273–286 (2003)
15. Kimery, K.M., McCard, M.: Third-party assurances: mapping the road to trust in e-retailing. Journal of Information Technology Theory and Application 4(2), 63–82 (2002)
16. Rifon, N.J., LaRose, R., Choi, S.M.: Your Privacy Is Sealed: Effects of Web Privacy Seals on Trust and Personal Disclosures. Journal of Consumer Affairs 39, 339–362 (2005)

17. Bakos, J.Y., Dellarocas, C.: Cooperation without enforcement? A comparative analysis of litigation and online reputation as quality assurance mechanisms. In: Proc. Internat. Conf. In-form. Systems, Barcelona, Spain, pp. 127–141 (2002)
18. Peterson, D., Meinert, D., Criswell II, J., Crossland, M.: Consumer trust: privacy policies and third-party seals. Journal of Small Business and Enterprise Development 14(4), 654–669 (2007)
19. Wash, R.: Folk models of home computer security. In: SOUPS 2010: Proceedings of the 6th Symposium on Usable Privacy and Security, SOUPS 2010, pp. 1–16. ACM, New York (2010)
20. Tan, Y., Thoen, W.: Toward a Generic Model of Trust for Electronic Commerce. International Journal of Electronics Commerce 5, 61–74 (2000)
21. Nielsen, J., Molich, R., Snyder, S., Farrell, C.: E-Commerce User Experience:Trust. Nielsen Norman Group, Fremont (2000)
22. Jarvenpaa, S., Tractinsky, N., Vitale, M.: Consumer trust in an internet store. Information Technology and Management 1(1-2), 45–71 (2000)
23. Hoffman, D.L.: Building consumer trust online. Communications of the ACM 42(4), 80–85 (1999)
24. Bolton, G.E., Katok, E., Ockenfels, A.: How Effective Are Electronic Reputation Mechanisms? An Experimental Investigation. Manage. Sci. 50(11), 1587–1602 (2004)
25. Ratnasingam, P., Pavlou, P.A.: Technology Trust in Internet-Based Interorganizational Electronic Commerce. Journal of Electronic Commerce in Organizations 1(1), 17–41 (2004)
26. Akerlof, G.: The market for lemons: quality uncertainty and the market mechanism. Quarterly Journal of Economics 84(3), 488–500 (1970)
27. Handy, C.: Trust and the Virtual Organization. Harvard Business Review 73(3), 40–50 (1995)
28. Shneiderman, B.: Designing trust into online experiences. Communications of the ACM 43(12), 57–59 (2000)
29. Stajano, F., Wilson, P.: Understanding scam victims: seven principles for systems security. Communications of the ACM 54(3), 70–75 (2011)
30. Riegelsberger, J., Sasse, M.A., McCarthy, J.D.: The researcher's dilemma: evaluating trust in computer-mediated communication. Int. J. Hum.-Comput. Stud. 58(6), 759–781 (2003)
31. Bacharach, M., Gambetta, D.: Trust as Type Detection. In: Castelfranchi, C., Tan, Y. (eds.) Trust and Deception in Virtual Societies, pp. 1–26. Kluwer, Dordrecht (2001)
32. Egger, F.N.: Affective Design of E-Commerce User Interfaces: How to maximise perceived trustworthiness. In: Proceedings of International Conference on Affective Human Factors Design, pp. 317–324 (2001)
33. Kirlappos, I., Sasse, M.A.: Security education against phishing: A modest proposal for a major re-think. IEEE Security and Privacy, 99(preprints) (2011)
34. Twyman, M., Harvey, N., Harries, C.: Trust in motives, trust in competence: Separate factors determining the effectiveness of risk communication. Judgment and Decision Making 3, 111–120 (2008)
35. Google Good to Know,
    http://www.google.co.uk/goodtoknow/online-safety/shopping/
36. Stay Safe, http://www.staysafeonline.org/
37. DirectGov UK, http://www.direct.gov.uk/en/N11/Newsroom/DG_180506
38. DirectGov UK,
    http://www.direct.gov.uk/en/Governmentcitizensandrights/
    Consumerrights/Protectyourselffromscams/DG_195960

39. Harvey, N., Harries, C., Fischer, I.: Using advice and assessing its quality. Organizational Behavior and Human Decision Processes 81, 252–273 (2000)
40. Action Fraud, UK,
    `http://www.actionfraud.org.uk/festival-lovers-must-beware-of-ticketing-fraud-mar11`
41. Strauss, A., Corbin, J.: Basics of Qualitative Research: Techniques and Procedures for Developing Grounded Theory. SAGE publications, London (1998)
42. Edelman, B.: Adverse selection in online "trust" certifications. In: Proceedings of the 11th International Conference on Electronic Commerce (ICEC 2009), pp. 205-212. ACM, New York (2009)
43. Verisign: Report Seal Misuse,
    `https://www.verisign.com/support/contact/seal-abuse/index.html`
44. TRUSTe,
    `http://www.truste.com/consumer-privacy/comparing-web-privacy-seals`
45. Beautement, A., Sasse, M.A., Wonham, M.: The compliance budget: managing security behaviour in organisations. In: NSPW 2008: Proceedings of the 2008 Workshop on New Security Paradigms, pp. 47–58 (2008)
46. Herley, C.: So long, and no thanks for the externalities: The rational rejection of Security advice by users. In: Proceedings of the New Security Paradigms Workshop 2009, pp. 133–144 (2009)
47. Whitten, A., Tygar, J.D.: Why Johnny can't encrypt: a usability evaluation of PGP 5.0. In: Proceedings of the 8th Conference on USENIX Security Symposium (SSYM 1999), vol. 8, p. 14. USENIX Association, Berkeley (1999)
48. GHD Repair, `http://www.ghd-repair.co.uk/fake_ghds.html`
49. Ebay, `http://pages.ebay.com/help/account/securing-account.html`
50. SOLID Authentication, `https://www.solidauthentication.com`
51. Wu, M., Miller, R.C., Garfinkel, S.L.: Do security toolbars actually prevent phishing attacks? In: Grinter, R., Rodden, T., Aoki, P., Cutrell, E., Jeffries, R., Olson, G. (eds.) Proceedings of the SIGCHI Conference on Human Factors in Computing Systems (CHI 2006), pp. 601–610. ACM, New York (2006)

Launching the New Profile on Facebook: Understanding the Triggers and Outcomes of Users' Privacy Concerns

Saijing Zheng[1], Pan Shi[1], Heng Xu[1], and Cheng Zhang[2]

[1] The Pennsylvania State University, University Park, Pennsylvania, United States
{suz128,pzs125,hxu}@ist.psu.edu
[2] Fudan University, Shanghai, China
zhangche@fudan.edu.cn

Abstract. While the body of privacy research on online social networks has been growing over the past several years, privacy problems emerged from the dynamism inherent in the launch of new features or interfaces have not been widely discussed. Drawing on the grounded theory approach, we aim to fill this gap by investigating the trigger conditions under which users may perceive the introduction of a new IT artifact as privacy threats. With the specific case of the New Profile introduced by Facebook, we conducted a content analysis of user responses posted on the official blog of Facebook. Results can be constructed as a process model including two stages. The first stage of the model presented four broad categories of trigger conditions of privacy concerns—information processing, increased accessibility, intrusion, and loss of control. The second stage describes three types of outcomes, including psychological outcomes, behavior outcomes, and suggested privacy mechanisms.

Keywords: Privacy Concerns, Online Social Networks (OSNs), Facebook, Grounded Theory, and Interface Design.

1 Introduction

The extensive display and sharing of personal information by users of social media such as online social networks (OSNs) span a number of years. During this time, significant changes and redesigns of various features and user interfaces have been made by the systems. This dynamism can trigger multiple expected and unexpected consequences that users of a site may experience and perceive. In particular, privacy problems emerged from the dynamism inherent in many changes of features and interfaces in OSNs have attracted significant attention. In 2006, the introduction of "News Feed" feature by Facebook resulted in an immediate privacy outcry from users [13]. Google Buzz, launched as an add-on to Gmail, was initially designed to opt-in its user base by publicly disclosing a friend list generated from users' Gmail contacts. The rollout of Google Buzz was strongly criticized for inadequate privacy protection [12]. Recently, Facebook is close to a settlement with the U.S. government [1], which stems from changes Facebook made to its privacy settings in December 2009 to make aspects of users' profile (i.e., name, picture, and friends list) public by default.

S. Katzenbeisser et al. (Eds.): TRUST 2012, LNCS 7344, pp. 325–339, 2012.

While the body of privacy research on OSNs has been growing over the past several years, privacy issues associated with the launch of new features or changes of interfaces have not been widely discussed in current literature. To our best knowledge, many privacy studies in social sciences and related disciplines [e.g., 15, 25] have focused on examining users' general privacy concerns without connecting to a specific IT event such as interface changes or specific feature launch. Drawing on the grounded theory approach, our work aims to fill this gap by investigating the trigger conditions under which users may perceive the changes of features and interfaces as privacy problems. With the specific case of the New Profile introduced by Facebook, we conducted a content analysis of user responses posted on sections of introducing the New Profile from the official blog of Facebook.

Contributions of this work are two-fold. First, our research will propose a process model to understand the emergence and outcome processes of users' privacy concerns triggered by the changes of features and interfaces in OSNs. Second, research findings can inspire technology-oriented researchers to develop more feasible privacy enhancing technologies that are embedded into the design specifications of systems, as well as aligned with organizational practices and user behaviors.

2   Conceptual Background

Solove [20] developed a taxonomy of information practices and activities, which maps out various types of privacy problems resulting from information collection, information processing, information dissemination, and invasion activities. These information practices and data activities "can potentially threaten an individual's ability to maintain a condition of limited access to his/her personal information" [2, p. 675]. Smith et al. [19] has identified four data-related dimensions to conceptualize and quantitatively measure individuals' privacy concerns on organizational information practices: data collection, unauthorized secondary use of information, data errors, and improper access to information.

In the context of OSNs, a service provider's success depends predominately on users' continuous interactions on its site, e.g., self-disclosure, information sharing, and communication [4, 15]. However, "organizational information practices (or poor organizational privacy programs) can result in a variety of privacy problems that can associate with consumers' concerns for information privacy" [23, p. 799]. From the end-user's perspective, many studies have been conducted to investigate users' privacy attitudes [e.g., 13, 14] and the possible risks that users face when they fail to adequately protect their information [e.g., 11].

Privacy concerns not only affect a user's willingness to disclose personal information, but also affect his or her acceptance of technology [24]. In the wake of privacy invasion, technologies "that are perceived as being privacy intrusive may also be perceived as being plagued with performance problems and usage uncertainties" [24, p. 140]. Thus, we argue that it is important to understand the trigger conditions under which an introduction of a new technological artifact (e.g., the change of an interface or the launch of a new feature) are perceived as a privacy threat.

3   Methodology

To achieve our research objectives, we adopted the grounded theory approach to understand privacy problems resulting from changes of interface and features in OSNs. Grounded theory approach has proved to be useful in developing contextual descriptions and explanations of phenomenon [8]. This methodology not only allows for the emergence of findings that are strictly tied to the data [17], but also offers a systematic approach for generating conceptual frameworks that are firmly grounded in empirical phenomena [22].

3.1   Research Context

The context of our study is Facebook, a popular social networking platform for information sharing, video sharing, photo sharing, tagging, blogging, creating and joining groups. According to the Facebook Statistics, Facebook has more than 800 million active users, fifty percent of whom log on to the site in any given day and people spend over seven hundred billion minutes per month [7]. Facebook's worldwide popularity and adoption make its frequent interface change and launch of new features susceptible to public criticisms.

In October 2010, Facebook introduced the New Profile, and gave users the option to upgrade to the New Profile early. Starting from Jan 10, 2011, Facebook was rolling out the New Profile to everyone in a compulsory manner. See Figures 1-2 for a comparison between early version of user profile and the New Profile on Facebook. The New Profile features [5]:

- ✓ A quick summary of who you are (like where you live, work and grew up), right at the top of your profile,
- ✓ A row of recently tagged photos so friends can see what you have been up to lately,
- ✓ Room to highlight meaningful friendships (like teammates, co-workers or roommates),
- ✓ More of your favorite activities and interests, and
- ✓ The ability to tag your friends in events and life experiences.

3.2   Data Collection

As soon as the New Profile was introduced to users on Facebook, it triggered users' privacy concerns, discontent, anxiety, as well as mass media's questioning of privacy issues. In Spring 2011, we conducted a content analysis of user comments posted on the Facebook Blog in response to the launch of the New Profile. Facebook Blog is not only a public platform for introducing new features and announcing significant events, but also enables users to discuss and give feedbacks towards these topics. We believe that analyzing actual users' reactions by using such a rich dataset enabled us to better understand users' collective privacy concerns. Such approach allowed us to not only obtain a large data set but also reach users who are sensitive in protecting their personal information.

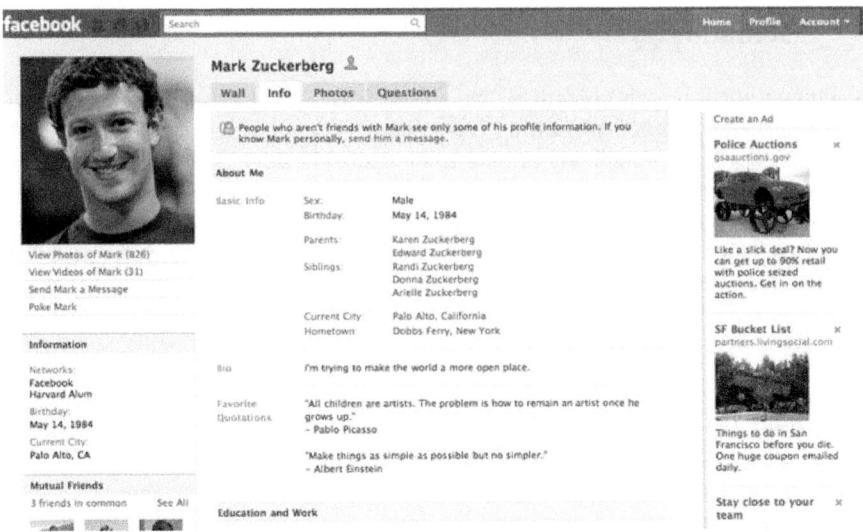

Fig. 1. Early Version of User Profile on Facebook

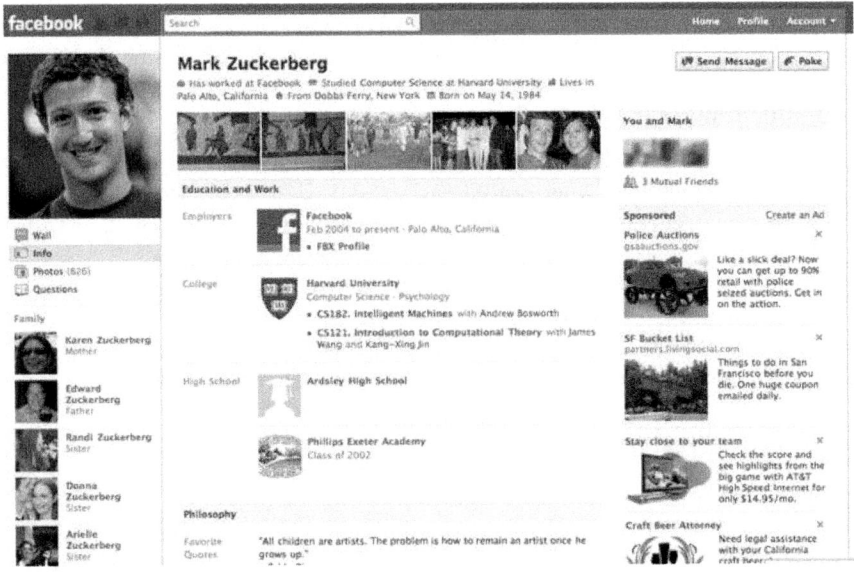

Fig. 2. The Facebook New Profile

We collected users' comments using Facebook API from two Facebook Blog entries: *Introducing the New Profile (Blog #1)* [5] and *New Profile is Here (Blog #2)* [6], both of which are the official channels that Facebook provided for users to express their opinions and suggestions on the New Profile. *Blog #1* was released on December 15th of 2010, which included 13,304 entries of user comments. *Blog #2* was released on January 10th of 2011, the date which Facebook started rolling out the New Profile to everyone in a compulsory manner. We crawled 8,949 pieces of user comments from *Blog #2*.

3.3   Grounded Theory Approach

In this section, for the purpose of clarity, we provide a brief overview of the steps undertaken using the grounded theory approach:

- Data Filtering: Data filtering was performed by two steps. First, we only included those user comments written in English. In addition, we eliminated those comments which were purely emotional icons (e.g., ☺), or offensive words, or advertisements. The first-step data filtering resulted in a data set of 8545 comments, with 4450 comments from Blog #1 and 4095 comments from Blog #2. Second, we manually scanned the data set by searching for specific comments related to users' privacy concerns or their perceived privacy violations. This process provided 835 comments related to privacy issues for in-depth review and coding (493 comments from Blog #1 and 342 comments from Blog #2).
- First Order Analysis: Two coders first developed a coding guideline with multiple concept categories and their corresponding explanations. This was followed by their independent grouping of the 835 privacy related comments into their identified categorizations. The coders were allowed to assign multiple categories to each user comment. For the first order analysis, we embraced an open coding approach in order to further identify new concepts that had arisen from the data. Our coding involved the identification and comparison of key concepts using Strauss and Corbin's constant comparative approach [21].
- Second Order Analysis: Based on results from our first order analysis, we found that there was the emergence of certain categories but not all relationships were defined. Corbin and Strauss refer to this step as axial coding which is the act of relating concepts and categories to each other and constructing a higher theoretical level of abstraction. This step involved an iterative process of collapsing our first order codes into conceptually distinct themes [3]. In terms of inter-coder reliability, Cohen's Kappa of 0.827 ($p<0.001$) suggested a high level of agreement between the coders.
- Conceptual Framework: Our final stage of data analysis consisted of determining how various themes we identified could be linked into a coherent framework identifying the trigger conditions under which the introduction of a new technological artifact (i.e., the launch of the New Profile on Facebook) are perceived as a privacy threat.

4   Findings

Results of data analysis could be summarized as a process model (Figure 3). This framework interweaved results from first and second order analyses to explain emergence and outcomes of a privacy problem resulting from the introduction of a new technological artifact (i.e., the New Profile) on Facebook.

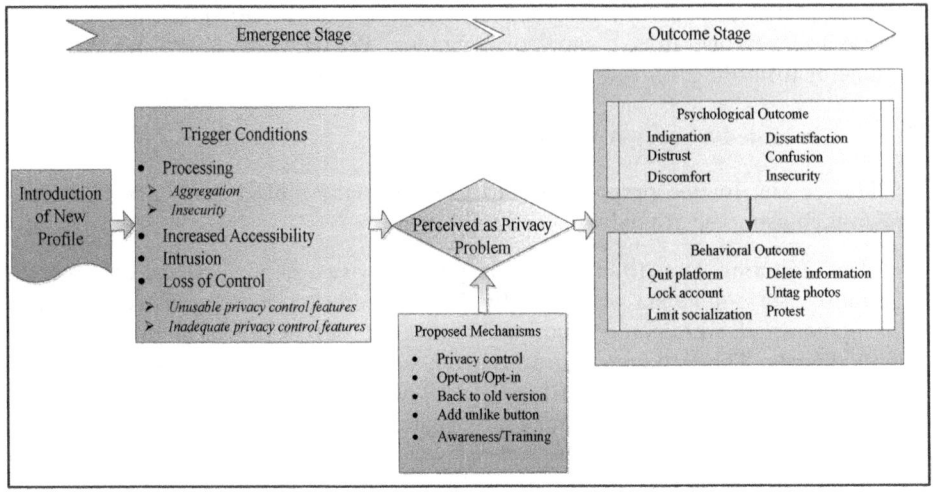

Fig. 3. Data Structure

4.1 First Stage: Emergence of a Privacy Problem

Our data analysis revealed a categorization of conditions that trigger users' privacy concerns due to the changes introduced by the New Profile. These trigger conditions include privacy problems resulting from information processing, increased accessibility, intrusion, and loss of control.

1) Information Processing refers to "the use, storage, and manipulation of data that has been collected" [20, p.504]. According to Solove [20], the practice of information processing often creates privacy problems through the consolidation of the information and linking it to the individual to whom it pertains. In the case of the New Profile, we identified two forms of information processing which triggered users' privacy concerns: *aggregation* and *insecurity*.

Aggregation refers to the combination of various pieces of users' personal data, such as their photos, videos, and basic information [20]. In the case of the New Profile, the new interface pulled tagged photos from a user's album and randomly displayed the newest five ones together with the user's profile information. Such change of the interface considerably triggered users' privacy concerns.

"I'm sure F/B creators are aware by now how utterly upset people are of the changes you focus on us. F/B had no right to select what displays in my account and you are so rude..."

"The display of tagged photos is the most stupid thing, if someone tags me in something offensive, that's the first thing people will see."

In our data set, *aggregation* was identified as the most salient concern triggered by the launch of the New Profile. A total of 203 comments were categorized as users' concerns over data aggregation, which led to their discomfort, distrust, even indignation toward Facebook. These users believed that the aggregation practice employed by Facebook invaded their privacy: *"aggregation will supply the stalkers paradise to invade users' privacy."*

Why did the aggregation of tagged photos stir up big complaints? In the old interface, the tagged photos were already located in users' albums. Why was it a problem for the New Profile to pull those tagged photos from users' albums and display them on users' profiles? The problem is on the activity of aggregating information – "the whole becomes greater than the parts" [20, p.506]. Combining data together could result in synergies, which can potentially reveal more details about a person in new and unexpected ways. Therefore, the aggregation practice introduced by the New Profile can cause privacy harms because it can potentially upset users' privacy boundary expectations on "what is known about them and on what others will find out" [20, p.507].

Insecurity describes the set of concerns over a service provider's "carelessness in protecting stored information from leaks and improper access" [20, p.516]. Results of our analysis revealed that users believe that Facebook should be responsible for preventing improper access to their disclosed data. In the context of the New Profile, privacy harms can potentially be introduced by the new feature of displaying tagged photos on users' profiles. For example, one user complained about the inadequate data protection:

"I had my pictures set for a certain "LIST" to view and found that someone else (who was not a friend on my page) was getting my pics and reposting them!!! There was a "mutual friend" between us but that person was not in the "LIST" that was allowed to view my pics and somehow with the changes they were able to do it. So they were allowing the other person to get the pictures."

With the compulsory adoption of the New Profile on January 10th of 2011, more and more users paid attention to the new feature of displaying tagged photos on users' profiles and complained about such change:

"It's ridiculous! You know what, today when I click my friend's tagged photo on her profile, I could access to the whole album of my friend's friend! Then, I made a test with my other two friends B and S, even S kick me out of her Facebook, and B is not in S's list who could access her album, I still could see the album! I can't believe this!!!"

In our dataset, a total of 124 comments were categorized as users' concerns over insecurity. According to Solove [20], insecurity is naturally related to aggregation, as "it creates risks of downstream harm that can emerge from inadequate protection of compendiums of personal data" (p.515). In the case of launching New Profile, although Facebook claimed that it did not change users' privacy settings and accessibility of information, the redesign of information display carelessly triggered users' security concerns by integrating tagged photos with their profile information. To users, this data practice in fact opened a new way to access information and potentially resulted in information leaks and improper access.

2) Increased Accessibility creates problems such as the enlarged scope of information disclosure and the enhanced risk of disclosure [20]. The New Profile reorganized the display of user information with a more visually attractive way to display a cluster of tagged photos and personal information on the top panel of the profile page. Although Facebook believed that this change could help users better portray themselves efficiently [10], some users disagreed with Facebook by arguing that the new interfaces would amplify the scope of information that may be viewed and accessed by unwanted audience. For example, some users pointed out that the aggregated information and tagged photos "shortened" the distance or "simplified" the procedures for "stalkers" to obtain information:

"Unless you are on purpose to search this stuff, otherwise you cannot see them directly. And in fact, your friends seldom go to see such kind of information; they just want to know what are you doing now? So this really increased the risk and possibility for stalkers to access."

Another user complained about increased accessibility:

"It seems that Facebook make a huge sign for every user, which reminds every visitor to look at here! Just one click! It makes me so uncomfortable! It's a violation of privacy!"

The breach of privacy often happened after users volitionally but unwittingly publicized information to a wider audience than they actually intended. The new design may increase the harms of unforeseeable visibility which was not only reflected in tagged photos, but also in newsfeeds. For example, if *User A* connected and interacted with a friend *B*, and *B* set his or her privacy settings to 'friends of friends' or 'everyone', then everything *A* did on *B*'s page would be broadcasted by the newsfeeds to all of *A*'s friends, no matter how tight *A*'s privacy settings were.

"Stop intruding on our privacy!!! What I post on a friend's wall is meant for that friend, not for everyone, please, quit posting stuff on my wall that i didn't intend to go there..."

Another user replied to this comment by saying that:

"I agree!!! When i go to a friend's house, and have a conversation with them, it isn't broadcast to everyone i know! it didn't used to be that way here either."

In our dataset, a total of 356 comments were labelled as users' worries on increased accessibility introduced by the New Profile. Interestingly, although the New Profile did not disclose any new personal information, increased accessibility widely triggered users' privacy concerns. Why? Disclosed information is made easier to exploit for purposes other than those for which it was initially made accessible [20]. As Solove notes: "Unlike disclosure, the harm (of increased accessibility) is not a direct revealing of information to another. Confidentiality is not breached; the cat is already out of the bag. With increased accessibility, a difference in quantity becomes a difference in quality—it enhances the risk of the harms of disclosure" [20, p.537].

3) Intrusion is defined as concern over invasions or incursions into one's life, making him or her uncomfortable and uneasy [20]. In the case of launching the New Profile, we identified two types of intrusion practices from our data. First, users considered the introduction of the New Profile as an intrusion to their information space because they viewed their profile page as their own belongings, in which Facebook has no right to change without users' explicit permissions.

"...i have begun deleting my photos online, and have untagged myself and all of my friends because ... i do not like the fact that you have a row of pictures at the top of my page that i did not approve"

Second, users believed that they themselves should have control to decide what types of information to be displayed on their profile. However, with the introduction of the New Profile, users were able to tag their friends in events and life experiences. In addition, those comments users posted on their friends' walls were also posted on their own walls. In our data set, some users considered the introduction of those new features as an intrusion to their information space, and believed that unwanted information cannot be posted by others.

"i don't need everyone to be able to see what i am commenting on. let that be the decision of each user ... as many fb users do, i have groups designated for games that i have blocked from seeing anything personal, but now they have access ... merely by the design of the page. not cool."

It seems that users have considered their online profiles as their virtual territory on Facebook. In offline settings, individuals often desire spatial distance, which provides comfort and relaxation, and enables them to stay away from the pressure of being in public. Similarly, in the context of Facebook, users claim ownership of their digital belongings that they are entitled to or that are created by them [25]. A user's profile page on Facebook is therefore considered as part of the virtual realm of the user. Therefore, interface changes which enable inappropriate access, unwanted posts, or information reorganization without users' explicit permissions, could be considered as intrusion.

4) Loss of Control. The element of control has been identified as an important predictor of individuals' privacy concerns [23]. In the context of privacy research, control has been defined as an individual's beliefs in one's ability to determine to what extent information about the self will be released and disseminated onto a website [23]. In the context of Facebook, Facebook offers its members with granular control on the searchability and visibility of their personal information and activities, which represents a large range of genres – including status information, photos, posts, bio and hobbies, family and relationships, permission to comment, places the user checked in, and contact information, etc. However, the privacy research community has criticized privacy control settings on Facebook to be too difficult to use, and to be inadequate for the protection of users' information [9].

Unusable Privacy Control Features: Given the frequent changes of user interfaces on Facebook, users have had difficulties in keeping pace to the corresponding changes of privacy settings. For example, some users were unclear about the changes of privacy settings introduced by the New Profile:

"so--if we switch to/are forced to switch to this new format, do all of our privacy settings automatically go back to 'allow,' forcing us to go back and redo them all? maybe folks who have made the switch can fill us in on this..."

Another user complained about the general complexity of privacy settings:

"is there any way to make a suggestion/request? i'd like to request one page with direct links to all the fb settings. it's crazy that we have to go to one place to set the privacy settings on our photos, and another place to set the privacy settings on apps, and another place for privacy settings on posts, etc. every website designer knows that navigation is supposed to work like a menu. and granted, you've got the little drop down menu in the upper right...but there's a lot of settings that aren't accessible from that (like photo album settings)."

In sum, even though Facebook did provide various settings to control privacy, users may not be able to make use of these settings due to their poor usability and thus users still perceived their privacy being jeopardized.

Inadequate Privacy Control Features: In our data set, users complained about the inadequate privacy control features to facilitate privacy management for different categories of information displayed on the New Profile. A large number of users expressed their discontent of losing control as well as great need for better privacy control mechanisms. For example:

"...we are feeling more and more like we have no control over what information is shared (despite privacy settings, which i am very familiar with given that i must now find ways to hide information that the site seems to think is important to share) and no way to personalize our profile."

Users' concerns about tagged photos displayed on the New Profile were mentioned most intensively. Users were bothered by the fact that tagged photos randomly appeared in the New Profile and that users cannot decide its visibility and arrangement of these photos. For users who care about their images, having no control over tagged photos (except untagging or deleting photos) made them angry:

"... i don't like that i don't really have control over which five pictures show in the line. i want to be able to select and order them as i can in an album. the five pictures you select aren't necessarily the ones i want and if i hide them until i get five i like, i'd still like to put them in the order i want. this random selection makes the pictures look sloppy..."

Another aspect of inadequate privacy control was revealed by users' needs for notification and consent for each change that Facebook made. For example, users want to be notified with the launch of new features, with options to accept or decline these new features. According to users' comments in our data set, losing right to consent new features is considered as an important aspect of inadequate privacy control.

"why no option to change back - there are so many flaws in this new design you should be ashamed of it not proud at all - actually you have invaded my privacy by putting my details in plain site without my permission."

4.2   Second Stage: Outcomes of a Privacy Problem

Users not only uttered their privacy concerns triggered by the New Profile, but also indicated their needs for desired control mechanisms as well as intended consequences or outcomes. As shown in Figure 4, we classified these comments as three categories of outcomes: 1) Psychological Outcomes, 2) Behavioral Outcomes, and 3) Suggested Privacy Mechanisms.

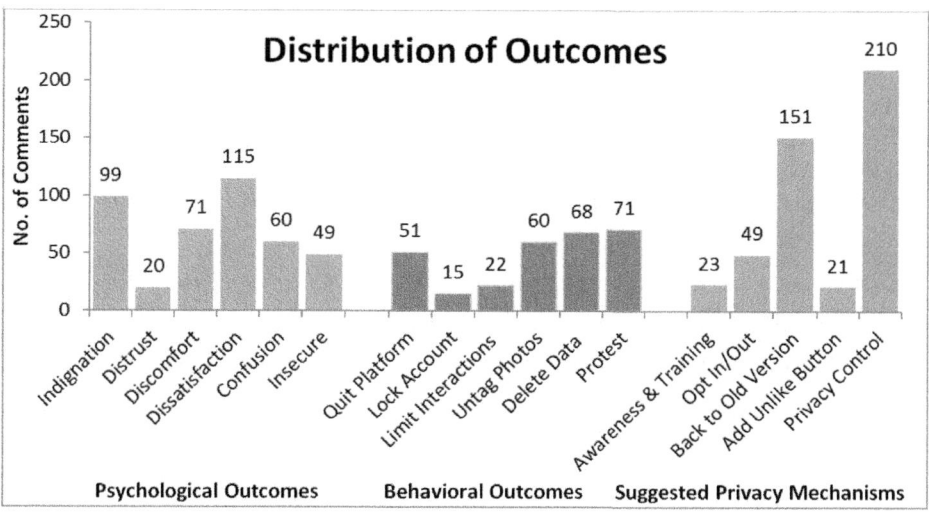

Fig. 4. Distribution of Psychological and Behavioral Outcomes, and Suggested Mechanisms

Psychological Outcomes

Psychological outcomes refers to affective reactions which include indignation to profile changes (99 comments), discomfort (71 comments) and dissatisfaction in using the platform and its services (115 comments), confusion in terms of how to use privacy settings (60 comments), insecurity during the interactions with the platform (49 comments), and distrust to the platform (20 comments). For example, a user cannot figure out how the new features worked and thus complained that *"I do not know how it changed...it is confusing cause of my security settings...i want to set it back."*

Some users indicated their distrust beliefs toward Facebook: *"it is obvious from the lack of response that fb doesn't care how many people hate the less informative and more intrusive new profile. what they do care about is income from their ads."*

Behavioral Outcomes

Behavioral outcomes refer to practical reactions which will be or have been done by users. These actions include quitting the platform, limiting socializing (e.g., online social interactions with friends, fan pages, groups etc.), locking account until Facebook grant them reasonable privacy control, deleting as much personal information as they can, untagging photos of themselves, and protesting Facebook with other users. Users applied an array of behavioral strategies to balance the tradeoff between publicness and privacy. For example, one user mentioned that:

"Our status from the top of the page is so you could get to our information first for advertisiing, so i removed mine too....hahaha...and i untagged all of my pictures, and removed everything you want to see...apps no longer allowed to..no more games to steal information...now i am strictly just friends i talk to...and i am getting bored with."

Other behavioral outcomes triggered by users' privacy concerns include less use of Facebook and even leaving the platform.

"While it's true that i won't immediately stop using facebook, because it has become a useful tool and has reached that critical mass where it seems that it's what everyone uses, i will in fact use it less if this new format is forced on us. and i will delete my personal info and untag photos of me rather than have them displayed in a manner that's beyond my control."

"This website has no privacy left what-so-ever. if this continues, screw facebook, i won't use it anymore."

Users even protested Facebook to fight against the introduction of the New Profile:

"Protest the forced 'New Profile' by deactivating your account for 2 hours. Perhaps that will finally get their attention. February 1, 2011 is 'Deactivation Day' Click here, like the page, and pass it on. Facebook is deleting these posts and shuffling the rest so fast it's very hard to keep track."

Suggested Privacy Mechanisms

As shown in Figure 4, users' suggested privacy mechanisms are those changes that users hope Facebook could make, including developing useful privacy control features, adding opt-out or opt-in, going back to the old profile, launching an "unlike" button on the feedback page, and promoting privacy awareness within user community.

"Change can be good, but putting the changes within the users' control would be a much wiser choice."

"Wish they'd make it optional or give the user more control over how things are displayed.   the new layout looks lame."

5   Discussion

This work depicts the emergence and outcomes of privacy concerns triggered by the changes of interface and features brought by the launch of the New Profile on Facebook. We argue that understanding the emergence and outcomes of a privacy problem is very important in understanding users' privacy needs and evaluating current designs of privacy enhancing features. Our findings indicate that changes of interface and features have different dynamics that may result in arousal of unique privacy challenges and interpretations.

In the emergence stage, there is no data showing that Facebook users would consider information collection as a harmful information practice, which is distinct from prior privacy literature [16, 19, 20] that usually considered information collection as a key dimension of privacy concerns perceived by users. This difference can be explained by the characteristics of the user population in this research, i.e., experienced users who have acquiesced to the data collection practices of Facebook.com. In an IT event which introduced various changes of interfaces and features, users' privacy concerns were found to be determined by the practice of information aggregation, as well as their perceptions of insecurity, ease of information access, intrusion, and privacy control.

Among the trigger conditions we derived from the users' comments, we found that Solove's taxonomy [20] is a useful framework that can cover most harmful information practices identified by our data set, e.g., information aggregation, insecurity, increased accessibility, and intrusion. Nevertheless, Facebook users interpreted these information practices with new meanings. Take the dimension of intrusion as an example. Solove's taxonomy interpreted intrusion from a non-territorial perspective, including the harmful practices of spam, junk mail, or telemarketing [20]. In our research context, users considered their online profiles as their virtual territory and thus claimed ownership of their digital belongings that they were entitled to or that were created by them. Interface changes which enabled inappropriate access, unwanted posts, or information reorganization without users' permissions, were considered as intrusion by Facebook users.

Loss of control, which is not covered by Solove's taxonomy, emerged as a very important trigger condition in this work, which raised users' privacy concerns in the launch of the New Profile. We identified two causes of loss of control—i) unusable privacy control features, and ii) inadequate privacy control features. Our results have indicated that even though Facebook did provide various settings to control privacy, users still complained about loss of privacy because they cannot make use of these settings due to their poor usability. In addition, many users expressed their discontent of losing control as well as great need for better privacy control mechanisms designed for new features launched by Facebook.

The outcomes of privacy problems revealed by our data vocalize a strong appeal toward practitioners of OSNs. Users are in great need of being notified and staying aware of new features and potential risks. However, it seems that users do not have much choice in reality. Practitioners of OSNs should be responsible to offer users with better control mechanisms and freedom of usage for the new features.

Another lens of defining privacy in the context of OSNs is from a boundary management perspective [23]. From this aspect, individual users make decisions in their information disclosure for the purpose of identity management [18]. The privacy issues introduced by the New Profile added complexity in privacy boundary management in OSNs. For example, tagged photos can potentially depict interaction information among tagged users, which automatically involves more stakeholders in privacy boundary formation and negotiation. The property of linking information from multiple parties blurs and complicates the process of privacy boundary management among users who co-own and co-manage their shared information. Thus, investigating users' interpersonal privacy concerns over shared information expects more careful designs to manage these privacy boundaries.

6   Limitations and Conclusion

The analysis of user comments posted on the official Blog of Facebook provides an overall picture of users' privacy concerns, attitudes, and intended behaviors pertaining to the launch of the New Profile on Facebook. However, this data set is not sufficient to provide us with insights regarding users' actual behaviour and social interactions in their daily online activities on Facebook. In future work, we should explore these issues at a fine-grained level through interview or field studies. In addition, our work is only limited with a specific IT event (i.e., the launch of the New Profile) on a specific social networking platform (i.e., Facebook.com). Future research should study other social networking platforms that offer similar sets of features to examine the generalizability of our findings. Third, our study focused on the user comments written in English and those non-English comments were excluded from data coding and analysis. Future work should extend to those non-English comments to explore cross-language or cross-culture differences. Lastly, the user population in our work is limited to a sub-sample of Facebook users who had posted their comments on Facebook's blog during the launch of the New Profile. In other words, data was only collected from those users who were willing to post their comments to express their privacy concerns. Care must be taken in any effort to generalize our results beyond the boundary of our sample.

Existing theories of privacy are conductive to understand the concept of information privacy in general terms. Our work goes beyond this high level of conceptualizations and explores the trigger conditions under which users perceive the changes of features and interfaces as privacy problems. In conclusion, our work not only adds to the growing literature of privacy in the context of social networking sites, but also offers practitioners wake-up calls and insights for further improvement.

Acknowledgements. The authors gratefully acknowledge the financial support of the U.S. National Science Foundation under grant CNS-0953749. Any opinions, findings and conclusions or recommendations expressed in this material are those of the authors and do not necessarily reflect the views of the National Science Foundation.

References

1. Angwin, J., Raice, S., Spencer, E.A.: Facebook Retreats on Privacy. The Wall Street Journal (2011)
2. Culnan, M.J., Williams, C.C.: How Ethics Can Enhance Organizational Privacy: Les-sons from the ChoicePoint and TJX Data Breaches. MIS Quarterly 33(4), 673–687 (2009)
3. Eisenhardt, K.M.: Building Theories from Case Study Research. The Academy of Management Review 14(4), 532–550 (1989)
4. Ellison, N.B., Steinfield, C., Lampe, C.: The Benefits of Facebook "Friends": Social Capital and College Students' Use of Online Social Network Sites. Journal of Computer-Mediated Communication 12(4), 1143–1168 (2007)
5. Facebook Blog: Introducing New Profile (2010),
   http://blog.facebook.com/blog.php?post=462201327130
6. Facebook Blog: New Profile Is Here (2011),
   http://blog.facebook.com/blog.php?post=479551972130
7. Facebook Statistics, http://facebook.com/press/info.php?statistics
8. Goulielmos, M.: Systems development approach: transcending methodology. Information Systems Journal 14, 363–386 (2004)
9. Grimmelmann, J.: Saving Facebook. Iowa Law Review 94, 1137–1206 (2009)

10. Gross, D.: Explaining Facebook's new profile pages,
    `http://articles.cnn.com/2010-12-`
    `06/tech/facebook.profile.update_1_profile-photo-facebook-`
    `friends-facebook-page?_s=PM:TECH`
11. Gross, R., Acquisti, A.: Information revelation and privacy in online social networks. In: Workshop on Privacy in the Electronic Society. ACM, New York (2005)
12. Helft, M.: Critics Say Google Invades Privacy With New Service,
    `http://www.nytimes.com/2010/02/13/technology/internet/`
    `13google.html`
13. Hoadley, C.M., Xu, H., Lee, J.J., Rosson, M.B.: Privacy as information access and illusory control: The case of the Facebook News Feed privacy outcry. Electronic Commerce Research and Applications 9(1), 50–60 (2010)
14. Jagatic, T.N., Johnson, N.A., Jakobsson, M., Menczer, F.: Social Phishing. Communications of the ACM 50(10), 94–100 (2007)
15. Krasnova, H., Hildebrand, T., Günther, O., Kovrigin, S., Nowobilska, A.: Why Par-ticipat. In: An Online Social Network: An Empirical Analysis. In: European Conference on Information Systems, Galway, Ireland (2008)
16. Malhotra, N.K., Kim, S.S., Agarwa, J.: Internet Users' Information Privacy Concerns (IUIPC): The Construct, the Scale, and a Causal Model. Information Systems Research 15(4), 336–355 (2004)
17. Orlikowski, W.J.: Case Tools as Organizational Change: Investigating Incremental and Radical Changes in Systems Development. MIS Quarterly 17(3), 309–340 (1993)
18. Palen, L., Dourish, P.: Unpacking "privacy" for a networked world. In: Proceedings of the SIGCHI Conference on Human Factors in Computing Systems, pp. 129–136. ACM Press, Ft. Lauderdale (2003)
19. Smith, H.J., Milberg, J.S., Burke, J.S.: Information Privacy: Measuring Individuals' Concerns About Organizational Practices. MIS Quarterly 20(2), 167–196 (1996)
20. Solove, D.J.: A Taxonomy of Privacy. University of Pennsylvania Law Review 154, 3 (2006)
21. Strauss, A.L., Corbin, J.: Basics of Qualitative Research: Grounded Theory Procedures and Techniques. Sage (2008)
22. Urquhart, C., Lehmann, H., Myers, M.D.: Putting the 'theory' back into grounded theory: guidelines for grounded theory studies in information systems. Information Systems Journal 20, 357–381 (2010)
23. Xu, H., Dinev, T., Smith, H.J., Hart, P.: Information Privacy Concerns: Linking Individual Perceptions with Institutional Privacy Assurances. Journal of the Association for Information Systems 12(12), 798–824 (2011)
24. Xu, H., Gupta, S.: The Effects of Privacy Concerns and Personal Innovativeness on Potential and Experienced Customers' Adoption of Location-Based Services. Electronic Markets 19(2), 137–140 (2009)
25. Zhang, N., Wang, C., Xu, Y.: Privacy in Online Social Networks. In: International Conference on Information System, Shanghai, China (2011)

Author Index

GPSR Compliance

*The European Union's (EU) General Product Safety Regulation (GPSR)
is a set of rules that requires consumer products to be safe and our
obligations to ensure this.*

*If you have any concerns about our products, you can contact us on
ProductSafety@springernature.com*

In case Publisher is established outside the EU, the EU authorized
representative is:

Springer Nature Customer Service Center GmbH
Europaplatz 3
69115 Heidelberg, Germany

Batch number: 09490872

Printed by Printforce, the Netherlands